Building a Web Site For Dummies®

Cheat Sheet

W9-BRI-169

The Seven Rules of Site Design

Rule #1: The Web is for reaching out to people.

Rule #2: Keep your Web pages lean and clean.

Rule #3: Don't make your visitors jump through hoops.

Rule #4: Never make an unnecessary link.

Rule #5: Always group necessary items together.

Rule #6: If you can give visitors an option, do so.

Rule #7: It's your Web site. It's your vision. Do it your way.

Web Site Design Tips

- Make your content as useful as possible.
- Use appealing graphics, but make sure that they support the content.
- Give your pages a consistent appearance.
- Install a search feature.
- Update your pages often so that people have a reason to return frequently.
- Stick to your topic.
- Know your audience and strive to please them.

CGI/Perl Resources

Site Name	Web Site
CGI Extremes	www.cgiextremes.com
CGI Made Really Easy	www.jmarshall.com/easy/cgi
CGI Resource Index	www.cgi-resources.com
CGI: Why Things Don't Work	www.raingod.com/raingod/resources/Programming/Perl/Notes/CGIDebugging.html
FREEPerlCode.com	www.freeperlcode.com
GetScripts.com	www.getscripts.com
Intro to CGI	www.mattkruse.com/info/cgi/
Matt Kruse's Intro to CGI	www.mattkruse.com/info/cgi
Matt's Script Archive	http://worldwidemart.com/scripts
Perl Primer	www.webdesigns1.com/perl
ScriptSearch	www.scriptsearch.com
www.perl.com	http://www.perl.com

Building a Web Site For Dummies®

HTML Resources

Site Name	Web Site
CNET Builder.com	www.builder.com
Compendium of HTML Elements	www.htmlcompendium.org
D.J. Quad's Ultimate HTML Site	www.quadzilla.com
HTML Goodies	www.htmlgoodies.com
HTML Specification	http://www.w3.org/TR/html
HTML Station	www.december.com/html
HTML Writers Guild	www.hwg.org
HTMLcenter	www.htmlcenter.com/tutorials/index.cfm
Index DOT Html	www.eskimo.com/~bloo/indexdot/html/index.html
Introduction to HTML	www.wdvl.com/Authoring/HTML/Intro/
Web Developer's Virtual Library	www.wdvl.com
WebReference.com	www.webreference.com

Java and JavaScript Resources

Site Name	Web Site
A1 JavaScripts	http://a1javascripts.com
Cut-N-Paste JavaScript	www.infohiway.com/javascript/indexf.htm
Freewarejava.com	http://freewarejava.com
Gamelan Java Directory	http://gamelan.earthweb.com/directories/pages
JavaScript Developer Central	http://developer.netscape.com/tech/javascript/index.html
JavaScript Made Easy	www.easyjavascript.com/javascript.html
JavaScript Search	www.javascriptsearch.com
JavaScript Source	http://javascript.internet.com
The Java Boutique	http://javaboutique.internet.com
Web Teacher JavaScript Tutorial	www.webteacher.com/javascript
Website Abstraction	http://wsabstract.com
WinMag JavaScript Resource Center	www.winmag.com/web/jsres.htm

For Dummies®: Bestselling Book Series for Beginners

Building a Web Site FOR DUMMIES®

by David Crowder and Rhonda Crowder

IDG Books Worldwide, Inc.
An International Data Group Company

Foster City, CA ◆ Chicago, IL ◆ Indianapolis, IN ◆ New York, NY

Building a Web Site For Dummies®

Published by
IDG Books Worldwide, Inc.
An International Data Group Company
919 E. Hillsdale Blvd.
Suite 400
Foster City, CA 94404
www.idgbooks.com (IDG Books Worldwide Web Site)
www.dummies.com (Dummies Press Web Site)

Library of Congress Control Number: 00-103647

ISBN: 0-7645-0720-6

Printed in the United States of America

10 9 8 7 6 5 4 3 2 1

1O/SU/QY/QQ/IN

Distributed in the United States by IDG Books Worldwide, Inc.

Distributed by CDG Books Canada Inc. for Canada; by Transworld Publishers Limited in the United Kingdom; by IDG Norge Books for Norway; by IDG Sweden Books for Sweden; by IDG Books Australia Publishing Corporation Pty. Ltd. for Australia and New Zealand; by TransQuest Publishers Pte Ltd. for Singapore, Malaysia, Thailand, Indonesia, and Hong Kong; by Gotop Information Inc. for Taiwan; by ICG Muse, Inc. for Japan; by Intersoft for South Africa; by Eyrolles for France; by International Thomson Publishing for Germany, Austria and Switzerland; by Distribuidora Cuspide for Argentina; by LR International for Brazil; by Galileo Libros for Chile; by Ediciones ZETA S.C.R. Ltda. for Peru; by WS Computer Publishing Corporation, Inc., for the Philippines; by Contemporanea de Ediciones for Venezuela; by Express Computer Distributors for the Caribbean and West Indies; by Micronesia Media Distributor, Inc. for Micronesia; by Chips Computadoras S.A. de C.V. for Mexico; by Editorial Norma de Panama S.A. for Panama; by American Bookshops for Finland.

For general information on IDG Books Worldwide's books in the U.S., please call our Consumer Customer Service department at 800-762-2974. For reseller information, including discounts and premium sales, please call our Reseller Customer Service department at 800-434-3422.

For information on where to purchase IDG Books Worldwide's books outside the U.S., please contact our International Sales department at 317-572-3993 or fax 317-572-4002.

For consumer information on foreign language translations, please contact our Customer Service department at 1-800-434-3422, fax 317-572-4002, or e-mail rights@idgbooks.com.

For information on licensing foreign or domestic rights, please phone +1-650-653-7098.

For sales inquiries and special prices for bulk quantities, please contact our Order Services department at 800-434-3422 or write to the address above.

For information on using IDG Books Worldwide's books in the classroom or for ordering examination copies, please contact our Educational Sales department at 800-434-2086 or fax 317-572-4005.

For press review copies, author interviews, or other publicity information, please contact our Public Relations department at 650-653-7000 or fax 650-653-7500.

For authorization to photocopy items for corporate, personal, or educational use, please contact Copyright Clearance Center, 222 Rosewood Drive, Danvers, MA 01923, or fax 978-750-4470.

is a registered trademark under exclusive license to IDG Books Worldwide, Inc. from International Data Group, Inc.

About the Authors

David and Rhonda Crowder have authored or coauthored nearly 20 books on computers and the Internet, including *Setting Up An Internet Site For Dummies* and the best-selling *Teach Yourself the Internet*. They were selling hypertext systems back in the days when you had to explain to people what the word meant. They have been involved in the online community for well over a decade and are the recipients of several awards, including *NetGuide Magazine*'s Gold Site Award.

ABOUT IDG BOOKS WORLDWIDE

Welcome to the world of IDG Books Worldwide.

IDG Books Worldwide, Inc., is a subsidiary of International Data Group, the world's largest publisher of computer-related information and the leading global provider of information services on information technology. IDG was founded more than 30 years ago by Patrick J. McGovern and now employs more than 9,000 people worldwide. IDG publishes more than 290 computer publications in over 75 countries. More than 90 million people read one or more IDG publications each month.

Launched in 1990, IDG Books Worldwide is today the #1 publisher of best-selling computer books in the United States. We are proud to have received eight awards from the Computer Press Association in recognition of editorial excellence and three from Computer Currents' First Annual Readers' Choice Awards. Our best-selling *...For Dummies®* series has more than 50 million copies in print with translations in 31 languages. IDG Books Worldwide, through a joint venture with IDG's Hi-Tech Beijing, became the first U.S. publisher to publish a computer book in the People's Republic of China. In record time, IDG Books Worldwide has become the first choice for millions of readers around the world who want to learn how to better manage their businesses.

Our mission is simple: Every one of our books is designed to bring extra value and skill-building instructions to the reader. Our books are written by experts who understand and care about our readers. The knowledge base of our editorial staff comes from years of experience in publishing, education, and journalism — experience we use to produce books to carry us into the new millennium. In short, we care about books, so we attract the best people. We devote special attention to details such as audience, interior design, use of icons, and illustrations. And because we use an efficient process of authoring, editing, and desktop publishing our books electronically, we can spend more time ensuring superior content and less time on the technicalities of making books.

You can count on our commitment to deliver high-quality books at competitive prices on topics you want to read about. At IDG Books Worldwide, we continue in the IDG tradition of delivering quality for more than 30 years. You'll find no better book on a subject than one from IDG Books Worldwide.

John Kilcullen
Chairman and CEO
IDG Books Worldwide, Inc.

Eighth Annual Computer Press Awards ≥1992

Ninth Annual Computer Press Awards ≥1993

Tenth Annual Computer Press Awards ≥1994

Eleventh Annual Computer Press Awards ≥1995

Dedication

For Solstice and her endless quest for knowledge.

Authors' Acknowledgments

Thanks are due to Steven Hayes and Jodi Jensen, our fine editors, who were there for us every step of the way. We also leaned heavily on the expertise of Carmen Krikorian, our permissions editor, who helped us put together all the marvelous material on the CD-ROM. Bill Barton, Sheri Replin, Diana Conover, and Yolanda Burrell all helped to make this the best book we could put together. And they're just the tip of the iceberg: About a zillion people work their tails off behind the scenes at IDG to bring you the finest books they can. Our hats are off to all of them. Last, but by no means least, we'd like to say once again how much we appreciate all the hard work done by our agent, David Fugate, and the rest of the folks at Waterside Productions, like Maureen Maloney and Wendy Dietrich, who keep everything flowing smoothly.

Publisher's Acknowledgments

We're proud of this book; please register your comments through our IDG Books Worldwide Online Registration Form located at http://my2cents.dummies.com.

Some of the people who helped bring this book to market include the following:

Acquisitions, Editorial, and Media Development

Project Editors: Jodi Jensen, Sheri Replin

Acquisitions Editor: Steven H. Hayes

Copy Editors: William A. Barton, Diana R. Conover

Proof Editor: Teresa Artman

Technical Editor: Yolanda Burrell

Media Development Specialist: Travis Silvers

Permissions Editor: Carmen Krikorian

Media Development Coordinator: Marisa E. Pearman

Editorial Manager: Kyle Looper

Editorial Assistant: Sarah Shupert

Production

Project Coordinator: Regina Snyder

Layout and Graphics: Amy Adrian, Barry Offringa, Jill Piscitelli, Julie Trippetti, Erin Zeltner

Proofreaders: John Greenough, Susan Moritz, Charles Spencer, York Production Services, Inc.

Indexer: York Production Services, Inc.

Special Help

Rebecca Senninger

General and Administrative

IDG Books Worldwide, Inc.: John Kilcullen, CEO

IDG Books Technology Publishing Group: Richard Swadley, Senior Vice President and Publisher; Walter R. Bruce III, Vice President and Publisher; Joseph Wikert, Vice President and Publisher; Mary Bednarek, Vice President and Director, Product Development; Andy Cummings, Publishing Director, General User Group; Mary C. Corder, Editorial Director; Barry Pruett, Publishing Director

IDG Books Consumer Publishing Group: Roland Elgey, Senior Vice President and Publisher; Kathleen A. Welton, Vice President and Publisher; Kevin Thornton, Acquisitions Manager; Kristin A. Cocks, Editorial Director

IDG Books Internet Publishing Group: Brenda McLaughlin, Senior Vice President and Publisher; Sofia Marchant, Online Marketing Manager

IDG Books Production for Branded Press: Debbie Stailey, Director of Production; Cindy L. Phipps, Manager of Project Coordination, Production Proofreading, and Indexing; Tony Augsburger, Manager of Prepress, Reprints, and Systems; Shelley Lea, Supervisor of Graphics and Design; Debbie J. Gates, Production Systems Specialist; Steve Arany, Associate Automation Supervisor; Robert Springer, Supervisor of Proofreading; Trudy Coler, Page Layout Manager; Kathie Schutte, Senior Page Layout Supervisor; Janet Seib, Associate Page Layout Supervisor; Michael Sullivan, Production Supervisor

Packaging and Book Design: Patty Page, Manager, Promotions Marketing

◆

The publisher would like to give special thanks to Patrick J. McGovern, without whom this book would not have been possible.

◆

Contents at a Glance

Introduction 1

Part I: Moving from Web Page to Web Site 7
Chapter 1: The Zen of Sites 9
Chapter 2: Pouring the Foundation 15
Chapter 3: Web Page Construction 101 27

Part II: Adding Sparkle to Your Site 49
Chapter 4: Plugging in Scripts and Applets 51
Chapter 5: Making Site Navigation Easier 65
Chapter 6: Making Things Look Great 91
Chapter 7: Web Sights and Sounds 105
Chapter 8: Web Aerobics: Tuning Up Your Site 123

Part III: Drop In and Stay a While, Folks 143
Chapter 9: Listening to Your Visitors 145
Chapter 10: Letting 'Em Have Their Say 165
Chapter 11: Just Plain Fun 183
Chapter 12: Using Content Providers 205

Part IV: Raking in the Bucks 223
Chapter 13: Stalking the Wild Dollar 225
Chapter 14: Love That Plastic: Taking Credit Cards 235
Chapter 15: Examining Affiliates Programs 255

Part V: Publishing and Publicizing Your Site 267
Chapter 16: Letting the World In 269
Chapter 17: Publicizing Your Site 279
Chapter 18: Keeping in Touch 295

Part VI: The Part of Tens 309
Chapter 19: Ten Great Places to Get Advice 311
Chapter 20: Ten Fabulous Tools for E-Commerce 323
Chapter 21: Ten More Great Add-Ins 335

Part VII: Appendixes 347

Appendix A: Glossary 349
Appendix B: About the CD 361

Index 369

IDG Books Worldwide End-User License Agreement.....385

Installation Instructions.............................387

Book Registration Information.......................Back of Book

Cartoons at a Glance

By Rich Tennant

page 7

page 309

page 49

page 223

page 267

page 347

page 143

Fax: 978-546-7747
E-mail: richtennant@the5thwave.com
World Wide Web: www.the5thwave.com

Table of Contents

Introduction *1*

About This Book 1

How to Use This Book 1

Foolish Assumptions 2

Conventions Used in This Book 2

How This Book Is Organized 3

    Part I: Moving from Web Page to Web Site 3

    Part II: Adding Sparkle to Your Site 3

    Part III: Drop In and Stay a While, Folks 3

    Part IV: Raking in the Bucks 4

    Part V: Publishing and Publicizing Your Site 4

    Part VI: The Part of Tens 4

    Part VII: Appendixes 4

About the CD-ROM 4

Icons Used in This Book 5

Where to Go from Here 5

Part I: Moving from Web Page to Web Site *7*

Chapter 1: The Zen of Sites 9

Achieving Unity: What Makes a Site Truly a Site 9

    Determining the underlying theme 10

    Setting limits 10

Keeping Them Coming Back 11

    Creating a comfortable site 11

    Keeping your site fresh 12

Tapping Creativity 12

Online Sources 14

Chapter 2: Pouring the Foundation 15

Drafting a Plan 15

    What do you want to accomplish? 16

    Who do you want to reach? 17

    What services do you need? 17

Setting the Look 18

    Appealing to your audience 18

    Avoiding clutter 19

Designing a Navigation Scheme 20
    Laying out the welcome mat 20
    Getting from here to there 21
The Big Rules 24
Online Sources 25

Chapter 3: Web Page Construction 101 ....**27**
Tagging Along 27
Examining Page-Building Programs 28
    Text editors 29
    WYSIWYG programs 31
Determining Your Web-Page Structure 33
    Normal elements 33
    Frames and framesets 35
Getting Wordy 36
    Paragraphs 36
    Headings 38
    Fonts 38
    Lines 40
Coloring Things 42
Linking Up 43
Picturing It 43
    Graphics programs 44
    Images 45
    Background images 46
    Image maps 47
Online Sources 48

Part II: Adding Sparkle to Your Site *49*

Chapter 4: Plugging in Scripts and Applets **51**
Making Sure That You Have CGI Access 51
    Why your ISP won't help 52
    Finding a CGI provider 53
    Using remotely hosted CGI scripts 53
Adding CGI Scripts 54
    Basic techniques 54
    Solving problems 55
Incorporating JavaScripts 56
    Basic techniques 57
    Facing problems 58
Dropping In Java Applets 59
    Basic techniques 60
    Troubleshooting applets 62
Online Sources 63

Chapter 5: Making Site Navigation Easier ...... .65

Adding a Search Function ...... .65
Getting a free search engine with FreeFind ...... .66
Putting the Atomz.com search engine on your site ...... .69
Dropping in Perl CGI scripts with Simple Search ...... .76
Showing the Way with Navigational Tools ...... .79
Shelving your links with Bookshelf ...... .79
Creating menus with VMaxNav ...... .85
Making drop-down lists ...... .88
Online Sources ...... .89

Chapter 6: Making Things Look Great ...... .91

Getting Graphics — for Free! ...... .91
Heeding copyrights and credits ...... .91
Differentiating between graphic file formats ...... .93
Ordering Graphics by Graziana Cipresso ...... .94
Creating a Logo with CoolText.com ...... .95
Using Some Elemental Applets ...... .99
Burning down the site ...... .99
Webbing in a winter wonderland ...... .100
Sitting by the lake ...... .101
Online Sources ...... .104

Chapter 7: Web Sights and Sounds ...... .105

Using Informatron's Cool Features ...... .106
Adding Informatron TV to your site ...... .106
Adding Informatron's Interactive Scoreboard to your site ...... .108
Adding Informatron News to your site ...... .110
Singing Karaoke-Style on Your Site ...... .111
Putting MIDI Radio on Your Site ...... .113
Getting Music ...... .115
Finding music houses ...... .115
Finding public-domain music ...... .116
Downloading MAGIX software ...... .117
Downloading a free version of iShell ...... .118
Online Sources ...... .120

Chapter 8: Web Aerobics: Tuning Up Your Site ...... .123

W3C HTML Validation Service ...... .123
Checking Those Links ...... .125
LinkPolice ...... .126
Linkbot Pro ...... .126
Putting Your Graphics on a Diet ...... .128
GIFWorks ...... .128
Spinwave ...... .132

Testing Your Site with NetMechanic 133
Statbot 136
Online Sources 141

Part III: Drop In and Stay a While, Folks 143

Chapter 9: Listening to Your Visitors 145

Taking Polls 145
    Alxpoll 146
    TallySite.com 152
Trying Out Form Makers 159
Privacy and Security 161
Online Sources 162

Chapter 10: Letting 'Em Have Their Say 165

Providing Guestbooks 166
Creating Message Boards 169
    Setting up a message board with Boardhost 170
    Modifying your Boardhost message board 172
Giving the Gift of Gab 178
Online Sources 182

Chapter 11: Just Plain Fun 183

Running RiddleNut.com's Random Riddles 184
Adding Bogglers to Your Web Page 187
Playing Around with Trivia Blitz 189
Placing Quotations on Your Site 192
    Quoting with The Quote Machine 192
    Quoting with Quoter 194
Setting Up EasyPostcard on Your Site 198
Goofing Off with Games 201
    Downloading free games from Loonyverse 201
    Playing games Jagex style 202
Online Sources 203

Chapter 12: Using Content Providers 205

Adding News to Your Web Site 206
    Taking advantage of 7am News 206
    Getting to know Moreover.com 209
Adding Weather Forecasts to Your Site 212
    Using Weather Underground 212
    Using Weather.com 214
Placing Cartoons on Your Web Site 216
    Not In My Backyard 216
    Toy Trunk Railroad 217
    The Deep End 218

Finding Copyright-Free Material 218
    The other Krishnamurti 219
    Project Gutenberg 220
Online Sources 221

Part IV: Raking in the Bucks 223

Chapter 13: Stalking the Wild Dollar 225

Learning the Real Secret to Internet Success 226
    Developing the attitude 226
    Focusing on your line 227
    Getting supplies flowing 229
Designing for E-Commerce 232
Online Sources 233

Chapter 14: Love That Plastic: Taking Credit Cards 235

Getting a Merchant Account 236
    Local banks versus online specialists 236
    How to sign up 239
    What to watch out for 240
Online Malls 244
Checking Out Alternative Payment Methods 245
    E-Cash 245
    Phone checks 245
    Phones, faxes, and snail mail 246
Converting Currencies 247
Online Sources 252

Chapter 15: Examining Affiliates Programs 255

Yeah, Sure, It's Free 256
Can I Join? 257
    Finding partners 257
    Working with a network 258
Profiting from Your Program 259
    Taking time 260
    Working the audience 261
    Adding value to your site 262
    Focusing on the topic 262
Running Your Own Affiliates Program 263
    Doing the math 263
    Using software to host affiliates 263
Online Sources 265

Part V: Publishing and Publicizing Your Site 267

Chapter 16: Letting the World In 269
Going Live 269
    ISPs 270
    Virtual and dedicated servers 270
    Finding your match 272
Keeping It Cheap: Free Web Site Providers 273
Getting Your Own Domain Name 274
    Picking a name 275
    Finding a registrar 276
Online Sources 277

Chapter 17: Publicizing Your Site 279
Working Keywords 280
    Adding meta tags 281
    Writing for keywords 281
    Writing for your audience 282
    Avoiding traps 283
    Playing games with keywords 283
    Analyzing keywords 284
Submitting to the Search Sites 286
    Do it yourself 286
    Submission services 287
    Keeping out of the search sites 288
Checking Your Search Site Position 290
    Manual checking 290
    ScoreCheck 291
Investigating Reciprocal Linking 292
    Joining Web rings 293
    Joining a banner exchange 293
Online Sources 294

Chapter 18: Keeping in Touch 295
Using Autoresponders 295
    WebMailStation.com 296
    GetResponse.com 298
Opt-In Newsletters 299
    Eurofreebies 300
    OakNet Publishing 303
Keeping Visitors Updated with Mind-it 304
Online Sources 307

Part VI: The Part of Tens *309*

Chapter 19: Ten Great Places to Get Advice .... .311

Web Watch 312
MyService Experts Avenue 313
grammarNOW! 314
geek/talk Forums For Webmasters 315
The Small Business Advisor 316
LawGuru.com 317
Bizy Moms 318
Ezine Factory 319
Poor Richard's Web Site 320
eBoz! 321

Chapter 20: Ten Fabulous Tools for E-Commerce 323

suite 7 323
AllCommerce 325
HumanClick 326
BayBuilder 327
ECommerce Guide 328
MapQuest 328
S&H Greenpoints 329
Systran Translation Software 331
TRUSTe 332
DMA Privacy Policy Generator 333

Chapter 21: Ten More Great Add-Ins 335

Intel Web Applets 335
Merriam-Webster 337
iSyndicate 338
Leonardo MediaBank 339
Recommend-It 340
Server Rat 341
@Watch 342
VoiceBlast 343
Tough Media 344
eCal*Now!* 345

Part VII: Appendixes *347*

Appendix A : Glossary .... .349

Appendix B: About the CD 361
   System Requirements 361
   Using the CD in Windows 362
   Using the CD with Mac OS 363
   What You Find 363
      Authors' links 363
      BBEdit and BBEdit Lite 364
      Bookshelf applet 364
      Dee Dreslough's Art Gallery on CD-ROM Web page graphics 364
      Dreamweaver 364
      Fire applet 364
      Fireworks 3.0 365
      Goddess Art of Jonathon Earl Bowser 365
      HomeSite 365
      Lake applet 365
      Lindy's Graphics 366
      Linkbot Pro and Linkbot Enterprise Server 366
      Macrobot 366
      Metabot 366
      Microsoft Internet Explorer 5.0 Web browser 366
      Netscape Communicator 4.7 Web browser 367
      Novagene's tiled background images 367
      Paint Shop Pro 367
      Snow applet 367
      Statbot 367
      WS_FTP Pro 368
   If You've Got Problems (Of the CD Kind) 368

Index *369*

IDG Books Worldwide End-User License Agreement *385*

Installation Instructions *387*

Book Registration Information . . . .*Back of Book*

Introduction

· ·

*M*aybe you already have your own Web site and you're not quite satisfied with it. Or perhaps you're still in the planning stages and want to know what you can do to make your site as good as it can be. You've been to Web sites that have all the bells and whistles, and you wouldn't be human if you weren't just a wee bit envious. Well, now you can have it all, too. In this book, we show you some of the best stuff around, and we tell you just how to go about putting it on your site.

About This Book

This isn't just another Web-design book. It's special. Really. We set out to write the one book we'd want by our side if we were looking to set up a really fancy Web site and not break the bank doing it. We tracked down and tested zillions of Web site enhancements and selected the top of the line to share with you. And we're honestly proud of the results. We've authored or coauthored nearly 20 books on computers and the Internet, and this one is our hands-down favorite.

It's full of things you're sure to love. It's packed with fun stuff like karaoke rooms and Internet television. It's got plenty of serious stuff, too, like how to get past the hype and really make money. You'll wonder how in the world you ever got along without having these features on your Web site.

How to Use This Book

Keep it next to your computer and never lend it to anybody. It's far too precious for that. Make your friends buy their own copies. If you need to make space on your bookshelf, throw away anything else you own to make room for it. When you travel, take it with you. Hold it in your arms at night and tell it how much you love it.

Each chapter is a stand-alone entity. (Don't you just love that word?) You don't have to read the whole thing, and it's a rare person who will read it from cover to cover right off the bat. Go ahead — hit the table of contents or the index and jump to the parts you're most interested in. But don't forget to explore the rest of the book after you're done with the parts that excite you most. You won't regret it — you'll find wonders in every chapter.

Foolish Assumptions

We figure that you have some kind of experience with creating Web pages. You don't need to be a wizard at it, just good enough to put together something that opens in a Web browser and to upload it to your Web site.

We assume that you have a favorite Web-page creation program — whether it's HomeSite, Dreamweaver, plain old Notepad, or the Unix-based text editor, vi — and you know how to use it. So when we say to copy and paste text or save your file, you know what you need to do. Just in case you don't have a good Web-authoring program, we've got that covered, too. The CD-ROM that accompanies this book has a passel of HTML editors on it.

Conventions Used in This Book

It's all organized, we promise. Even though it's rather plebeian compared with finding free content for your site, lots of people worked very hard to make sure that this book follows some straightforward rules, like typographical conventions.

Code listings, of which we have plenty, look like this:

```
<HTML>
<HEAD>
<SCRIPT>
...
</SCRIPT>
<TITLE>
...
</TITLE>
</HEAD>
...
```

HTML elements in this book are in uppercase and their attributes are in lowercase, as in this example:

```
<INPUT type="hidden" name="answer" value="yes">
```

If the value of an attribute is in normal type, you enter it exactly as shown. If it's in italics, it's only a placeholder value, and you need to replace it with a real value. In the following example, you replace *myownimage* with the name of the image file you intend to use:

```
<IMG src="myownimage">
```

Whenever you see the URL for one of the top sites we've tracked down, it appears in a special typeface within the paragraph, like this: www.dummies.com. Or it may appear on a separate line, like this:

```
www.dummies.com
```

How This Book Is Organized

This book is divided into seven parts. We organized it that way, with a little help from the folks you see in the Acknowledgements. You did read the Acknowledgements, didn't you? Don't tell us that you're the kind of person who reads the Introduction but doesn't read the Acknowledgements. Please tell us that you didn't miss the Dedication, too?

Each part has between three and five chapters in it. And each chapter has headings and subheadings. All the sections under these headings and sub-headings have text that enlightens the heart and soul. This book is so organized, you wouldn't believe it. Here, take a look.

Part I: Moving from Web Page to Web Site

Part I shows you how to transform a bunch of Web pages into a coherent Web site. It spills the secrets of how to plan a successful site from the ground up and tosses in a quick refresher course in basic HTML.

Part II: Adding Sparkle to Your Site

Part II gives you a ton of ways to make your site work, look, and sound great. It covers the different ways that you add new features to your Web site. Then it covers different ways to add search and navigation features to your site, where to get great graphics and multimedia, and how to keep your site in tip-top shape.

Part III: Drop In and Stay a While, Folks

Part III is about getting your visitors involved in your site so that they keep coming back for more. It shows how to get feedback from your site visitors with surveys, forms, message boards, and chat rooms. If that's not enough, there's fun and games and a guide to getting fresh content for your site.

Part IV: Raking in the Bucks

Part IV takes a look at making money from your site. It explodes the myths about Internet income and shows you how to really make a profit, how to get a credit card merchant account, and how to work both ends of the affiliates game.

Part V: Publishing and Publicizing Your Site

Part V shows you all you need to know about getting your site online and helping people find it. It covers Web-hosting options, getting listed in search engines, and establishing reciprocal links with other sites. It also shows how to keep in touch with your visitors after they leave without falling into the spam trap.

Part VI: The Part of Tens

Part VI is The Part of Tens. Well, it just wouldn't be a *For Dummies* book without The Part of Tens, right? We've got three chapters in this part, so you've got 30 extra bits here that tell you all sorts of wonderful things, like where to go for Web site design advice and ways to add value to your site.

Part VII: Appendixes

Part VII has a glossary of all the tech terms that might leave you baffled and a guide to what's on the CD-ROM that's tucked into the back of this book. Which leads us to. . . .

About the CD-ROM

We put together plenty of nice stuff for you on the CD-ROM that accompanies this book. You'll find all sorts of things that make jazzing up your Web site easy — from sophisticated HTML editors to some of the finest Web art you've ever seen. We included programs for Windows and programs for Macs. And wherever possible, we included the Web site add-ins that we discuss in the book, including some Java applets that'll knock your socks off.

Icons Used in This Book

The icons in the margins of this book point out items of special interest. Keep an eye out for them — they're important.

Psst! Listen, pal, we wouldn't tell just anybody about this, but here's a way to make things a bit easier or get a little bit more out of it.

Time to tiptoe on eggshells. One false step and things can get pretty messy.

You don't really need to know this stuff, but we just plain like to show off sometimes. Humor us.

Well, of course, it's all memorable material. But these bits are ones you'll especially want to keep in mind.

You don't need to bother downloading this applet or feature because we already did it for you.

Where to Go from Here

Well, keep turning pages, of course. And use the material to make your own Web site the hottest thing there ever was.

One of the hardest parts about getting this book together was categorizing the material in it. Many times, a Web site add-in could have been slotted into a different chapter than the one it ended up in because it had multiple features or attributes. So when you're at any of the sites that we mention in this book, be sure to take a good look around. A site that has a great chat room might also have a fine affiliates program. One that offers a good series of Java applets could have some solid tutorials on Web design. A site that has good information on dedicated servers may have the best e-commerce solution for you. We encourage you to browse up a storm.

Part I
Moving from Web Page to Web Site

"Sales on the Web site are down. I figure the server's chi is blocked, so we're fudgin' around the feng shui in the computer room, and if that doesn't work, Ronnie's got a chant that should do it."

In this part . . .

We start off by covering all the things that you need to know to put together a Web site. Chapter 1 shows you the differences between a bunch of Web pages and a coherent Web site. Chapter 2 spills the secrets of how to plan a successful site from the ground up. And Chapter 3 is a quick refresher course in basic HTML.

Chapter 1

The Zen of Sites

In This Chapter

▶ Creating unity of content

▶ Building visitor loyalty

▶ Unearthing your personal creativity

"**Y**ou're a really good Web designer," we told a client's Webmaster recently. He shrugged it off and went on to the next topic on the meeting's agenda. Whether he was just being modest or thought we were playing corporate politics with cheap compliments, we don't know. We meant what we said, however, and the reason is simple. It wasn't that his pages were filled with nice graphics. It wasn't that the elements were finely balanced. It wasn't that the JavaScript popups added an involving level of interactivity.

None of these things — not individually or in combination — can make a site fly. The reason we were impressed with the Webmaster's work was because he clearly understood that a Web site isn't just a bunch of pages that happen to reside on the same server.

Achieving Unity: What Makes a Site Truly a Site

No matter what technology you use to build your site, you can make it a great one — or a real loser. You can base it on HTML (HyperText Markup Language), CFML (Cold Fusion Markup Language), ASP (Active Server Pages), DHTML (Dynamic HTML), or any other alphabetical wonders you care to work with. It may sound blasphemous to a world that's used to worshipping at the altars of the latest high-tech advances, but the real secret to making a Web site work is simple human insight.

Determining the underlying theme

Long before you set out to choose background colors or font types or graphical styles, you must get a solid grasp on the theme of your site. The theme is the unifying idea on which everything else in your site rests. Sometimes, it's simple and obvious. For a corporate recruiting site, the theme is why this company is the best place to work. For a genealogical site, the theme is the history of a single family and its offshoots.

Other times, it's a bit more complex. For an e-commerce site, you may choose a theme of great prices and saving money. If you're aiming for a different market, however, you may charge high prices and base your theme on either higher-quality products or just plain snob appeal. The underlying mechanics of both sites may well be identical — navigational methods, order-processing systems, and so forth — but the sites' editorial content and graphical look and feel would have to be totally different.

Your low-cost bargain site may, for example, have bright and simple graphics that show a happy-go-lucky cartoon character using scissors to whack dollars in half. The high-roller site, on the other hand, would do well with richer, deeper colors. Although both sites, as in any selling situation, need to display photographs of their products, the higher-priced site is most likely to appeal to its intended audience with photographs of well-dressed people using its products in sophisticated settings.

Setting limits

If you've ever participated in newsgroups or mailings lists, you know how annoying it is when someone gets way off topic. There you are on `http://alt.citrus.cosmetics`, trying to find out the latest tips for using orange juice as a hair conditioner, and some guy starts blathering about the high price of gasoline or which cell-phone company has the best roaming plan. It's usually not very long before someone else reminds him that's not what he's there for.

When it comes to the material on your site, unless you're part of a Web development team, there's nobody who's going to keep you from drifting off-topic but you. This is the flip side of determining your theme — determining where to stop and what not to cover.

Take an e-commerce site devoted to personal electronics, for example. You'd need to decide whether to sell the entire spectrum of available devices or just to target a specific niche, such as MP3 players or digital cameras. For a religious site, you may need to choose among covering the activities of your local church, the wider issue of the tenets of the sect to which it belongs, or the broadest range of world religious beliefs. If you don't know in advance what you're going to do — and not do — then you're really hampering yourself. Designing a Web site is much easier if you know what specific parameters your efforts must meet.

Keeping Them Coming Back

Practically every human endeavor depends on repeat customers. Even if you're not actually selling your site visitors anything, the number and frequency of return visits are generally good indicators of success or failure.

You've got to think from two perspectives if you're going to make your site into a place that people want to visit again and again. You have to wear your developer's hat, of course, but you also need to pretend that you're one of the people visiting your site. Put aside your awareness of the site's structure and mechanics; come at it as though you have just stumbled across it and have never seen it before.

Ask others whose judgment you trust to visit and critique your site. You don't have to change things to suit them, but getting outside perspectives on your work never hurts.

Creating a comfortable site

Keeping visitors around for even a little while, let alone making them want to return, depends on the level of comfort that you provide. If they're not comfortable moving around your site to begin with, what makes you think that they're going to bookmark it and come back for a return engagement? In creating comfort in your Web site, you need to consider the following questions:

- ✔ **Does the site maintain a consistent layout from page to page?** If not, you'll create stress and annoyance for your visitors.

- ✔ **Is the type and style of content consistent over time?** This point is a critical one. A large part of visitor comfort comes from always finding what they expect when they visit your site.

- ✔ **Is it easy to navigate from one page or section to another?** Visitors usually don't appreciate being forced to jump through hoops or follow a preset path (see Chapter 2 for site navigation tips).

- ✔ **If the site is larger than a few pages, does it include a search feature?** Most people are either legitimately busy or just plain impatient. Unless your site enables visitors to run a search so that they can quickly and easily find the material they're looking for, you run the risk that they simply won't bother to use your site.

Keeping your site fresh

If your material never changes, the odds are pretty good that most people won't come back to it very often, if ever. Unless your sole topic is a rock-solid reference subject, you can't get away with anything less than constant updating. Sure, the *Oxford English Dictionary* can come out with a new edition only every few generations. (The first edition came out in 1928 and the second one in 1989, with only two supplements in between.) But such cases are very rare. Even if you deal with a modern high-tech equivalent, such as a site on the Java programming language or the current HTML standard, you need to stay on your toes.

If your core material is something that doesn't change often, you need to add some peripheral material that you can replace more frequently. Consider adding a Tip of the Day, fresh links, a Did You Know? column, or something along those lines so that you can avoid offering only totally stale content to your return visitors.

How often you need to update your site is dependent partially on your topic and partially on your site policy. With sites that deal with volatile topics such as breaking international news, you need to update on a minimum of an hourly basis. On the other hand, sites that analyze the news can stand a more leisurely pace — daily, weekly, or even monthly — because their scope is considerably wider.

Even if your topic doesn't absolutely demand a certain update schedule, you should still establish a regular policy for how often you add fresh material to your site. Whatever schedule you establish, make sure you stick with it. Remember the comfort factor, and bear in mind that your site's visitors will be less comfortable if they don't know what to expect from you. Consistency on your side will help build trust on theirs.

Rock bottom: A Web site must change at least once a month in order to keep anybody interested in coming back to it.

Tapping Creativity

Although much of what goes into making a Web site function is pretty much simple, mechanical, left-brain stuff, there's another level. You need to reach that level if you're going to stretch beyond the basics and create sites that really shine. Fortunately, you can use a lot of simple techniques to get from here (the basics) to there (an extraordinary site).

You don't need to sit around in a lotus position, chanting mantras in order to reach your own hidden creative resources. If that's your particular cup of tea, by all means do it, but whatever means you employ, the goal's the same — to stop doing just plain "thinking" and reach a different level of understanding.

Now, we've got nothing against day-to-day thinking. We do a fair amount of it ourselves. But *standard* thinking means that you're only using half of your brainpower. Peoples' brains have two different halves. The left brain is the one that we "live in" most of the time — the one that handles numbers and words and sees everything as sequential. The right brain, on the other hand, sees everything as symbols and images that are free-floating and nonsequential.

People actually have five brains, not just two, but we promised our editor that we wouldn't use the word *paleomammalian* in this book.

The basic upshot of all this right-brain/left-brain stuff is that the left brain is such a loudmouth that you don't often hear what your right brain says. And it's got so much to tell you. Because the right side of the brain isn't stuck in the same patterns as the left brain, it gives you an entirely different perspective on the world — and on your work — that can often provide valuable insights and show you patterns that you didn't even realize existed before. Perhaps it can identify the perfect background color to go with a particular topic or the kind of navigation buttons that would appeal most to your audience — things that would be very difficult to achieve by linear thinking alone.

At any rate, your right brain's there for you to use, free of charge, and you ignore it at your peril. So how do you muzzle the left brain long enough to hear what the right brain has to say? Here's a handful of tips for you:

- ✔ **Meditate:** You can use an official, ritualistic method of meditation, if you want, where you study for years under a guru. On the other hand, you can just sit in a comfortable chair and let your mind drift. If your left brain just refuses to stop chattering, try subvocalizing or humming nonsense syllables such as "dum-de-dum" to override it, or listen to music to occupy its attention.

- ✔ **Brainstorm:** If you're fortunate enough to be a member of a loose, relaxed team, sit around with other team members and shoot the breeze about the problem. Feel free to get off-topic. Let the humor roll — nonsense often leads to sensible results.

- ✔ **Doodle:** If you're on your own, take your mind off the straight-and-narrow path by drawing whatever pattern comes to mind. Try doodling with your left hand (if you're right-handed) to jog your right brain into action. It's an odd fact that your left brain controls the right side of your body and the right brain controls the left side.

✔ **Do other things:** Take on any activity that has nothing — nothing at all — to do with your work. Play solitaire. Read a novel. Play a video game. After you take a break from your nonwork activity, the answer to your problem often comes to your mind.

✔ **Take a nap:** Your right brain often speaks to you when you're in an unconscious or semiconscious state. You may well wake up with all the inspiration that you need.

Online Sources

Table 1-1 lists some places on the World Wide Web where you can find more information on the topics that we cover in this chapter.

Table 1-1	Online Resources
Web Site Name	*Web Address*
The BrainWaves Center	www.mentalmuscles.com/
Creating a Successful Web Site	www.hooked.net/~larrylin/web.htm
DevSearch	www.devsearch.com/
Left vs. Right: Your Brain Takes Sides!	http://curiocity.com/brainstorm/ rightleft/
Project Cool	www.projectcool.com/

Chapter 2

Pouring the Foundation

- -

In This Chapter

▶ Determining your purpose

▶ Analyzing the audience

▶ Figuring your needs

▶ Appealing to visitors

▶ Keeping it lean

▶ Making main pages work

▶ Creating effective navigation

- -

*P*eople argue about what the number-one factor in quality Web site design is, and they probably always will. Some say great graphics are the key. Others say worthwhile information is everything. Still others think that ease of use is the most important factor. We're not so sure that there's such a thing as a linear ranking for these kinds of things. After all, a good-looking site that doesn't work well is useless. A site with a combination of good content and lousy graphics is nothing to crow about either.

In this chapter, we walk you through the fundamental things that you should consider as you create your Web site. And at the end of the chapter, we give you seven basic rules for creating Web sites that work. Take 'em with a grain of salt, and remember — you're the ultimate judge.

Drafting a Plan

Are you publicizing a political candidate? Trumpeting your favorite cause? Looking for a job? Selling shoe polish? Notice the verbs in each example. They're the key factors in determining your site's *purpose,* as opposed to its *topic.*

What do you want to accomplish?

Just having a topic isn't enough — you need a purpose, too. The *topic* is merely what the site is about, while the *purpose* is what the site does. Say, for example, that you want to create a site about penguins. Okay, that's a nice starting point. You like penguins — they're cute, unusual, and pretty interesting; many people share your interest in them. But why do you want to create a Web site about them? Do you have something to say? Do you have information to give, an opinion to share, or a particular point of view that you want to put across?

You don't need to have a Ph.D. in aquatic ornithology to create such a site. Maybe you just like funny-looking birds that swim. But you still need a purpose, or the site just isn't going to work out in the long run. Perhaps you spent ages plowing through the search engines, and you've gathered together the world's greatest collection of penguin links. But why did you go to all that trouble? What's your purpose?

If the purpose for creating a penguin site is for your own personal enjoyment, then you really don't need to do much with the site. In fact, you can just create a Web page on your own hard drive or even settle for leaving the links in your Web browser's bookmarks. If you do want your page on the World Wide Web, however, it's there for everyone to see, so you need to take the needs of your potential visitors into account, as well as your own needs for creating such a site.

Suppose that you're putting your penguin page on the Web for the purpose of sharing everything you know about these birds with the whole world. How does that purpose change your approach to site design? You need to include more on the Web site than a bare list of links, for one thing. Everything that you do with the site must help people understand its purpose. If you're setting up your own domain name, for example, you want to pick one that clearly describes your site's content — like www.allaboutpenguins.com. (Grab it quick — it still wasn't taken at press time.)

The purpose of your site trickles down through each step that you take in creating it. You want the title of each page in the site to specify how it supports the site's purpose. The textual content of each page needs to lead naturally into some specific aspect of the topic that furthers your goal. Each graphical image must be just the right one to drive home or emphasize a critical point.

Who do you want to reach?

Who are the people you expect to visit your site? What geographical or cultural groups do you want the site to appeal to? Without at least a general idea of your potential audience, you can't have much of an idea about what type of site to create.

If data is available about the audience for similar sites, you want to track it down. But where do you find it? Surprisingly, most of it's available from the people you're competing with. (Even if you're not running a commercial site, similar sites are your competitors.) Anyone who's been involved in any type of intelligence work would be shocked at the way people on the World Wide Web casually throw around valuable information, instead of keeping it under lock and key.

Many sites offer links to their visitor data. Even a quick perusal of the server logs can provide you with priceless insights into the sort of people who visit sites similar to the one you're creating. If the sites you want information on don't list links to their log data, send an e-mail message to the Webmaster asking how to access it. Most Webmasters aren't the slightest bit security-conscious about their customer data, and the number who're more than willing to spill the beans about their visitors may surprise you.

Check out StatBot Micro, a log analyzer written especially for the readers of this book, on the CD-ROM that accompanies this book.

What services do you need?

How much of your own time and effort are you going to put into your Web site? Presumably, you're going to at least control the general design and make the key decisions about content, or you wouldn't be reading this book. Most likely, you're doing the actual page creation as well. If not, you need to make sure that the people who *are* doing the coding know what they're doing and exactly what you expect of them.

When searching for qualified people to create your Web site, don't rely on college degrees, paper certifications, and the like. Make candidates show you their previous work. Go to their Web sites and explore them thoroughly. Test everything that you find to determine whether a candidate has the necessary skill and experience to implement the features you want to include on your site.

If your site means anything to you at all, do *not* place it in the hands of your Aunt Sophie's extremely clever cousin who, although he's only 11 years old, knows just *all sorts of things* about computers. (If you care to figure out what relationship he is to you, by the way, you may want to check out *Genealogy Online For Dummies*, published by IDG Books Worldwide, Inc.)

Beyond the question of creating the Web pages and other files that make up your site, you need to consider where the site itself is going to reside. Chapter 16 contains more detail on this point, but you basically have to figure out if you're going to commit to the task of running your own Web server or house your site on someone else's server. The pro side of doing it yourself is that you maintain total control. The pro side of leasing either an entire Web server or space on a virtual Web server is that you have about 20 million fewer things to worry about, leaving you free to concentrate on your main task — managing your site.

Setting the Look

All great art depends on having every necessary component in place and nothing — not one thing — that you don't need there. Great literature doesn't add extraneous characters or pad its plot lines. Great paintings don't have a bunch of extra brush strokes or colors thrown in for no particular reason. When you're practicing the art of Web design, strive for that kind of purity.

Appealing to your audience

The audience — the visitors you hope to attract to your site — determines the content. To set some basic limits, think of these visitors as being at a beginning, intermediate, or advanced level, and gauge your content accordingly. If you're aiming advanced content at a beginning audience or vice versa, you're looking at failure from the word go.

Not only does your audience determine your content, but its preferences influence your visual-design requirements as well. If your audience consists of high school students whose interests revolve mainly around the latest musical sensations, you need a far different look than if it consists of retired naval officers who want to know about international events.

For the young music lovers, for example, you need to strike a tone that's lighthearted and exciting, both in your words and graphics. Brighter colors and a more relaxed and informal tone for the text are the call here. For the old salts, on the other hand, you need to take a heavier approach, with darker, duller colors and a middling-formal approach to language.

Whatever the group you're aiming for, ask yourself the following questions:

- ✔ **How do they talk among themselves?** Roller hockey players don't communicate quite the same way as cartographers do. What's the level and style of language usage in the group? Do its members have a particular jargon, slang, or regional dialect? If so, can you use it comfortably and correctly?

- ✔ **What kind and color of clothes do they wear?** This kind of information tells you volumes about their preferences. People who are willing to wear suits and ties in midsummer don't think the same way as those who prefer casual clothing. The colors they choose to wear also indicate the color ranges they're likely to feel comfortable with on your site.

- ✔ **What's their world view?** For many people, the world consists of their apartment or house; the road between it and their workplace; their cubicle, office, or factory floor; and a couple of restaurants somewhere along that pathway. For others, the world consists only of Wall Street and the Asian financial markets. For some, the world is a series of airports, cell phones, and e-mail messages. Anything that exists outside your audience's worldview is totally invisible to them and probably doesn't belong on your Web site.

Find out all that you can — from what kind of cars your visitors drive to the hours they wake and sleep. Any kind of information that you can nail down about your audience and their lives helps you to understand them, and that understanding can't help but improve your site's appeal.

Avoiding clutter

If you're one of those people who keeps a perfectly clean desk where your speakers line up exactly perpendicular to the edge of your monitor, whose laundry basket is more than occasionally empty, and who always knows where to find everything that you own, we probably can't tell you much about organization. If you're like the rest of us, however, read on.

Far too many Webmasters seem to think that the best kind of Web page is one that has everything in the world crammed into it. It's like a novel that introduces 27 characters in the first two pages — the overkill ruins it, and your mind is left swimming.

Perhaps you absolutely must put together a Web page containing a dozen frames, several JavaScript pop-ups, numerous Java applets running in the background, and a bunch of animated GIFs that all move around the screen using CSS positioning. If so, please, please, *don't* put in an image map, too.

The line between losing and winning is very fine if you're considering using Web "gadgetry." Without it, most sites seem a bit on the dull side, and Web designers exhibit a really strong Keep-Up-with-the-Joneses streak that usually results in a frenzy of site changes whenever some new technique becomes popular. Too much of a good thing — or too many good things in one place — can, however, become a real problem.

The key is to remember your site's purpose as you're designing any page. If anything you're considering adding to the page doesn't serve that purpose, then don't add it. If you discover some fun or glitzy gizmo that you simply *must* put on a page — and we show you plenty in this book to tempt you — first determine if you can make it fit in with what you already have on that page. If you absolutely can't fit it in, but you still want to add it, maybe you can take something else out to make room for it.

This doesn't mean that you can't have more than one unusual feature on a page — just make sure that you follow a path of moderation.

Designing a Navigation Scheme

Clean navigation, we're sorry to say, isn't very common. There are an astonishing number of Web pages out there that don't even include a link back to the site's main page. If you leave out even this one simple navigational tool on your pages, you force people to go through the hassle of chopping bits off the URL in their Web browser's Address bar in order to get around on your site. Most people just don't bother with that kind of barrier — they give up and go somewhere else instead. And what's the point of having a site that people just want to leave?

Conversely, make sure that people can get to all the pages on your site by starting from the main page. Orphan pages that can't be reached through your site's normal navigational setup are a waste. Sure, you can just sit back and hope that a search engine catalogs it. In that case, people will probably just go right to that page without ever seeing the rest of your site. But that strategy's got nothing to do with Web site design — it's just wishful thinking and hoping that, somewhere, someone else is going to fix what you did wrong.

Laying out the welcome mat

How many times have you clicked a link to go to a site only to find yourself looking at some glitzy image with those inane words <u>Click Here to Enter the Site</u> staring at you? It makes you want to take the Webmaster aside, and with a gentle pat on the head, quietly explain, "I *am* in the site. Don't you realize that?" Where does the Webmaster think that page is — on someone else's site?

Sometimes you find not even a word of explanation — or anything else. Just a picture. Okay, you don't need to be a rocket scientist to figure out that you just need to click that picture, but that just ain't right. Think about it: If you're going to bookmark that site, you're going to bookmark the page that comes *after* the one where you must click the image, right? And the reason for placing your bookmark there is so that you don't need to go through a wasted step whenever you return to that site. It's important to avoid unnecessary links anywhere in your site, but it's most important on your site's main page. The instant that a page loads, you want a visitor to begin *using* your site, not waste time clicking extra links to find the good stuff. If the site offers a function such as a search engine, visitors want the capability to run a search right there, on the spot — not several pages and links away. If the site is informational, you want to give them access to the information immediately. This stipulation doesn't mean that you must include a link to every page on the site from the main page, but you do want to provide some clear and easy ways for visitors to get from the main page to any other page on the site.

We must, however, cite a slight exception to this general rule — one in which you don't have much choice but to offer extra links. If your site displays a lot of images, such as an art gallery, putting all the images on a single page is practically impossible. Sure, you can code the page to accomplish this feat, but the page is going to take forever and a day to download. The only real solution is to use a bunch of links to the images. But you can still offer instant gratification to your visitors by using *thumbnail-image links*.

Figure 2-1 shows such thumbnail links in action. By using smaller versions of the images as the links to the full-sized versions, you give your visitors some idea of how the full-sized pictures look without the wait for the actual images to load. Better yet, your visitors don't need to bother with any images that don't interest them. They can pick and choose which ones they want to view by examining the thumbnails and then clicking the links of their desire.

Getting from here to there

The basic idea for setting up good navigation is that you should group together all the links that your site visitors need to get around. That doesn't mean that they must all be packed together like links in a navigation bar, or even that they all have to be on the same Web page; the only real limit is your own imagination. But it does mean that you have to set them up in some rational manner, preferably one that's intuitive to use. (See Chapter 5 for more details on navigational tools.)

The Web site for the comic strip *User Friendly* (at www.userfriendly.org) is a classic example of a great navigational setup that's also very creative. No matter what you want to do, you find it easy to manage on this site. The main page offers a directory of text links running down the left side, and the link to the current day's cartoon — the main point of interest for most visitors — sits right at the top of a column of image links, as shown in Figure 2-2.

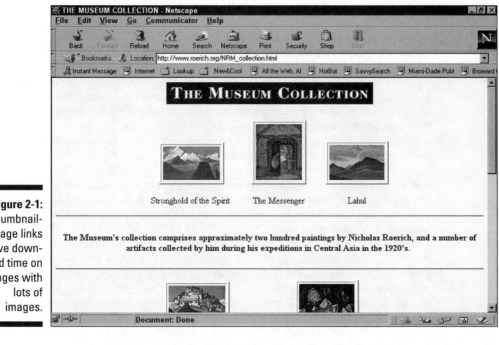

Figure 2-1: Thumbnail-image links save download time on pages with lots of images.

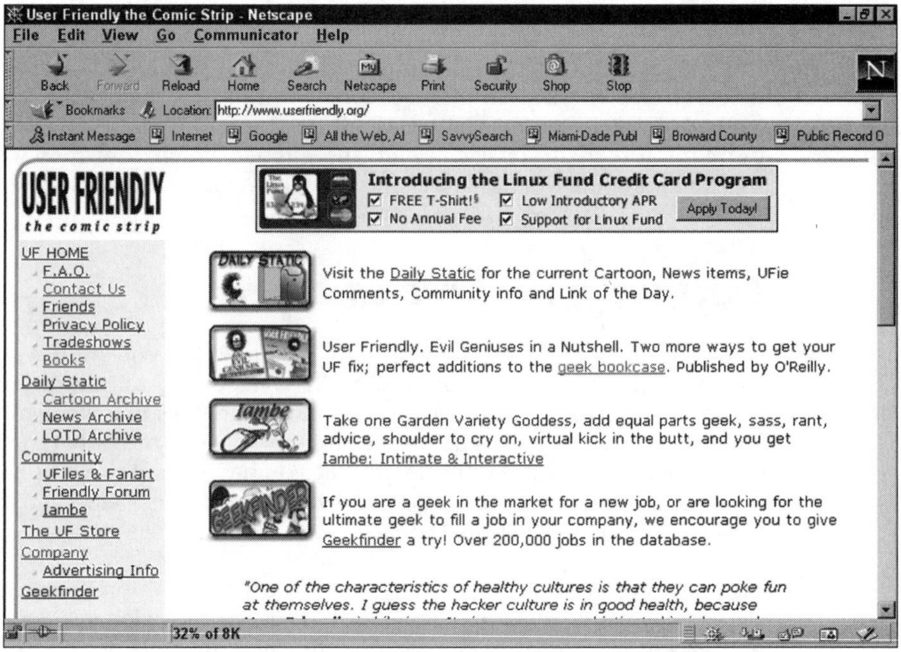

Figure 2-2: Both text and image links are used to good effect.

User Friendly Media Inc. (UserFriendly.org)

The basic archive page for the site (at www.userfriendly.org/cartoons/
archives) enables you to jump to any strip in the current month by clicking
the calendar or to jump to annual archives, as shown in Figure 2-3. The
annual archive pages (which you access by clicking the year links in the
middle of the page) list strips from 12 monthly calendars on each page. And
to really ice the cake, you can scroll down the archive page a bit and search a
database to find any strip by topic or content. Just punch in **Dust Puppy**, and
you get a list of links showing every strip featuring that character, from the
first appearance to the latest.

As you view any day's strip, the links above the cartoon enable you to move
forward or backward to follow a particular line, as shown in Figure 2-4. (Of
course, you find no forward link from the most current strip because tomorrow's installment isn't on the Web site until tomorrow.) You can also click the
Up link to go to the archive page or the Daily Static link to jump to the current day's cartoon or the Home link to go to the home page.

And all this is done without cluttering up the page. Any time that you can add
to the capabilities of your page without detracting from its form or function,
it's great.

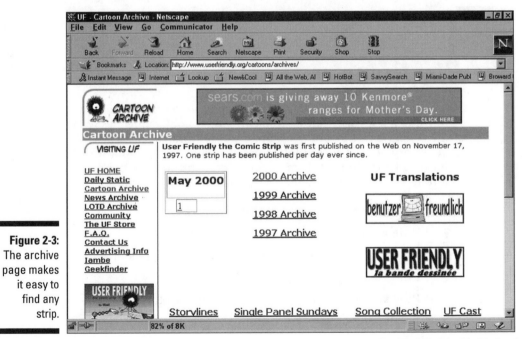

Figure 2-3:
The archive
page makes
it easy to
find any
strip.

Figure 2-4:
Links over the strip comprise a comprehensive navigation scheme.

The Big Rules

We created some short lines to condense the information in this chapter down to a few rules that we think are pretty good guidelines going by our own experiences as both designers and visitors. Make these rules a part of your very being. Cross-stitch them and hang them on your wall. Use a woodburning kit to engrave them on your desk. Tattoo them backward on your forehead so that you see them in the mirror every morning.

- ✔ **Rule #1:** The Web is for reaching out to people.
- ✔ **Rule #2:** Keep your Web pages lean and clean.
- ✔ **Rule #3:** Don't make your visitors jump through hoops.
- ✔ **Rule #4:** Never make an unnecessary link.
- ✔ **Rule #5:** Always group necessary items together.
- ✔ **Rule #6:** If you can give visitors an option, do so.

Remember that design and content are a matter of art more than they are of science, which means that your own personal gut feelings count for more than anything else. If someone tells you that your design decisions are wrong, and they're someone whose input you respect, you certainly want to give their opinion some consideration. But if you're firmly convinced that you're right, never let anyone else's concepts override your own. This brings us to The Big Rule:

✔ **Rule #7:** It's your Web site. It's your vision. Do it your way.

Online Sources

Table 2-1 lists some places on the World Wide Web where you can find more information on the topics that we cover in this chapter.

Table 2-1	Online Resources
Web Site Name	*Web Address*
Echo Web's Web Development Articles	`http://echodev.com/articles/dev.shtml`
HTML Web Tips	`www.projectcool.com/developer/tips/design01_tips/index.html`
Web Pages That Suck	`www.webpagesthatsuck.com`
Yale Style Manual	`info.med.yale.edu/caim/manual/contents.html`

Chapter 3

Web Page Construction 101

In This Chapter

▶ Taking a look at tags

▶ Checking out page-building programs

▶ Figuring out your Web-page structure

▶ Using HTML tags to format text

▶ Getting the lowdown on links

▶ Adding graphics to your Web site

This chapter's here just in case you need a refresher on basic Web page building before plunging ahead into all the wonderful add-ons that we cover in the rest of the book. Here, we touch on how you use HTML to create Web pages and to populate them with text and images. We show you how to format text, set the colors on your Web page, set up links between pages using both text and images, and guide you to some great programs for creating image maps.

We also cover the different kinds of programs that you can get your hands on to create Web pages and to either create or modify graphics.

Even if you already know all about these things, you may want to browse through the chapter and check out some of the links you can find in the tables.

Tagging Along

Web pages are built primarily by writing instructions in *HyperText Markup Language (HTML)*. HTML is a simple programming language; its main aim is to tell a Web browser, such as Netscape Navigator or Microsoft Internet Explorer, how a Web page should look on-screen. As with any other topic, you can go much deeper into HTML and get into all kinds of arguments about the details. Don't worry, however — all we cover here is the bare minimum that you need to know to create Web pages and link them together to make Web sites.

You can always find the most recent version of the HTML specification at www.w3c.org/TR/html.

HTML is composed of *elements*. A paragraph, for example, is an element. So is an image. Elements, in turn, are composed of *tags*, *attributes*, and — sometimes — *content*. A tag is a simple descriptive term that tells a Web browser what element it's dealing with. The beginning of each element is shown by the name of that element within angle braces. This is called a *start tag*. The start tag for a paragraph, for example, is <P> ; for an image, it is <IMG>. The end of an element is shown by the *end tag*, which is just like the start tag except that the end tag has a slash before the element's name. The end tag for a paragraph, therefore, is </P>. Some elements, such as IMG, don't have an end tag. An *attribute* is a modification of the basic element. You specify the width and height of an image, for example, by adding attributes to the tag, as in the following example:

```
<IMG width="100" height="30">
```

Content is simply anything that goes between the start tag and the end tag, as in the following example:

```
<P>This is a paragraph.</P>
```

We cover the tags and attributes that you need most during the course of this chapter, but you need to know this much now in order to understand the choices that you face among different Web page-building programs.

Examining Page-Building Programs

These days, everyone wants to jump on the Web bandwagon, and it seems like every program under the sun can be used to make Web pages. You can use word processors such as Microsoft Word and dedicated page-creation software such as Dreamweaver, GoLive, or FrontPage. Every program has its quirks, and not all of them produce high-quality, clean HTML code.

Leaving out the Johnny-come-latelies, such as word processors that tack HTML onto their older functions, there are two basic kinds of page-building programs. The first is a *text editor* — which is kind of like a word processor without the frills. The second is a *WYSIWYG* (What You See Is What You Get) editor that lets you develop the Web page visually instead of by working directly with the code.

Both proponents of pure text editors and WYSIWYG enthusiasts can get about as raucous defending their favorite approach as a bunch of baseball fans can get about the World Series. The plain fact, though, is that sometimes you'll want to use one type of editor and sometimes you'll prefer the other kind of program. The following sections describe the differences between these two types of programs.

Text editors

HTML files are simple text files. They contain nothing but the plain, old letters, symbols, and numbers that you find on your keyboard. HTML is so simple, in fact, that you don't need any kind of specialized Web page-building program. You can create Web pages perfectly well by using nothing but Windows Notepad — assuming that you have the knowledge of the language that you need to type code without making any mistakes, that is (see Figure 3-1).

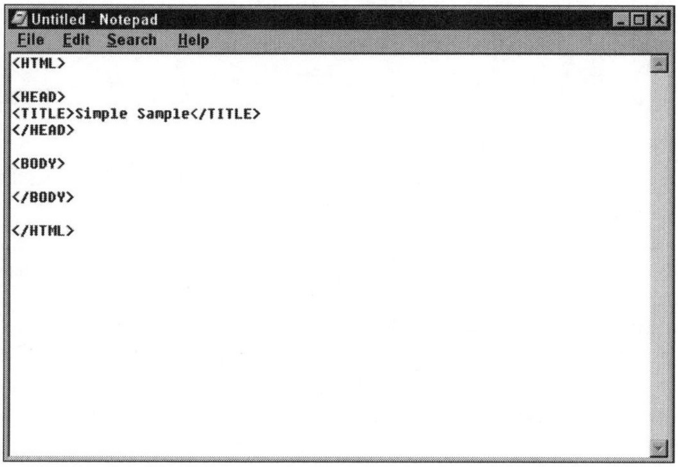

Figure 3-1:
Windows Notepad is really all you need to make a great Web page.

```
Untitled - Notepad
File  Edit  Search  Help
<HTML>

<HEAD>
<TITLE>Simple Sample</TITLE>
</HEAD>

<BODY>

</BODY>

</HTML>
```

You don't have to settle for total simplicity, however, to get the raw power of working directly with the HTML source code. A number of high-powered text editors are designed specifically for creating HTML code. In our opinion (and that of the major computer magazines such as *Windows Magazine* and *PC Magazine*, which constantly road test all the competitors), the best of all the text editors is HomeSite, as shown in Figure 3-2. We had the pleasure of working with Nick Bradbury, the program's creator, on the book *HomeSite 4.5 For Dummies* (published by IDG Books Worldwide, Inc.), and before that, we used the program for our own projects for years.

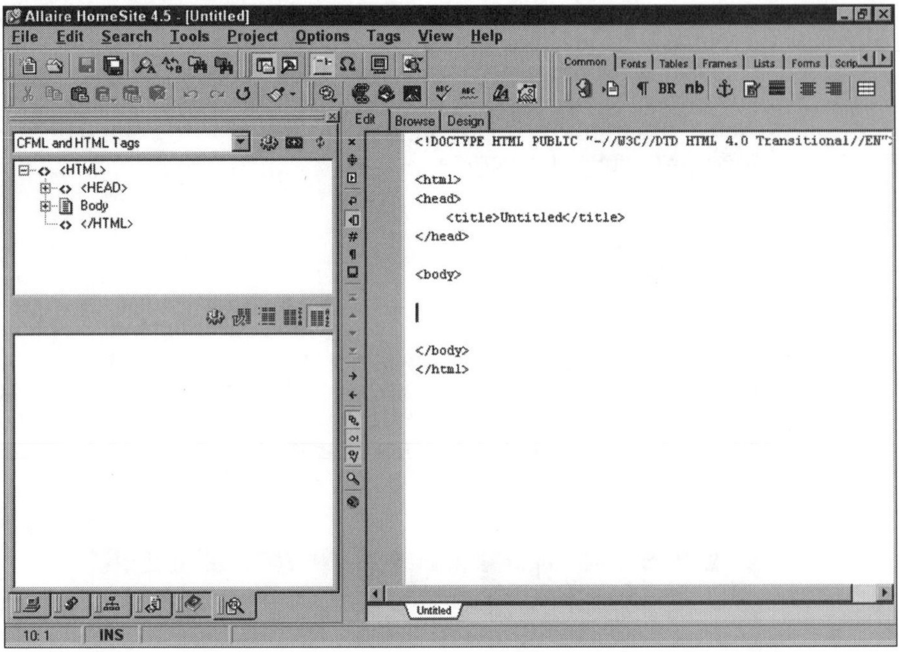

Figure 3-2:
HomeSite
is a great
program,
used for
working
with Web
page source
code by
more pro-
fessionals
than any
other text
editor.

You can find an evaluation version of HomeSite 4.5 on the CD-ROM that
accompanies this book.

At its most basic, you can use HomeSite as a plain old text editor, but it also
has some really shining qualities that can make your Web programming life a
lot easier. For starters, the text is color-coded, which means that elements,
attributes, and content appear in different colors, making the HTML code
easier to read and understand. It also comes with a host of helpful tools built
into it, such as context-sensitive lists of the attributes that you can use with
the tags that you type.

Table 3-1 shows where to find several additional text editors that make creating Web pages easy.

Table 3-1	HTML Editors
Program	*Web Address*
Arachnophilia	www.arachnoid.com/arachnophilia/
Coffee Cup HTML Editor	www.coffeecup.com

Program	Web Address
HomeSite	`www.allaire.com/products/` `homesite/index.cfm`
Hot Dog Professional	`www.sausage.com/hotdog5/` `overview_hdpro5.html`
HTML Assistant Pro	`http://exit0.com/ez1/products/` `pro2000.html`
HTMLed Pro	`www.ist.ca/htmledpro.html`

WYSIWYG programs

WYSIWYG programs are easy for novices to use in the early stages of Web site creation, but they can quickly prove less than satisfactory. The reason for both factors is the same — the program makes a bunch of choices for you. Although this feature may seem a comfort at first, it quickly becomes a limitation. If you go for a WYSIWYG program, make sure that it's sophisticated enough that you can still use it as your skills advance.

You can take a dip in the WYSIWYG waters without investing any money. Netscape Communicator, the suite of programs that includes the Navigator Web browser, also includes a built-in WYSIWYG Web page creator called Composer, as shown in Figure 3-3. To fire it up, just click the Composer icon in the lower-right corner of Navigator. Microsoft offers a similar program, FrontPage Express, which is a stripped-down version of its FrontPage Web-building software.

Most WYSIWYG programs have at least some degree of depth beneath their surface simplicity. Both GoLive and Dreamweaver, for example, let you set the attributes for every element, in case you don't like the default choices. Dreamweaver (see Figure 3-4) actually gives you the best of both worlds because it comes with — and interfaces directly with — HomeSite (or BBEdit for the Mac version). That means that you can enjoy both the quickness of WYSIWYG creation and the total control of text editing in the same page-creation session. Table 3-2 lists several WYSIWYG programs that you can use to build Web pages, along with the Web addresses where you can find them (or information about them).

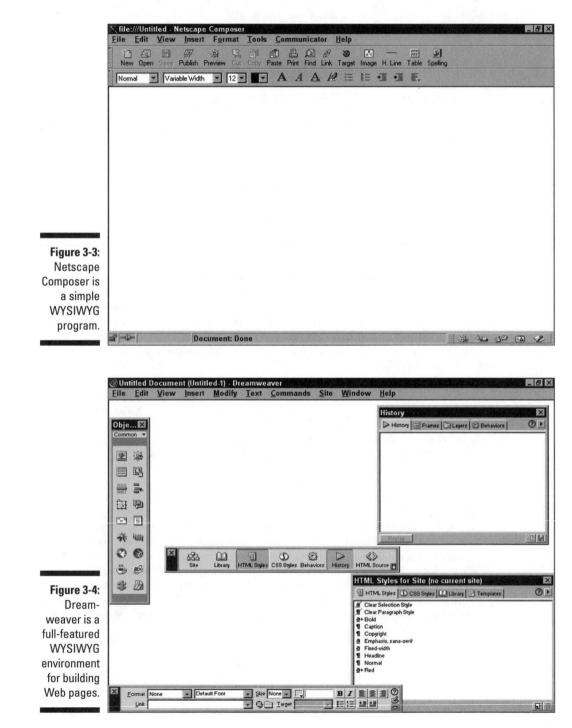

Figure 3-3:
Netscape
Composer is
a simple
WYSIWYG
program.

Figure 3-4:
Dream-
weaver is a
full-featured
WYSIWYG
environment
for building
Web pages.

Table 3-2	WYSIWYG Programs
Program	*Web Address*
Adobe PageMill	`www.adobe.com/products/pagemill/main.html`
Dreamweaver	`www.macromedia.com/software/dreamweaver/`
FrontPage	`www.microsoft.com/frontpage/`
GoLive	`www.adobe.com/products/golive/main.html`
Hot Dog PageWiz	`www.sausage.com/pagewiz/overview.shtml`
HoTMetaL PRO	`www.hotmetalpro.com`

Determining Your Web-Page Structure

There are two basic kinds of Web-page structures: *regular* and *framed*.
Regular gets better mileage on highways, and framed looks nice on a wall.
No? Okay. A regular Web page is a stand-alone structure, as shown in Figure
3-5. Frames, on the other hand, are a way to place more than one Web page
on-screen at a time. To the visitor, a framed site appears as one coherent
whole, no different from a regular page, something like the horizontally
framed example shown in Figure 3-6. (Frames can run vertically, too.) Frames
give you more capabilities — and a few extra headaches just to balance
everything.

Normal elements

As we mention in the section "Tagging Along," earlier in this chapter, Web
pages are built with *elements*. A typical Web page features a basic structure of
three elements: HTML, HEAD, and BODY. The HTML element contains both the
HEAD and BODY elements, as the following example demonstrates:

```
<HTML>

<HEAD>
</HEAD>

<BODY>
</BODY>

</HTML>
```

Figure 3-5:
A regular
Web page is
composed
of a single
HTML file.

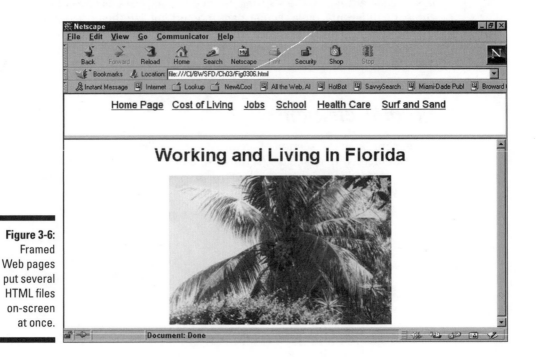

Figure 3-6:
Framed
Web pages
put several
HTML files
on-screen
at once.

You can actually make a Web page without using the HTML, HEAD, and BODY tags, but we don't recommend it. It's technically possible and is even legitimate under the HTML standard; leaving them out can't help anything, however, and putting them in helps you to keep the other elements in their proper places.

All the code for everything that's visible on the Web page goes into the BODY element. The HEAD element contains things such as the page's title, which goes between the <TITLE> and </TITLE> tags like this:

```
<HEAD>
<TITLE>This is the page title.</TITLE>
</HEAD>
```

The title doesn't appear on the actual Web page — it's displayed in the title bar at the top of the visitor's Web browser.

Frames and framesets

Framed sites work a bit differently than regular ones do. You build them out of *framesets,* which set off different areas of the screen. Each one of these areas is known as a *frame,* and each frame contains its own Web page. The following HTML code sets up the pair of frames that you see in Figure 3-7:

```
<HTML>

<FRAMESET cols="80,*">
  <FRAME name="leftFrame" src="navigation.html">
  <FRAME name="mainFrame" src="main.html">
</FRAMESET>

</HTML>
```

The "80,*" in the preceding code listing means that you're setting aside 80 pixels for the first frame, while the rest of the screen is available for the second frame. You can also specify a specific pixel amount for the second frame if you want. On the other hand, you can specify a percentage of the screen for each frame instead of specifying exact pixel sizes, as in the following example:

```
<FRAMESET cols="20%,*">
```

To create horizontal frames instead of vertical frames, you use the rows attribute instead of cols in the first frameset tag. Everything else works just the same way.

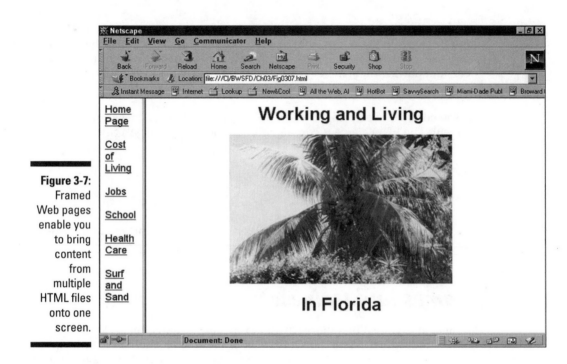

Figure 3-7:
Framed
Web pages
enable you
to bring
content
from
multiple
HTML files
onto one
screen.

Getting Wordy

Words are the foremost method of communication on the World Wide Web, and it's a rare Web page indeed that hasn't got a passel of 'em scattered over it.

In the examples that we provide in the following sections, we show only the code necessary for creating the particular elements that we talk about.

Paragraphs

Paragraph elements are what you normally use to place text on a Web page. You put the text between the `<P>` and `</P>` tags, as in the following example:

```
<P>This is where the textual content goes.</P>
```

Technically, the end tag for a P element is optional in HTML — you don't need to include it, although most Web page creation programs add it automatically.

Web browsers automatically add a bit of space between paragraphs. If you want some extra space, you can add it by using the line break, or BR, element, as the following example shows:

```
<P>This is the first paragraph.</P>
<BR>
<P>This paragraph has a space above it.</P>
```

Figure 3-8 shows the results of using the BR element.

You can usually get away with using an empty P element — one with no content between the start and end tags — to create a blank line between paragraphs instead of using a BR element. Unfortunately, this technique doesn't work for all Web browsers. Because empty P elements are not allowed under the HTML standard, browsers that strictly follow the standard ignore them and don't insert a blank line.

If you want the best of both worlds, the standard solution to this problem is to put some invisible content into the P element. Because Web browsers ignore plain white space, you can't just press your space bar. What you need to do is to put in a nonbreaking space with a special code. Here's how you do it:

```
<P>This is the first paragraph.</P>
<P> </P>
<P>This paragraph has a space above it.</P>
```

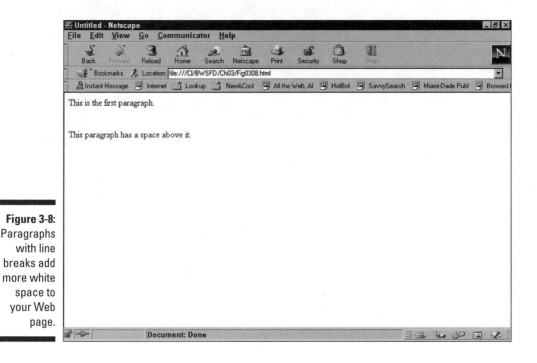

Figure 3-8:
Paragraphs
with line
breaks add
more white
space to
your Web
page.

If you use a nonbreaking space, make sure that you don't leave off the semi-colon at the end. If you do, you end up with the characters   on-screen instead of a blank space.

Headings

Headings are also elements that contain text. Different headings create different sizes of text and make that text bold. HTML uses half a dozen heading elements, ranging from the humongous H1 size all the way down to the teeny-weeny H6. You can probably guess that H2, H3, H4, and H5 are between H1 and H6 in size, so we won't bother to explain that.

You use headings to differentiate one section of text from another. Smaller headings designate subsections under larger headings. Say, for example, that you're running a news Web site. You use H1 for the main headline and follow it with the text in P elements. Any subheads in the article use H2 headings, any subheads under those headings use H3, and so on, as the following example demonstrates:

```
<H1>Clown Runs Amok</H1>
<P>In a surprising development today, Clown of the Year Toby
        O'Dell-Gonzalez went on a rampage through the
        Hideyoshi Circus, spraying at least 17 elephants
        with whipped cream.</P>
<H2>Echoes Earlier Incident</H2>
<P>Highly placed sources within the circus confirm that this
        is not the first time the famed performer has
        committed such an act. "Toby just kind of has a
        thing about dairy products," said one of the
        co-owners of the circus.</P>
```

Figure 3-9 shows how the preceding code listing looks on your Web page.

Fonts

Font is a fancy term that describes the way a letter is shaped. **This** word is in a different font than *this* one is. You can just go with the default fonts — those fonts that are automatically set in the Web browser — or you can specify which ones you want. For casual Web-page development, the default fonts work just fine, but you may find that you prefer to make your own choices to get just the "right look."

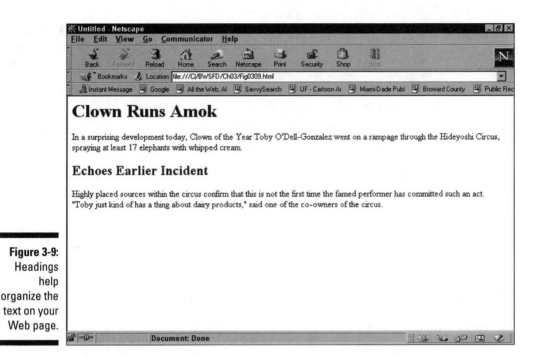

Figure 3-9:
Headings
help
organize the
text on your
Web page.

A couple of the elements that you use most often for altering fonts are B and I. Respectively, these set the enclosed lettering to bold or italic print, as in the following example:

```
<P>This is normal print. <B>This is bold print.</B> <I>This
       is italicized print.</I></P>
```

You can also use the FONT element to set the *face* of the text, which is the basic appearance of the lettering (whether it's Arial, Times New Roman, and so on), as well as the size and the color. (See the section "Coloring Things," later in this chapter, for more information on setting color.) The following example shows how to use the FONT element to set face, size, and color:

```
<P><FONT face="Arial, Helvetica, sans-serif" size="5"
       color="blue">This is blue-colored Helvetica in
       size 5.</FONT> <FONT face="Times New Roman, Times,
       serif" size="3" color="red">This is red-colored
       Times Roman in size 3.</FONT> <FONT face="Courier
       New, Courier, mono" size="7" color="black">This is
       black-colored Courier in size 7.</FONT></P>
```

Figure 3-10 shows the results of the two preceding code examples.

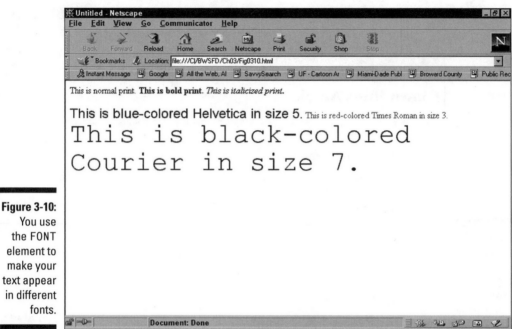

This is normal print. **This is bold print.** *This is italicized print.*

This is blue-colored Helvetica in size 5. This is red-colored Times Roman in size 3.

This is black-colored
Courier in size 7.

Figure 3-10:
You use
the FONT
element to
make your
text appear
in different
fonts.

Although we use the FONT element on whole sentences in the code example, it can be applied to smaller stretches of text — even to a single character.

The reason for the face attribute's several choices is that many different computer systems are hooked up to the Internet, and Windows doesn't offer the same options as do Macs or Unix boxes. If the font you specify isn't available, the visitor's Web browser has to make its best guess about what font to substitute for it. By offering a series of font options for the browser to use, you improve the chances of a visitor seeing just what you intend. The preceding code example includes all you need to cover the three main types of font faces common on the World Wide Web.

Lines

Okay, a horizontal line isn't really a word, but this part of the book is the least unlikely place we can think of to discuss this element. In HTML, these lines are technically known as *horizontal rules*, so the element that represents them is called HR. Horizontal rules visually separate one section of a page from another, underline an image, and do just about anything you normally do with lines.

You can set the width of horizontal rules as either a percentage of the width of a screen or as an exact pixel value. The default width value of a horizontal line is 100 percent of the screen width, so if you don't specify the value of the width attribute, that's what you get. To specify a width of 50 percent, for example, use the following code:

```
<HR width="50%">
```

To specify a width of 400 pixels, you do it like this instead:

```
<HR width="400">
```

The height, or thickness, of the line in pixels is set via the size attribute, as the following example shows:

```
<HR size="6">
```

By default, the line is hollow, or *shaded*. (The hollow line is called "shaded" because, back in the days when Web pages weren't so colorful and all there was to work with was black text on a medium gray background, hollow horizontal lines appeared to sink into the page, creating a shaded, or 3D, effect. Against most other background colors, the effect isn't apparent.) To make a line solid, you need to add the noshade attribute, as in the following example:

```
<HR noshade>
```

The following code creates the Web page shown in Figure 3-11:

```
<HR>
<HR width="100%">
<HR width="50%">
<HR width="200">
<HR width="400">
<HR size="10">
<HR size="6" noshade>
```

Many Web designers use graphics, such as GIF files, to create horizontal lines instead of relying on HTML. See the clip-art sources in the section "Picturing It," later in this chapter, for some examples.

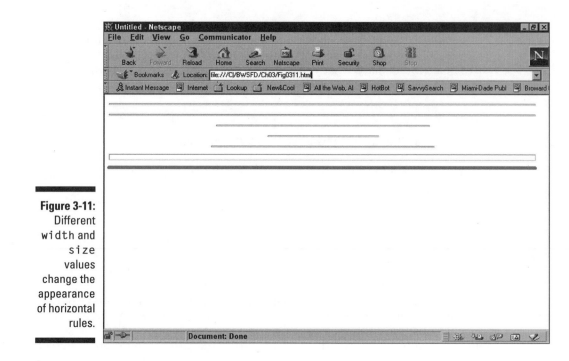

Untitled - Netscape
File Edit View Go Communicator Help
Back Forward Reload Home Search Netscape Print Security Shop Stop
Bookmarks Location: file:///C|/BWSFD/Ch03/Fig0311.html
Instant Message Internet Lookup New&Cool All the Web, Al HotBot SavvySearch Miami-Dade Publ Broward
Document: Done

Figure 3-11:
Different
`width` and
`size`
values
change the
appearance
of horizontal
rules.

Coloring Things

Unless you're really into television reruns or artsy photography, you probably don't see much of anything in black and white these days. The world's a colorful place, and you may disappoint your visitors if they don't see color on your Web site.

We touch on color in the section "Fonts," a bit earlier in this chapter, but you can use color in many places. As more time goes by, you will doubtlessly be able to color every element in HTML.

If you use *Cascading Style Sheets (CSS)*, you have a great deal more control over color than you do with normal HTML. CSS is far beyond the scope of this book, but you can find out more in *Dreamweaver 3 For Dummies*, by Janine Warner and Paul Vachier (published by IDG Books Worldwide, Inc.).

If you read the section "Fonts," earlier in this chapter, you already know that you can set the color of a particular set of letters, but you can also set the base color for all the text. Other than fonts, you can also set the color for a page's background and its links. The links actually use three different colors: one for links a visitor hasn't clicked, one for a link that they are clicking, and one for links that they have already visited.

All these color changes are accomplished by setting the values for various attributes of the BODY element. You set the text color with the text attribute, the background color with the bgcolor attribute, the unvisited link color with the link attribute, the visited link color with the vlink attribute, and the color for a link that someone's clicking (the *active link*) with the alink attribute. Setting all of them at once looks like this:

```
<BODY text="black" bgcolor="white" link="blue" vlink="red"
      alink="purple">
```

Linking Up

When it comes to the World Wide Web, *links* (which connect different files) are everything. Without them, there couldn't be a Web at all. You create links with the A (anchor) element. That element's href (hypertext reference) attribute gives the Web address of the file you want to link to. This address is called a *URL*, which is short for Uniform Resource Locator. Here's what a link looks like in HTML:

```
<A href="http://www.dummies.com/">content</A>
```

The part that reads content is where you put words or images that people can click to go to the linked file. This content appears as blue underlined letters if it's a text link and as a blue outlined image if it's an image link.

Picturing It

You can have a Web page with nothing but words on it, but most people think that's a bit dull. It's pretty rare to find a site that's not filled with images of one kind or another. When it comes to placing images on the World Wide Web, you need to use graphics files in one of three common formats: *GIF, JPEG* (also called *JPG*), or *PNG*.

Where do you get images? You can create them from scratch, or you can download ready-to-use files from some of the Web sites that we list in Table 3-3. If you use other people's images — and most Web designers do — make sure that you first read all the fine print on their Web sites. Unless they state otherwise, the original artist owns the copyright on an image. You can't use it without permission. Fortunately, the vast majority of artists on the Web are eager to give that permission in exchange for nothing more than a link from your Web site back to theirs. This arrangement gives them free publicity and gives you free, high-quality artwork. Everybody's happy.

If the artist isn't willing to let you display their copyrighted art in exchange for a link, you may need to pay to use the image. Sometimes, too, the image is free to use on noncommercial sites but costs to use on commercial ones. To reemphasize the point, *make sure that you read the fine print*. Don't — we repeat, *don't* — just grab an image that's not free, use it, and figure that you can get away with it. You can do that — after all, you can download any image that you can see in a Web browser — but you're cheating the artist and running the risk of serious repercussions, like Federal charges. Plenty of freely available art's out there. Stick with it and you're unlikely to run into problems.

Table 3-3	Clip Art Sources
Web Site Name	*Web Address*
Barry's Clip Art Server	www.barrysclipart.com
Clip Animations	www.animation.arthouse.org
Clip Art Connection	www.clipartconnection.com
Cool Archive Free Clip Art	www.coolarchive.com
Graphic Maps	www.graphicmaps.com/clipart.htm
Noetic Art	www.noeticart.com

Graphics programs

Even if you're not a digital artist who creates your own graphics from scratch, you need a good graphics program so that you can modify images. You may, for example, find a good image that's not in one of the three common file formats. You may find an image that's too big for your purposes and that you need to resize. You may want to crop out most of a picture or change its contrast, brightness, or whatever.

You can go whole hog and grab a copy of PhotoShop or Fireworks, or you can go with a less-expensive shareware program, such as Paint Shop Pro. Table 3-4 gives you some URLs where you can find out about graphics programs or even grab demo versions to try out.

Table 3-4	Graphics Programs
Program	*Web Address*
Fireworks	www.macromedia.com/software/fireworks/
Paint Shop Pro	www.jasc.com

Program	Web Address
Painter	www.metacreations.com/products/painter6/
PhotoShop	www.adobe.com/products/photoshop/
Ulead Web Razor Pro	www.ulead.com/wrp/runme.htm
Xara WebStyle	www.xara.com/webstyle/

Trial versions of both Fireworks and Paint Shop Pro are on the CD-ROM that accompanies this book.

Images

The most common item other than text on Web pages is the *image,* represented by the IMG element. The only absolutely required attribute for that element is the src attribute, which specifies the name and, if located somewhere other than in the same directory as the HTML file that links to it, the location of the graphics file.

Thus, you code the simplest image on a Web page like this (see Figure 3-12):

```
<IMG src="cats16.jpg">
```

To specify a graphics file in another folder, you need to add the path to the folder, as in the following example:

```
<IMG src="pets/cats16.jpg">
```

If the graphic file's on another Web server entirely, you need to add the full path to that URL, as follows:

```
<IMG src="http://www.anotherserver.com/cats16.jpg">
```

We mention in the section "Linking Up," earlier in this chapter, that you can use an image as a link just as you can use text for one. To do so, just put the IMG element right between the start and end tags for the A element, as the following example shows:

```
<A href="http://www.dummies.com/"><IMG src="cats16.jpg"></A>
```

IMG elements don't have an end tag.

Figure 3-12:
An image of
a kitty in a
JPEG file
format.

Background images

A background image follows the same rules as a regular image, except that you create it by using the background attribute of the BODY element instead of using an IMG element, as shown in the following example:

```
<BODY background="cats2.jpg">
```

Background images *tile*, which is to say that they repeat themselves across the page until they reach the edge of the screen. They then begin tiling again in the next available space below the first line of images and so forth until they fill the entire page from side to side and top to bottom. Because of this characteristic, most people prefer to use small background images, like those shown in Figure 3-13.

You want to choose Background images with care. Make sure that they don't interfere with the other elements on the Web page. You want the color muted, the lines indistinct, and the content supportive of the overall theme.

Figure 3-13:
A page with
a tiled
background
image.

Image maps

We discuss image links in the preceding sections on linking and images. However, you can also use a special kind of image link called *image mapping*. If you use a normal image link, you have one link that goes with one image. By using image mapping, you can add several links to a single image.

By using an image-mapping program, you draw shapes over specific areas within an existing image. You then assign a particular URL to each of these areas. When visitors click the part of the image that links to a URL, they're sent to that URL. You may, for example, use a map of the world as your image map. When your visitors click England or Scotland, they go to a page about the U.K. If they click Africa, they go to a page about that continent. And so on and so on. . . .

You don't need to stay purely geographical, however. You can just as easily take a diagram of the human body and click the abdomen to go to a page about appendectomies or click the mouth to go to a page about dentistry. Any kind of logical connection works with image maps.

Many graphics programs, such as Fireworks, include image-mapping capabilities. If you don't own one of those programs, however, you may want to check out some of the dedicated image-mapping programs that we list in Table 3-5.

Table 3-5	Image Mapping Programs
Program	**Web Address**
Image Mapper	`www.sausage.com/supertoolz/image_manipulation/stimage.html`
LiveImage	`www.mediatec.com`
Mapedit	`www.boutell.com/mapedit/`
MapMaker	`www.tns.lcs.mit.edu/cgi-bin/mapmaker`
Web Hotspots	`www.concentric.net/~automata/hotspots.shtml`

Online Sources

Table 3-6 lists some places on the World Wide Web where you can find more information about the topics that we cover in this chapter.

Table 3-6	Online Resources
Web Site Name	**Web Address**
Compendium of HTML Elements	`www.htmlcompendium.org`
HTML Goodies	`www.htmlgoodies.com`
HTML Specification	`www.w3c.org/TR/html`
HTML Writers Guild	`www.hwg.org`
Index DOT Html	`www.eskimo.com/~bloo/indexdot/html/index.html`
Introduction to HTML	`www.wdvl.com/Authoring/HTML/Intro/`
Learn HTML Home	`http://awest.jeffco.k12.co.us/learnhtml/00conten.htm`

Part II
Adding Sparkle to Your Site

The 5th Wave   By Rich Tennant

"I have to say I'm really impressed with the interactivity on this car wash Web site."

In this part . . .

Here, we give you a ton of ways to make your site work, look, and sound great. Chapter 4 talks about the different site add-ins that you can use and shows you how to handle the different kinds that you'll encounter. Chapter 5 covers different tools that you can use to add search and navigation features to your site. Chapter 6 tells you where to snag some cool graphics. Chapter 7 introduces you to the world of Web multimedia. And Chapter 8 shows you how to keep your site in tip-top shape.

Chapter 4

Plugging in Scripts and Applets

. . . .

In This Chapter

▶ Checking for CGI access

▶ Implementing CGI scripts

▶ Using JavaScript

▶ Adding Java applets

. . . .

*W*e show you how to add cool features to your Web site in this book. These features are, of course, programs of one kind or another. Relax, though — you don't have to be a programmer to use them. Many of them are programs written in the Perl language, which you hook up to your Web page using the *Common Gateway Interface*, or CGI for short. There's nothing mystical or particularly difficult about using CGI, and we give you the basics in the section "Adding CGI Scripts," later in this chapter.

A *script* is a short program.

Java applets are also popular for adding new capabilities to Web pages. They're programs written in the Java programming language, and plenty of them are free for you to use.

Another common method for adding new functions to your Web pages is with scripts written in the JavaScript programming language. Unlike Perl and Java, JavaScript was specifically designed solely for writing programs for the World Wide Web. You can go all the way and learn to write your own JavaScripts, or you can take advantage of the zillions of existing ones and just plug them in. The code goes right into the same file as your own Web page code — it's just a matter of copying and pasting it.

Making Sure That You Have CGI Access

If you're going to use CGI with your Web pages, you have to make sure that you have the capability to do so. Sounds obvious, of course, but you may or may not have CGI access for your Web site. CGI access means that you can run programs on your Web server that use the Common Gateway Interface, a method of sending form data from a Web page to an external program for processing.

Nine times out of ten, these programs are kept in a subfolder called `cgi-bin`, so your first step is to look to see if you have such a subfolder on your server. If you do, odds are that you have CGI access because that subfolder doesn't have any other purpose. If it's there, go ahead and try to use a CGI program. If you follow all the instructions carefully and it still won't work, you may need to have a talk with your network administrator or ISP.

Even if you do have CGI access, you still may not be able to run the scripts you want. Your CGI access also should have the ability to handle *SSI*, or server-side includes. This simply means that the server that processes the script can include data of its own, which is sent back to your Web page. Without that capability, most CGI scripts are useless.

Why your ISP won't help

When your Web site is hosted by the same ISP that you get your Internet access from, you'll probably find that they're not too supportive of your desire to run CGI scripts. There are a couple of reasons for this, which make good sense to your ISP, but don't help you at all.

First off, badly written programs using CGI can represent a security hazard, poking holes in the normal running of things. Because the ISP wants everything to run smoothly and under its control instead of someone else's, ISPs tend to frown on this possibility.

Second, most ISPs don't really care about your Web site. They're not bad people, but they're mostly in the business of providing Internet access to their dial-up customers and anything else they have to deal with is just an annoyance that gets in the way of their main job. (See Chapter 18 for more info.)

If your ISP allows you to run CGI scripts at all, it may be a painful and expensive process on your end. We once had an ISP that wanted to approve the scripts in advance, put them on the server themselves sometime over the next couple of days, and charge us $25 a pop for doing so. From an ISP's point of view, that's reasonable. From our point of view, it was a definite no-go. For starters, we like to do things right away instead of taking days to get around to it. On top of that, you often have to monkey with a CGI script before you get it working just the way you want. Every time we wanted to make a change, it would cost another $25 and set us back a couple of more days.

Finding a CGI provider

Fortunately, not all Web space providers feel this way. If you live in a city or large town, you can easily shop around and find a new ISP if the one you're using isn't on your side, CGI-wise. If not, thanks to the way the Internet works, you don't need to deal with your local ISP at all.

You can go with a virtual server or other commercial remote Web-space provider (see Chapter 18 for details), or you can easily find free Web-space providers by using the search engine at FreeWebspace.net. Go to the main page at www.freewebspace.net and click the <u>Advanced Search</u> link, or just go straight to www.freewebspace.net/search/advanced.shtml. In the search form, click the CGI check box under Features, as shown in Figure 4-1. Select any other options you desire and click the Search button. Our test search, using the default options except for the CGI check box, came up with 30 free providers who grant CGI access.

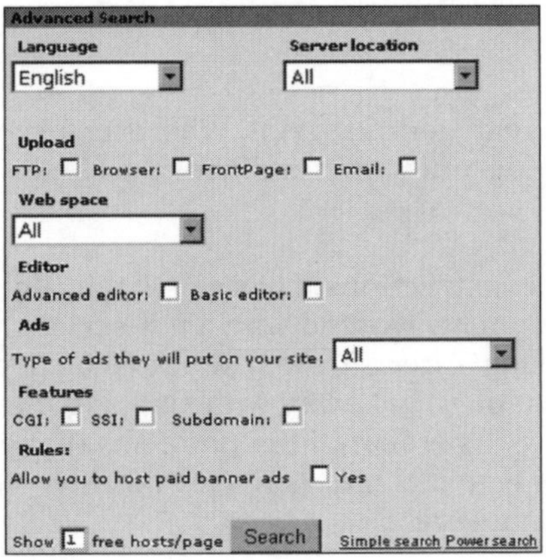

Figure 4-1:
FreeWeb-
space.net's
Advanced
Search form
can help you
find a
provider
who gives
you CGI
access.

Using remotely hosted CGI scripts

There's another solution to these difficulties. The CGI scripts you use don't have to reside on the same server that houses your Web pages. This is good, because CGI scripts are run by the Web server where the script is located, and using them puts an added load on your server. If you have lots of visitors, the data processing demands on it can be pretty strenuous. If you don't have your Web site on a dedicated server with plenty of power, things can get really slow.

When the script is on someone else's server, however, you don't have to worry about the server load. Happily, there are lots of remotely hosted CGI scripts, which means that you can still add their capabilities to your own pages while avoiding the server overload problem. Many of the add-ons in this book are remotely hosted.

Adding CGI Scripts

A CGI script works by taking input from your Web page and sending that input out to an external program for processing. Usually, it returns a new Web page that has the results of that processing on it. The input is most often data from a form, but it can sometimes just be a link that a user clicks to activate the program. CGI Free, for example, provides some free scripts that work via links to its server (see Figure 4-2). Check out the technique at `www.cgi-free.com`.

Basic techniques

Before you do anything, you have to get the script. Wherever a script is described in this book, we provide you with the URL of the site from where you can download it.

After you have the files, read the instructions. Let's say that again: Read the instructions. It's tempting, after you've worked with a few scripts, to just plunge right ahead without looking. After all, most scripts plug in pretty much the same way, and you can often get away with skipping the instructions. That's the cause of about 812 percent of the problems that people have with scripts, though. All it takes is to misunderstand or misinterpret one little setting, and the whole thing won't work.

The instructions are often in the standard `readme.txt` file. Sometimes, the script doesn't have a `readme` file, though, and the instructions are embedded in the text of the script itself in the form of *comments*. (Comments are notes the programmer adds to provide information, and they're marked so that they're differentiated from the program code and don't interfere with the running of the program.)

Next, open the file in a text editor and make any necessary changes so that it works with your own particular setup. You may, for example, need to add a list of URLs for a link menu, an e-mail address to send a message to, or the location of your site's main Web page. You don't need to understand the programming in order to do this. Just follow the instructions and replace the sample values in the script with your own values. After you do this, save the modified script.

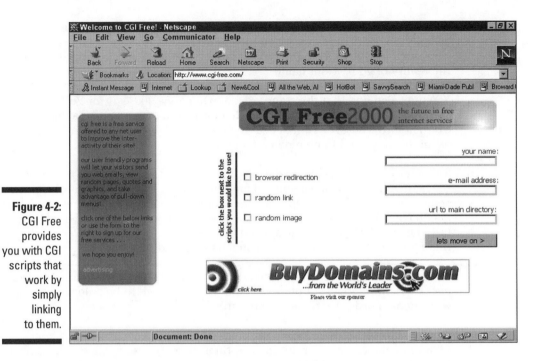

Figure 4-2:
CGI Free
provides
you with CGI
scripts that
work by
simply
linking
to them.

If you use a word processor to make the changes, make sure that the script gets saved as plain text, and that the original file extension doesn't get changed either. You don't want a bunch of word processing formatting codes embedded in the script!

Now, add the HTML code that the script's instructions say to add to your Web page. As with the script, you probably need to change a few sample values to the actual values. The HTML code is usually nothing more than the location of the CGI program, entered as the action attribute of a form.

Finally, upload the script and the modified HTML file to your Web server. The HTML file goes in the normal HTML folder, and the script goes into the cgi-bin folder.

Solving problems

Those basic techniques work in almost all cases, but there are some situations where you may need to modify things a bit more to get everything working just right.

For example, nearly every script you find assumes your cgi-bin directory is called `cgi-bin`. Yours may be simply named `cgi`, for instance. If that's the case, you need to change the typical folder references in the script to match the reality of your folder name.

You may also find that the standard file extensions, like `.pl` for Perl files, aren't allowed in your CGI setup. In that case, you have to change the file extension to whatever your server demands. A file named `search.pl`, for example, may need to be renamed `search.cgi`.

If you try to run the script and nothing happens, you need to go back over the instructions and see if you did anything wrong. Nine times out of ten, it's something simple but so small and insignificant that it's easy to overlook. You may have left out a required comma between two values, or forgotten a quotation mark. Perhaps you misspelled the URL of a Web site. Go over everything you did very carefully, and you'll usually find the problem.

If there's nothing wrong with the script, make sure that you uploaded all the necessary files. Some scripts have data files that need to be uploaded along with them in order for them to work properly.

If none of these steps solves the problem, check to see that your cgi-bin folder has the correct permissions settings. If you're not familiar with permissions, ask your ISP to check them for you.

If all else fails, send an e-mail message to the author of the program explaining the nature of the problem and ask for help. Because most of these programs are free, don't expect too much in the way of technical support, though. Nobody can afford to both give away programs and spend all their time providing free technical support as well. The best approach is to be polite, perhaps tell them how much you want to use their program (if you don't feel that way about it, you haven't come this far), and make sure that you give all the information you can about the settings you used.

Incorporating JavaScripts

JavaScript has a tremendous advantage over other methods of adding "beyond HTML" features to your Web pages. It was designed for no other purpose, and it's so tightly integrated with HTML that it's a joy to use. The processing takes place in the visitor's Web browser, so it's both fast for them and no problem for your Web server. You don't have to understand the language in order to add other people's scripts to your Web site. In many cases, no alterations to the code are needed. In some cases, however, you may have to change the name of a file or add some URLs to a list. Figure 4-3 shows The JavaScript Source at `javascript.internet.com`, one of the many places on the Web to get free JavaScript code.

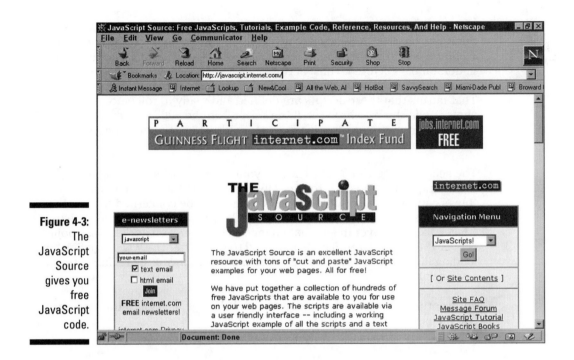

Figure 4-3:
The
JavaScript
Source
gives you
free
JavaScript
code.

Some JavaScript is contained in an external .js file, which is referenced from within your HTML file, but this capability is almost never used. You'll probably see it rarely or never, and none of the JavaScript programs in this book use an external file. Perl scripts, on the other hand, are external. They may not even be on your Web server.

Basic techniques

You need to add two things to your Web pages when you work with JavaScript. The first is the script itself, which has to go in the HEAD element of your Web page, like this skeleton script named "whatever":

```
<HEAD>
<Script Language="JavaScript">
/*
You will usually find comments here.
*/

function whatever()
{
Actual code is found here.
}
</Script>
</HEAD>
```

Scripts can be placed within the BODY element instead of in the HEAD element, but it can be risky. A JavaScript needs to be *interpreted* — translated by a Web browser from the human readable code into something a computer can understand — before it runs. Scripts in the HEAD element are processed before the Web browser processes the elements within the BODY element. That means that these scripts are defined and ready to roll before anything shows up in the Web browser. If the script is in the BODY element, it's possible for a visitor to attempt to trigger it before it's defined, which begs for a malfunction. Better to stick with the safer, usual approach.

The second thing you need to add to your Web page is something to trigger the script, which causes it to run. This goes within the BODY element. Many things can trigger a script, but you don't need to be concerned with all the possibilities. The script you add is most likely designed to have a particular trigger, like a rollover image that changes whenever a visitor's mouse pointer is over the image. Or it may be intended to work after the Web page finishes loading into the browser. You can alter the trigger if you're familiar with JavaScript.

For a script that executes as soon as the Web page loads into the browser, use the onload attribute of the BODY element:

```
<BODY onload="whatever()">
```

For a script where you want the visitor to click an element, use the onClick attribute. This example uses the A element, but onClick is a ubiquitous attribute, and you can use it with just about anything:

```
<A onClick="whatever()">Click here for whatever.</A>
```

There are lots more triggers, such as onMouseOver and onMouseOut, which are, respectively, used to execute scripts when a mouse pointer moves onto and away from an element. The documentation for a script normally specifies which one(s) it's intended to use. If you want to explore JavaScript, try *JavaScript For Dummies*, 2nd Edition, by Emily A. Vander Veer (published by IDG Books Worldwide, Inc.).

Facing problems

Fortunately, practically any JavaScript that you pick up is pretty well guaranteed to work — under the right conditions. When it comes to JavaScript, zillions of things can go wrong. The biggest problem is that there are so many different versions of Web browsers out there. Not only do Netscape Navigator and Internet Explorer handle scripts a little bit differently, but also, different versions of the two major Web browsers don't work the same either. That means that a script that works fine in the latest version may not work at all in an older one. Unfortunately, there are still lots of older Web browsers out there — not everyone is in a hurry to tie up their system downloading the newest versions all the time.

If a browser doesn't recognize JavaScript, the script won't run. There's no harm done, just a missed experience for the visitor.

Unless you want to put in the time and effort to really master the language and do your own debugging, your best bet is to simply try out the script you want to use. Test it in Netscape Navigator, Internet Explorer, and any other Web browser you think your target audience uses. If it works well in all of them, you're home free. If it causes problems in any of them, you need to decide how important that segment of the audience is to you. For example, if your site is dedicated to Microsoft products and your script won't work in Netscape Navigator, you're probably pretty safe in going ahead with it, anyway, because the vast majority of your visitors are likely to use Microsoft's Internet Explorer.

Dropping In Java Applets

Java applets run the gamut from the trivial and useless to the fabulous. Many of them perform some type of image modification, like the popular Lake applet. (See Chapter 6 for more info.) Others add rotating banner ads or scrolling tickertape-style messages. The really nice thing about Java applets is that, like JavaScript, they run on the visitor's machine, which reduces the load on your Web server. One drawback, however, is the length of time that they take to be downloaded to the visitor and the slight delay on their end while Java starts up (if it isn't already running). Figure 4-4 shows the main Java page for Sun Microsystems (java.sun.com), the company that invented the language.

Major programs are called *applications*. Your word processor or spreadsheet program, for example, is an application. Although Java is indeed used to write applications, the kind of Java programs written for the Web tends to be very small, so they're known by the diminutive *applet*.

Despite the similarity in their names, Java and JavaScript are only vaguely similar, and they work quite differently. They do have one important thing in common, however — they're both executed on your visitors' computers, which takes the load off your server.

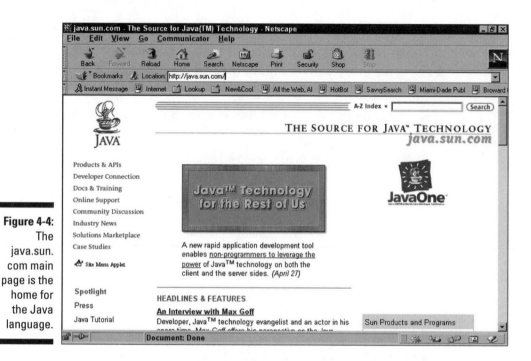

Figure 4-4:
The
java.sun.
com main
page is the
home for
the Java
language.

Basic techniques

Java applets are composed of `.class` files (rarely, you see a `.cls` extension instead). The file may be downloaded by itself, but you often find it in a `.zip` or other compressed file along with some other supporting files — documentation and perhaps graphics or sound files as well, depending on the function of the applet.

After you have the files, you need to add code to your HTML file to activate the applet. This is done with the `APPLET` element, and there are many different attributes that may or may not come into play, depending on the particular applet involved. Almost invariably, the applet's documentation provides the HTML code you need, and all you have to do is to cut and paste it, changing only a few items, such as the names of image files, to make it fit your site. No applet included in this book does it any other way.

Sometimes, an applet's author doesn't include a documentation file but has all the necessary information on the Web page you download the applet from. Make sure to print out a copy of that page. Better yet, save it to your own system so you can easily cut and paste the HTML code and refer to the instructions if you have any problems.

You can never count on any Web site being operational all the time. If you don't make your own copy of the Web page that shows the instructions, you'll be out of luck if the Web server is down the next time you try to go back.

At its most basic, you add a Java applet contained in a file called `bongo.class` like this:

```
<APPLET code="bongo.class">This would have been
          drumming.</APPLET>
```

The content between the start and end tags is phrased the way it is because that content is ignored by any Web browser that supports Java and won't show up on them. It's displayed only by browsers that aren't Java-capable (or that have Java turned off). It's not necessary to add any content between the start and end tags, but it's a nice gesture because it lets visitors know to turn on Java or upgrade their browsers if they want to get the full benefit of your site.

Optionally, the applet may have a `name` attribute. This is used when you have multiple interacting Java applets and one of the applets needs to send information to another one. Each applet's name gives them all the capability to identify one another.

```
<APPLET code="bongo.class" name="HitIt"></APPLET>
```

You also need to specify the `width` and `height` attributes for the applet. These values are found in the accompanying documentation:

```
<APPLET code="bongo.class" width="200" height="100"></APPLET>
```

If the `.class` file isn't in the same folder as the `.html` file that calls it, you need to use the `codebase` attribute as well. It tells the Web browser where to find the Java applet. If the example file were in the `drumming` subfolder, the HTML code would look like this:

```
<APPLET code="bongo.class" codebase="/drumming" width="200"
          height="100"></APPLET>
```

Unlike most URLs in HTML, the `codebase` location must be within either the same folder as the `.html` file or a subfolder of it. This means that you can't access a Java applet on another server with it.

In most cases, the applet will also require that you add some other information to the HTML code. This information, called a *parameter,* is added via the `PARAM` element. In the following example, we add a particular sound file to our bongo applet:

```
<APPLET code="bongo.class" width="200" height="100">
<PARAM name="CurrentSound" value="quickroll.au">
</APPLET>
```

The parameter is usually the name of an image or sound file, the URL of a Web page, or the text of a message. There can be lots more in the way of parameters, depending on what the particular applet does — the parameters may set font size, background color, speed of change, or just about anything else. Some parameters are optional; others are required. As with everything else, read the documentation carefully.

Troubleshooting applets

When you upload the .class file and any supporting files to your Web server, make sure that you have carefully checked the documentation to see where the files should go. Many Webmasters carefully separate different file types into different folders. It's a good and useful technique, for example, to keep your image files in a different folder from your .html files. If nothing else, it makes it easier to read the file listings and helps avoid using the wrong file type settings when you upload files.

This approach can cause problems, however. For example, say that you're using an applet that manipulates images. If the Java applet expects to find the .html file it's called from, the image files, and itself all in the same folder, you need to make an exception to your usual filing technique and keep all the necessary files in the same place.

Another common problem that may occur during the uploading of the files is that .class files must be uploaded as binaries. If you upload them as ASCII, they won't work. Also make sure that any image or sound files are uploaded as binaries and that any text files — and, of course, the .html file — are uploaded as ASCII.

Even if an image file is uploaded correctly, you can still have trouble. First, check the documentation to see if the applet works with that file type. If everything is okay, it's possible the file itself is the problem. Not all graphics programs create files that can be read by other graphic programs. UMAX scanner software, for instance, makes TIFF files that can't be read by some viewers. JPEGs created with PhotoShop 4 won't work with all Java applets. The solution? Load the image into another program — you may have to try a couple of them — and save it again from the second program. Upload it again and the new file may work.

Objectifying applets

The APPLET element is no longer in favor with the World Wide Web Consortium (W3C), the body that issues the official HTML standard. This doesn't mean that it won't work — it still works fine, and most Web designers still use it. In fact, you almost never find a Java applet to put on your Web page where the documentation uses anything but the APPLET element. All the applets in this book use it.

If you want to be on the latest bandwagon, though, you could add Java applets by using the more complex OBJECT element instead. APPLET is specifically geared to Java applets, just like it sounds, while the newer OBJECT element is capable of adding many different kinds of objects, including Java applets, to Web pages. This new element does make sense because otherwise HTML would end up with tons of different elements for each and every kind of object that gets invented in the future.

There is a problem with the OBJECT element, though, that you should keep in mind. If a visitor is using Internet Explorer 3 and encounters an OBJECT element that refers to a Java applet, IE crashes.

With this warning in mind, it's still probably best to go with the method suggested by the applet's documentation.

Online Sources

Table 4-1 lists some places on the World Wide Web where you can find more information on the topics that we cover in this chapter.

Table 4-1	Online Resources
Web Site Name	**Web Address**
CGI Resource Index	www.cgi-resources.com
CGI: Why Things Don't Work	www.raingod.com/raingod/resources/ Programming/Perl/Notes/CGIDebugging.html
Freewarejava.com	http://freewarejava.com
Intro to CGI	www.mattkruse.com/info/cgi/
Java Boutique	http://javaboutique.internet.com
JavaScript Made Easy	www.easyjavascript.com/javascript.html
Perl Primer	www.webdesigns1.com/perl/

(continued)

Table 4-1 *(continued)*

Web Site Name	Web Address
Steal My JavaScript	www.geocities.com/~team-5150/mirror/
WDVL: The Perl You Need to Know	http://wdvl.com/Authoring/Languages/Perl/PerlfortheWeb/
Website Abstraction	http://wsabstract.com

Chapter 5

Making Site Navigation Easier

In This Chapter

▶ Adding a search engine

▶ Improving your site with navigational tools

*Y*ou can expect two kinds of visitors to your site: those who want to get what they want fast and those who want to take the time to explore.

For the first kind of visitor, you need to provide a way for them to quickly find what's interesting. A *search engine* is the answer for these people. And we don't mean the kind that gives them links to the entire World Wide Web, but one that searches only your site (although you can have both).

For the second type of visitor, you need to provide an easy way to browse around your site. You can just slap a bunch of plain old links everywhere, but there are a lot of neater and cooler ways to do it.

In this chapter, we show you how to add some glitz and function to your site that makes the surfing experience a whole lot easier for your visitors.

Adding a Search Function

Unless your whole site is just a single Web page, you need a search engine for it. Sites that don't offer search functions are at a real disadvantage compared with those that do have them. Put yourself in a visitor's shoes and ask, "Do I want to spend hours browsing this site in the hope that I may stumble across the information I want? Or do I want to spend a few seconds running a search to get the information I need right away?"

All the search options that we describe in the following sections have their own strengths and weaknesses. Similar programs and services offer varying features. One service automatically updates its database of search terms for your site daily, while another does so only on a weekly basis. Yet, the search engine that updates daily requires you to post banner ads, while the engine that updates weekly doesn't. Both of them enable you to go to their sites and initiate an instant update at any time. The importance of each feature is a matter for you to decide. We recommend checking out all of them. Because none of them requires much effort to install and use, you may as well road-test every one to see which you like best.

Getting a free search engine with FreeFind

After you take a look at the capabilities of FreeFind's search engine (www.freefind.com), you may not bother to look at anything else (except that we describe some others well worth a peek, too). It's a beautifully designed, full-featured, honey of a search feature that you can add to your site in a few minutes. It's customizable, creates a site map for you, keeps an up-to-date What's New list that shows visitors what you added lately, gives you extensive reports on what people are looking for, and does pretty near everything else you can want, except fry your eggs for breakfast. The cost? Nothing.

After you finish drooling over the search engine, you may ask, "What's the catch?" Advertising supports it, which means that an ad banner appears at the top of the search page on your site. If your site also has its own advertisers, you can't show any of your ads in competition with FreeFind's ads on that page.

On most sites, an advertising banner's a pretty small point to consider. Even if you do have your own sponsors, you can still place their ads on every other page on your site, and FreeFind helps your visitors get to all those other pages more easily. FreeFind imposes a site limit of about 2,000 Web pages (32MB), but a polite e-mail message to the folks at FreeFind generally gets them to raise the limit.

You do face one other restriction with FreeFind: FreeFind doesn't allow anyone to use its search engine on adults-only sites, because its advertisers don't want to appear on such sites.

Still with us? Okay, FreeFind's search engine runs on its servers, not on yours, so tons of people can use it simultaneously without tying up all your server resources.

You can set up FreeFind to search just your site, just the World Wide Web outside your site, or both your site and the Web in the same search. You can modify the search form, and FreeFind makes the job extremely easy for you by providing online wizards that help you make custom choices, such as designating link colors (either by name or hexadecimal value).

Joining FreeFind

To sign up for FreeFind, all you need to do is to fill out a simple form, as the following steps describe:

1. **Go to FreeFind's home page (**www.freefind.com**) and enter your Web site address, your e-mail address, and the category of your site (entertainment, sports, travel, and so on) in the appropriate text and drop-down list boxes (see Figure 5-1).**

   FreeFind keeps your e-mail address confidential; your address won't be sold to anyone.

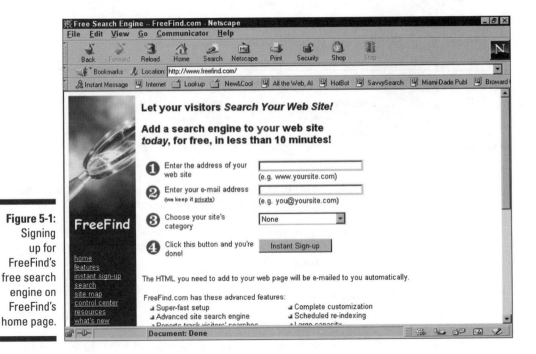

Figure 5-1:
Signing up for FreeFind's free search engine on FreeFind's home page.

2. **Click the Instant Sign-up button.**

   FreeFind sends you an e-mail confirmation message right away. The message contains your password, site ID, and all the links you need to use its service.

3. **Click the link in the e-mail confirmation message to go to the FreeFind Control Center.**

4. **On the Control Center page, you need to enter your Web site address, e-mail address, and the password from the e-mail confirmation message in the form, as shown in Figure 5-2.**

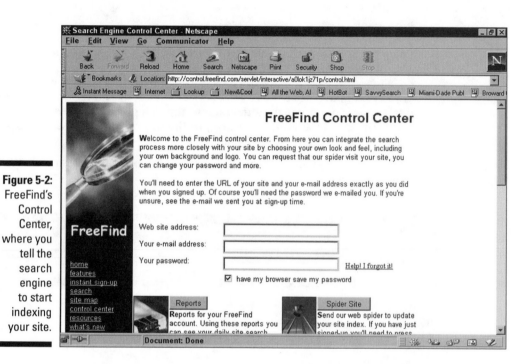

Figure 5-2:
FreeFind's
Control
Center,
where you
tell the
search
engine
to start
indexing
your site.

5. **Click the Spider Site button, and then click the Finish button in the dialog box that appears to have FreeFind index your site.**

FreeFind now indexes your site and e-mails you after it completes the indexing. At the same time it does the indexing, FreeFind also creates a site map and What's New page for your Web site.

Adding the search engine

The first e-mail message that you receive from FreeFind contains the HTML code for a basic search panel. An attachment to the message, `searchpanel.html`, contains the code for several more versions as well. Figure 5-3 shows `searchpanel.html` as it appears in a Web browser. The top search panel version is the same as the one in the e-mail message. All you need to do is to cut and paste the version that you want (either from the e-mail message or the attachment) onto the Web page on which you want to use it, upload the page to your site, and your search engine is fully functional.

You can't use the search engine until FreeFind completes the indexing of your site. If you try it before FreeFind is finished, you receive an e-mail message saying that the spider's indexing of your site isn't complete, and you just get a page reminding you to wait.

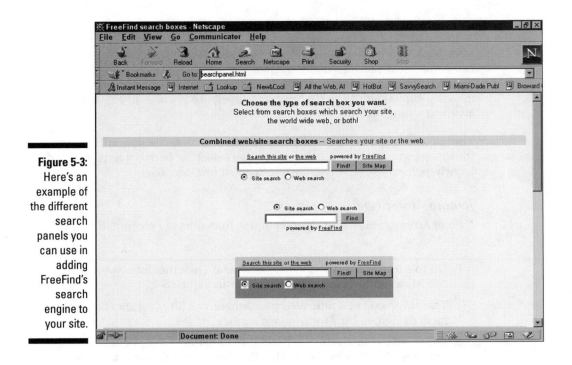

Figure 5-3:
Here's an example of the different search panels you can use in adding FreeFind's search engine to your site.

If you want to customize and pretty up the search page, go to the Control Center page and click the Customize button. You can specify background colors and images, the type of logo that appears, the positioning of the search results, and many other options. The choices that you make there also affect your site map so that both the search page and the site map share the same look.

Putting the Atomz.com search engine on your site

If you're dead set against hosting someone else's advertising on your site, you may want to consider using Atomz.com's search engine (www.Atomz.com), another site that runs on its servers instead of yours. Atomz.com doesn't have banner ads but requires only that you put its logo on the search page. The company also doesn't accept adults-only sites or any other site it deems inappropriate.

As is the case with FreeFind, Atomz.com's service is free, but the company also offers a paid service for sites that contain more than 500 pages. The rates are quite reasonable, however. For a 5,000-page site, the cost is only $1,200 per year. (If you have a site with that many pages and you can't generate $100 a month from it, you may want to take a careful look at what you're doing.)

You can set certain pages so that all searches exclude them, assign greater weight to different items (like alt text in images), and enable a visitor to limit the search to a particular section of the site. Atomz.com also offers a few features that most services don't, such as the capability to search inside Flash and PDF files. They also have a feature called Sound Alike matching that matches similar words so that using misspelled keywords in a search doesn't give you wrong results.

The service keeps track of search requests and provides you with reports of the top keywords that visitors use. You can select the period that is reported — anywhere from the past two days to the last few months.

Joining Atomz.com

Joining Atomz.com is a bit more complex than joining FreeFind; follow these steps to join:

1. **Go to Atomz.com (**www.Atomz.com**) and click the Join Now! button on the Atomz.com main page, as shown in Figure 5-4.**

   This takes you to a new Web page where you fill out a short and simple form to sign up for Atomz.com's service.

2. **Enter your e-mail address (which the company keeps confidential) and the URL of your site in the Join form, and then click the Join button, as shown in Figure 5-5.**

   Next, you see the same form, but this time, a Confirm button appears beneath it.

3. **Double-check the information that you just entered and click the Confirm button.**

   Atomz.com sends you an e-mail confirmation message within a few minutes, containing your password.

   Keep your password somewhere safe. You need it whenever you want to log in again after you join.

4. **Click the link in the confirmation message to confirm receipt.**

   This link takes you to the Atomz.com Welcome page, as shown in Figure 5-6.

5. **Click the Next: Review Our Service Agreement button.**

   Next, you see the Service Agreement page, as shown in Figure 5-7.

6. **Read the service agreement, using the scroll bar on the side of the text area to access all the text, and click the I Agree to These Terms button.**

   The next screen is the Contact Information page, as shown in Figure 5-8.

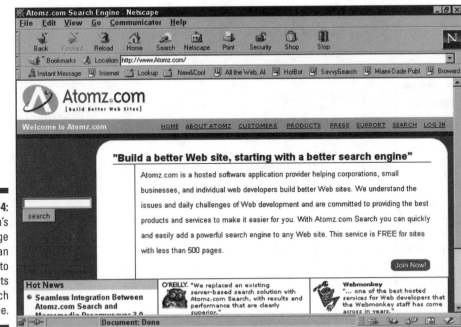

Figure 5-4:
Atomz.com's
main page
— you can
join here to
receive its
search
engine.

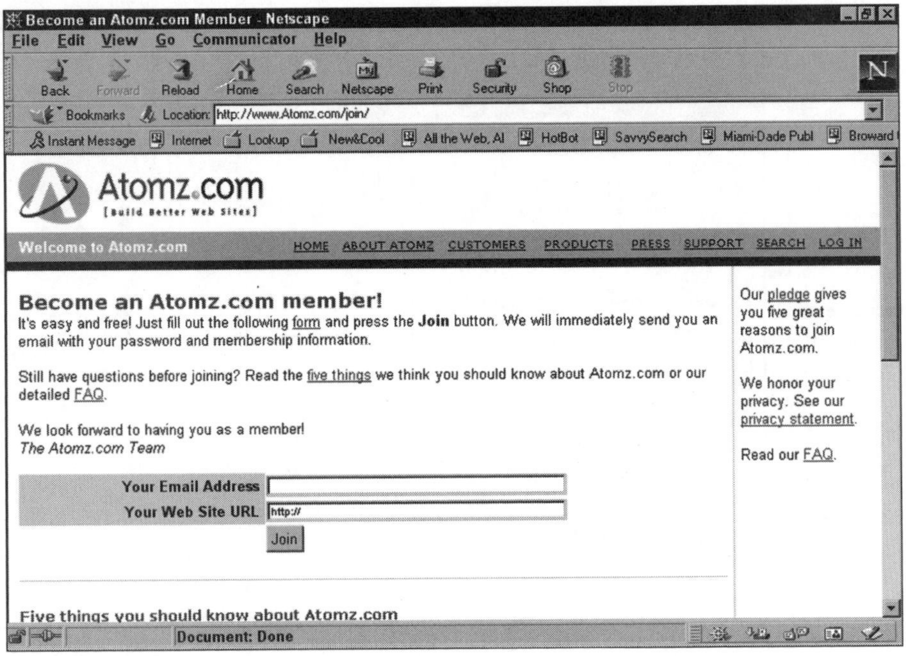

Figure 5-5:
You need to
fill out the
Join form to
sign up for
Atomz.com.

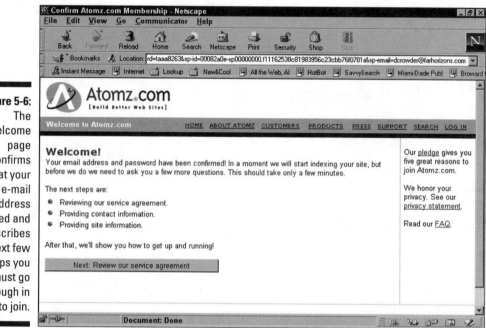

Figure 5-6:
The
Welcome
page
confirms
that your
e-mail
address
worked and
describes
the next few
steps you
must go
through in
order to join.

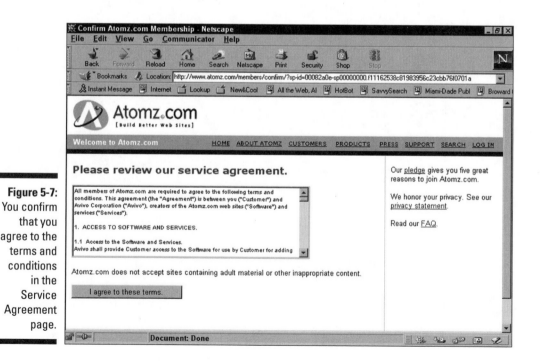

Figure 5-7:
You confirm
that you
agree to the
terms and
conditions
in the
Service
Agreement
page.

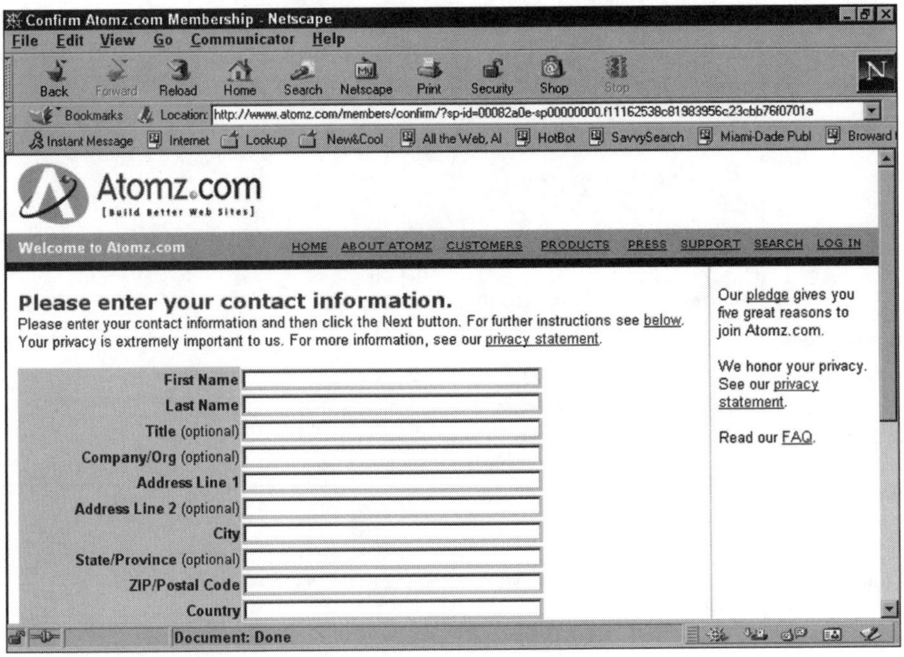

Figure 5-8:
You enter
your name,
address,
and so on in
the Contact
Information
page.

7. **Fill in all the information that the Contact Information page requires and click the Next button.**

   The Site Information page appears, displaying the URL that you entered when you first joined, as shown in Figure 5-9.

8. **If your URL is incorrect on the Site Information page, change it; if it's fine, move on to Step 9.**

9. **Enter the name of your site in the Web Site Name text box.**

10. **Choose a category for your site from the Web Site Category drop-down list (Business, Games, and so on).**

11. **Click the Next button.**

    The Welcome page appears, meaning that the sign-up process is complete, as shown in Figure 5-10.

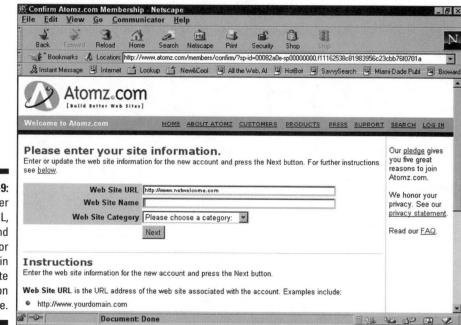

Figure 5-9:
You enter
the URL,
name, and
category for
your site in
the Site
Information
page.

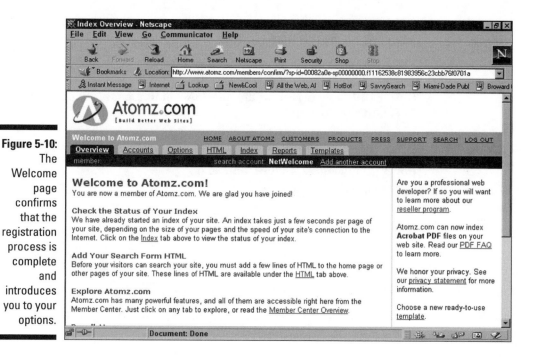

Figure 5-10:
The
Welcome
page
confirms
that the
registration
process is
complete
and
introduces
you to your
options.

Adding the search engine

At this point, Atomz.com is busily indexing your site. If you want to watch the process, you can click the Index tab on the Welcome page. The important thing to do, though, is to actually add the search engine form to your site. To do so, click the HTML tab and follow these steps:

1. **On the HTML Overview page, pick either the Standard or the Advanced Search Form and click the <u>HTML code</u> link for the form that you pick (or just scroll down the page to the HTML code), as shown in Figure 5-11.**

2. **Copy the appropriate version of the HTML code and paste it into the Web page that you want to use as the location for your search feature.**

3. **Upload the page to your site and run a search to test it.**

For some variations on these options, you can click the Templates tab to get some additional choices of search forms for your site. If none of these pre-designed forms meets your needs, however, you can modify them to suit yourself.

Don't monkey with the `input type=hidden` line. That's the code by which Atomz.com recognizes your site. If you change it, the search can't work.

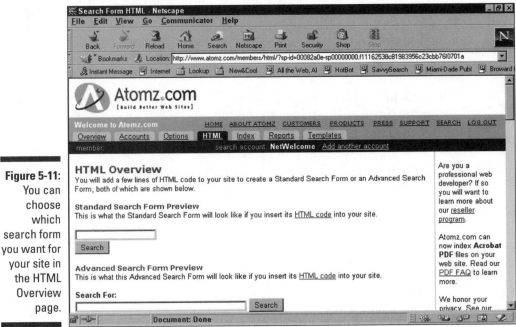

Figure 5-11: You can choose which search form you want for your site in the HTML Overview page.

Dropping in Perl CGI scripts with Simple Search

If you're a go-it-alone type who doesn't want to rely on outside servers to process your site searches, you can drop in a Perl CGI script instead (see Chapter 4). It requires a bit more technical skill than some tasks, or a little bit of help from your ISP or network administrator, but it's definitely doable, even if you don't know anything about CGI. One of the best and easiest to use is *Simple Search*. Written by Matt Wright, one of CGI's greats, it's been a venerable mainstay of many a Web site. Figure 5-12 shows Simple Search on a Web page.

You can download Simple Search from Matt's Script Archive (`http://worldwidemart.com/scripts/search.shtml`). To add Simple Search to your site, you first need to uncompress the main file for the program (`simple.zip`, `simple.tar`, or whatever) and then make a few alterations in the enclosed sample files.

You need to change a few settings in the script in order to make it work on your site. Make sure that you follow the exact format of what appears in these settings as you replace the sample values in the script with the actual information for your own site, or the script won't work. This mostly means that you must leave all quotation marks and semicolons in place just as they appear in the following examples. Don't replace single quotes with double quotes or vice versa. Keeping a hard copy of the file handy while working on it may help you to remember what to do — and what not to do.

To prepare the Perl script of Simple Search for use, follow these steps:

1. **Go to** `http://worldwidemart.com/scripts/search.shtml` **and open the file** `simple.pl` **in a text editor.**

2. **Scroll down until you reach the section with the heading** `# Define Variables`.

3. **Replace the** `$basedir` **value with the base directory path of your own site.**

   In the following script line, the sample value for this variable is `/mnt/web/guide/worldwidemart/scripts/`. Remember to replace only the value itself, not the variable (`$basedir`) or any of the punctuation marks.

   ```
   $basedir = '/mnt/web/guide/worldwidemart/scripts/';
   ```

   The *base directory path* is the path on your Web server, not your Web site's URL, which you add in the following step. If you don't know this value, ask your ISP or network administrator. Make sure that you include the trailing slash at the end (`/`).

4. **Replace the** $baseurl **value with the base URL of your own site.**

   The value you need to supply for the $baseurl variable is the URL of
   the directory where your site's main page resides. The base URL for
   Dummies.com, for example, is http://www.dummies.com/ — and using
   both http:// and the trailing slash is important here, too, even if you're
   not used to using both in Web addresses. In the following line from the
   script, the value you need to replace is
   http://worldwidemart.com/scripts/:

   ```
   $baseurl = 'http://worldwidemart.com/scripts/';
   ```

5. **Replace the sample values for the** @files **variable with the paths and
   files that you want Simple Search to process as part of its search.**

   In the following line from the script, the values you need to replace are
   .shtml, demos/links/.html, and demos/guest/*.html:

   ```
   @files = ('*.shtml','demos/links/*.html','demos/
              guest/*.html');
   ```

   This is one of the easiest places to create a typographical error that will
   keep the script from working because the @files variable can have more
   than one value. Each value is between single quotation marks, as usual,
   but it's also separated from the other values by a comma. If you use more
   than one value here, pay careful attention to the sample code's syntax.

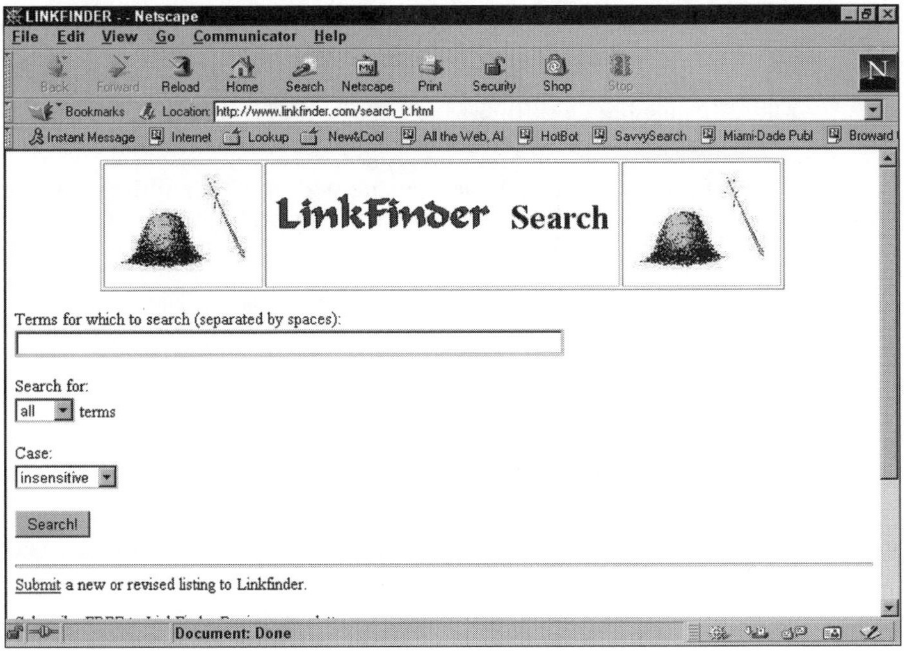

Figure 5-12:
Simple
Search adds
keyword-
searching
capabilities
to your site.

If you want to search only HTML files in the main directory, for example, you enter the value that the following example shows:

```
@files = ('*.html');
```

To search both HTML and SHTML files in the main directory, you use the following example instead:

```
@files = ('*.html','*.shtml');
```

To search for HTML and SHTML files in a subdirectory called `fauna` as well, you use the following example:

```
@files = ('*.html','*.shtml','*/fauna.*html','/
        fauna/*.shtml');
```

6. **Replace the value of the** `$title` **variable with the name of your site. In the following line from the script, the sample value you need to replace is** `Matt's Script Archive`.

```
$title = "Matt's Script Archive";
```

This value appears along with the search results, and the next step makes the text into a text link.

7. **Replace the value of the** `$titleurl` **variable with the Web address of your main page. In the following line from the script, the value you need to replace is** `http://worldwidemart.com/scripts/`.

```
$title_url = 'http://worldwidemart.com/scripts/';
```

This value is usually the same as the `$baseurl` value, although you may want to add the page's filename as well. For example, if your `$baseurl` value is `http://www.mysite.com/` and your main page is `index.html`, you could use either `http://www.mysite.com/` or `http://www.mysite.com/ index.html` as the value for `$titleurl`.

8. **Replace the** `$searchurl` **value with the Web address of your search page. In the following line from the script, the part you need to replace is** `http://worldwidemart.com/scripts/demos/search/ search.html`.

```
$search_url = 'http://worldwidemart.com/scripts/demos/
        search/search.html';
```

9. **Save the file.**

To prepare the HTML search page for use, follow these steps:

1. **Open the file** `search.html` **in a text editor.**

2. **Change the** `action` **attribute of the** `FORM` **element to the URL where you're locating the Perl script on your Web server.**

In the following line from the `search.html` file, the value you need to replace is `http://worldwidemart.com/scripts/cgi-bin/demos/search.cgi`.

```
<form method=POST action="http://worldwidemart.com/
           scripts/cgi-bin/demos/search.cgi">
```

3. Save the file.

Now upload both files to your server. Make sure that you send `search.pl` in ASCII form and that you put it in your `cgi-bin` directory. Send `search.html` in ASCII form and put it in your Web page directory.

Okay, remember we told you this one took a bit more tech savvy than most? This is where that comes into play. You need to set permissions for the files so they'll work on your Web server. If you don't know what that means, don't worry about it. Just ask your ISP or network administrator to do it for you. Tell them that you need to chmod `search.pl` to 755 and to chmod `search.html` to 744. They'll know what you mean, and they can take care of it in about ten seconds.

Showing the Way with Navigational Tools

The more complex your Web site is, the more you need to use good navigational tools. Although a search engine provides quick answers to specific questions, there's nothing like browsing your way through a site to really get to know what treasures it's got tucked away. You can help your visitors find their way around your site with some of these handy navigational helpers.

Shelving your links with Bookshelf

Bookshelf (also known as Webshelf) is an applet created by Nick Sakva, and it's one of those joys that you run across from time to time. It's not only functional, but it's also attractive and clever to boot. It's a Java applet that sets up a list of links that looks like a 3D bookshelf — similar to the one shown in Figure 5-13. Each link gets its own volume on the shelf, and the books' titles show the names of the links. You can set individual details, such as the size and color of each book, and you can even add graphical icons to the bindings. The coolest part, though, comes when someone clicks a link — just before the link activates, the book slides out a bit to show that it's selected.

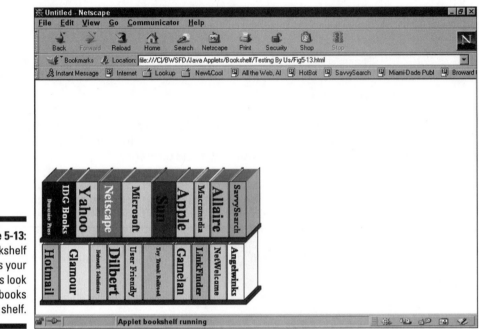

Figure 5-13:
Bookshelf
makes your
links look
like books
on a shelf.

Bookshelf is a Java applet that you'll find on the CD that accompanies this book. The class files for it are compressed within the file shelf.jar, so when you go to put it on your Web page, your HTML code for the start tag needs to read as follows:

```
<APPLET name="bookshelf" archive=shelf.jar code="ru.sakva.
          bsh.Webshelf.class" width=400 height=400>
```

When there are several files needed to make a Java applet work, they often come packed together within a jar (or Java Archive) file, which is simply a zip file with a different extension. You don't need to unzip the jar file for the class files to work.

You can change the width and height values for this applet, by the way. As a matter of fact, you probably want to monkey with these values in order to get the right look for your shelves of books. Depending on how many links you want on a page, the number of books varies, and any time that you have more than can fit on one shelf, the applet generates a new shelf. Two shelves take up twice as much height, of course. Likewise, setting the applet for thicker books means that fewer titles can fit on a given width of shelving; taller books also need more height per shelf . . . and so on. Doing a bit of experimenting with the width and height values, changing them and reloading the page to see the results, is often well worth your time and effort.

If you end up with an extra shelf displaying only one or even a few books on it, you can just increase the `width` value of the shelf a little bit. Doing so usually makes enough room to move the book(s) on the second shelf back up onto the shelf above it and eliminates the need for the extra shelf.

Now for all the stuff that comes before you reach the `</APPLET>` end tag. This applet uses lots of parameters. If you look at the sample Web pages (`SHELF_E1.HTM` and `SHELF_E2.HTM`) that come with the applet, you see that the first several parameters are for setting the overall look and default values. After you get beyond these settings, you find several different groups of parameters, each group separated from the others by a blank line. These are the settings for each individual book on the shelf. That blank line isn't required in the code, by the way, but it does make it easy to see where the settings are for each book.

You don't need to use all the parameters that are available for this applet. Any parameter for which you fail to specify a value simply reverts to its default value.

First off, you want to choose what happens after a visitor clicks a link. You do so by using the `frame` parameter. If you want the linked page to open over the current one, you use the following code:

```
<PARAM name=frame value=_self>
```

To open the linked page in a new browser, you instead use the following code:

```
<PARAM name=frame value=_blank>
```

Other options for the value include the standard `_parent`, `_top`, or `_bottom`, or the name of any frame you have created.

Next, you want to set the color of the wall on which the shelf "hangs" and the color of the shelf as well. You set all colors in this applet by using hexadecimal values. You probably want to set the wall color to match your own page's background color. The following code example shows how to set the color of the wall and shelf:

```
<PARAM name=wall.color value=FFFFFF>
<PARAM name=shelf.color value=602010>
```

To set the arrangement of the books on the shelf, you specify the `putBooks` parameter. Here's how to tell Bookshelf to set the books upright:

```
<PARAM name=putBooks value=vertical>
```

A value of `horizontal`, on the other hand, means that the books are stacked sideways on the shelf. The default value is `horizontal`, so you really only need to specify this parameter if you want them upright. If you do go for vertical books, you can also set whether they're right-side up or upside down. You do so by using the `book.turned` parameter, and the only possible values are `yes` or `no`. The following code makes the books sit right-side up:

```
<PARAM name=book.turned value=no>
```

The previous code sets the default value for the entire shelf, but you can override it for each book. You can also set any individual book to stand right-side up or upside down as well, regardless of the default setting, as we'll show you when we get to the part of the code that handles individual books.

The `title.direction` parameter is closely related to a book's direction. If the books stand in a normal, upright position, using the value `downward` for this parameter means that the title of a book runs from top to bottom, and using `upward` for it sends the title from the bottom to the top. The default value is `upward`, so you really only need to specify this parameter if you want downward titles. This is the way to do it:

```
<PARAM name=title.direction value=downward>
```

If the book is upside down, the title is also going to run in the opposite direction. An upward title on a book that's upside down looks the same as a downward title.

You set the colors of the book covers and titles with the `cover.color` and `title.color` parameters, using hexadecimal color values, like this:

```
<PARAM name=cover.color value=00008B>
<PARAM name=title.color value=000000>
```

Several parameters deal with the dimensions of the books, all of which require pixel values. The height of the books is set via the `book.size` parameter, so if you want books that are 100 pixels high, you use this code:

```
<PARAM name=book.size value=100>
```

You set the default, minimum, and maximum thickness by using three different parameters, as the following example shows:

```
<PARAM name=book.thickness value=20>
<PARAM name=book.min value=10>
<PARAM name=book.max value=100>
```

A fourth parameter, `book.volume`, works in concert with these and each individual book's thickness settings to calculate their size. You're best off leaving this value set at about 10, as in the following example, although it can be interesting to experiment with different values:

```
<PARAM name=book.volume value=10>
```

The total number of books showing is set by specifying the `books.number` parameter. If you have 20 books on the shelf, this is what you type:

```
<PARAM name=books.number value=20>
```

You need to make sure that the number of books is accurate. If you set this parameter's value to less than the number of books you have, only that number shows. For example, if you have 12 books and set this value to 10, 2 books won't show up — and that means there'll be two links that can't be used.

If you set it to more books than you have, Bookshelf generates enough extra books, using the default settings, to match the number. The extra books have blank spines, of course, and no links will be associated with them.

Next, you need to detail each individual book. In many cases, the parameters work exactly the same as the default ones that we describe in the preceding paragraphs. The only difference for some is a prefix that tells which book the parameter applies to.

The two most important things that you need to have on each book are its link and its title. A link that leads to another site has to use the full URL (like `http://www.dummies.com/`), but local links can use a relative URL, like this:

```
<PARAM name=$1.ref value="index.html">
<PARAM name=$1.title value="Home Page">
```

The `$1.` part of the parameters' names means that this particular book is the first book on the shelf. If it's the second book you're detailing, you use `$2.` instead (and so on).

You don't even need to list the books in order. The book number that's a part of the parameter names is all that Bookshelf needs to sort them out.

If you want a two-line title on the book's spine, you need to separate the lines with a semicolon, as in the following example:

```
<PARAM name=$1.title value="JavaScript;Resources">
```

You can't have more than two lines in a book's title. If you try to create multiple lines, the attempted third line stays on line two, including the semicolon.

You can override the default cover and title colors for each book by specifying the book's own colors:

```
<PARAM name=$1.cover.color value=00008D>
<PARAM name=$1.title.color value=000FD0>
```

You can also set the direction in which the book and title faces for each individual book:

```
<PARAM name=$1.turned value=no>
<PARAM name=$1.title.direction value=downward>
```

The settings for an individual book take precedence over the default settings for all the books as a unit. If you decide, for example, to set a certain book so that it doesn't turn over, it stays standing upright even if you set all the others to flip upside down.

You set the width of a particular book like this:

```
<PARAM name=$1.volume value=20>
```

You can add an image to the book's spine, too, by telling the book's icon parameter what file to use:

```
<PARAM name=$1.icon value="spine.jpg">
```

This file must be either a GIF or a JPG image, and you don't want it to be very large, although Bookshelf can shrink it quite a bit to make it fit.

Finally, you can place boxes, as well as books, on the shelves. This effect looks like a shrink-wrapped software package instead of a book. All you need to do to specify that the link's in a box is to set up its parameter value, as shown here:

```
<PARAM name=$1.box value="yes">
```

The following example combines all the previous code, showing it as it needs to appear in the code on your Web page:

```
<APPLET name="bookshelf" archive=shelf.jar code="ru.sakva.
        bsh.Webshelf.class" width=400 height=400>
<PARAM name=frame value=_self>
<PARAM name=wall.color value=FFFFFF>
<PARAM name=shelf.color value=602010>
```

```
<PARAM name=putBooks value=vertical>
<PARAM name=book.turned value=no>
<PARAM name=title.direction value=downward>
<PARAM name=cover.color value=00008B>
<PARAM name=title.color value=000000>
<PARAM name=book.size value=100>
<PARAM name=book.thickness value=20>
<PARAM name=book.min value=10>
<PARAM name=book.max value=100>
<PARAM name=book.volume value=10>
<PARAM name=books.number value=20>
<PARAM name=$1.ref value="http://www.dummies.com/">
<PARAM name=$1.title value="Dummies Press">
<PARAM name=$1.cover.color value=00008D>
<PARAM name=$1.title.color value=000FD0>
<PARAM name=$1.turned value=no>
<PARAM name=$1.title.direction value=downward>
<PARAM name=$1.volume value=20>
<PARAM name=$1.icon value="spine.jpg">
<PARAM name=$1.box value="no">
<PARAM name=$2.ref value="http://www.idgbooks.com/">
<PARAM name=$2.title value="IDG Books">
<! Remaining Books Go Here >
</APPLET>
```

The part that says `<! Remaining Books Go Here >` is just a placeholder. You don't need it in your code. That's where you put the parameters for the other 18 books in this example.

Creating menus with VMaxNav

VMaxNav, a Java applet from Virtual Max, creates an Explorer-style menu that makes site navigation a breeze. As you can see in Figure 5-14, it's attractive, space-saving, and useful. It's also easy for Webmasters to work with. You can control the colors and fonts that it uses and even throw in a background image if you want. You can download it from `www.geocities.com/siliconvalley/lakes/8620/vmaxnav.zip`.

The basic code for adding the VMaxNav applet is as follows:

```
<APPLET code="vmaxnav.class" width="200 height="294">
```

You can alter the `width` and `height` attributes, but if you're using a background image, you must make sure that you use one that either fits the new dimensions or that looks good as it tiles, or your nice, new navigational tool won't look too good.

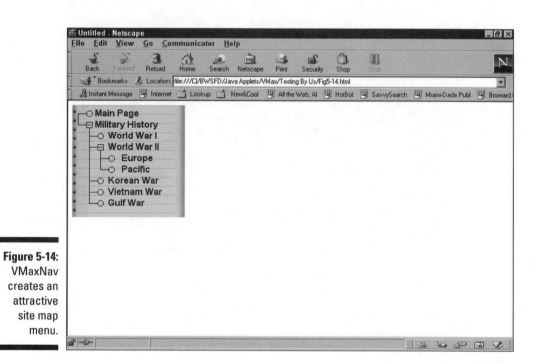

Figure 5-14:
VMaxNav creates an attractive site map menu.

The two parameters shown in the following example are required by this applet:

```
<PARAM name="AUTHOR" value="Virtual_Max
          (http://come.to/vmax)">
<PARAM name="KEY" value="Free Version">
```

The AUTHOR parameter is self-explanatory. The KEY parameter value changes only if you register the applet. (The only difference between registered and unregistered versions is that the unregistered one adds a link to Virtual Max's Web site at the end of your own links.)

VMaxNav requires one file other than the class file — a text file that lists the links that you want to add. If you want the background image, that's another external file, but the applet doesn't require it. The following examples show you how to specify these files in your code:

```
<PARAM name="URL" value="vmaxnav.txt">
<PARAM name="BGIMAGE" value="vmaxnavbg.gif">
```

We cover the structure of the text file after we're done discussing the parameters. If you use the name vmaxnav.txt for this file, you don't need to list the URL parameter because that name is hard-wired into the applet, meaning that the applet automatically looks for a file with that name, unless you specify otherwise. If you use another name, then you do need to specify the URL.

You can set the colors for the navigation tree through the TEXTCOLOR, ACTIVECOLOR, and BGCOLOR parameters. You need to enter these values in hexadecimal format. The following code example shows the default color values:

```
<PARAM name="TEXTCOLOR" value="C0C000">
<PARAM name="ACTIVECOLOR" value="80FF00">
<PARAM name="BGCOLOR" value="000080">
```

If these colors suit your design scheme, you don't need to specify them.

You can choose the font face, style, and size by setting the values of the FONT parameter. The font-face options are TimesRoman, Helvetica, Courier, Dialog, or DialogInput.

You must use the exact same capitalization because of the applet's case-sensitivity for these font names. Font style values are 0 for normal, 1 for bold, 2 for italics, and 3 for bold italics. Font size values are in pixels.

You put the three values together, separating each by a space. To set Helvetica bold, 20 pixels high, for example, use the following example:

```
<PARAM name="FONT" value="Helvetica 1 20">
```

To specify how the linked file opens, you use the TARGET parameter. The values are the standard _top, _self, _blank, and _parent, or any window name that you have created:

```
<PARAM name="TARGET" value="_blank">
```

Here's the whole shooting match in one place:

```
<APPLET code="vmaxnav.class" width="200 height="294">
<PARAM name="AUTHOR" value="Virtual_Max
          (http://come.to/vmax)">
<PARAM name="KEY" value="Free Version">
<PARAM name="URL" value="vmaxnav.txt">
<PARAM name="BGIMAGE" value="vmaxnavbg.gif">
<PARAM name="TEXTCOLOR" value="C0C000">
<PARAM name="ACTIVECOLOR" value="80FF00">
<PARAM name="BGCOLOR" value="000080">
<PARAM name="FONT" value="Helvetica 1 20">
<PARAM name="TARGET" value="_blank">
</APPLET>
```

To set up the external text file that VMaxNav draws its information from, you need to follow a strict but simple format. One line in the text file creates one equivalent line in the applet display's tree. You specify the level of the line in the tree by the number of blank spaces in the line's beginning. As the following example shows, a top-level line has no spaces before the text. If it's a second-level line, you add one space before the text; if it's a third-level line, you add two spaces, and so on.

```
Top Level
  Second Level
    Third Level
  Another Second Level
    Third Level
      Another Third Level
Another Top Level
```

Make sure to save the applet as an unformatted, plain-text ASCII file.

The text on each line has to follow the format *text|URL*, like this:

```
Main Page|index.html
```

After you finish, upload the `html` file, the `class` file, the `txt` file, and the background image file (if you use one). Don't forget that you need to upload the `html` file and the `txt` file in ASCII format and the other two as binary files.

Making drop-down lists

Well, we've got just about everything else in this chapter, so it's probably time to throw in a bit of JavaScript, too. The drop-down list shown in Figure 5-15 is easy to add to your site. It's a form that contains a selection menu. When a visitor makes a selection from the list, the form calls the JavaScript code and loads the selected page.

To add this to your Web page, you first need to put the script into your `HEAD` element, so your code looks like this:

```
<HEAD>
<SCRIPT language="JavaScript">
<!--
// Hide from old browsers
function golinks(where){
self.location = where;
}

// stop hiding -->
</SCRIPT>
</HEAD>
```

Of course, you'll probably have some other stuff in the `HEAD` element, too, like your title, but we're keeping this down to the basics.

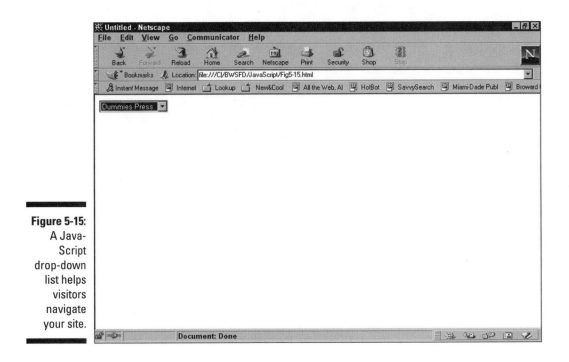

Figure 5-15:
A Java-
Script
drop-down
list helps
visitors
navigate
your site.

Next, put the form into your BODY element:

```
<BODY>
<FORM>
<SELECT onchange="golinks(this.options
          [this.selectedIndex].value)">
<OPTION value="http://www.dummies.com/">Dummies
          Press</OPTION>
<OPTION value="http://www.idgbooks.com/">IDG Books</OPTION>
</SELECT>
</FORM>
</BODY>
```

Change the values of the OPTION elements to the URLs you want to link to. Of course, you'll want to change the descriptive content, too. To add more links to the list, just add more OPTION elements.

Online Sources

Table 5-1 lists some places on the World Wide Web where you can find more resources like those that we cover in this chapter.

Table 5-1	Online Resources
Web Site Name	*Web Address*
LinkBar	www.consultcom.com/Java/Applets/LinkBar.html
NavBar	http://lktoh.tripod.com/
Searchbutton	www.searchbutton.com
whatUseek	http://intra.whatUseek.com
ZoneCoaster Search	www.zonecoaster.com/shop/?c=Free_Perl_Scripts&p=Search_Version_2.03

Chapter 6

Making Things Look Great

In This Chapter

▶ Getting free graphics

▶ Getting Graziana Cipresso graphics

▶ Ordering and creating free logos

▶ Using graphical applets

*Y*ou can have a perfectly functional Web site without images. But if you put your site side by side with another one that's just as functional but also uses graphics, you lose. Most people go to the other site and leave yours gathering electronic dust.

In this chapter, we take you on a whirlwind tour of places where you can download images by the bushel, Java applets that modify images in fabulous ways, and lots of other add-ins that improve the appearance of your site.

Getting Graphics — for Free!

Most of us aren't artists, and even if we know an artist or three, most of them spend their time mucking about with paint brushes and canvases. Many aren't really comfortable with electronic media. So how does the average person who wants nice graphics for their Web site get them? The good news is that they're all over the place. In recent years, the World Wide Web has become increasingly graphical, and the quality of those graphics has improved tremendously from the early days of the Internet.

Heeding copyrights and credits

Every Web browser is a funnel for graphics. Any image that you can see in it, you can download and put on your site. You need to keep in mind a few considerations, though. Yes, you can grab every image file that you find. But you can't necessarily use them all without consequences.

When an artist creates an image, that artist owns the *copyright* to that image. Just like the word says, that gives the artist — and the artist alone — the right to make copies, electronic or otherwise. They can give other people permission to make copies of the image — or even sell the copyright to someone — but unless they do so, the artist retains total control over the image.

Never take legal advice from anyone who spells copy*right* as copy*write*.

One of the few ways in which someone can lose a copyright is if artists state that they're placing a work in the *public domain*, which means that they're surrendering their copyright and others can do anything that they want with the work. A lot of people don't understand what public domain means, though, and you sometimes run across a statement on a Web site that says something incredible like, "I retain the copyright to all these images, but I'm placing them in the public domain, so feel free to use them." If you find one of these contradictory disclaimers, and you really want to use the images, your best course is probably to contact the artist for clarification.

Typically, though, you find five different situations with fine print on an artist's Web site, as the following list describes:

- ✔ The artist states that you can't use the images. Just walk away — you can find plenty of others out there.

- ✔ The artist states that you can use the images without any conditions on their usage. Go ahead and download to your heart's content.

- ✔ The artist states that you can use the images if you do certain things, such as include a link back to the page they're on or include a copyright notice under the image. Do what the artist asks and use the images.

- ✔ The artist states that you can use the images freely if you run a noncommercial site but that commercial sites must pay. If you're commercial and the work is good, pay up — it's not going to break the bank. After all, you're not buying a Renoir original here.

- ✔ The artist provides no information at all about usage. Either walk away or e-mail the artist to find out the policy.

Online sources that we list at the end of this chapter show some great places where you can get your hands on lots of high-quality Web images.

Differentiating between graphic file formats

Sometimes it seems that there are about as many different graphic file formats as there are people in Manhattan on a Monday afternoon. Every company from Adobe to Kodak has its own way of showing electronic images. When it comes to the Web, though, you really only need to consider three formats — the three that work in all major (and most of the minor) Web browsers.

GIF

The venerable, old *GIF* (*G*raphics *I*nterchange *F*ormat) file format still sees a lot of usage on the Web. Because GIF limits you to 256 colors, it's best to use for images that don't have lots of colors or much in the way of subtle shifts between colors. GIF also has a unique capability — it can contain several images in a single file. These images appear sequentially as you view the GIF file, resulting in a cheap and easy form of animation.

JPEG

The relatively newer *JPEG* (*J*oint *P*hotographic *E*xperts *G*roup) format, also commonly known as *JPG* because people still have the habit of using DOS 8.3-type filenames, has radically different capabilities. JPEG's a true color format, so you don't need to worry about any color limitations. It also stores image information in a different way, resulting in a highly compressed file that's usually much smaller than a GIF file of the same image.

PNG

The latest puppy in the window is the *PNG* (*P*ortable *N*etwork *G*raphics) format. (You pronounce it "ping.") This format came about as a response to the increasing legal mess over the GIF format. (See the accompanying sidebar, "Licensing Web sites.") PNG does everything that the GIF format does, except for creating animated images, and does quite a few things much better, such as providing better transparency capabilities. Best of all, it's totally free of all legal entanglements. (A more sophisticated format known as *MNG* — *M*ultiple *N*etwork *G*raphics — that's currently in the works will include the capability to create animated images, too.) Although PNG support in Web browsers tends to be a bit spotty right now, it's definitely improving. PNG is the native format of Macromedia Fireworks, a major graphics program, and will probably become the Web standard.

Licensing Web sites

The GIF format has become the center of a lot of legal contentions over the years. Although these disputes generally haven't affected the end user in the past, that time is now over. Unisys Corporation, the owner of the compression algorithm that GIF images use, has decided to charge many Web-site owners a minimum of $5,000 each for the right to use GIFs on their sites. (No, we're not making this figure up. We wish that we were.) You can read the gory details at www.unisys.com/unisys/ lzw/lzw-license.asp. In a nutshell, if Unisys doesn't license the software that you use to create GIFs, you owe them thousands of dollars. Even if it is licensed, you may not be out of the woods — Unisys says only that you're "probably covered."

For a company intranet or a noncommercial Web site, the fee is $5,000. We're warning you again that we're no lawyers, but from what Unisys says, we gather that even a child putting up a single Web page on a kindergarten site that shows an image of their latest finger painting has to cough up the bucks. (See "Definitions of Sites That Qualify for Intranet/Billboard LZW License," at www.unisys.com/unisys/ lzw/lzw-def.asp, for details.) Other Web sites, including Internet stores and hosting services, must "negotiate separate written license agreements" that presumably cost more than $5,000. (See "Types of Web Sites That Do Not Qualify for This License," at the same URL.)

Now, all this controversy presents a tremendous difficulty for all involved. First off, Unisys is obviously biting off more than anyone can chew. If we were given the job of tracking down all GIF images on the Web that people create with non-licensed software, we'd ask for something much easier to do — like counting all the grains of sand in California — so you probably don't need to worry about much in the way of active prosecution. Even if you do want to cooperate, though, how can you possibly tell whether every image you lay your hands on has ever passed through an unlicensed program?

As you can imagine, this whole idea doesn't sit too well with most people, and you can see the kind of reaction the situation has prompted at http:// burnallgifs.org.

Ordering Graphics by Graziana Cipresso

Want a free logo for your site? Some really cool and professional animations? Just ask Graziana. This site, at www.enteract.com/~graziana, really does offer custom logos and banners at no cost. All you have to do is exert a little bit of patience — for about five days — because paying work must come first for this skilled artist. To order a logo or banner or to explore the download-able art, go to the home page and click the Free Stuff link.

In addition to the animated clip art and custom services, this site includes some graphics we're tempted to call "standard icons" except for the fact that they're so well done. The icons come in color-coordinated suites, such as the one shown in Figure 6-1. They include a variety of background images, along with the most commonly used buttons on a Web site (Home, E-mail, Links, About, and so on). On top of this, you also find directional indicators, a colored ball, and a pair of horizontal divider lines for each suite.

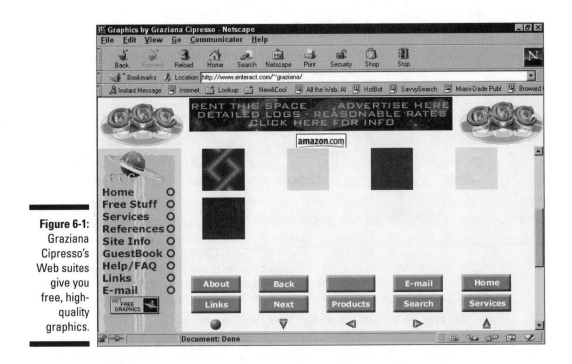

Figure 6-1:
Graziana
Cipresso's
Web suites
give you
free, high-
quality
graphics.

Creating a Logo with CoolText.com

If you want a free logo fast and you don't mind doing it yourself, try CoolText.com at — you guessed it — www.cooltext.com. This Web site generates graphics while you wait according to the options that you choose. The process is simple and fun, and there's no limit to the number of logos you can experiment with.

Not only are its logos cool but so are the site's legal requirements: none, zip, nada. There's no copyright issue to deal with, no ads stuck in the middle of things, no fine print of any kind. As an act of gratitude for such a great service, you may want to add a link back to this site from yours, but even that's not required.

Although CoolText.com doesn't hold a copyright on the logos you create, you probably do. We're not lawyers (and we don't even play them on TV), but it seems to us that the decisions you make during the course of designing the logos qualify them as artistic creations. Don't take our word for it, though — if this point is important for your situation, check with an attorney who really knows copyright law or e-mail the federal Copyright Office at copyinfo@loc.gov.

To make a custom logo at CoolText.com, follow these steps:

1. **Go to** www.cooltext.com **and then click any logo style in the list at the left side of the main page, as shown in Figure 6-2.**

   You go to the logo design page, as shown in Figure 6-3.

2. **Type the text for your logo in the Logo Text text box on the design page.**

   You usually type the name of your site or company here, although you can type anything that you want. If you need to make more than one line, you can put a new line symbol (\n) in the text, as in the following example:

   ```
   First Line\nSecond Line
   ```

   It doesn't really matter which logo style you start with because you can change your mind at any time without starting over. We're using the Cutout style in our example. To change the style, you just select new ones by clicking the icons on the right side of the logo-design page. In fact, doing this is a good way to get to know the different styles quickly.

3. **Next, pick a font from the Font drop-down list.**

   If you want to browse through images of the available alphabets, click the Font List button in the lower-right corner of the Web page. The Texture List button is even better — of course, it shows the textures that the various logo styles use, but you can download them and use them for Web page background images, too.

4. **Enter a font size in the Font Size text box.**

   Different logo styles offer different options from here on. Depending on the style that you choose, these options may set colors, determine whether text is engraved or raised, and so forth. For the Cutout style, for example, you next select a foreground color.

5. **Select a foreground color from the Foreground Color box in the lower-left of the screen.**

   You can do this by either entering numerical values in the R, G, and B text boxes to indicate the RGB (red, green, and blue) components, or by clicking the displayed color at the bottom of the box to access a color picker.

   The color picker appears, as shown in Figure 6-4.

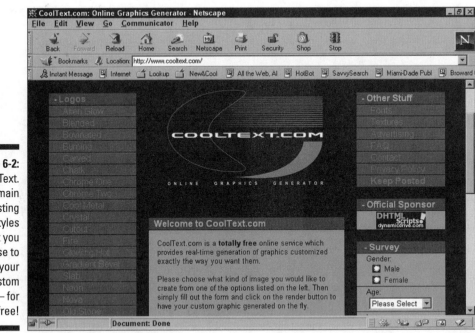

Figure 6-2:
CoolText.
com's main
page, listing
the styles
that you
can use to
create your
own custom
logo — for
free!

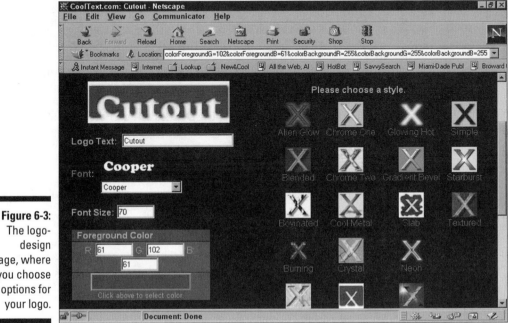

Figure 6-3:
The logo-
design
page, where
you choose
options for
your logo.

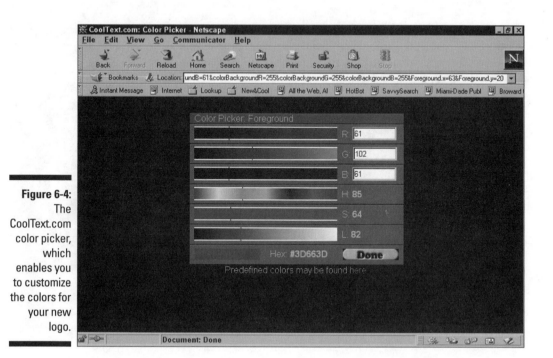

Figure 6-4:
The
CoolText.com
color picker,
which
enables you
to customize
the colors for
your new
logo.

6. **Click anywhere along the R (Red) line to select the amount of red, along the G (Green) line to select the amount of green, and so on.**

Each time that you do this, the page reloads with the new value show-ing. As an alternative to the red, green, and blue (RGB) approach, you can also set colors by using the *HSL* model (hue, saturation, and lumi-nance). Hue basically sets the color itself — whether it's red or blue, for example. Saturation is how pure the color is. Luminance is how much white is added to the color. You click the H, S, and L lines to set their values the same as you do for the R, G, and B lines. You can't, however, enter numerical values yourself, because these lines don't have text boxes after them.

If you're not certain how much to enter in the R, G, and B text boxes (or where to click on the lines in the color picker), you can click the link at the bottom of the color picker that reads *Predefined colors may be found here* to go to HYPE's Color Specifier. (You can go directly to it at `www.users.interport.net/~giant/COLOR/ColorSpecifier.html` whether you're in CoolText.com or not.) This Web page shows you a long list of named colors, with examples of each — and their RGB values. Just decide which one you like and note its RGB values; then click the Back button to return to CoolText.com.

7. When you're satisfied with the foreground color, click the color picker's Done button to return to the logo design page.

8. Repeat Steps 5 through 7 for the background color box.

9. After you set all the options for your logo, click the Create Logo button.

Now, all you have to do is sit back and wait until your logo shows up. If you like it, download it right away because it only exists on CoolText.com's server for about an hour. If you don't like it, back up and monkey with the settings until you get what you're looking for.

While you're at CoolText.com, check out the bullet generator, too. You get to it by clicking the <u>Bullets</u> link from the main page.

Using Some Elemental Applets

The three applets that we describe in the following sections are on the CD-ROM that accompanies this book. They all come from David Griffiths, and you may want to spend some enjoyable time checking out his other ones at www.spigots.com/spigots.htm. If you want to save yourself some typing, the Spigots site has Drop Dead Simple code-generating wizards for each of its applets.

These applets are free to use on your site. If you do feel the urge to shell out a few bucks for them, the author requests that you make a donation to the Ty Hafan Children's Hospice at www.tyhafan.org/donations/ instead of paying him.

All three applets work on either GIF or JPEG images.

Burning down the site

Where there's water, there should be fire, right? Or is that the other way around? Whatever, the Fire applet is one pretty cool effect to add to your site. It takes a GIF or JPEG image and sets all the light-colored parts aflame, as in the example shown in Figure 6-5.

Figure 6-5:
The Fire
applet
makes
the light-
colored
parts of
an image
appear to
catch fire.

The best kind of image to use with the Fire applet is one with a totally black background and a plain white foreground.

With only three possible parameters, it's a really simple Java applet to add. Just use the following code (substituting your own image file and link destination, of course):

```
<APPLET code=fire width=200 height=200>
<PARAM name=image value="hotwords.gif">
<PARAM name=href value="http://www.dummies.com">
<PARAM name=target value="pics">
</APPLET>
```

The one parameter that the applet absolutely requires is image. Without it, you're not going to see anything. You don't need the href parameter unless you want the applet to serve as an image link; its value is the URL of the file you want to link to. You don't need the target parameter unless you also use the href parameter. The target parameter specifies the name of the window in which you want the linked file to open.

After you get the Fire applet running, try dragging your mouse across the top half. Next, try dragging it across the bottom half.

Webbing in a winter wonderland

The Snow applet turns any image into a winter wonderland, kind of like those water-filled snow globes with the tiny villages in them (see Figure 6-6).

Figure 6-6:
The Snow applet turns images into winter scenes.

Like the Fire applet that we describe in the preceding section, the Snow applet's simple to add to your Web page. Three of its parameters are the same as for the Fire applet. You have to specify a value for the image parameter in order to have anything to show. The href parameter, which sets a URL to link to if a visitor clicks on the image, is optional. The target parameter is useful only if you also use the href parameter. You use the target parameter to set the name of the window in which the linked file opens.

The one new parameter for this applet is the strength setting, which determines whether your image is hit by a gentle snow flurry or a raging blizzard. The low setting is 1, and the high setting is 10. Use the following code to create this applet (substituting your own image file and linkdestination):

```
<APPLET code="snow" width=200 height=134>
<PARAM name=image value="palmsnow.jpg">
<PARAM name=strength value="10">
<PARAM name=href value="http://www.idgbooks.com/">
<PARAM name=target value="pics">
</APPLET>
```

Sitting by the lake

The Lake applet is one of the most popular of all the visual effects that you find on the Web. It's the darling of postcard shops (see Chapter 11), romantic sites, and just about anyplace else that wants to set a gentle mood. Lots of different applets of this type are floating around on the Web, but this one by David Griffiths is the original, and its most recent incarnation offers tons of fabulous features.

Figure 6-7 shows the basic Lake applet, but you really have to see it in motion to appreciate the effect. It adds a reflective surface to the bottom of an image (thus increasing its height, by the way), and throws in a ripple effect so that the bottom half of the image appears as though you're seeing its reflection in water that a gentle breeze is stirring.

Figure 6-7:
The Lake applet makes any image appear to be on the shoreline.

Of course, you may want some different effects instead. Say, for example, that you want to give the impression of being on a boat on the lake. Set the rocking parameter and hang on to the gunwales. Or you may want to show a submerged scene reflecting on the bottom of the surface. No problem — just set the underwater parameter and strap on your scuba tanks.

It's a good idea to take a tour along the Ring of Lake Applets, a series of Web sites, to see what other folks have done with this applet. Get your start at http://viperspit.com/lake.html.

You can put this applet in your page very simply, or you can spend a lot of time and effort fine-tuning it for artistic effects. Rock bottom (no pun intended), the only parameter that you really need is image. Use the following code to create this applet, substituting your own image for duck01.jpg:

```
<APPLET code=lake width=200 height=360>
<PARAM name=image value="duck01.jpg">
</APPLET>
```

You should set the width attribute so it's the same as the width of the image, while you set the height attribute to about 1.8 times the height of the image. You may need to adjust the height up or down for a particular image.

As with the earlier two applets, you can also set the optional href and target parameters, as in the following examples:

```
<APPLET code=lake width=200 height=360>
<PARAM name=image value="duck01.jpg">
<PARAM name=href value="http://www.idgbooks.com/">
<PARAM name=target value="pics">
</APPLET>
```

The href parameter sets a URL to link to if a visitor clicks the image, and the target parameter sets the name of the window in which the linked file opens.

To set the scene rocking as if you're viewing it from a boat on the lake, add the rocking parameter to the applet's other parameters, as follows:

```
<PARAM name=rocking value="true">
```

To view the scene from beneath instead of on top of the lake, add the underwater parameter, as follows:

```
<PARAM name=underwater value="true">
```

If you have an image that already shows a lake (or sea or whatever), you can crop out the water portion and go with the usual settings. Or you can leave the wet part in and use the horizon parameter. This setting makes things work a bit differently. You're not adding an extra bit at the bottom of the image, so you set the height and width attributes both equal to the height and width of the image — no multiplying the height by 1.8 as you normally do. You then set the horizon parameter's value as the number of pixels from the bottom of the image to where you want the lake effect to begin. In the following example, we set a 200 x 200-pixel image to show a horizon 80 pixels from the bottom:

```
<APPLET code=lake width=200 height=200>
<PARAM name=image value="duck01.jpg">
<PARAM name=horizon value="80">
</APPLET>
```

Finally, the overlay parameter gives you some special options — not in the code, but in your graphics choices. There are two basic uses for an overlay. The first, and most common, use is to add some lettering over the image. You may, for example, want to say "Boat Rentals" or "Come to Our Lovely Island Paradise." To do this, make a GIF image that holds the message and give it a transparent background. When it's laid over the base image, you get the lake effect underneath the message.

Don't use a transparent GIF for the base image — that is, for the image parameter. If you do, the top half ends up upside down. It works fine for the overlay parameter, however.

The second use of the overlay parameter is to add a covering image that covers over something in the base image. You may, for example, want to add a curving edge to your shoreline. Because the Lake applet provides only a straight line for the lake edge, you need to create an image in which you erase every other part of the picture except for the part of the shoreline that curves below the straight edge that the Lake applet creates. By laying this partial picture over the base image, you cover over part of the water and reestablish the land in that part.

Whatever purpose you may have for adding an overlaid image, use the following code example to do so:

```
<APPLET code=lake width=200 height=360>
<PARAM name=image value="duck01.jpg">
<PARAM name=overlay value="shorecurve.gif">
</APPLET>
```

Online Sources

Table 6-1 lists some places on the World Wide Web where you can find lots of high-quality graphics for your site.

Table 6-1	Online Resources
Web Site Name	*Web Address*
CoolNotions.com	www.coolnotions.com
Free Grafix	www.kevdebin.atlnet.com/Free/FreeGfx.htm
Brandi Jasmine's Digital Art Gallery	www.brandijasmine.com
Dee's Art Gallery	www.dreslough.com/dee/index.html
Gliebster.com	www.gliebster.com/free/graphics/
Goddess Art of Jonathon Earl Bowser	www.jonathonart.com
Graphics Attic	www.graphicsattic.com/gahome.htm
Lindy's Graphics	www.theiowa.net/lindy/
Moyra's Web Jewels	www.moyra.com/jewels/minentrance.html
Novagene's Web Oasis	www.novagene.com/gallery.html
Unseengraphics	www.unseengraphics.com

We don't list any *image repositories* in this table. An image repository is a Web site that simply provides about a zillion images for download without any regard for where they come from or what kind of legal troubles they may cause for you. They typically involve all sorts of copyright and trademark violations, and the fact that such a repository provides the Donald Duck images that you put on your site doesn't keep Disney's lawyers off your back. Stick with sites like the ones in this table and you'll keep out of trouble.

Chapter 7

Web Sights and Sounds

In This Chapter

▶ Adding Informatron's features to your site

▶ Setting up karaoke rooms

▶ Plugging into music through MIDI Radio

▶ Creating a musical site

▶ Downloading iShell

*W*eb pages don't just sit there any more. They've come a long way since the early stages of just displaying text on your computer screen. New forms of multimedia experiences crop up all the time. Television and radio stations, for example, have broadcast on the Web for a long time, but most of them only target individual users. Few TV and radio broadcasters have yet realized the importance of allying with Webmasters to get more exposure for their signals, but we dug up a couple of sites for you that are Web-based themselves, existing only on the WWW instead of being traditional broadcast or cable stations and they do understand how much you, the Webmaster, mean to them.

We also point you to plenty of sources for sound files that you can use on your own Web site. Of course, as with any innovation, there's a certain amount of debate about the use of sound on Web pages. Aside from the carping of die-hard traditionalists who just plain insist that you shouldn't use it, there are some serious considerations. Sound doesn't necessarily go with every site. If you do decide to use it, you need the ability to match the mood of the music with the theme of the page. The right song can add a new dimension; the wrong one can sound ridiculous — and maybe even make your site a bit of a joke.

If you do use sound, make sure that you give your visitors the capability to turn it off. Embedded sound with no controls is an annoyance to many visitors. You may as well give them the option, anyway, because they can simply turn off their speakers to get rid of the sound. (Either that or they just leave your site in disgust, never to return.)

Using Informatron's Cool Features

Informatron offers three different Web-site add-ins that you may want to check out: Informatron TV is streaming-video content; the Interactive Scoreboard is a way for sports-addicted visitors to keep up to date on the latest happenings; and Informatron News gives you links to three separate news sites, each presenting a different focus on the news. The following sections describe each of these nifty features in detail.

If you do add any of these features to your site, make sure that you sign up as an Informatron affiliate. The company doesn't pay you, but it does plug your Web site, which is possibly better than cold, hard cash.

Adding Informatron TV to your site

Do you want the kind of independent content that makes Web-based television so much more interesting than plain, old broadcast or stale cable TV — and do you want it to show up on your Web site? If so, Informatron TV is the ticket for you.

The Informatron TV add-in places a series of banner-like buttons on your site, as shown in Figure 7-1. You can go to three different channels (the three top buttons), each of which launches RealPlayer when a visitor clicks it. The three channels have somewhat similar content: Channel 1 carries concerts; Channel 2's a bit of a grab bag, carrying (at the time of writing) such programs as a video of a building being demolished, and interviews with comedian Shawn Majumder and the rock group Aerosmith; Channel 3 carries concerts and interviews.

At last count, approximately 88 million people use RealPlayer, so most of your visitors can watch this content without downloading the plug-in first. If they don't have it, however, they'll be prompted to download it when they try to view a program. You may want to help your visitors by putting in a link on your site to www.real.com/player/index.html so those who don't have RealPlayer can download it ahead of time.

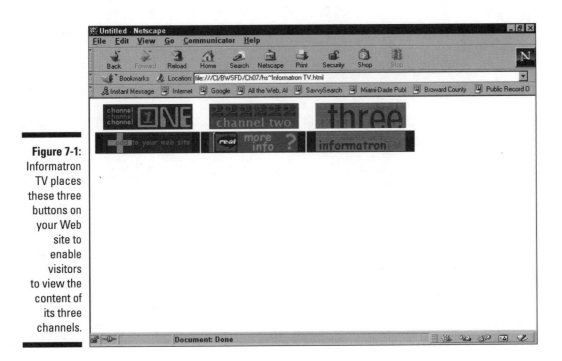

Figure 7-1:
Informatron
TV places
these three
buttons on
your Web
site to
enable
visitors
to view the
content of
its three
channels.

To add Informatron TV to your site, follow these steps:

1. **Go to** www.informatron.com/itvaddthree.htm **to access the Informatron TV page.**

2. **Copy the JavaScript code that you see in the first text area on the page (see Figure 7-2).**

3. **Paste the code into your Web page inside the** HEAD **element.**

   The instructions on the site tell you to paste the script in after the </HEAD> end tag. Although this method also works, it's a nontraditional approach and there's no guarantee that future Web browsers will overlook the error like the current ones do.

4. **Copy the HTML code from the second text area on the Informatron TV page (refer to Figure 7-2).**

5. **Paste this code into your own Web page's source code inside the** BODY **element where you want the channel buttons to appear.**

6. **Save your Web page and upload it to your site.**

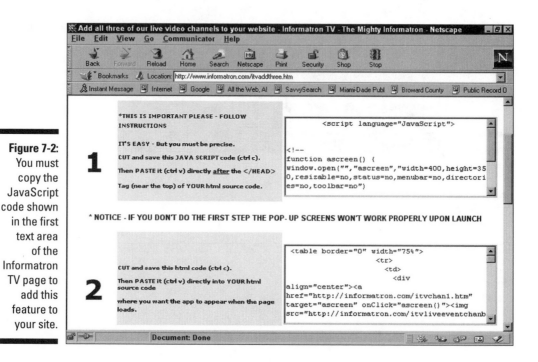

Figure 7-2:
You must
copy the
JavaScript
code shown
in the first
text area
of the
Informatron
TV page to
add this
feature to
your site.

Adding Informatron's Interactive Scoreboard to your site

The Informatron Interactive Scoreboard opens a medium-sized window over your page that shows the scores of today's sporting contests one at a time for a few seconds each. Anyone with an interest in the details of a particular game can click the scoreboard to open a new, full-sized window. The new window shows *USA Today*'s complete report on the event.

Although the scoreboard icon says "pop-up" on it, you may want to put your own text over, under, or next to it to explain that it's not just an image, but is waiting to be clicked.

To add the Interactive Scoreboard feature to your site, follow these steps:

1. **Go to** www.informatron.com/quicklink2.htm **to access the Informatron Interactive Scoreboard page.**

2. **Copy the JavaScript code from the text area on the page.**

3. **Paste the code into your own Web page's source code, inside the** HEAD **element.**

The instructions on the site tell you to paste the script in after the </HEAD> end tag. Although this method works, it's a nontraditional approach and there's no guarantee that future Web browsers will overlook the error like the current ones do.

4. **Scroll down the Informatron Interactive Scoreboard page to find the buttons shown in Figure 7-3. Copy the HTML code next to the button that you want to use on your site.**

5. **Paste the code into your Web page's source code, inside the** BODY **element.**

6. **Save your Web page and upload it to your site.**

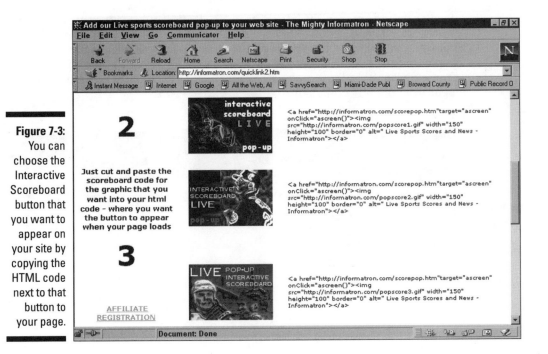

Figure 7-3: You can choose the Interactive Scoreboard button that you want to appear on your site by copying the HTML code next to that button to your page.

Adding Informatron News to your site

The news add-in isn't quite as good for you as the other Informatron offerings, because it actually sends visitors away from your Web site. The news sites that the add-in links to are darn good, however, so if you don't mind your visitors leaving your site to view them (temporarily, at least), this link is still a worthwhile addition to your site.

You can change this behavior by simply adding `target` attributes to the links to specify a new instance of a visitor's Web browser as the target. The following code causes the news site to open in a new window:

```
<A href="http://informatron.com/ncframes.htm"
          target="_blank">
```

Similar to Informatron TV, Informatron News offers three different segments: News, Sports, and Finance. At first glance, each button looks the same, but they're all two-frame animated GIFs, and the second frame specifies the news topic that the button links to. Figure 7-4 shows the three buttons in their first-frame phase. We added explanatory text next to each of them on the page to spare visitors any confusion.

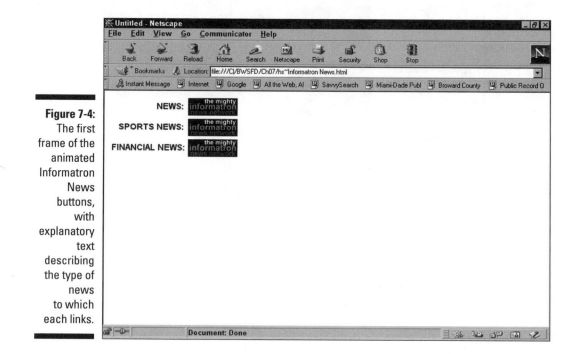

Figure 7-4:
The first frame of the animated Informatron News buttons, with explanatory text describing the type of news to which each links.

To add the Informatron News buttons to your site, follow these steps:

1. **Go to** `www.informatron.com/quicklink.htm`.

2. **Copy the HTML code that you find next to the button for the news site that you want to link to.**

3. **Paste the code into your Web page's source code, inside the** `BODY` **element.**

4. **Repeat Steps 2 and 3 for any other buttons that you want to add to your site.**

5. **Save your Web page and upload it to your site.**

Singing Karaoke-Style on Your Site

Now, here's a unique idea — setting up karaoke rooms on your Web site. And it works right from your own Web site without leading any of your visitors to another site. Like a lot of free services, the karaoke package from a company that's charmingly named eatsleepmusic.com includes advertising banners that you must display to incorporate the add-in on your site. But the folks behind this service are different from most such companies in one nice way: They share the ad revenue with you. And they plug your site through their own banner-exchange program, too. Pretty cool, huh? This add-in is worth getting even without those incentives; with them, however, it's simply a must-have — unless, of course, you can't figure out any way to work music into your site.

Before you start adding the karaoke rooms to your pages, you need to register with eatsleepmusic.com. Follow these steps to sign up:

1. **Go to** `www.eatsleepmusic.com/community/links/player_addsite.cfm`.

2. **Fill out the registration form that you find on that page.**

3. **Read the terms of service and select the check box directly above the Submit button if you agree to the terms.**

4. **Click the Submit button.**

   The subsequent Web page that appears lists different karaoke players, such as rock, country, and so on.

5. **Click the link beneath each player description to see and hear what your visitors will experience if you put that karaoke player on your site.**

6. **Hit the Back button in your Web browser to return to the player page, and copy the JavaScript code under the name of the player that you want on your Web page.**

7. **Paste the code into your page's source code where you want the karaoke player to appear.**

8. **Save your HTML file and upload it to your site.**

9. **Repeat Steps 5 through 8 for any other karaoke players that you want to add to your site.**

You receive an e-mail message containing your password and site ID after you register at the eatsleepmusic.com site. The e-mail also includes the code for adding the pop player to your site, just in case you skipped copying and pasting the code for a room when you signed up. Keep this message — you need to provide your password and ID if you want to change your registration information later.

Figure 7-5 shows the easy-listening karaoke room on a Web page.

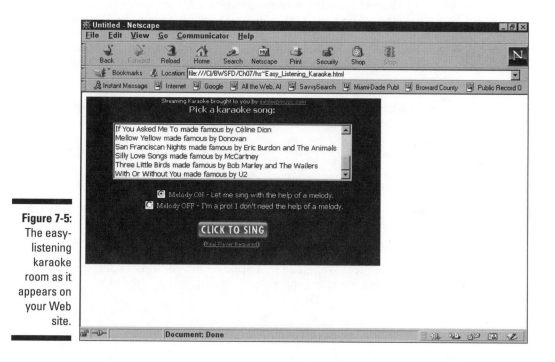

Figure 7-5:
The easy-listening karaoke room as it appears on your Web site.

Putting MIDI Radio on Your Site

MIDI Radio wants to put music on your site — for free. This is a nice add-in that enables your visitors to click a button on one of your pages to launch a pop-up window that plays a continuous stream of music in whatever category a visitor selects. Because it's a pop-up window, your visitors can still wander your Web pages while they listen to music.

To add MIDI Radio to your Web site, follow these steps:

1. **Go to** www.chesworth.com/midi/radio/signup.htm.

2. **Fill out the registration form that you find on that page.**

3. **Click the Submit button.**

   The next page shows the buttons that you can put on your site to activate MIDI Radio, as shown in Figure 7-6. In the text above the buttons, you also find a link that enables you to choose an AutoStart feature. If you choose this option, you don't need a button, because MIDI Radio starts automatically as soon as a visitor enters any Web page you put MIDI Radio on.

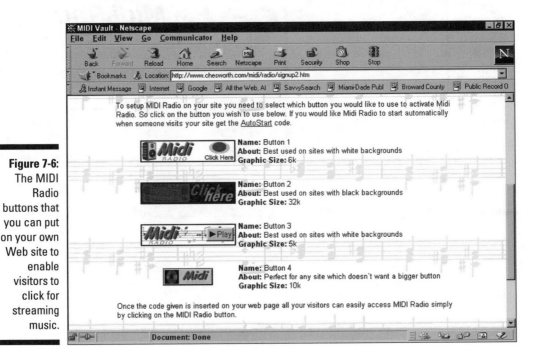

Figure 7-6: The MIDI Radio buttons that you can put on your own Web site to enable visitors to click for streaming music.

4. **Click either the <u>AutoStart</u> link or the MIDI button that you like best.**

   A new page appears that lists the JavaScript code for the button you chose or for the AutoStart code if you chose that option.

5. **Copy the JavaScript code from this page and paste it into your own Web page's source code where you want the button to appear.**

   If you chose AutoStart, it doesn't matter where you paste the code.

6. **Save your file and upload it to your site.**

Figure 7-7 shows the MIDI Radio pop-up window over a site displaying one of the buttons that MIDI Radio supplies.

Figure 7-7:
MIDI Radio in action — click the button in the upper-left corner to open the pop-up window, which enables you to preview and play songs in each category.

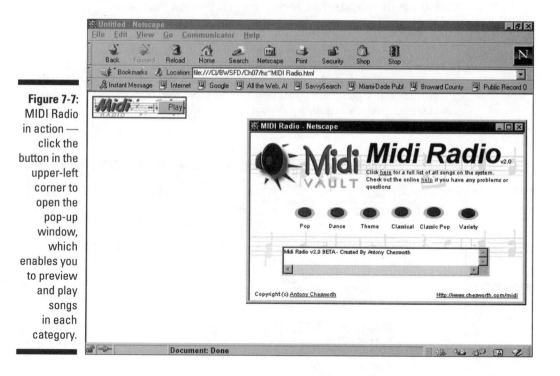

Getting Music

First things first — you gotta get the music before you can add it to your Web site. Okay, grabbing music off the Web or off a newsgroup or through FTP or just about any other way that data moves on the Internet is a pretty easy thing to do, but you face two problems with taking just any old song that you can get your hands on. First off, if you can snag it with no trouble, so can everyone else — and you presumably want your site to stand out from the crowd. Second, you face the question of copyright. The odds are pretty good that you have no idea who owns the copyright to a song that you snag from some music site or whether that song's in the _public domain_ (for everyone to use) instead of under copyright.

You can avoid this copyright mess by following these few simple suggestions:

✔ Get your own custom music by hiring professionals to create it for you — totally new, completely unencumbered. That way, you won't have any legal hassles, and nobody else can use it on another site either.

✔ Buy or download royalty-free music collections.

✔ Use public-domain music (if you don't mind everyone else using the same music on countless other Web sites, too).

✔ Create your own music.

The following sections describe how to get these different types of music for your site.

Finding music houses

Professional music suppliers can accommodate your desires to play unique music on your site, either by selling you custom compositions that they design to serve your own particular needs or by providing you with music that they already have on-hand for you to buy or license. The exact deal you strike depends on the company's policy and how much money you're willing to part with. Some companies license you to use the music only in certain ways (sort of like the way software licenses say things like you can only use a program on a single computer), so be sure to specify that it's going to be used on Web pages when you talk to them. You should not, however, have to pay any royalties — fees for every time you play the music — just the flat fee when you get the music.

Table 7-1 lists some good Web sites where you can find or order some royalty-free music.

Table 7-1	Royalty-Free Music Suppliers
Web Site Name	*Web Address*
Applause	http://cnvi.com/applause/linksmig.htm
Classiclips	www.buy-out-music.com
DoReMix	www.edirol.com/support/demorol.html
Fresh Music Library	www.freshmusic.com/home.html
LicenseMusic	www.licensemusic.com
Music 2 Hues	www.music2hues.com/flagship.html
Partners In Rhyme	www.partnersinrhyme.com
PBTM Library	www.pbtm.com
Prime Cuts!	www.productionmusic.com
Royalty Free Music	www.royaltyfree.com
SoundSurf	http://soundsurf.com

Finding public-domain music

Not all music is currently under copyright. Music's been around a long time, and most of it's in the public domain — meaning that nobody holds the copyright to it. Copyright can, however, prove to be a tricky issue. If you make a mistake, you can end up in federal court, paying hundreds of thousands of dollars in fines. Rest assured, however, that very few copyright infringers ever go to prison, although the law provides for that eventuality. On the other hand, some of them find themselves spending all their time talking to lawyers. And paying lawyers. Paying lawyers lots. So before you add some public-domain music to your Web site, make absolutely sure that it *is* in the public domain.

Table 7-2 lists some good public-domain music sources.

Table 7-2	Public Domain Music Sources
Web Site Name	**Web Address**
Classical Piano Free Downloads	`www.sheetmusic1.com/NEW.GREAT.MUSIC.HTML`
PDMusic.org	`http://pdmusic.org`
PD Info	`http://pdinfo.com/default.htm`
Public Domain Music	`www.web-helper.net/PDMusic`
The Choral Public Domain Library	`www.cpdl.org`
Virtual Sheet Music	`www.virtualsheetmusic.com/Downloads.html`

Some public domain music sites provide copies of sheet music that you can use to create new recordings of your own. Others have music files that you can download and use right away. There's a catch, however — a recording of a public domain song is not in the public domain. The written music is, but the recording isn't. Yes, we're repeating ourselves, but it's critical for you to remember that. The legal reasons are so convoluted that any two lawyers have three opinions about why it's so, but it's a fact. So, unless the site specifically states that it's releasing its music files into the public domain, you probably have to pay for the download. Some of the sites that charge for commercial sites to use their recordings are willing to let noncommercial sites use them for free.

Downloading MAGIX software

If you create a song, you own the copyright to it. No need to bother with negotiations, no need to pay anyone — you're the artist and that's that. Well, that's a great idea, but what if you're not a musician? No problem. (Really!) You can buy software to help you make music — and the people who wrote the programs realize that not everyone is Mozart. All you need to do is to make a few choices, and the computer does the rest. Of course, if you're into composing music or you just plain get into playing around with program settings, you may find some pleasant surprises about just how versatile these programs are.

You can use a wide range of software from MAGIX Entertainment Products to create music for the Web. The company offers everything from programs for children who want to create their own music videos to ones for professional musicians who want to mix their own songs. And you don't need to break the piggy bank either. The most expensive program the company sells goes for $250, but most of them are much less expensive — around $29.99. Better yet, the MAGIX Web site offers free demo versions of its software that you can download to see which program suits you best. Follow these steps to get hold of the MAGIX free demo versions:

1. **Go to** www.magix.net.

2. **Click the appropriate link to select the language you want to view the Web site in.**

3. **On the main page, click the Download button.**

   The download page appears and lists all the available demo files.

4. **Click the links to download all the programs marked Demo.**

   The other programs are patch files. These files are used to upgrade the programs. You can download them, too, if you want to make sure that you have the latest bug fixes.

You can skip the entryway and just go straight to www.magix.net/new/downloads/downloads-main-us.html to look for the U.S. English demo versions, but poking around the main page first is more fun. Besides, exploring all the product information helps you decide which demos you want to download. And the site has the same navigation bar on the left of every page, so the Download button is always there.

If you teach music, you can get free software from MAGIX for your school to use. Fax a request on your school letterhead for the company's free educational CD-ROM to 310-656-0234.

Downloading a free version of iShell

Tribeworks' iShell is pretty much unbelievable. It's so cool that you just can't wrap your mind around the concept that it's free. It's a multimedia application that you can use to create Web content, although it can do even more than that. (It can, for example, make stand-alone interactive CD-ROMs and DVD-ROMs.) It's so powerful and so sophisticated that many full-time professional multimedia developers use it. They pay lots of money for membership in a developers' society that supplies them with product enhancements, advanced technical support, and access to the program's source code. (If you're interested in that level of activity, Full Membership status costs $2,000 for the first year and $1,000 for each subsequent year.) If you're not a real multimedia pro, however, you can just sign up for the Free Membership status instead.

To sign up as a free member and download iShell, follow these steps:

1. **Go to** www.tribeworks.com.

2. **Click the Register Now! button on the Tribeworks home page, as shown in Figure 7-8.**

3. **On the next page, enter your e-mail address, name, phone number, and, optionally, your company in the appropriate text boxes.**

4. **Click the Submit button.**

5. **On the next page, enter your job description, physical address, and information about the kind of projects you work on in the appropriate text boxes.**

Leave the check box above the Submit button selected to receive a subscription to the Tribeworks newsletter.

6. **Click the Register button.**

On the next page, you may enter information about your work if you want, but Tribeworks doesn't require you to do so.

Leave the check box above the Register button selected to subscribe to the iShell users' mailing list.

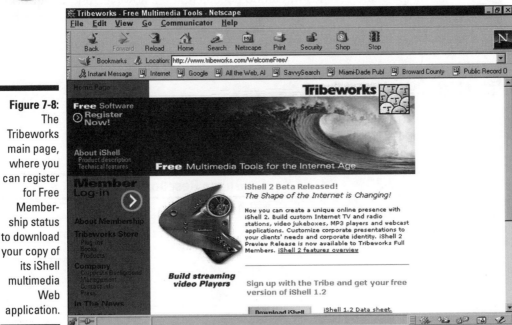

Figure 7-8:
The Tribeworks main page, where you can register for Free Membership status to download your copy of its iShell multimedia Web application.

7. **Click the Submit button at the bottom of the page.**

   You receive an e-mail message giving you a password.

8. **After you get your password, go to the main page at** www.tribeworks.com **and click Member Log-in.**

9. **Enter your e-mail address and password into the log-in form.**

10. **Click the Log-In button.**

   If you have cookies enabled, you won't have to re-enter your log-in information the next time you come back. It'll be automatically stored on your hard drive and read back when you return.

11. **Click the <u>Click here to download iShell</u> link, or the <u>Download Products and Licenses</u> link in the member's area.**

12. **On the download page, click the link for either the Mac or Windows version of iShell.**

13. **After you download the program, click the link to download the license file (which is necessary to run the program).**

With the iShell program's level of sophistication, you also get a certain amount of complexity. If you're not experienced in any kind of application development, you may find the learning curve a bit on the steep side. The iShell application comes with good documentation, however, and Tribeworks provides a line of free tutorials and examples that you can download, as well as an official book that you can purchase online.

Online Sources

Table 7-3 lists some places on the World Wide Web where you can find more resources like the ones that we cover in this chapter.

Table 7-3	Online Resources
Web Site Name	*Web Address*
10 Questions About MP3	www.cnet.com/category/ 0-4004-7-294825.html
Anvil Studio	www.anvilstudio.com
Cakewalk	www.cakewalk.com
Coda Music Technology	www.codamusic.com/coda

Web Site Name	Web Address
Cool Edit	www.syntrillium.com
GoldWave Digital Audio Editor	www.goldwave.com/index.html
PG Music	www.pgmusic.com/products.htm
Simple Server:Shout	www.analogx.com/contents/download/network/ssshout.htm
SoftStep	www.geneticmusic.com/algoart/index.htm

Chapter 8

Web Aerobics: Tuning Up Your Site

In This Chapter

▶ Validating your HTML

▶ Finding broken links

▶ Optimizing graphics files

▶ Fine-tuning your site

▶ Analyzing your traffic

Making Web pages is pretty easy, but the one thing lots of people over-look is that about a hundred zillion things can go wrong with them. Even if your Web pages work perfectly on your favorite Web browser, they may not work on all browsers. Even if all your links are functional, some of the sites they're aimed at will go down or out. Even if you have great graphics on your site, they may slow down your page load so much that nobody is willing to wait for them to download.

So this chapter takes a look at several tools that make your pages work better:

✔ Sites that shrink your graphics files — not the width and height, but the number of bytes they eat up

✔ Places that examine your HTML code and point out errors or possible problem areas

✔ Programs that follow all your links for you and let you know which ones are working right and which ones aren't

✔ Some handy tools that make shoor yore spelling things right

Don't miss this tour — your visitors will appreciate what these tools can do for your site.

W3C HTML Validation Service

This one's the official site, the straight-from-the-horse's-mouth place. W3C is the short form of World Wide Web Consortium, and the folks there are the ones who put out the HTML standard. Now, anyone who's done much with Web pages already knows that there are things that work on Netscape Navigator that don't work on Internet Explorer and vice versa. (And that's not even taking third-party Web browsers into consideration.) If you write your HTML to fit the official W3C standard, you'll miss out on some capabilities, like setting page margins, but you'll also be guaranteed that your Web pages will work in every browser. Okay, there may be some odd browsers out there on the fringes that don't support the W3C standard, but they're not much of a concern.

To check whether your Web page meets the official standard, follow these steps:

1. **If the Web page you want to check is on the World Wide Web, go to** `http://validator.w3.org`**; if it's on your hard drive, go to** `http://validator.w3.org/file-upload.html`**.**

2. **Enter the URL of the Web page in the Address text box (see Figure 8-1).**

   If you're testing a file on your local drive, the form is just a little bit different. A Browse button will appear to the right of the Address text box. Click that button to search your hard drive and select the file you want to test. From here on in, both approaches are identical.

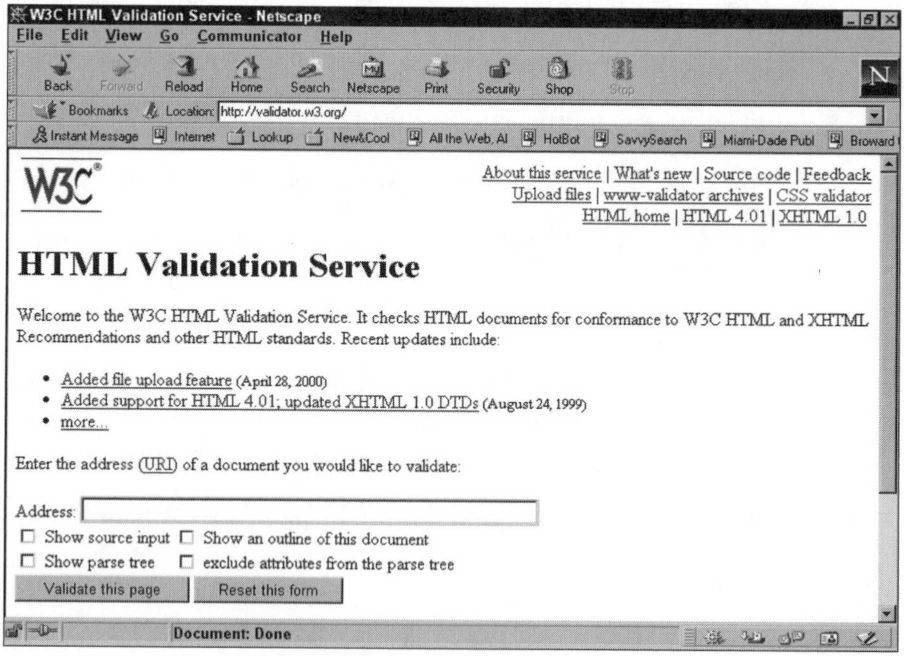

Figure 8-1:
The W3C validation form helps you check your pages for conformance to the HTML standard.

3. **Select the Show Source Input check box if you want the HTML source code from the tested document to show up on the report.**

   This is most useful if you want to sit down with a hard copy of the report, especially if you need to go over it with other members of a Web design team.

4. **Select the Show an Outline of This Document check box if you want to have the hierarchy of heading elements (H1 through H6) shown on the report.**

   If no heading elements are on the page, this option will not show any results.

5. **Select the Show Parse Tree check box to get a diagram of element and attribute relationships on your page; select the Exclude Attributes from the Parse Tree check box to show only elements in the diagram.**

6. **Click the Validate This Page button (or, for the file-upload version, the Validate This Document button).**

   The results of the test appear on a new page.

If your pages don't fit the official standard, it doesn't necessarily mean that your pages are bad. The most important thing is to find out whether your pages work properly in the Web browser(s) you expect your site visitors to be using.

The official standard is much stricter than the coding on a Web page has to be in order for the page to work. Both of the major Web browsers will gleefully overlook all sorts of variations from the standard (or even outright errors) and still display the page as you intended. And in many instances, the people who wrote the standard just plain disagree with the majority of Web-page authors on how things should be done.

Checking Those Links

Few things are more irritating than a bunch of broken links. Visitors won't mind the occasional click that takes them to a Page Not Found error — after all, the Web is a fast-changing place. But when broken links show up over and over again, visitors are going to decide that your site isn't worth all the trouble you put them through.

So what can you do? You can take all the care you want with your own site's internal links, but the links that lead to other people's sites are totally out of your control. Sites go down, and pages and files change location, but the

Webmasters in charge of those sites aren't likely to keep you notified. One possible solution is to use the Mind-it service (see Chapter 18) so that you always know when a site you have a link to is updated. However, if you have lots of links, keeping track of all those updated links could be a full-time job for you.

The real solution is to click every single link in your entire site on a regular basis. Fortunately, you don't have to wear out your mousing finger, though. This is the kind of thing that computers excel at. After all, one of their main purposes is to perform repetitive actions rapidly so that we don't have to.

LinkPolice

LinkPolice (`http://linkpolice.mycomputer.com`) is a paid service that lets you check through zillions of links without any hassle. It can handle anything up to and including a thousand pages on a single site. Annual fees range from $59 for 2 sites to $399 for 40 sites, but you can try it out for free. The basic service lets you log on to their site and run a check anytime you want. With all pricing plans, for an extra $20 a year, LinkPolice checks your sites automatically once a week.

To try out the LinkPolice service on one Web page, follow these steps:

1. **Go to** `http://linkpolice.mycomputer.com/view_demo.html`.

2. **In the text box that appears, enter the URL of the page you want to check.**

3. **Click the Check Page button.**

The results take a minute or so to come up, depending on the complexity of the page being checked. The demo test works like the paid LinkPolice service, but the demo is limited to checking the first 50 links it finds and only processes one Web page. The report is also limited in that it shows only the first five bad links. Figure 8-2 shows a report on the Dummies Press home page.

Although you may think of links as being only the ones you put in with A elements, image files are linked to Web pages, too, not embedded in them. That means LinkPolice also checks IMG elements to make sure that the graphics files they specify are where they're supposed to be.

Linkbot Pro

Linkbot Pro is a Windows program from Watchfire (formerly Tetranet Software) that checks your links for you and then generates a report.

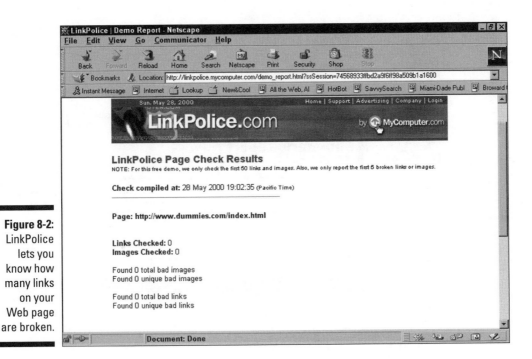

Figure 8-2:
LinkPolice
lets you
know how
many links
on your
Web page
are broken.

Although the report is great, Linkbot goes beyond just telling you about broken links. Linkbot checks your HTML syntax and some other important factors (such as file download times) along with digging up broken links. It also finds orphan pages for you — ones that are on your server but are not linked to any other page. With Linkbot Pro, you can repair broken links by using a search-and-replace feature to take care of all instances of bad links throughout your site. Because Linkbot Pro remembers the results of its searches and compares the current search with previous ones, you can track how much improvement or decline there is in several different factors that influence the quality of the site. And you can customize just about every aspect of the program.

To use Linkbot Pro, launch the program and follow these steps:

1. **In the URL box, enter the URL of the site you want to check; then press Enter.**

   After the check is complete, you're asked whether you want to publish the report (that is, to create a Web page from it).

2. **Click the Yes button.**

3. **Navigate to the directory in which you want to store the file, give the file a name, and click the Save button.**

   Linkbot Pro generates a detailed report like the one in Figure 8-3 and shows the report in your Web browser.

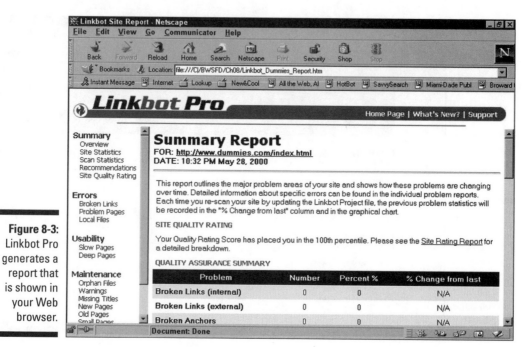

Figure 8-3:
Linkbot Pro
generates a
report that
is shown in
your Web
browser.

You can find a trial version of Linkbot Pro at `www.watchfire.com/products/linkbot.htm` or on the CD-ROM that accompanies this book.

Putting Your Graphics on a Diet

Fat files. They're embarrassing. They slow down a page like nothing else. They turn a fabulous site into a sluggish turkey. A really good graphics program can trim your overweight files down, but a really good graphics program will also set you back a pretty penny — and you have to work with it for a while in order to get the most out of it. Instead of putting all that money and effort into solving this problem, try some of the following Web sites that do the job for you — for free.

GIFWorks

GIFWorks is absolutely one of the best tools you'll find on the Web. Period. You get the idea we like it? A lot? There's a good reason. This is one truly full-featured program, and it's something you may not be familiar with yet, but we think it's the wave of the future on the Web. This program isn't one you download and use on your computer. It stays put, and you use it right there on the GIFWorks site.

With GIFWorks, you can do everything to GIF files, from reducing colors to adding special effects. So what does it cost? Nothing, nada, zip. And to top it all off, the same folks have a couple of other sites that do everything from making postcards (Media Builder, at www.mediabuilder.com) to letting you get your hands on more than 10,000 high-quality GIF images (The Animation Factory, at www.animfactory.com). We're not exaggerating when we say *quality*, either. This is some of the best stuff we've seen.

The Animation Factory's images are also free — for noncommercial use. Aha! A catch at last? Nah. If you want to use the images on a commercial site, all you have to do is cough up $29.95 for a year's download privileges. There's no further fee for using the images. And that $29.95 fee also gives you access to about another 100,000 images at the Animation Factory's premium site located at www.animfactory.net. The Animation Factory is well worth the price, even if you don't run a commercial Web site, and GIFWorks shows the same attention to quality but costs nothing at all.

Here's how to use GIFWorks to slim down your image files:

1. **Go to** www.gifworks.com.

2. **On the menu shown in Figure 8-4, choose File⇨File Open.**

   Come back to this page later and check out the File⇨New 3D Text option. It's a great way to create animated text banners.

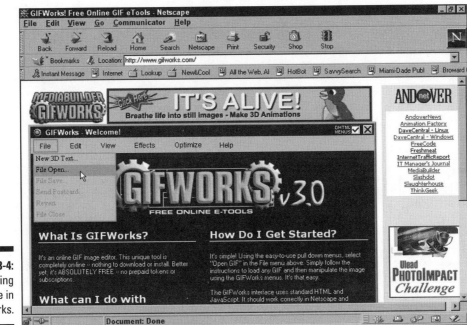

Figure 8-4: Opening a file in GIFWorks.

3. **On the next screen, open a file from the Web by entering its URL and clicking the Fetch Image button. Or, upload a file from your local drive by clicking the Browse button, selecting the file, and then clicking the Upload Image button.**

GIFWorks operates on a *copy* of the image you specify. It doesn't change the original file in any way.

After the image is at GIFWorks, you'll be looking at it in the program (see Figure 8-5). We're using a torch from the collection at `www.animfactory.com` for this example. The torch is animated, by the way, and that points out one of the great strengths of GIFWorks. Many programs can modify and optimize individual GIF images, but an animated GIF is composed of many different images — eight of them, in this case — and GIFWorks can simultaneously modify all of them, thus altering the animated image.

Before you begin to work with the image, click the Help menu and take a look at the FAQ.

From here, what you do depends on your exact situation.

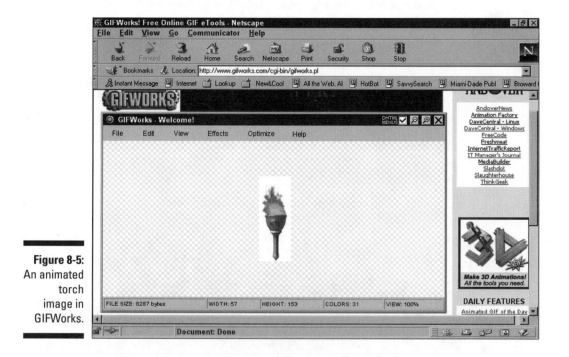

Figure 8-5:
An animated torch image in GIFWorks.

✔ **To reduce the file size quickly:** Choose Optimize⇨Reduce Colors from the menu. You get a whole page full of different versions of the original image, each with fewer colors than the preceding ones. You also get information about the file size, number of remaining colors, and percentage reduction. Scroll down the page, look at each of the images, and download the one that represents the best compromise between image quality and file size.

✔ **To make a color transparent:** Choose Edit⇨Add Transparency from the menu. In the pop-up window that appears, click the color you want to clear. To make a transparent GIF totally opaque, do the same thing, but start off with Edit⇨Remove Transparency.

✔ **To view information on file size, width, height, and so forth:** Choose View⇨Image Info.

Okay, that's all the practical stuff that most Webmasters need. Now for the fun part. After you're done being responsible, head for the Effects menu (refer to Figure 8-5) and start playing. You can do so many things to your images that you may have a hard time choosing among them. Unless you're dead set on just trying anything that comes to hand, choose Help⇨Effects Gallery to get a look at some examples. Speaking of which, Figure 8-6 shows what some of the effects did to the torch image shown in Figure 8-5. Enjoy.

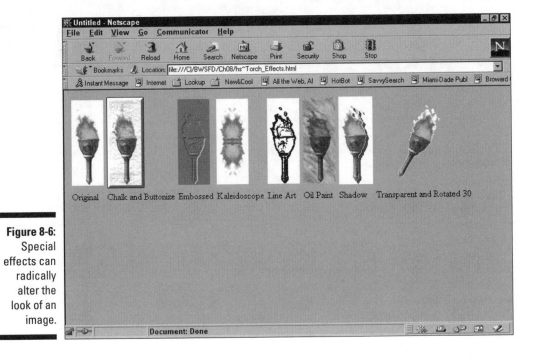

Figure 8-6: Special effects can radically alter the look of an image.

Spinwave

Spinwave does just one thing, but it does it very well. It optimizes image files to save space and decrease download time. Spinwave not only handles GIFs, it handles JPEGs as well, each file type having its own "image cruncher." Both an online version and a regular program that you can run on your own computer are available. The online version is free.

Here's how Spinwave works:

1. **Go to** www.spinwave.com/crunchers.html.

    JPEG Cruncher is on top. Beneath it is GIF Cruncher (see Figure 8-7) .

2. **Click the Browse button in the cruncher that matches the file type that you want to work with.**

3. **Select the file on your system.**

4. **If you're using JPEG Cruncher, choose a JPEG image quality setting from the drop-down list to the right of the Crunch button.**

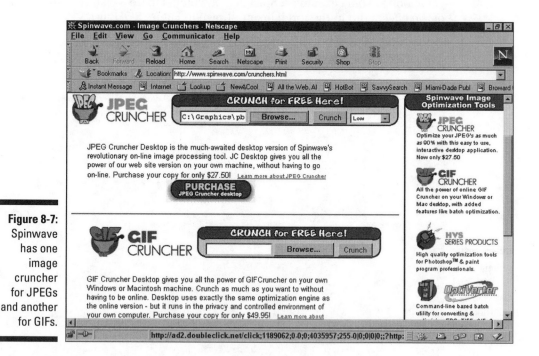

Figure 8-7:
Spinwave has one image cruncher for JPEGs and another for GIFs.

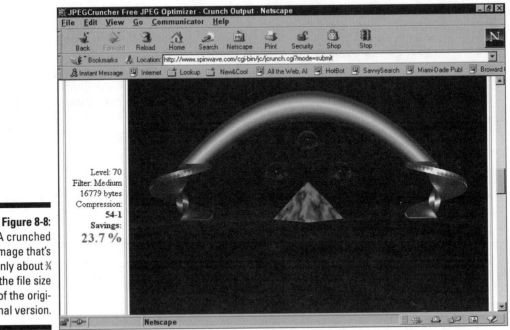

Figure 8-8:
A crunched image that's only about ¾ the file size of the original version.

5. **Click the Crunch button.**

   In a few moments, a new page appears, showing a series of images. The top one is the original one, for comparison purposes. Each lower one is of slightly lesser quality but has a smaller file size. (Notice the compression ratio shown beside the image in Figure 8-8.)

6. **Scroll down until you find an image that still looks good but takes up less space than the original and download it.**

Testing Your Site with NetMechanic

Although the tightly focused sites are very popular and extremely useful, there are also some really nice places on the World Wide Web that are like smorgasbords of Web tools. Sites like these are mostly fond of automotive metaphors — NetMechanic and the Web Site Garage, for instance. The Web Site Garage also includes GIF Lube. You get the idea. There's just not much of anything along the lines of The Site Garden or The Page Salon. Well, whatever they're called, go to them, bookmark them, and return to them often. You'll be glad to have them handy.

NetMechanic does a whole bunch of things for you, all in one simple move. Or you can go to a bit of effort and customize the process, like using a custom dictionary for the spell checker, for example. NetMechanic has both a free version and a paid one. The freebie is limited to a maximum of 20 pages, while the paid version handles up to 400 pages on one site. If you have 100 or fewer Web pages, it costs $35; for a site with 101 pages to 400 pages, the price makes a sudden jump to $200.

Five different tests are run on the page or site you choose:

- ✔ Link Check
- ✔ HTML Check & Repair
- ✔ Browser Compatibility
- ✔ Load Time Check
- ✔ Spell Check

To run the site test with all the default settings, follow these steps:

1. **Go to** `www.netmechanic.com`.

2. **Enter the URL of the page or site you want to check in the Enter Your URL text box (see Figure 8-9).**

3. **If you want to receive a report via e-mail, enter your address in the Enter Your Email Address text box; if you want to view the report on screen, don't enter anything here.**

4. **If you're checking a single page, select the One Page radio button; if you're checking a site, select the 20 Pages radio button.**

5. **Click the Go button.**

NetMechanic runs its suite of tests on your site and generates a report, either on-screen or sent to your e-mail account, depending on which option you choose in Step 3. The on-screen version shows a progress bar while you're waiting. The more complex your site is, the longer the process takes to complete. If you want to abort the process, the progress screen has a Cancel button you can click.

To run a customized test, try this instead:

1. **Go to** `www.netmechanic.com/toolbox/power_user.htm`.

2. **Enter the URL of the page or site you want to check in the Enter Your URL text box (see Figure 8-9).**

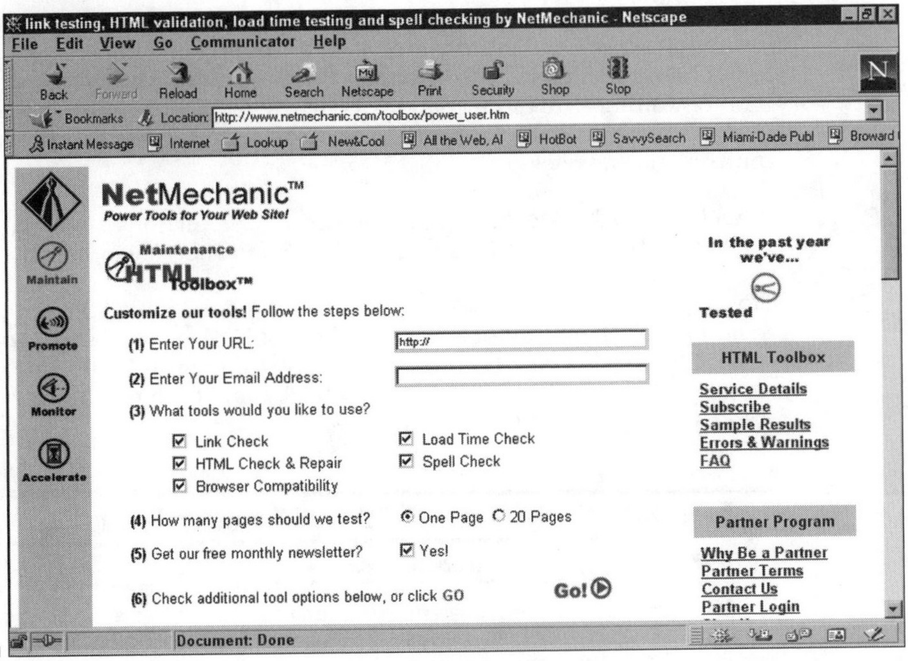

Figure 8-9:
You can customize NetMechanic so that it runs only the tests you want.

3. **If you want to receive a report via e-mail, enter your address in the Enter Your Email Address text box; if you want to view the report on-screen, don't enter anything here.**

4. **Deselect the check boxes for any tests you don't want to run.**

5. **If you're checking a single page, select the One Page radio button; if you're checking a site, select the 20 Pages radio button.**

6. **Choose whether to subscribe to the newsletter.**

7. **If you don't want to set any further options, click the Go button; otherwise, scroll down the page.**

8. **Under HTML Check & Repair, select the check box if you want to test for handicapped accessibility.**

   Under Browser Compatibility, NetMechanic lists the percentages of people who use different versions of the two major Web browsers when visiting its site.

9. **If you have different figures available from the site you're testing, enter those numbers for each of the listed Web browsers.**

10. **Under Spell Check, enter the URL of a custom dictionary (if you have one relating to the topic of the site you're testing) in the text box; if you don't want words in uppercase to be spell-checked, leave the Ignore words in UPPER CASE check box selected.**

11. **Click the Go button.**

NetMechanic runs the selected tests on your site and generates a report, either on-screen or sent to your e-mail account, depending on which option you choose in Step 3. The on-screen version shows a progress bar while you're waiting. The more complex your site is, the longer the process takes to complete. If you want to abort the process, the progress screen has a Cancel button you can click.

Check out the NetMechanic image file optimizer, GIFBot, at `www.netmechanic.com/accelerate.htm`. It handles both GIF and JPEG file formats.

If you just go to `www.netmechanic.com`, you don't get all the options you could have. There's actually a second set of NetMechanic sites, co-branded with Ziff-Davis' ZDNet, that work a little bit differently. Which one you use is up to you, but you definitely should check them both out. Table 8-1 lists the URLs of the different tests.

Table 8-1	ZD/NetMechanic Sites
Test	*Web Address*
Browser Check	`www.netmechanic.com/cobrands/zdnet/browsercheck`
GIFBot	`www.netmechanic.com/cobrands/zdnet/gifbot`
HTML Check	`www.netmechanic.com/cobrands/zdnet/htmlcheck`
Link Check	`www.netmechanic.com/cobrands/zdnet/linkcheck`
Load Check	`www.netmechanic.com/cobrands/zdnet/loadcheck`
Spell Check	`www.netmechanic.com/cobrands/zdnet/spellcheck`

Statbot

Boy, it's hard to pick a favorite out of all these Web-site tools, but we're kinda partial to a program called Statbot from the Moorglade Design Group at `www.moorglade.com` (especially because the Moorglade folks were kind enough to create a special version of their program for you folks reading this book). It's true freeware that will never time out, and you can get support for it on the Moorglade Web site.

Every time that people visit your Web pages, the server at your site gathers information about them (such as which Web browser they use, what site they came from, and which of your pages they visited) and records this in a log file. The log file holds a massive amount of data, especially on a really busy site, but it's full of information that you can use to better serve your visitors — if only you could somehow make sense out of it all.

If you run your own Web server, you already know all about log files. If not, check with your Web space provider to find out whether a separate log of your site's activity exists or can be set up for you, as well as the name and location of the file. If your site is housed on either a dedicated server or a virtual server, you should definitely have a log file.

That's where Statbot comes into play. It's a log analyzer that crunches all those numbers and facts for you and translates them into easy-to-understand charts and graphs.

Statbot is a Windows program, and it's easiest to use if you're on a Windows Network that includes the Web site you're analyzing. However, you can still use Statbot on your local Windows computer to analyze log files kept on remote Unix or Linux boxes. You just need to download the log file from your server first. If that's the case, you can either use your favorite FTP program or use the included file upload/download capability in Statbot.

If you have direct access to your log files, you can use Statbot to download a log file to your local Windows machine by following these steps:

1. **Click the Transfer Remote Files button in the toolbar or choose Tools⇨Remote File Transfer from the menu.**

2. **In the resultant dialog box, as shown in Figure 8-10, enter the remote host, your username on that host, your password, the path to the log file, and the path to the local file you want the log to be received as.**

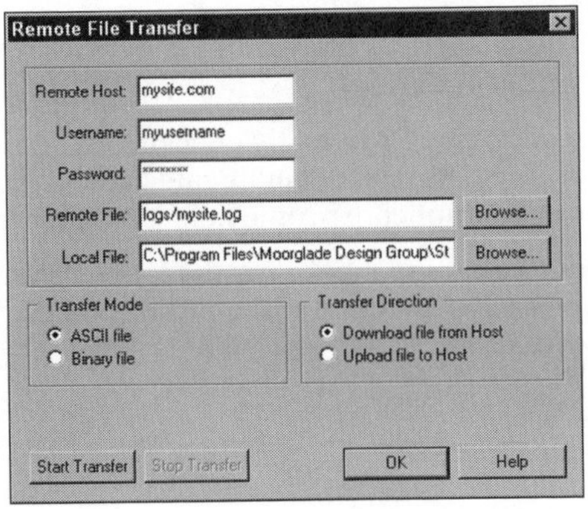

Figure 8-10:
The Remote
File Transfer
dialog box
lets you
download
a remote
log file.

3. **Make sure that the ASCII File and Download File from Host radio buttons are selected.**

4. **Click the Start Transfer button.**

If your Web space provider only lets you look at your log's raw data via a Web page, follow these steps:

1. **Type the URL provided by your Web hosting company into your browser and press Enter.**

   Your browser downloads the log file. As it does, you see the first lines of the log file displayed as text in the browser. Wait until the browser finishes loading the log file page.

2. **On the main browser toolbar, choose Edit⇨Select All to select and highlight all log entries (even those you can't see).**

3. **On the main browser toolbar, choose File⇨Save As to save all log entries into a single log file.**

   At this time, you choose the directory in which you want the log file saved, as well as the name of the log file itself. Click OK and the log file is saved.

When the log file has been downloaded, you're ready to proceed with processing the log file.

The steps are the same from this point, no matter whether the file was downloaded from a remote host or created on your local system or network. To process a log file, follow these steps:

1. **Click the New Profile button in the toolbar or choose File⇨New from the menu.**

   This action brings up the New Profile Wizard.

2. **Click the Begin button.**

3. **In the next screen of the wizard, as shown in Figure 8-11, enter a name for the profile you're creating.**

   Statbot creates the default name ProfileX by checking to see if one already exists. If a Profile1 exists, the default name Profile2 appears. Statbot won't let you create duplicate profile names.

4. **If the defaults don't suit you, type a path for the work directory and output directory either by typing the pathnames or clicking the Browse buttons to locate them.**

5. **Click the Next button.**

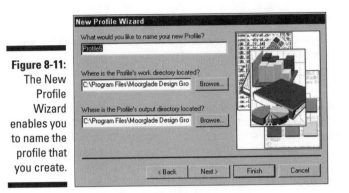

Figure 8-11:
The New
Profile
Wizard
enables you
to name the
profile that
you create.

6. **In the screen shown in Figure 8-12, select the time range for your report.**

The options cover any time span from today to the previous year.

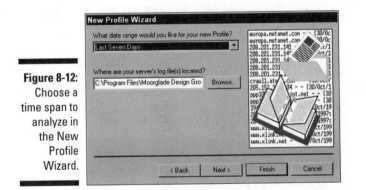

Figure 8-12:
Choose a
time span to
analyze in
the New
Profile
Wizard.

7. **Enter the location of the server log to be processed or click the Browse button to navigate your local system to find it.**

If you enter a directory name here instead of a single log file, all files found in the directory will be processed. This is very handy if your readers have numerous log files that span many weeks or months. Some Web servers (Microsoft IIS, for example) even generate a new log file for each day. At the end of a year, you could have 365 log files on your system.

It's much nicer entering a single log directory here than 365+ file names! Statbot Micro is even smart enough to ignore non-log files found in a log directory.

8. **Click the Next button.**

9. **In the following screen, click the check boxes next to the actions you want to see performed.**

10. **Click the Finish button.**

The program generates a series of graphs, as shown in Figure 8-13. Six graphs are actually displayed, but you have to scroll down to see the final two. If you'd rather have all six on-screen at once, you can choose View⇨ Graph Layout⇨3 columns. This puts the bottom two graphs to the right of the others and eliminates the white space that you now see. The latest version defaults to a 2-by-2 display of graphs, and the main window is actually reduced in width.

In addition, several reports are created as HTML files, and your default Web browser launches to display them, as shown in Figure 8-14.

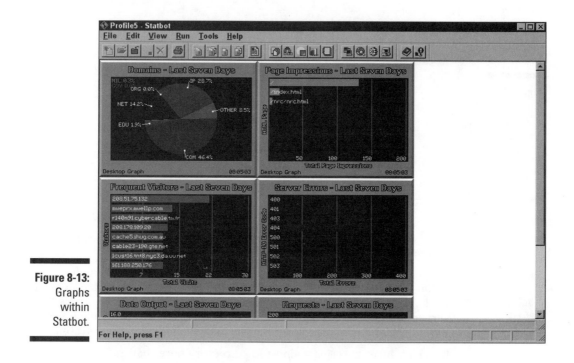

Figure 8-13:
Graphs
within
Statbot.

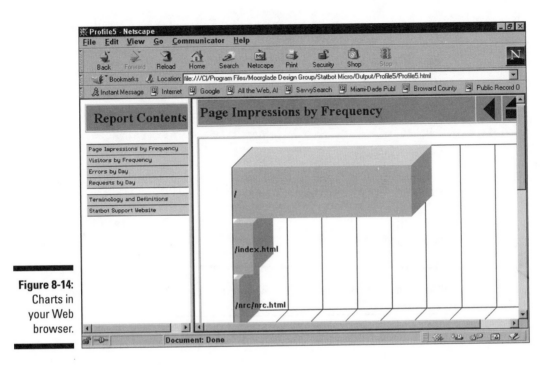

Figure 8-14:
Charts in
your Web
browser.

Online Sources

Table 8-2 lists some places on the World Wide Web where you can find more resources like the ones we cover in this chapter.

Table 8-2	Online Resources
Web Site Name	*Web Address*
Bobby	www.cast.org/bobby
Document Validation Service	www.stg.brown.edu/cgi-bin/ validate/validate.pl
Doctor HTML	www2.imagiware.com/RxHTML
Dr. Watson	watson.addy.com
GIF Wizard	www.gifwizard.com

(continued)

Table 8-2 *(continued)*

Web Site Name	Web Address
HTMLWorks	www.htmlworks.com
LinkAlarm	www.linkalarm.com
Site Check	www.siteowner.com/sitecheck.cfm
Virtual Stampede	http://virtual-stampede.com/tools.htm
W3C CSS Validation Service	http://jigsaw.w3.org/css-validator
WDG HTML Validator	www.htmlhelp.com/tools/validator
Web Site Garage	http://websitegarage.netscape.com
WWWeblint	www.unipress.com/cgi-bin/WWWeblint
XML Syntax Checker	www.xml.com/xml/pub/tools/ruwf/check.html

Part III
Drop In and Stay a While, Folks

The 5th Wave   By Rich Tennant

IT'S THEIR CHAT ROOM, ALL RIGHT, AND I THINK THEY'VE FIGURED OUT WHO "STRANDED" IS, SO BE CAREFUL WHAT YOU SAY.

In this part . . .

This part is about getting your visitors involved in your site so that they keep on coming back for more. Chapter 9 is all about getting input from the folks who come to your site through surveys and forms. Chapter 10 continues this topic but with an important difference — the add-ins here put the visitor in control. Chapter 11 goes for the fun stuff — quotation applets and even video games. And Chapter 12 shows you where to go to get fresh content for your site.

Chapter 9

Listening to Your Visitors

- -

In This Chapter

▶ Setting up surveys

▶ Using form makers

▶ Ensuring privacy and security

- -

*W*hen the Web first started, it was strictly a one-way street. You, as the Web designer, put up information for others to view — and that was it. Nowadays, feedback from site visitors is critical, and they expect you to provide them with the capability to give it. Most Web sites use some kind of form to get information from visitors. This chapter shows you a few easy ways to use forms on your site.

Taking Polls

Hardly a day passes without someone announcing the results of some kind of poll: "Thirty-two percent of city residents prefer smog." "The IDG nerd's approval rating climbed by four percent in the past week." "Quantum physics confuses nine people out of five." For whatever reason, people are fascinated by other people's feelings about different things. And people love to toss in their two bits worth whenever they see a survey form. Here are a few common uses for Web site surveys:

- **Feedback on product quality:** "How do you rate our new release?"

- **Opinions on social issues:** "Should we pay more attention to threatened species?"

- **Preferences between political candidates:** "Do you plan to vote Democrat, Independent, or Republican?"

- **Requests for new site features:** "Check the services you want us to add."

Alxpoll

With Alxpoll (www.alxpoll.com), you can easily create a survey to place either on your site or on the Alxpoll server. Alxpoll uses a simple wizard that walks you through the survey-form creation process. Unlike most of the other survey services on the Web, Alxpoll doesn't slap an advertising banner onto your site — and they don't charge you anything, either.

The way Alxpoll does this for free is by asking you to join one or more opt-in mailing lists (see Chapter 18) during the survey creation process. You don't have to join, but many people do and the mailing list messages carry advertising. This is a unique, if roundabout, way for Alxpoll to earn its bread. It keeps everybody happy because no one sees an ad unless they choose to subscribe.

As you create your poll, don't worry too much about the choices that you make. If you decide that you don't like anything after you finish, you can change it then. To create a poll by using Alxpoll's service, follow these steps:

1. **Go to** www.alxpoll.com **and then scroll down until you see the Quick Sign-Up form, as shown in Figure 9-1.**

   You can also click the <u>Create A Poll</u> link at the bottom of the page, after the Quick Sign-Up form, but doing so takes you to a nearly identical form.

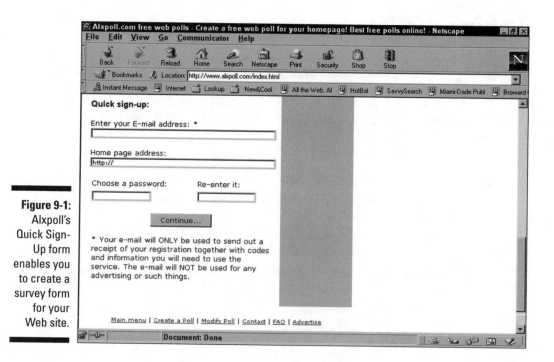

Figure 9-1:
Alxpoll's
Quick Sign-
Up form
enables you
to create a
survey form
for your
Web site.

2. **Fill in the information that the form requests.**

You don't have to enter your e-mail address if you don't want to. You can still create the survey without this information. Alxpoll, however, automatically sends a backup copy of the HTML code for the survey form to the e-mail address that you enter. If you don't enter an e-mail address, you don't receive a backup copy. Similarly, providing the URL for your home page isn't necessary for the survey form to work, but including it is a wise move because Alxpoll puts a link to this page at the bottom of the survey. If you don't provide your Web site's address, no one can link to your page from the survey form.

You may not want to take the term *home page* too literally here. Enter the URL of whatever page on your site you want people to visit after completing the survey.

3. **Enter a password in the Choose a Password text box and enter it again in the Re-enter It text box.**

You don't pick a username — Alxpoll automatically assigns a number to each new poll, and that number's your user ID.

4. **Click the Continue button.**

You jump to the Create a Polling page.

5. **On the Create a Polling page, type a title for the survey in the first text box, as shown in Figure 9-2.**

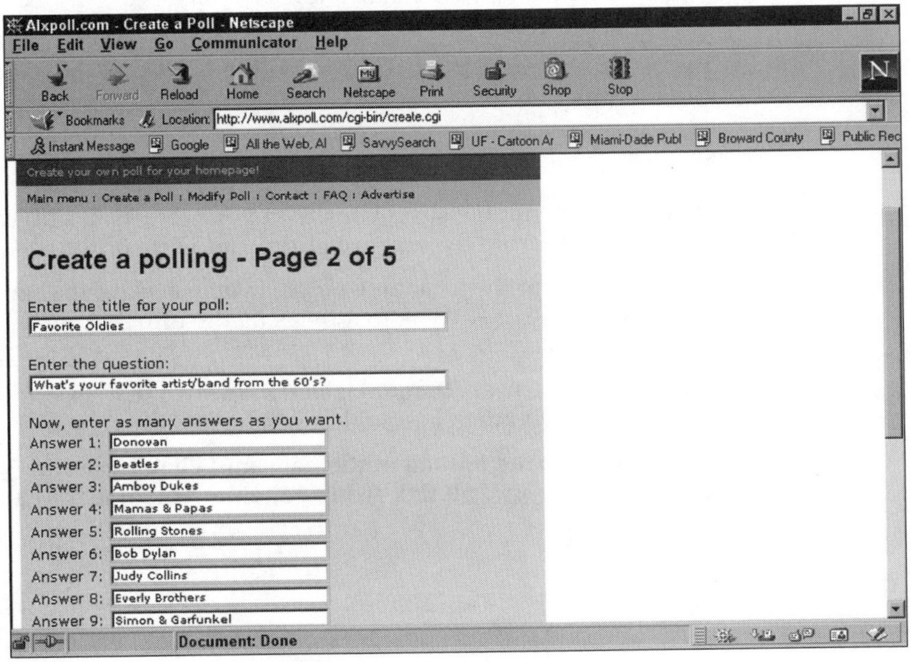

Figure 9-2:
The Create a Polling page enables you to name the poll that you create and provide questions and possible answers.

6. Type the survey question in the Enter the Question text box.

7. Type each possible response to the question in the Answer text boxes.

   You can enter up to 20 possible answers for each survey.

8. Click the Continue button to go to the next page of the survey form.

9. Pick one of the four standard color schemes from the Choose Color Scheme drop-down list, as shown in Figure 9-3.

10. Click the Continue button to access the next page of the form.

11. Click one of the radio buttons to select the type of form controls you want in your poll, as shown in Figure 9-4.

12. Click the Continue button.

    At this point, you may suddenly find yourself wondering what happened to the poll you're creating. You just left a form that read Page 4 of 5, and now you're looking at one that reads Sign Up — Page 2. Not only does the numbering system jar, but the colors and content are different, too. Everything's okay, however. This page is where Alxpoll asks you if you want to join the opt-in mailing lists we mentioned in the beginning of this section.

    If nothing on the page interests you, just don't select any of the lists. If you do find something that you like — and this page does offer a nice selection — you can safely join and unsubscribe later. PostMasterDirect.com, the company that runs the lists for Alxpoll, doesn't give or sell your e-mail address to anyone.

13. Whether you do or don't subscribe to any of the mailing lists on this page, you still need to scroll down to the bottom of the page and click the Continue button.

    Now you're at the final page for setting up your poll, as shown in Figure 9-5.

14. If you want to put the survey form on your own Web site, you need to copy the code from the text area here and paste it into a Web page.

    If you don't want the form on your site, you can leave the survey form on Alxpoll's server and link to it by using the URL that appears after the HTML code to create a link from your site to Alxpoll's site.

15. Write down the user ID number and password that appear on this page or just print the page so that you have a copy.

16. Scroll down to the bottom of the page and click either the <u>View Poll</u> link or the <u>Modify Poll</u> link (which enables you to make changes to your poll).

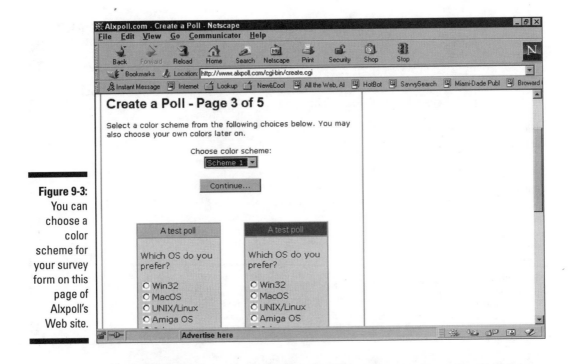

Figure 9-3:
You can
choose a
color
scheme for
your survey
form on this
page of
Alxpoll's
Web site.

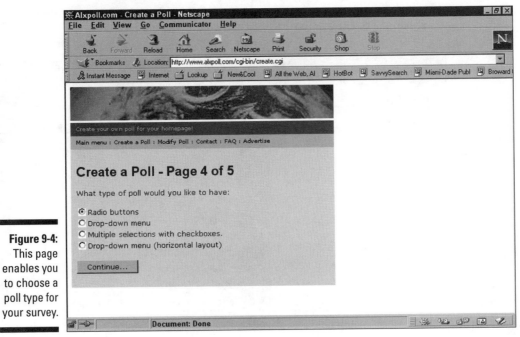

Figure 9-4:
This page
enables you
to choose a
poll type for
your survey.

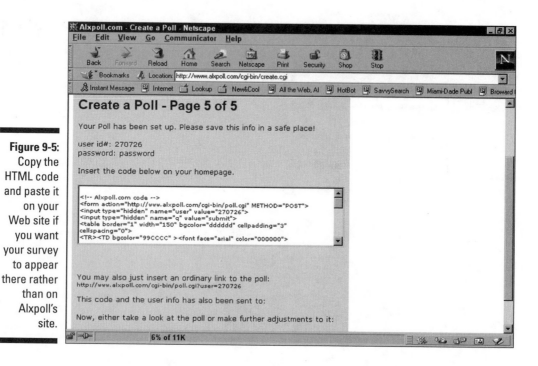

Figure 9-5:
Copy the
HTML code
and paste it
on your
Web site if
you want
your survey
to appear
there rather
than on
Alxpoll's
site.

If you chose to view your poll by clicking the Under Poll link, you see something similar to the sample survey shown in Figure 9-6.

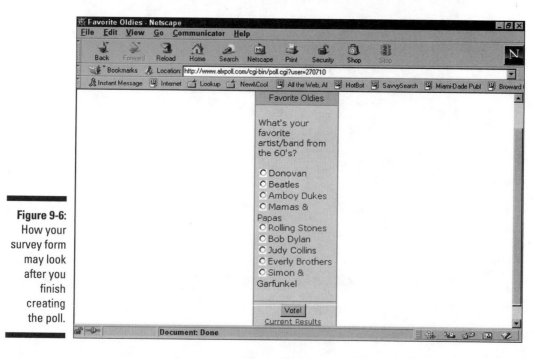

Figure 9-6:
How your
survey form
may look
after you
finish
creating
the poll.

You probably notice that the form can use a bit of widening to accommodate the size of some of the responses. This change is simple. If you decide to put the HTML code on your own site, you can just change the value of the form's `width` attribute. If your site links to the survey form on Alxpoll's site, however, you need to use the site's poll-modification options to change the poll's width.

If you choose to modify the poll at this time by clicking the <u>Modify Poll</u> link, you have many options. If you don't want to modify it now, you can still access the modification page later. Log back on to Alxpoll's Web site (at `www.alxpoll.com`), scroll down to the bottom of the page, and click the <u>Modify Poll</u> link that you find there. Either way you get there, you need to follow these steps to access your poll so you can modify it:

1. **Enter in the appropriate text boxes the user ID number and password that you got in Step 15 of the preceding set of steps describing the poll-creation procedure.**

   You did follow our earlier advice about this information, right?

2. **Click the Log On button.**

Now that you're at the modification page, you see that it has different areas where you can change your poll in the following categories:

✔ **Personal information:** You can modify your password, name, e-mail address, home-page title, and home-page URL. You also find a drop-down list for Site Category, but the only option it offers is Other. After you finish making changes, click the Update button for them to take effect.

✔ **Poll questions and answers:** You can modify the poll title, question, and answers. Oddly, you can alter only the first 10 answers, even though you can have up to 20 answers in the survey. Click the Update button after you finish making your changes.

✔ **Vote blocking:** Alxpoll's surveys include a feature that prevents (or at least limits) people from stuffing the ballot box. The default method is to keep track of voters' IP addresses. If someone tries to vote and that person's IP address is already on file for that survey, Alxpoll politely informs him that he can't vote twice and shows the current results of the survey instead. You can choose to use cookies for vote blocking instead or use both methods (or neither one). Just select On or Off from the drop-down list next to each option. The vote-blocking timeout sets how long Alxpoll keeps the address on record. Click the Update button after you finish making your modifications.

✔ **Poll appearance:** You can change your color settings for the page background, poll background, header background, header text, body text, link, and Results bar. You can select colors by name from the drop-down list for each item. If none of these colors suit your Web site's color scheme, you can type either a hexadecimal code or a color name in the Other Colour text boxes.

The Results bar may also be replaced with a small custom image. (You can, for example, use a human figure or the outline of a car.) You can also enter new sizes for the poll border and width and choose a new poll type (radio buttons, check boxes, and so on). Click the Update button after you finish.

✔ **Advanced JavaScript appearance menu:** This menu offers most of the same options as the regular appearance settings but uses a color chart that you can click that shows color choices as you make them. Click the Save Settings button after you complete your choices.

✔ **Get HTML code:** Click this button and you go to a Web page where you can copy the HTML code for the survey. You can also fill in an e-mail address and click the Mail Me the HTML Code button to have Alxpoll send you a message containing a copy of the code.

✔ **Reset counters/remove poll:** Selecting the Reset Vote Counts radio button sets all the results back to zero. Select the Permanently Remove Poll radio button if you don't want Alxpoll to keep the poll. This option is useful if you test the system and don't want the test to clutter up the server. For either option to take effect, you must click the Reset/Remove Poll button.

The Main Menu link at the bottom of the page doesn't return you to the home page, but keeps you on the Modify page. Use the link at the top of the page instead to return to the home page.

TallySite.com

TallySite.com (www.tallysite.com) offers a service similar to that of Alxpoll (see the preceding section), except that it's advertiser-supported, so your polls feature someone else's advertising banner. Aside from the fact that Alxpoll doesn't use advertising, there's another important difference between the two sites. Alxpoll assigns each poll its own ID number, and you need to keep track of all the passwords for all your surveys. At TallySite.com, you set up only one username and password, and you manage all your polls from one central Web page.

To create a survey form by using TallySite.com, follow these steps:

1. **Go to** www.tallysite.com **and click the New User button.**

   Next, you see the User Profile page.

2. **Type a username, password, and an e-mail address in the appropriate text boxes on the User Profile form, as shown in Figure 9-7.**

   TallySite.com keeps your e-mail address confidential. The form only requires these three items of information, but you can optionally enter your zip code, gender, and birth year.

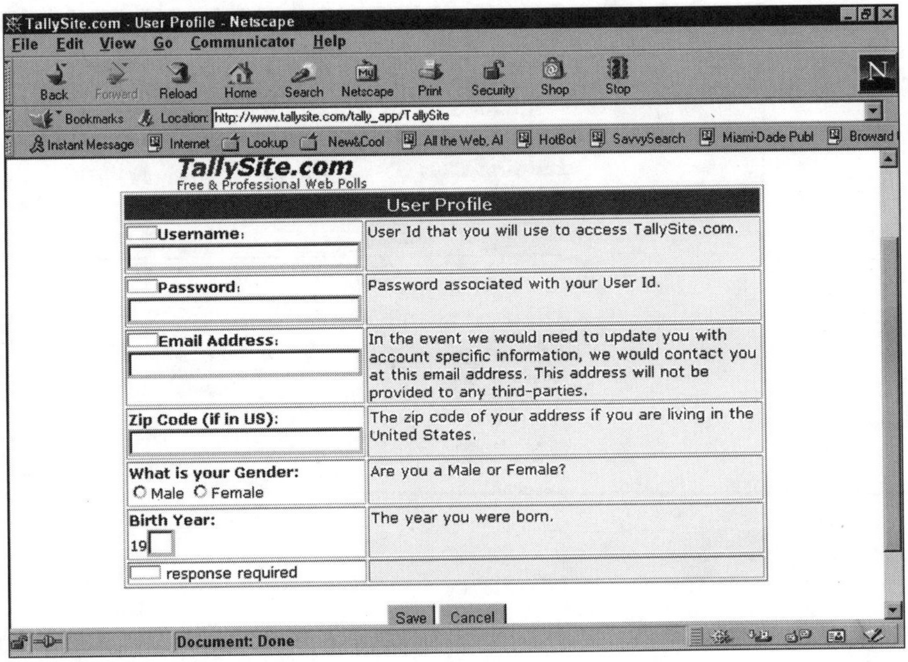

Figure 9-7:
TallySite.
com's User
Profile page,
your starting
point for
creating
your survey.

3. **Click the Save button.**

4. **Click the Create Your First Poll button.**

5. **In the Poll Question form that appears next, enter a name for the survey in the Poll Name text box and then the question in the Question text area, as shown in Figure 9-8.**

6. **Click the appropriate radio button to choose either a single-answer poll (one using radio buttons as alternatives) or a multiple-answer poll (using check boxes to enable more than one response).**

7. **Enter each possible answer on a separate line in the Possible Answers text area.**

8. **Scroll down the page and click on a radio button to select either the Single Column List or a Drop-Down List.**

   The latter is available only for single-answer polls (meaning you chose radio buttons in Step 6). Oddly, what this really means is that the survey form won't use radio buttons but — like this option says — a drop-down list.

9. **Select a Poll Category from the drop-down list at the bottom of the form.**

   Options range fromUnknown to Travel & Places.

10. **Click the Save button.**

11. **Click the Show My Polls button.**

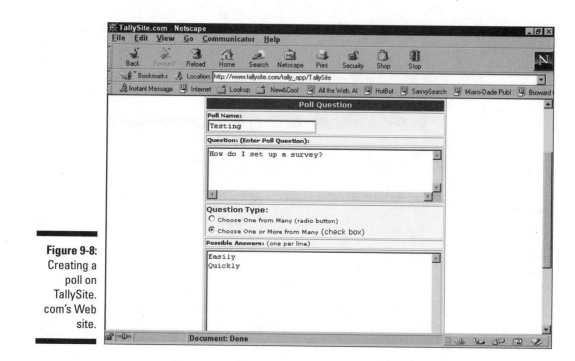

The My Polls page that appears next is shown in Figure 9-9. It is the central location from which you manage all your surveys.

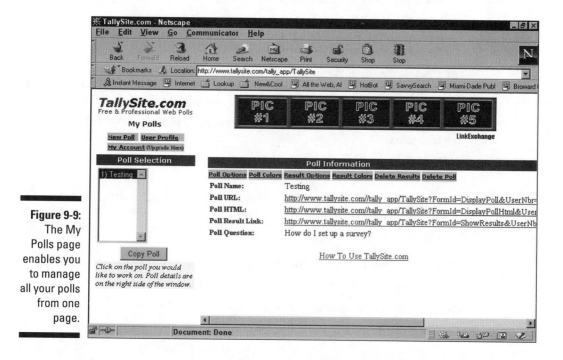

In the upper-left corner of the My Polls page, you see three buttons. The first, New Poll, is what you click to create a new survey. The second, User Profile, lets you change your username, password, and so forth. The third, My Account, just takes you to a page that tells you that you're using the free version, which you presumably already know. If you want to get rid of the advertising banner, a link on that page lets you upgrade to commercial service for a small fee.

The remainder of the My Polls page consists of two sections: *Poll Selection* and *Poll Information*. Poll Selection lists all the surveys that you create through TallySite.com. If you click a poll name in the list, you see its data appear in the Poll Information section of the page. The Copy Poll button beneath the poll list duplicates a poll that you have selected from the list so that you can use that poll as the basis for another one.

You can use three links in the Poll Information section. The first link, Poll URL, takes you to the poll, and the third one, Poll Result Link, takes you to the poll results. The second link, Poll HTML, opens a page that shows the HTML code for the survey form. Copy and paste this code into your Web page to place the form on your site.

The buttons above the links let you modify the survey. These buttons are

- **Poll Options:** Modifies the selected poll.
- **Poll Colors:** Changes the survey form's colors.
- **Result Options:** Customizes the voting results page.
- **Result Colors:** Changes the colors on the voting results page.
- **Delete Results:** Clears all the current voting and resets the results to zero.
- **Delete Poll:** Deletes the poll.

Poll Options

The first button, Poll Options, takes you back to the same form that you used to create the poll. Make any necessary changes in the poll right on the form and then scroll down and click the Save button.

Poll Colors

The second button, Poll Colors, takes you to a page where you can set colors for the following items:

- Question background
- Question text
- Choice background

- Choice text
- Result background
- Result link

The current colors appear in a sample poll on the right side of this page, and text boxes on the left side list the current color values for each item in the preceding list. To change the current (default) colors, follow these steps:

1. **Type either a hexadecimal color code or a color name in one of the text boxes and then click another color text box or press Enter or the Tab key to see the results of the change in the sample poll.**

2. **Repeat Step 1 for any other color you want to change.**

   Optionally, you can click the Choose Color link next to the text box for the element that you want to change. If you use these links, you access a Color Chooser, as shown in Figure 9-10. You click the cell containing the color that you want and then click the Choose button. TallySite.com automatically enters the hex code for the color that you pick in the appropriate text box on the form.

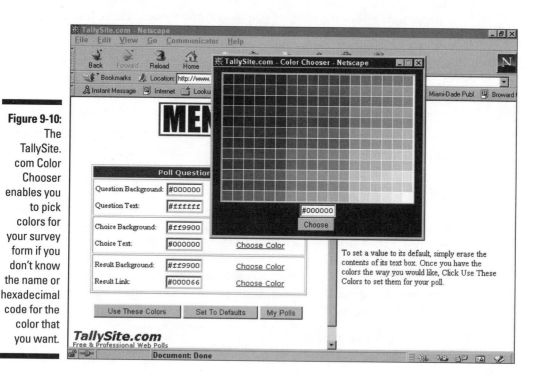

Figure 9-10:
The
TallySite.
com Color
Chooser
enables you
to pick
colors for
your survey
form if you
don't know
the name or
hexadecimal
code for the
color that
you want.

If you change your mind about any changes that you make to the colors on your survey, you can easily revert to the original settings. To reset all the colors to the default values, just click the Set To Defaults button under the color listings; to reset only one color to its default without affecting other colors, erase its current value from the text box. You can then enter new colors into the text boxes for any of these elements. To abort your color changes, click the My Polls button, which returns you to your poll-management page.

3. **To accept the color changes that you make on this page, click the Use These Colors button.**

   This action takes you to another page with a single button on it.

4. **Click the Return To My Polls button to return to your poll-management page.**

Result Options

The Result Options button lets you customize your voting-results page. To do so, click the link to access the Result Options page and then follow these steps:

1. **In the Header HTML text area at the top of the Result Options page, enter whatever text you want to appear above the voting results, as in the example shown in Figure 9-11.**

   You can use HTML, as well as plain text, for the header material.

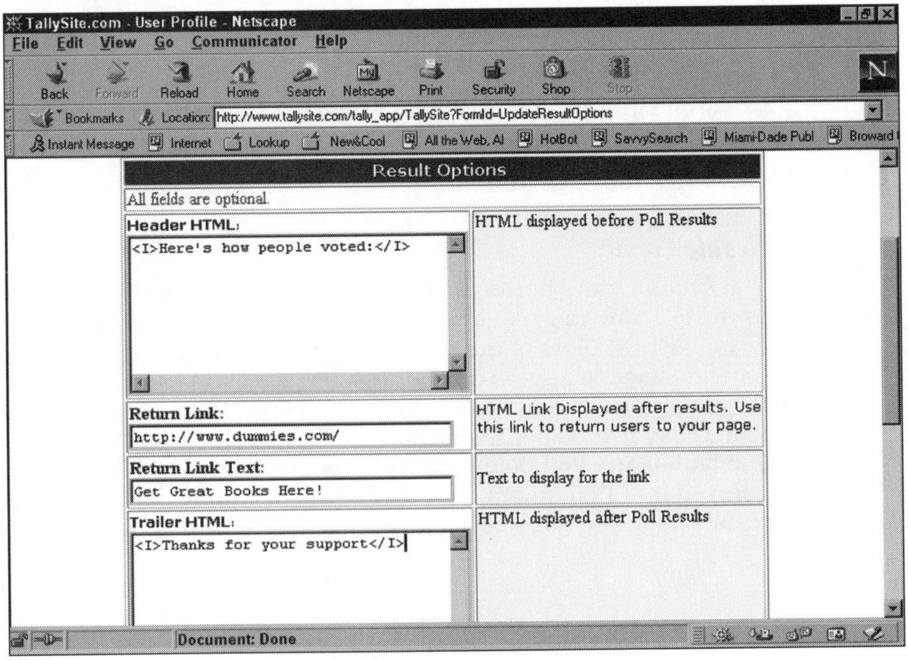

Figure 9-11: Adding text to the Results Options page adds more information to your survey results.

2. **In the Return Link text box, enter the URL of the Web page that you want visitors to go to after they finish voting.**

3. **In the Return Link Text text box, type the words that you want to appear as the link to the page you specify a URL for in Step 2.**

4. **In the Trailer HTML text area, enter anything you want to appear after the voting results.**

   As with the header, you can use either plain text or HTML here.

5. **Scroll down to the Prevent Multiple Submissions option and select either the Yes or No radio button.**

   This option is set to No by default, but you generally want to choose Yes so that the same people can't vote repeatedly and skew the results (unless you like rigged elections, of course).

6. **For the Open New Window To Display Results option, select either the Yes or No radio button.**

   If you do choose to open a new window, the results will be displayed in a new instance of the visitor's Web browser. This option is set to No by default.

7. **Select either the Yes or No radio button for the Show Number Of Results For Each Answer option.**

   The default is Yes, which means that both the number of votes and the percentage of votes appear on-screen. If you choose No, only the percentage of votes shows.

8. **If you want to set the date to end voting, specify a date in the Closing Date text box.**

   You must enter this closing date in YYYY-MM-DD format, so if you want to end the voting on January 5, 2019, you enter **2019-01-05**.

9. **Click the Save button.**

Result Colors

The Result Colors button takes you to a page that works essentially the same as the Poll Colors page . . . well, with one or two new wrinkles. In addition to changing the colors of the results page, you can enter the URL for a background image to appear on your results page. You can also click a <u>Pre-Defined Backgrounds</u> link and choose from some ready-made backgrounds. Other than those two points, everything else on this page works the same as what you find on the Poll Colors page that was discussed back in the — you guessed it — Poll Colors section (except, of course, that they apply to your results page and not to your survey page).

Deleting results and polls

The Delete Results button clears all the previous voting statistics. After you click it, you go to a page displaying two more buttons. Click the Delete All Results button to confirm that you want to clear the current voting statistics or click the Cancel button to abort and retain the current results.

Finally, the Delete Poll button takes you to a page identical to the Poll Questions page that you used to create the poll. This page serves as a safety feature because it shows you precisely which poll you're deleting. To confirm the deletion, scroll down to the bottom of the page and click the Delete Poll button. No Cancel button exists here, but you can abort the deletion by simply clicking your Web browser's Back button — as long as you do so before you click the Delete Poll button on this page.

Trying Out Form Makers

Surveys aren't the only use of forms on the Web, of course. In fact, the amount and types of information that are gathered are staggering. Visitor information, prospect inquiries, and product orders are only a few uses of forms. If the idea of using forms interests you, but you're not comfortable with CGI, or Common Gateway Interface (see Chapter 4), you may want to try out some of the form makers and processing services that we describe in this section.

A tremendous amount of overlap exists between the folks who offer free forms and those who offer form-processing services. Many of the form makers also provide CGI services, although they usually limit them to servicing their own custom forms. A pure form-processing service, however, handles forms that you create on your own. This type of service gives you a whole lot more control and power over your Web site contents.

The same folks who bring you the polling service at TallySite.com also run a form maker called FormSite.com (www.formsite.com). It works almost exactly like their other service, and it's free if you accept its accompanying advertising — or you can pop for a few bucks to get rid of the advertising banners and pick up some extra features, such as secure forms.

Response-O-Matic, which you predictably find at www.response-o-matic.com on the Web, is one of the best form-processing firms around, and it gives you a lot of flexibility. It handles any form that you want to throw at it. Well, okay, it does have a few restrictions. But they're minimal and reasonable. You can't, for example, transmit more than 50 kilobytes of data with one form submission. That's plenty, however, with scads and bunches to spare.

The questions that you add to the form are up to you, but they require a bit of HTML knowledge. (If you're totally at sea when it comes to HTML, try Freedback.com instead, which we list in the "Online Sources" section at the end of this chapter.)

To create a form by using Response-O-Matic's service, follow these steps:

1. **Go to** www.response-o-matic.com **and then click the** <u>Create A Template</u> **link.**

   This action takes you to the site's Form Wizard page.

2. **Scroll down the page until you see the heading** Go!, **as shown in Figure 9-12.**

3. **In the Enter Your E-Mail Address text box, type the e-mail address you want form data sent to.**

4. **In the Enter Your Name text box, type the name that you want users of your form to see on the Thank You page.**

5. **In the third text box on the Form Wizard page, type the subject line that you want to appear on the e-mail that you receive from this form.**

6. **Type a title for the form's Thank You Page in the fourth text box.**

   This title appears at the beginning of the page that users of the form see after they submit their information.

Figure 9-12:
Response-O-Matic's Form Wizard page, where you begin creating your customized form.

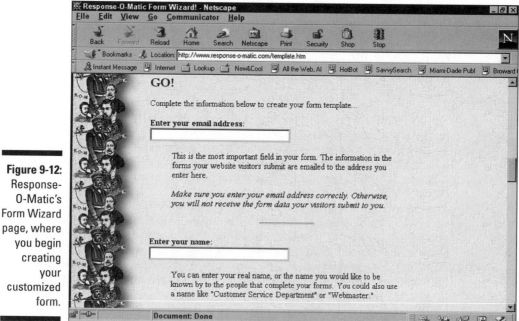

7. **In the next text box, type the URL of the page that you want form users to go to after they submit their information.**

   This URL will be placed in a link on the Thank You page. It can link to any page you want. It's probably a good idea to link back to the page you have your survey on so that visitors can continue their surfing without any disorientation, but where it leads to is entirely up to you.

   Make sure not to overwrite the `http://` at the beginning of the URL that appears in the text box. This prefix is a necessary part of the URL.

8. **Type a name to go with the return page URL in the next text box.**

   This name will be displayed as the text in the link that leads to the return page.

9. **Choose a background color for the Thank You page by clicking one of the radio buttons in the next section.**

10. **Choose a text color for the Thank You page by clicking one of the radio buttons in the next section.**

11. **Choose an unfollowed link color for the Thank You page by clicking one of the radio buttons in the next section.**

12. **Choose a followed link color for the Thank You page by clicking one of the radio buttons in the next section.**

13. **Click the Submit button to complete the form template.**

14. **On the page that appears, scroll down and copy the HTML code, paste it into your HTML editor, and save it.**

15. **Edit the template code in your HTML editor so that it contains the questions that you want.**

After you finish modifying the code in your HTML editor, upload the Web page that contains it to your Web server. Test it.

Privacy and Security

First off, if you submit your site's input to someone else for processing, you surrender control over that information. Make sure that you check out the form processor's privacy policy before you commit yourself. Look for a link that says something like <u>Privacy Statement</u> or <u>Privacy Policy</u>, click it, and carefully read the fine print that you find there. Print out a hard copy to keep in your files.

If the form processor doesn't post a clearly stated privacy policy on their site, you probably don't want to use its services. If the company doesn't promise in writing to keep your information and your users' information confidential and you still go with it, you may end up feeding everything from your site's forms right into a spammer's or telemarketer's data bank.

Another concern is that most form-processing services send the form contents to you by e-mail. Because the information in the form travels through the Internet's e-mail systems, anyone running one of the servers through which it passes as it traverses the Internet can read the information. Now, your average network administrator has better things to do than read other people's passing e-mail, but you've got to keep in mind that this ain't exactly the most secure approach possible. *Sniffer programs,* software that filters through e-mail as it passes through a server, can grab sensitive information from those messages.

Obviously, using form-processing services isn't the ideal approach if you're getting information that would be useful to crooks — such as credit-card numbers, for instance.

If you handle sensitive information, you need to make sure that any form-processor that you use collects your data via a secure form and keeps the data on its server until you can pick it up yourself by logging on to a secure page at the processor's site, like with the professional-level version of FormSite.com (see the section "Trying Out Form Makers").

Online Sources

Table 9-1 lists some places on the World Wide Web where you can find more resources like the ones that we cover in this chapter.

Table 9-1	Online Resources
Web Site Name	**Web Address**
aBooth	`www.abooth.f2s.com`
Beseen Quizlet	`http://beseen.com/quiz`
CN FormBuilder	`www.commercialnetworks.com`
EZPolls	`http://ezpolls.mycomputer.com`
FormMailer	`www.formmailer.net`
Freedback.com	`www.freedback.com`
Freepolls.com	`www.freepolls.com`
Glory's Form Maker	`http://gloryscreations.com/formmaker.html`

Web Site Name	*Web Address*
GuestVote.com	www.guestvote.com
Insta-Poll	www.insta-poll.com
NetVotes	www.netvotes.com
Nytebyte's Online Form Maker	www.nytebyte.com/business/ cgisamp/formaker.htm
Pollit.com	http://pollit.com
SiteGadgets.com	www.sitegadgets.com
Survey Engine	http://mail.infotrieve.com/isurvey

Chapter 10

Letting 'Em Have Their Say

. . . .

In This Chapter

▶ Providing guestbooks

▶ Constructing message boards

▶ Creating chat rooms by using QuickChat

. . . .

*I*n Chapter 9, we explain polls and forms and how they can add value to your Web site; the add-ins in this chapter (guestbooks, message boards, and the like) are similar to the polls and forms in Chapter 9 but with one really important difference. With polls and forms, you have total control over the topics and possible responses. But when it comes to guestbooks, message boards, and chat rooms, you give up a bit of control over your Web site's content. You turn that control over to your visitors by providing them with a forum where they can express themselves.

Censorship and your Web site

Censorship is an ugly word to most people, especially in connection with the Internet. Unfortunately, in running your own Web site, you sometimes find that you need to limit in some way what others can post to your site. In extreme cases, you may even need to bar a particularly disruptive person from posting in, for example, your chat room. Is this act — and that of setting up filters — a form of censorship? The answer to this question depends on why it's done. If your intention is simply to keep someone from voicing an opinion, you're engaging in censorship, plain and simple. If your intention is to defend the free speech rights of the rest of the members against someone who's interfering with them, that's another matter entirely.

This topic isn't an idle philosophical matter but a very real consideration that you'll likely need to face as a Webmaster. It's a sad fact that someone, sometime, will probably jump into the middle of your nice, happy online community and try to mess it up. Although you may expect a certain amount of disagreement and even heated discussion in any group, personal attacks and deliberate disruption of discussions are different matters. As a Webmaster, your responsibility is to act for the benefit of your peaceful visitors. And there are times when that means you have to ban a troublemaker from your site.

Providing Guestbooks

Guestbooks are the digital equivalent of a graffiti wall, which doesn't necessarily mean that they're going to contain limericks or dirty words. But they *are* designed so that people can leave short messages for all to see.

Many guestbooks offer an additional option that allows users to create messages that only the guestbook owner — the Webmaster — can view. This enables people to leave private comments for you.

The guestbook stacks the messages that people post one after the other, with the vast majority of guestbooks putting the newest message on top and moving all the others down. A few guestbooks work the other way around, but we don't recommend that type because you have to scroll too much to get to the most recent message.

You may want to use a couple of e-mail features built in to most guest books:

- ✔ **Thank-you note:** This feature sends a nice note to each visitor who leaves a message.

- ✔ **Message copies via e-mail:** This feature e-mails the Webmaster a copy of each message posted. This is a nice timesaver; otherwise, you have to constantly go to the guestbook to see what new messages have been posted.

Guestcities (www.guestcities.com) is one of the easiest guestbooks in the world to set up. It's free, and the only catch is that an unobtrusive advertising banner appears at the top of your Web page. Guestcities remotely hosts the guestbook on its own site, so the guestbook requires absolutely no knowledge of CGI scripts for you to run.

To set up your Guestcities guestbook, follow these steps:

1. **Go to** www.guestcities.com **and click the** <u>Join!!</u> **link, as shown in Figure 10-1.**

2. **Enter your name and e-mail address in the appropriate text boxes.**

3. **Enter the URL and name of your Web site and make sure that the Make Title a Link Back to Site check box is selected.**

4. **Pick a type for your Web site from the Category drop-down list.**

5. **Choose either Yes or No from the Allow HTML drop-down list.**

   If you choose No, all entries that people make in the guestbook are just plain text. If you want your visitors to be able to format the text in their messages, you should choose Yes.

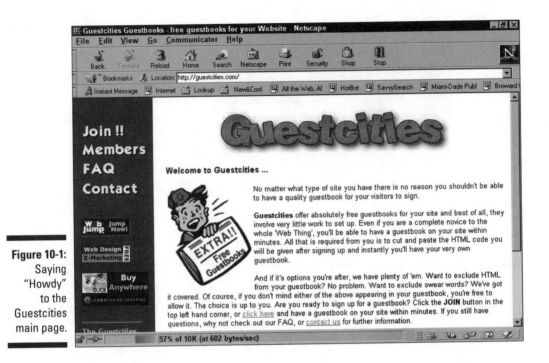

Figure 10-1:
Saying
"Howdy"
to the
Guestcities
main page.

6. **Choose Yes or No from the Censor Bad Words drop-down list.**

7. **Select colors from the Font Color and Link Color drop-down lists.**

8. **Enter either a color or the URL for an image in the Background text box, as follows:**

   - Entering a color gives you a plain color as the background for your guestbook.

   - Entering the URL for an image gives your guestbook a background image.

   The next five text boxes contain the questions that you want your visitors to respond to.

9. **If the questions are ones you want to ask, do nothing to them; if not, change the text to suit your needs.**

   Figure 10-2 shows the default guestbook form that you create if you make no changes to any of the questions in these text boxes.

   The first two text boxes, Name and Email, do nothing but display the answers that are typed into them by a visitor. However, the third question's text box, Website URL, converts its answer to a hyperlink, so you shouldn't use it unless you need to ask a question that can be answered with a URL.

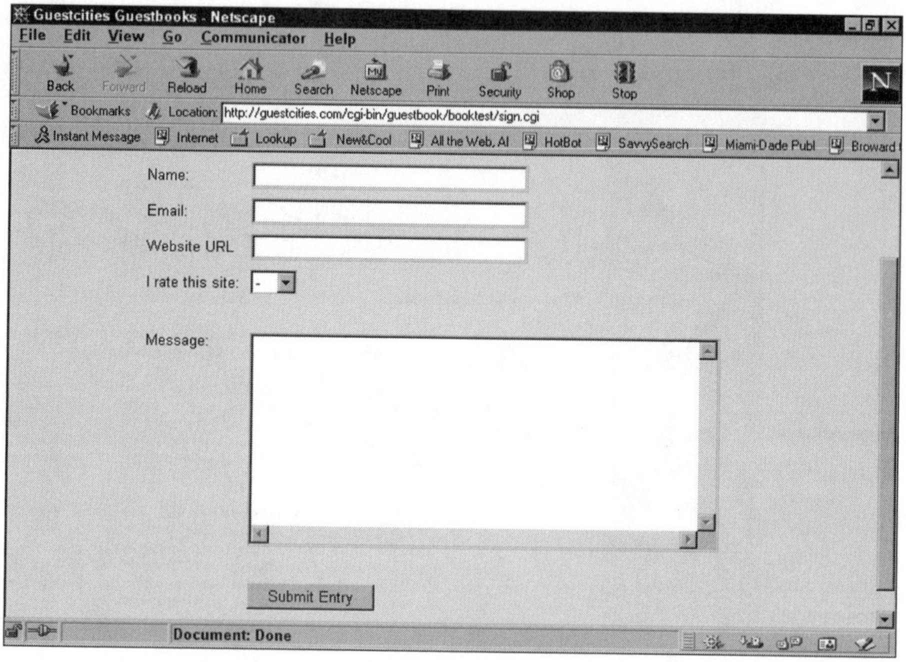

Figure 10-2:
The
Guestcities
guestbook
form that
you get if
you accept
the defaults.

The fourth question's text box, I Rate This Site, has a special function. It offers guests the option of picking a rating between 1 and 5. You can change the text of the question, but you want to always make sure that a guest can sensibly answer it by choosing one of those numbers.

Only the last question's text box, Message, is actually required. If you don't want to ask your visitors one or more of the other questions, simply delete all the text in those text boxes, leaving only the text in this one.

10. **Select the radio button next to the icon that you want to use for the I Rate This Site question.**

You use this icon to graphically display the visitors' rating answers. If you use a star icon and a visitor gives you a rating of "3," three stars will be displayed in the message.

11. **Enter a username and password in the appropriate text boxes at the bottom of the page.**

12. **Click the Create My Guestbook button.**

13. **Copy and paste the HTML code that appears into your Web page and then upload it to your site.**

Guestcities e-mails you a copy of the HTML code so that you have a backup copy of it. Just in case, though, you should probably print out the final page in the creation process.

You can change any of the guestbook options that you select by going to www.guestcities.com and clicking the <u>Members</u> link. Enter your username and password to get access to the options page.

Creating Message Boards

Message boards provide the structure that simple guestbooks lack. Most of the messages that people post on message boards tend to be fairly short, but unlike in a guestbook, messages aren't just listed in a simple top-down or bottom-up order that's based on when they're posted. Instead, a message board lists its postings by topic. In fact, the whole intent of a message board is different from a guestbook's: Both guestbooks and message boards let people leave messages, but message boards also let people interact with one another.

Before a new message is posted, the poster chooses a subject or *topic line* for it. As other people respond to the message, that topic automatically carries over and the reply is connected to the original message. Usually, the board lists these postings in a *hierarchy*, where each response is indented beneath the message it replies to, and the series of messages on one topic is called a *thread*. Visitors to your site can follow a thread from beginning to end, jump in and reply to any message in the thread, or start an entirely new discussion by posting a new message.

Message boards almost always deal with a particular field of interest that visitors to a Web site have in common. Some common examples are

- ✔ Professional discussions
- ✔ Political issues
- ✔ Regional concerns
- ✔ Hobbies
- ✔ Current events
- ✔ Technical support

Obviously, a publicly available forum on controversial topics gives people who are less than polite an opening to be disruptive. A worthwhile message board program includes a filter feature where you can specify any terms you want to prohibit. (You know — like if you run a board for wild turkeys, you may not want them to have to see words like *stuffing* or *Thanksgiving*.) Filters prevent messages containing the terms you list from going onto your message board.

Setting up a message board with Boardhost

Boardhost (www.boardhost.com), like the name says, gives you a place to host your message boards. Although the company remotely hosts the boards it provides, the boards are customizable so that you can mimic the look and feel of your own Web site. You get a well-designed message board with all the bells and whistles you expect from a paid service — but for free. As usual, in such cases, it's advertiser-supported, but if the banner ads bug you, you can ditch them for a small fee. In this case, that fee is eminently reasonable — only $8 a month.

Boardhost has a whole mess of nice features that you can activate or kill at will during or after setup. Some examples of these features include

- ✔ Setting up the board so that your users receive an e-mail message after someone else replies to a post of theirs.
- ✔ Offering a keyword search so that nobody has to manually go through all the messages to find a topic that they're looking for.
- ✔ Adding your own logo to all the board's pages.
- ✔ Adding password-protected access so that you can hold private discussions.

To create a message board with Boardhost, follow these steps:

1. **Go to** www.boardhost.com **and click the** <u>Join Free!</u> **link, as shown in Figure 10-3.**

   This link takes you to the Terms of Service page.

2. **Read the Terms of Service and click the check box below them that says that you agree to abide by them.**

3. **Scroll down and type a username in the appropriate text box.**

   The username is case-sensitive, so typing **ImInCharge** isn't the same thing as **imincharge**.

4. **Click the Check It! button.**

   If the username you choose is already in use, Boardhost tells you that you must enter a different one. After you enter a new username, click the Check Database button to determine whether it's in use.

   You can run around in circles forever if you're not imaginative with your username. Make it unusual but something that you can remember.

5. **After you create an acceptable username, enter your real name and e-mail address in the appropriate text boxes and click the Submit Info button.**

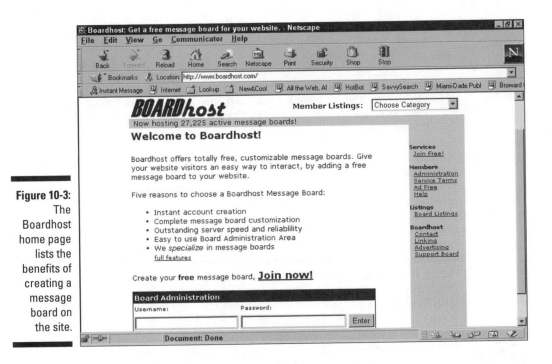

Figure 10-3:
The
Boardhost
home page
lists the
benefits of
creating a
message
board on
the site.

6. **Click the button that appears asking if your e-mail address is correct; if the address is wrong, click the Back button in your Web browser instead and then re-enter your e-mail address correctly, clicking the Submit Info button again.**

   Boardhost now sends you an e-mail message with your activation code.

7. **Click the first link in the e-mail that Boardhost sends you to automatically sign on to the Account Creation page.**

   If your e-mail doesn't support embedded links, you can just copy the URL and paste it into your Web browser instead. You can also click the second link to go to a page where you manually enter the information from the e-mail, but why bother?

   The Account Creation page provides you with the final stage for creating your message board.

8. **Under Website Info, enter the name and URL of your Web site in the appropriate text boxes and pick a category for your message board from the drop-down list.**

9. **Under Message Board Info, type a title for the message board into the text box and pick your time zone from the drop-down list.**

   Remember: The messages show the time when they're posted.

10. **Under Personal Info, select the check box if you do not want to receive e-mail messages from Boardhost.**

    If you do select this check box, you won't get notification when Boardhost upgrades its capabilities.

11. **Finally, you must type a password into the two text boxes under Password and click the Finish Creation button to go to the Account Created page.**

Your message board is now up and running. You may want to explore your new message board to see how it works. Click the link that shows the URL of your message board and see how the basic board setup looks. Enter some messages if you want. Play around a bit.

Once you feel comfortable with the message board, click your browser's Back button to return to the Account Created page, and then scroll all the way down and click the Generate HTML Codes button. On the resulting HTML Codes page, take a minute to look at the appearance of the links, buttons, and icons that Boardhost provides. Copy and paste the one(s) that you like into your Web pages so that your visitors can click them to go to your message board. If you don't like any of them, the HTML code is easy to modify.

You can also generate the HTML code later by using the Administration functions. (See the following section.)

Modifying your Boardhost message board

You may decide at some point that you want to modify your message board. Fortunately, Boardhost enables you to modify it whenever you want. To get started modifying your board, you just click the <u>Enter Administration</u> link on the Account Created page. If you've gotten hopelessly separated from that page while exploring your new message board, just follow these steps to log on from scratch:

1. **Go to** www.boardhost.com.

2. **Enter your username and password in the appropriate text boxes of the Board Administration area.**

3. **Click the Enter button.**

The Boardhost Administration page appears, as shown in Figure 10-4.

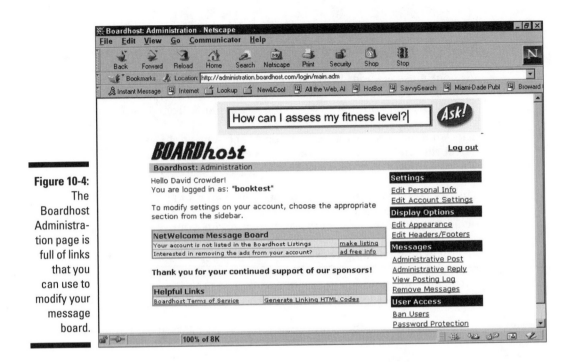

Figure 10-4:
The
Boardhost
Administra-
tion page is
full of links
that you
can use to
modify your
message
board.

This page has a column of links on the right side and a few more in boxes in the main area of the page. There are two links in the Test Board box:

✔ **Make listing:** Takes you to a page that lets you add your board to the public listings on Boardhost if you don't want a private board.

✔ **Ad free info:** Takes you to a page that gives you information on upgrading to ad-free service.

The Helpful Links box has four links:

✔ **Boardhost Terms of Service:** Takes you to a page that shows you the Terms of Service.

✔ **Generate Linking HTML Codes:** Takes you to a page that duplicates the HTML code that you receive when you sign up for your message board.

✔ **Create a new message board:** Takes you to the Account Creation page.

✔ **Boardhost Account Removal:** Takes you to a page where you can cancel your message board.

The remaining links, which lead to Web pages where you can modify your message board, are found in a panel at the right side of the Administration page. They are described in detail in the following sections.

The Edit Personal Info link

The Personal Info page is divided into three sections. The first, E-mail Address, simply contains the e-mail address that you list when you sign up for your message board. You can change it if you've changed ISPs or wish to receive Boardhost's messages at a different address. The check box beneath it enables you to opt out of receiving any mailings from Boardhost.

The Administrative Notifications section contains only a single check box. Select this check box if you want to receive an e-mail message that notifies you each time someone posts a message to your board.

The Contact Information section lists your name and password. (The password is displayed as a series of asterisks, of course, so no one can read it over your shoulder.) You can optionally provide your physical address.

After you finish making your changes to this page, scroll down to the bottom of the page and click the Save Personal Info button. You don't, oddly, go back to the Administration page but to one that has the same set of links on the right side, which is just as good.

You can get back to the Administration page by clicking the Back button in your browser twice.

The Edit Account Settings link

This link leads to a page containing five sections. The first section, Webpage Info, simply lists the name, URL, and category of your Web page that links to Boardhost.

The Message Board Info section displays the title of your board as well as its settings for the time zone, time format, and date format. This area also lets you set the maximum number of messages your board can hold. The default is 200, but you can set it to hold up to 300 by entering the desired number in the text box.

If your board exceeds the maximum number of messages it can hold, it automatically deletes the oldest message to make room for the newest message, so make sure to set it high enough to accommodate your message traffic.

The Boardhost Header section contains one drop-down list and one text box. The drop-down list enables you to choose the type of header that you want on your message board. The available options are to display the board title as your header (the default option), to display a graphical file as your board header (the Display Header With Logo option), or to display no header at all. If you use a graphics file as a logo, you need to enter the URL of that file in the text box. If you don't want either a title or a logo but still want to display links to your message area and home page, select the Display Header With Logo option and then enter `http://boardhost.com/images/invisible. gif` as the image URL in the text box.

The Optional Features section contains half a dozen check boxes:

- ✔ **Message Search:** Enables a search feature that lets visitors find messages by entering keywords.

- ✔ **Links Allowed:** Lets visitors enter a link to a Web site (selected by default).

- ✔ **Images Allowed:** Adds the capability to include images in messages (selected by default).

- ✔ **Allow E-Mail Notifications:** Gives visitors the option to receive e-mail messages when other visitors reply to their posts.

- ✔ **Allow HTML:** Allows visitors to use HTML code to format their messages (selected by default).

- ✔ **Admin Posts Only:** Makes it impossible for visitors to post new messages. They can, however, still reply to existing messages. If this option is selected, only you, the message board administrator, can post a totally new message rather than merely make a reply.

The Display Options section contains three check boxes and one drop-down list. All three check boxes are selected by default, so you must deselect them if you don't want these options. The check boxes are

- ✔ **Quoted Message Replies:** Quotes the message that is being replied to.

- ✔ **IP Address Stamping:** Adds the IP address of the person posting the message to the top of the message.

- ✔ **Convert Smiley Faces to Images:** Turns textual smiley faces like :-) into graphical icons.

You use the drop-down list to set spacing options between messages. You may choose, for instance, to put a line between messages or to have a blank line separate them.

When you're satisfied with the options you choose, scroll down to the bottom of the page and click the Save Account Settings button. You don't go back to the Administration page but to one that has the same set of links on the right side, which is just as good.

You can get back to the Administration page by clicking the Back button in your browser twice.

The Edit Appearance link

This link takes you to a page containing four sections, as follows:

- ✔ **Board Colors:** This section enables you to set the colors on your message board by entering the appropriate hexadecimal codes in the

Background Color, Link Color, Visited Link Color, and Text Color text boxes. Click the <u>Click here for a color hex number chart</u> link for a view of the colors you can choose.

- ✔ **Message Board Fonts:** This section contains three text boxes that enable you to enter values for the font faces that you want to use for your board and for the size of those fonts.

- ✔ **Advanced Board Options:** This section contains five text boxes. The first is for entering a URL of a background image for the board. The second is for the board title. The title here is not the same as the one you set on the Account Settings page; this creates the HTML TITLE element for the message board — the title that is displayed at the top of your visitors' Web browsers when they're on your message board. The third text box sets the length of the text areas. (The default is 20.) The fourth and fifth text boxes set the number of rows and columns for the message area itself. (Default values are 9 rows and 50 columns.)

- ✔ **Custom Messages:** This section has more than a dozen text boxes that contain the text currently used as labels for the message board. By typing over the defaults, you can specify your own labels for all the text in the message-entry areas, including the Submit button.

When you're done making modifications on the Appearance page, scroll down to the bottom of the page and click the Save Appearance Settings button. You don't go back to the Administration page but to one that has the same set of links on the right side.

You can get back to the Administration page by clicking the Back button in your browser twice.

The Edit Headers/Footers link

This link leads to a page where you find three different text areas. The first text area enables you to set the header for the message board index page. The second one lets you set the header for all message pages. The final text area is for setting the footer for all message pages. You can use HTML as well as plain text in all three text areas.

After you finish adding or modifying headers and footers, scroll down to the bottom of the page and click the Save Headers and Footers button. You don't go back to the Administration page but to one that has the same set of links on the right side.

You can get back to the Administration page by clicking the Back button in your browser twice.

The Edit Meta Tags link

This link leads to a page where you can enter a description and keywords for the message board that search engines can use to index it. You need to enter the full HTML code, including the META element, into a text area. (See Chapter 17 for more information on Meta tags.)

If you don't want to type the code yourself, click the <u>Meta Tag Generator</u> link. You can then enter the description and keywords into text boxes in a pop-up window. Click the Create Meta Tags button within that window and the HTML code you need will appear. Copy the code, click the <u>Close Window</u> link, and paste the code into the text area.

After you enter your Meta tags, click the Save Meta Tags button. You don't go back to the Administration page but to one that has the same set of links on the right side. It also has links to the submission pages of a few popular search engines.

You can get back to the Administration page by clicking the Back button in your browser twice.

The Messages links

The next four links on the right side of the Administration page are

✔ **Administrative Post:** Takes you to a page where you can post a message to the board in an especially noticeable way. An administrative posting is just like a normal posting except for three differences. The first difference is that you can choose the color in which your name appears by selecting a color from the drop-down list next to the Name text box. The second difference is that if you have enabled IP stamping (see the section "The Edit Account Settings link," just a bit earlier in this chapter), the title "Administrator" will show instead of your IP address on this message. If IP stamping is not allowed, your title won't appear. The third difference is that you can select the check box near the bottom of the page to prevent anyone from replying to the message.

When you're ready to send your administrative posting, scroll down to the bottom of the page and click the Preview button to check the message's appearance before sending it or click the Post Message button to send it without previewing.

After clicking the Post Message button, you go to a page that has one link for going to the message board and another link for reading the message you just posted.

You can get back to the Administration page by clicking the Back button in your browser twice.

🖊 **Administrative Reply:** Takes you to a page that shows a listing of current messages. Click any message to make a reply from the Administration IP address.

🖊 **Remove Messages:** Takes you to a page listing the current messages. Selecting the check box next to one or more messages and then clicking the Remove Selected Messages button deletes those messages from the board. Clicking the Remove All Messages button clears everything from the message board.

🖊 **Posting Log:** Leads to a page containing links for viewing message logs from today, yesterday, and two days ago.

The Access Options links

The final two links at the right side of the Administration page are

🖊 **Ban Users:** Takes you to a page where you can enter the IP address that you can note from a message if you have IP stamping enabled (see the section "The Edit Account Settings link," a bit earlier in this chapter); click the Add Ban button to ban a particular IP address from posting new messages. You can also review currently banned IP addresses, select those you want to unban, and click the Remove Ban button to enable them to post on the board again.

🖊 **Password Protection:** Takes you to a page where you can change the Message board from an open board to one that requires users to log in with a username and password. To enable this option, click the Install Password Protection button. You then have to enter the first username and password (your own, of course). Afterward, whenever you click the Password Protection link, you can add new users by entering their usernames and passwords and then clicking the Add User button. To remove a user, you simply click the name and then click the Remove User button. To restore things to their original state, you scroll to the bottom of the page and click the Uninstall Password Protection link.

You don't go back to the Administration page but to one that has the same set of links on the right side.

You can get back to the Administration page by clicking the Back button in your browser twice.

Giving the Gift of Gab

Chat rooms provide a way for visitors to your site to engage in live, real-time communication. Like message boards, chat rooms enable lots of users to leave messages on the same topic — but these messages don't appear in topic-related threads. Instead the messages appear as they're sent, and the various conversation threads run together in the same area. You may think that this sounds a bit chaotic, and we can't agree more. Chat room discussions are totally unstructured, and the more people that are in a chat room, the more confusing trying to follow a conversation gets.

But chat rooms are fun and popular — and even chat novices quickly get used to picking out the specific conversation they're a part of. Still, carrying on a conversation in a chat room is kind of like talking to one or two people in the middle of a large party. This isn't your problem as a Webmaster, though, except that you may want to recommend these rooms mainly for smaller gatherings. People who regularly hang out in chat rooms understand and accept their peculiarities, and if your visitors really want chat rooms, providing them is easy enough. Several sources on the Web offer their services to help you add a chat room to your site. In this section, we cover QuickChat, but there are others listed in Online Sources at the end of this chapter.

QuickChat (www.planetz.net/quickchat) is one source that gives you a fast way to slap a Java chat room onto your Web site. To add QuickChat to your site, follow these steps:

1. **Go to** www.planetz.net/quickchat **and click the <u>Make Code</u> link (second in the list of links at the left side of the page), as shown in Figure 10-5.**

   This link takes you to the registration page.

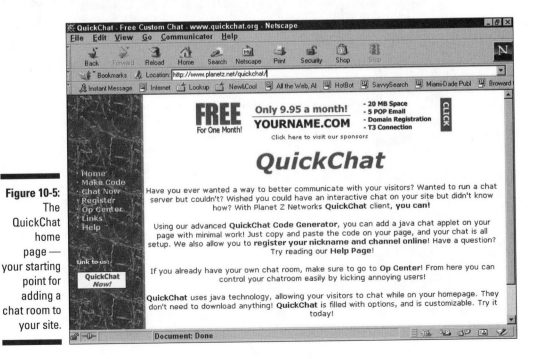

Figure 10-5: The QuickChat home page — your starting point for adding a chat room to your site.

2. **Enter your name, e-mail address, and the URL of your Web site in the appropriate text boxes and any comments that you have in the text area.**

3. **Click the Register button.**

4. **On the Generate Code page that appears, enter values for the width and height of the chat room in the first two text boxes, as shown in Figure 10-6.**

5. **Select the background and foreground colors that you want for your chat room from the first two drop-down lists and then pick the font size for the text of the messages from the third drop-down list.**

6. **Enter in the text box at the end the name of the chat channel (the particular room that you're creating) that you want to use, making sure that you preface it with a hash mark (#).**

By default, QuickChat enters you into the #Webchat channel. Click the More Info link to view information about picking a channel name. In the pop-up window that appears, use the Click Here To View Existing Channels link to find what names are already in use.

7. **Leave the Restrict To One Channel check box selected unless you want to enable your chat users to access the other channels (different chat rooms also hosted by QuickChat).**

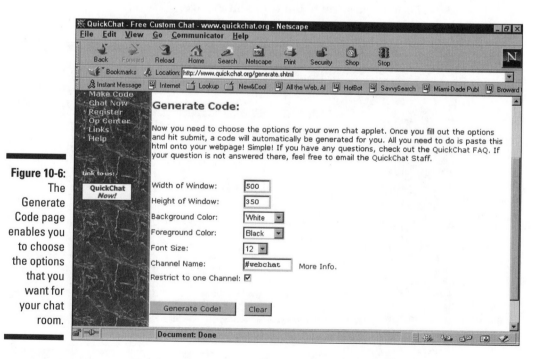

Figure 10-6:
The Generate Code page enables you to choose the options that you want for your chat room.

8. **Click the Generate Code! button.**

9. **Copy and paste the resulting code into your Web page and then upload it to your site.**

After you fire up the Web page in which you pasted the chat room code, all you — or any of your visitors — must do is to wait for the chat applet to load, enter a nickname in the appropriate text box (the e-mail address is optional), and click the Connect button, as shown in Figure 10-7.

You can click the Show User Settings button if you're a pro at chat rooms and want to adjust settings, such as Receive Wallops and Block DCC Connections. If these terms mean nothing to you, don't bother with this button.

If the nickname that you choose is already in use at QuickChat, you will be asked to pick a new one before proceeding into the chat room.

After you connect to the chat room, you go to the chat screen, as shown in Figure 10-8. The people currently in the chat room are shown in the area on the right side. Enter your messages in the long text box at the bottom of the chat window. Click one of the colors to the left to set a color for your text to appear in. Click B to make the text bold, U to underline it, R to reverse it (white against black, for example), and N to remove all formatting. Press Enter to send your message. The message will appear, along with all the other participants' messages, in the top area of the screen.

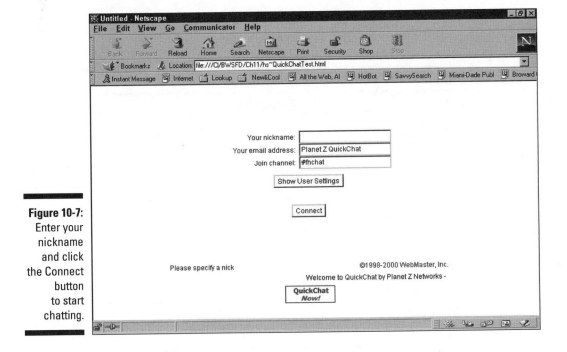

Figure 10-7:
Enter your nickname and click the Connect button to start chatting.

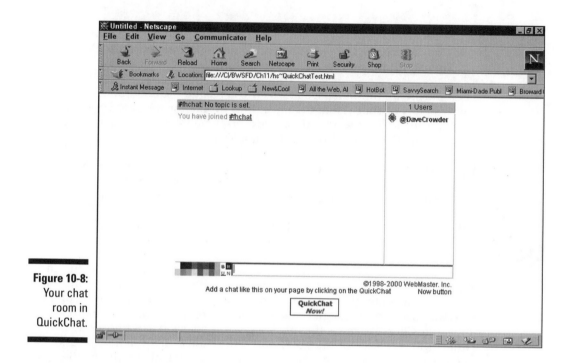

Figure 10-8:
Your chat
room in
QuickChat.

Online Sources

Table 10-1 lists some places on the World Wide Web where you can find more resources like those that we cover in this chapter.

Table 10-1	Online Resources
Web Site Name	*Web Address*
aGNeS News Forum	www.vestris.com/agnesbbs/
Boards2Go	www.boards2go.com
CountZ.com	www.countz.com/guestbooks
Dreambook	www.dreambook.com
Echelon Guestbooks	http://web.eesite.com/guest
GuestForum.com	www.guestforum.com
htmlGear	http://htmlgear.lycos.com/
InsideTheWeb	www.InsideTheWeb.com
MyForum	www.myforum.net
ParaChat	www.parachat.com/

Chapter 11

Just Plain Fun

In This Chapter

▶ Using riddles on your site

▶ Enticing your visitors with brainteasers

▶ Adding trivia to your site

▶ Placing quotations on your site

▶ Setting up a postcard shop on your site

▶ Adding online games to your site

*H*ey, life can be just a bit too serious at times — people like to kick back and have fun once in a while. If you're looking for fun things that you can add to your site, however, it almost seems like the Web just doesn't get it. Everything's so . . . well, so darned functional. Where's the stuff that doesn't actually do anything? Where's the stuff that's a totally and completely delightful waste of time?

It's our job to keep you up to date on the latest and greatest of everything Web-related, so we went out looking for Web site add-ins that take a step away from the serious side of things.

If you need to justify these kinds of things to your boss, point out that they help pull people to your site in the first place, and they make it more "sticky," too, so that visitors come back for more.

Running RiddleNut.com's Random Riddles

Ever wonder how seven batters from one baseball team can come up in the same inning, but nobody scores a run? Oh, and the team didn't use any substitutions either. Got you wondering? Good.

How about this one?

> One of us falls and never breaks.
>
> One of us breaks but never falls.
>
> What are we?

The answer to the first riddle is that, of the first five batters, two are out, while three get on base. Now the bases are loaded with two outs. The sixth batter hits a grand slam. Wait a minute! Didn't we say that nobody scores? But here are four runs. Except for one thing: The guy who hit the grand slam fails to touch first base. That means that he's the third out and the grand slam never happened. All right, so what about the seventh batter? Well, the player who hit the grand slam isn't called out until the pitcher protests to the umpire that he missed the base, and the pitcher's not allowed to protest until the next batter comes up.

The answer to the second riddle is *night and day*. There can be nightfall and daybreak but never nightbreak and dayfall.

If you like riddles, the Random Riddle from RiddleNut.com (at, of course, `www.riddlenut.com`) is a gold mine. More important, if your visitors like riddles, you can hook them by adding these Random Riddles to your pages. You don't even need to sign up or give them an e-mail address or anything.

These riddles are okay for all ages.

The people at RiddleNut.com honestly appreciate riddles as an art form. And they want you to help spread the word by adding riddles to your Web page. For free. Here's how you go about it:

1. **Go to** `www.riddlenut.com/build.php.`

2. **In the form on that page, select a text color from the first drop-down list, as shown in Figure 11-1.**

3. **Select a link color from the second drop-down list and a background color from the third.**

4. **In the final drop-down list, pick a width (in pixels) for the table that holds the riddle.**

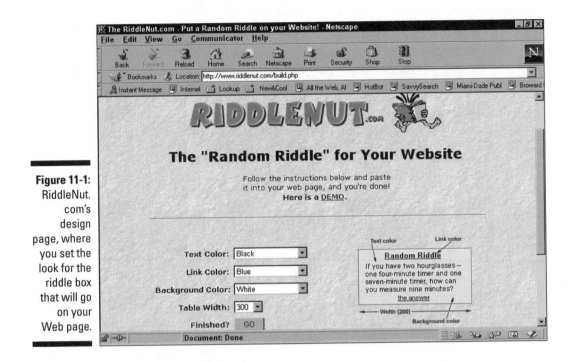

Figure 11-1:
RiddleNut.
com's
design
page, where
you set the
look for the
riddle box
that will go
on your
Web page.

5. **Click the GO button.**

6. **On the resulting page, copy the HTML code, paste it into your own Web page within the** BODY **element, and then upload the Web page to your site.**

Yes, we know that we say in Chapter 4 not to put JavaScript code in the body of your page because somebody may activate it too soon. But this one is different. Really. No visitor can do that with this because it doesn't appear until it's ready to use.

The resulting code is like the following example, allowing for differences in color and table-width choices:

```
<CENTER>
<SCRIPT LANGUAGE="JavaScript1.1"
SRC="http://www.riddlenut.com/include/riddle.php?fontcolor=Bl
            ack&linkcolor=Blue&backcolor=White&tabwid=300">
</SCRIPT>
</CENTER>
```

The Random Riddle on your page looks something like the one shown in Figure 11-2.

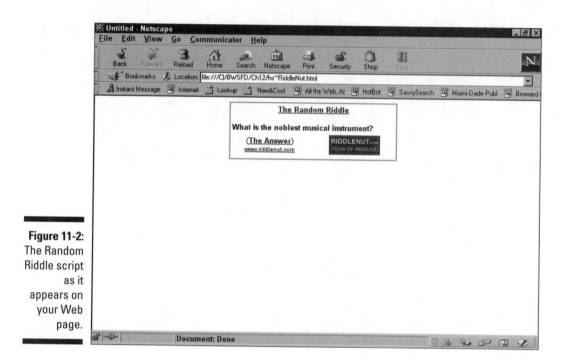

Unlike some remotely hosted Web site add-ins, this one has no control center where you can go to adjust your settings. You can, however, manually adjust the settings in your own page's source code. The key items here are the fontcolor, linkcolor, backcolor, and tabwid attributes. Each attribute, of course, corresponds to the color and table-width choices that you make on the RiddleNut.com design page. By changing the values of the three-color attributes on your site, you can alter the riddle box without going back to the RiddleNut.com site. You can enter either named colors or hexadecimal values, as in the following example:

```
SRC="http://www.riddlenut.com/include/riddle.php?fontcolor=Gr
              een&linkcolor=0000FF&backcolor=White&tabwid=300">
```

Don't alter the RiddleNut.com code's punctuation in any way at all. You may feel that you need to place quotation marks (" ") around the attributes' values or add a hash mark (#) in front of a hexadecimal number. If you do any of these things, you mess up the table's size and color characteristics. In one test where we played around with the punctuation by adding single quotes (' ') around the attributes, we even managed to make the entire riddle box disappear. If the precision needed to alter the source code makes you uncomfortable, you can just go back to the RiddleNut.com design page, redo your settings, and repaste the code with the new values into your own page. That's the safest way to do it.

The minimum table width in the RiddleNut.com drop-down list is 200 pixels, but it appears to create a riddle box 220 pixels wide in actual practice. No matter how small a number you put in the code as the value for `tabwid`, it reverts to this default minimum. The maximum width, however, can go well beyond the 450-pixel mark, which is the highest one on the riddle setup page. We lost interest after pushing it to 800 pixels, which is a good deal wider than you need for this add-in on any normally designed page, but you're welcome to see how far it will go.

Adding Bogglers to Your Web Page

Do you like a good brainteaser? Bogglers.com (at — you guessed it — `www.bogglers.com`) comes from the same folks who brought you the RiddleNut.com site. Like riddles, brainteasers are cool additions to any site. But brainteasers offer a different sort of amusing exercise than riddles do. Riddles, after all, come in a particular form in which the answer is usually disguised in the way the question is phrased. Bogglers, on the other hand, are word games, plain and simple, and they mostly depend on the graphical placement of words or the arrangement of letters. Often, the answer is a wonderfully terrible pun.

What, for example, is the meaning of PODIVEOL or UGOME? If you can't figure them out, drop in to the Bogglers.com Web site and run through the brainteasers until you find the answers — we'd never spoil your fun by telling you. (What's that? You say that we told you the answers to the riddles, so why not give you these answers, too? Oh, all right. Here they are: "dive in pool" and "you go before me." Still, it's worth your while to go there and browse through the tons of brain food that you'll find.)

Better yet, slap a Boggler on your own site and play with it there. You'll see what a blast it is, and appreciate how much your visitors will like it. Adding Bogglers to your site is even simpler than adding a riddle — just follow these steps:

1. **Go to** `www.bogglers.com/buildboggler.php`.

2. **In the form on that page, select a frame color from the first drop-down list, as shown in Figure 11-3.**

3. **Optionally, select a background color from the second drop-down list.**

   You probably want to leave it at the default setting of Invisible (no color) because some of the word games rely on the color of the lettering. Because you don't know what that's going to be in advance, you're best off covering all future bets by sticking with the default. If you must pick a color, go with White.

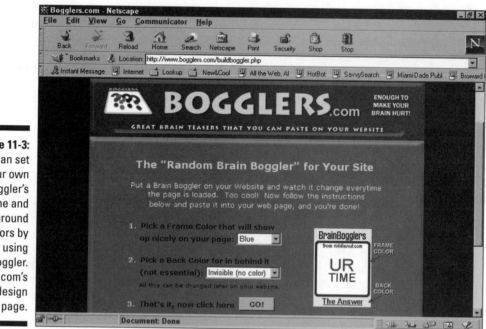

Figure 11-3:
You can set
your own
Boggler's
frame and
background
colors by
using
Boggler.
com's
design
page.

4. Click the GO! button.

5. On the resulting page, copy the HTML code, paste it into your own Web page's body, and then upload the page to your Web site.

Yes, paste it in the BODY element. (See the Technical Stuff note in the RiddleNut.com section if you don't trust us. Sniff.)

Here's the code that you get if you go with the default choices:

```
<CENTER>
<SCRIPT LANGUAGE="JavaScript1.1"
SRC="http://www.bogglers.com/bogglers.php?color=
          blue&tbcolor=">
</SCRIPT>
</CENTER>
```

Again, you can alter the values of the attributes just by typing in new ones, but this time, there are only two attributes: color, meaning the border color, and tbcolor, meaning the background color. And we can't repeat this warning enough — *don't* mess with the syntax. Don't go adding anything to the source code that Bogglers generates. Just type in new color names without quotation marks or type in hexadecimal values without hash marks.

Figure 11-4 shows a Boggler that's on a Web page and ready to be enjoyed.

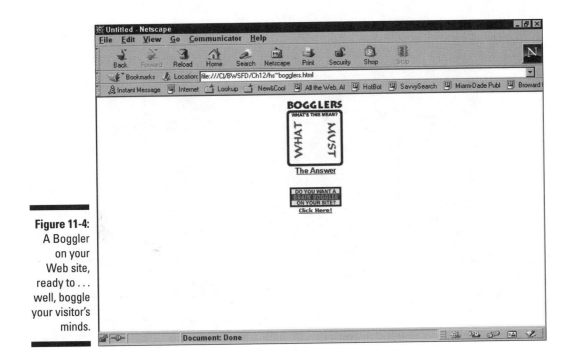

Figure 11-4:
A Boggler
on your
Web site,
ready to . . .
well, boggle
your visitor's
minds.

Playing Around with Trivia Blitz

Surely you're up to date on international politics? The latest news — like who's at war with whom? Sports? The world of entertainment? Certainly, at any rate, you're deeply into *something* or other. If so, you're probably pretty good at trivia. Trivia Blitz is a game from Uproar.com that, in addition to being fun, offers prizes to your site's visitors and a profit for you as an affiliate. (See Chapter 15 for more info about affiliate programs.)

Even if you're not into any kind of trivia at all, you can bet that your site visitors are, and that means you can make them happy by giving them what they like. To add Trivia Blitz to your Web pages, follow these steps:

1. **Go to the Free Games For Your Website page at** www.uproar.com/webdevelopers/special.html.

2. **Scroll down to the bottom of the page and click the Add It Now! button.**

   The resulting page is shown in Figure 11-5.

3. **Select the check boxes for all the versions of the game that you want to include and enter in the accompanying text boxes the URLs of the pages that are going to contain the games.**

4. **Scroll down to the bottom of the page and click the Submit button.**

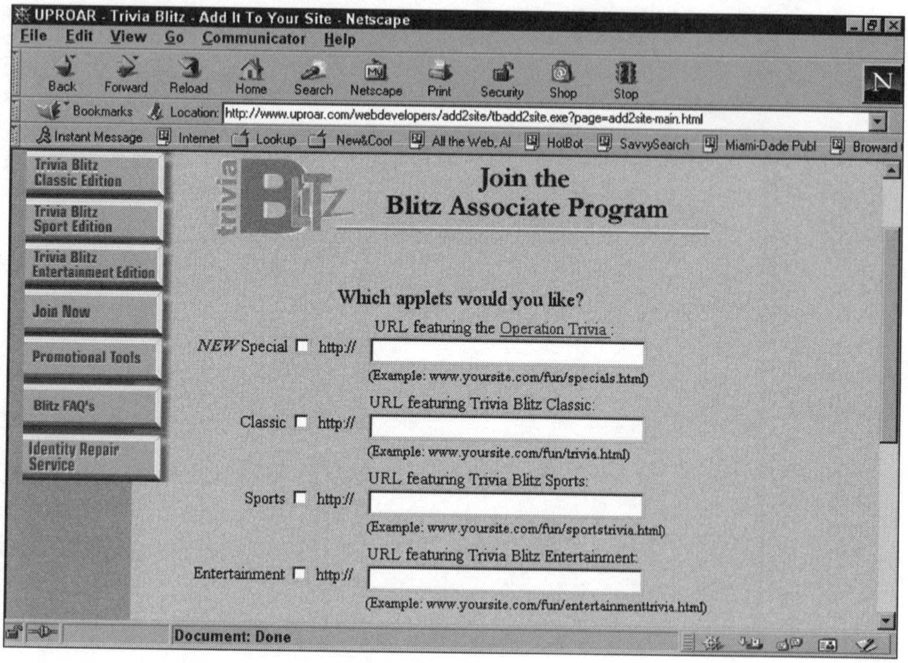

Figure 11-5:
The Trivia
Blitz sign-up
page offers
several
different
trivia
games.

If you've already signed up with Trivia Blitz and only want to add a new version instead of signing up again, you need to enter your ID number and password in the appropriate text boxes at the bottom of the page before you click the Submit button.

5. **Fill out the name and address information in the resulting form, as shown in Figure 11-6.**

6. **Choose a password and re-enter it for confirmation.**

7. **Read the legal agreement and select the check box that says you read it.**

8. **Click the Sign Me Up button.**

9. **Print the page that includes your new ID number (writing your password on it) and then put it in a file folder for safekeeping.**

In a little while, you receive a separate e-mail message for each program you're signing up for at the address that you specified on the form. Each message contains the HTML code that you use to add that particular Trivia Blitz game to your Web pages.

10. **Copy and paste this code into your own Web pages and then upload the pages to your site.**

Don't make any changes to the HTML code that's in the message(s). If you do, the game won't work.

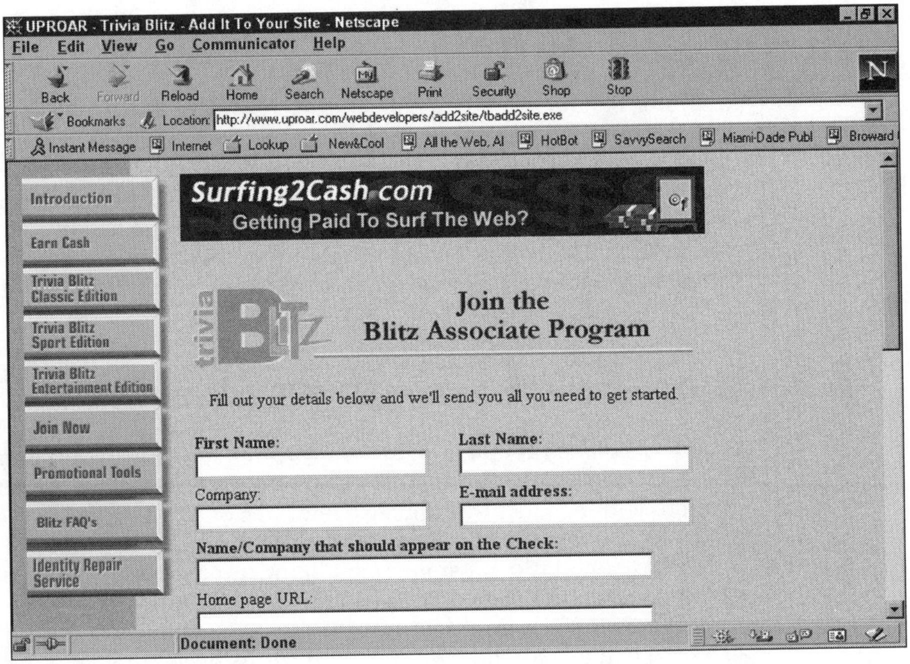

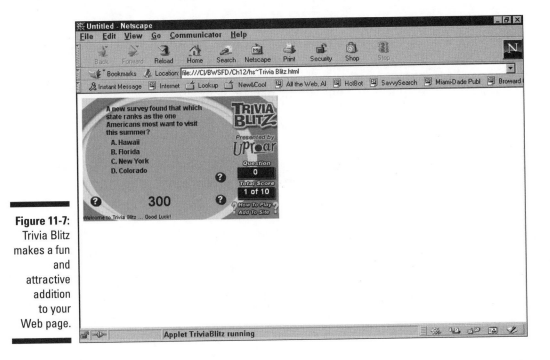

Figure 11-6: Fill out your personal information in this section of the Trivia Blitz registration.

Figure 11-7 shows Trivia Blitz ready and waiting for a visitor to play it.

Figure 11-7: Trivia Blitz makes a fun and attractive addition to your Web page.

Placing Quotations on Your Site

Quotations, *bon mots*, memorable lines — the world is full of them, and we're all fond of spouting them on occasion: Benjamin Franklin's simple wisdom, "When you're finished changing, you're finished." The Duc de La Rochefoucauld's famous, "One is never as unhappy as one thinks, nor as happy as one hopes." And who can forget the immortal line of President Richard Nixon, "I have often thought that if there had been a good rap group in those days, I might have chosen a career in music instead of politics."

Quoting with The Quote Machine

The Quote Machine (at `www.artigen.com/newwire/qmachine.html`) spouts out a new quotation twice an hour. It's a remotely hosted Java applet that you can add to your site just by copying a few lines of HTML code. Artigen provides this nice little gizmo for free. The company may add an advertising banner along with the quotation at some point in the future, but currently, all they get out of the deal is that someone who clicks on the quotation on your site goes to their news site. The down side to The Quote Machine is that Artigen's site doesn't open in a new window but takes visitors away from your site.

The Quote Machine is incredibly simple to add. You don't even need to fill out any forms. The three following steps describe the entire process:

1. **Go to** `www.artigen.com/newswire/qmachine.html`.

2. **Copy the HTML code from the How Do I Add It to My Pages? section of that page.**

3. **Paste the code into your own Web page where you want the quotation to appear and upload the page to your site.**

Figure 11-8 shows The Quote Machine as it appears on your Web site.

You can use the following code to insert The Quote Machine. Like we said before, you don't actually have to do anything but paste the code where you want the quotation to show up on your page. If you want to monkey with a few of the settings, however, go right ahead. First off, the `width` and `height` values aren't cast in stone. You can adjust them to suit your own design needs.

```
<APPLET CODE="QMachine.class"
        CODEBASE="http://www.artigen.com/newswire"
        WIDTH=550 HEIGHT=100>
<PARAM NAME="topic" VALUE="scitech">
<PARAM NAME="textcolor" VALUE="0,0,128">
<PARAM NAME="backcolor" VALUE="255,255,255">
</APPLET>
```

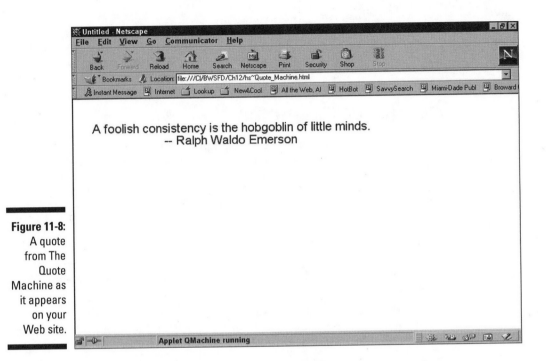

Figure 11-8:
A quote
from The
Quote
Machine as
it appears
on your
Web site.

When it comes to the code's parameters (topic, textcolor, and backcolor), you don't actually need to have any PARAM at all in your source code. All the parameters have default values in the applet, so you can just delete the PARAM elements and let the defaults stand, or you can specify values for one or two parameters if you don't want to specify all three.

The topic parameter can have a value of scitech or an optional value of wisdom. Each value draws from a different database of quotations. If you don't specify one, scitech is the default value.

You can put the applet on your page twice: one with the topic parameter set to scitech and the other set to wisdom. That way, you get both quotations.

The textcolor parameter sets — you guessed it — the color of the lettering. Although the HTML code that you copy off The Quote Machine site sets this parameter's value to a medium blue, the default color is actually black, so that's what you get if you don't include this PARAM. The backcolor parameter, which sets the background color, is white by default.

To change either the textcolor or backcolor parameter, you need to enter a new color value as an *RGB triplet*. RGB triplets denote colors by specifying the amount of red, green, and blue in the color. The possible values range from 0 to 255. Thus, if you want to make red lettering, you use a value of 255,0,0. This setting tells the applet to use as much red as possible and no green or blue.

Don't put spaces after the commas in the RGB triplets. If you do, you'll end up with black text and a white background, regardless of which color you wanted.

Quoting with Quoter

Quoter, a Java applet by Paul Lutus, is simple and versatile. It's a stand-alone, not connected to any service, so it's considerably "stickier" than The Quote Machine because there's nothing about Quoter that can lead people away from your site. It's also a freebie that its creator distributes under a *careware* license. (What's careware? Check out www.arachnoid.com/careware for details.)

To add Quoter to your site, follow these steps:

1. **Go to** www.arachnoid.com/quoter, **where you can see the applet in action.**

2. **Scroll down to the bottom of the page and click the word** Quoter **in the sentence that says Download Quoter With Installation Instructions (10KB).**

3. **After you've downloaded the file** quoter.zip, **unzip it into the directory that contains the Web page you plan to add it to.**

   You now have two new files: the applet itself (quoter.class) and a text file of quotations (quoter.txt).

4. **Add the following code to your Web page where you want the quotation box to appear:**

   ```
   <APPLET code=quoter.class name=quoter width=500
           height=300 >
   </APPLET>
   ```

5. **Upload your Web page and the** quoter.txt **file as ASCII files and upload** quoter.class **as a binary file.**

The code in the preceding steps gets you the basic setup, as shown in Figure 11-9.

Now comes the fun part. If you want more than just the plain vanilla installation, there's plenty of room for more control. As with many applets, you can set the width and height values to suit your Web page's layout. And Quoter comes with a whole bunch of parameters that you can monkey with.

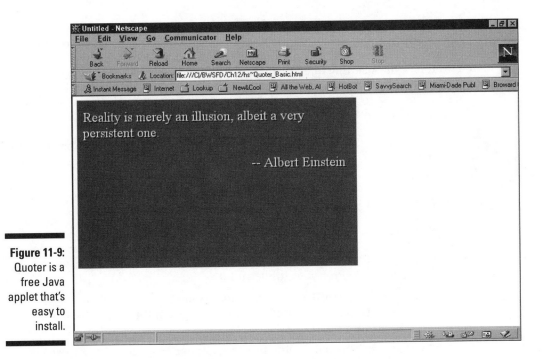

Reality is merely an illusion, albeit a very persistent one.

-- Albert Einstein

Figure 11-9:
Quoter is a
free Java
applet that's
easy to
install.

The following four parameters control the quote's lettering:

- ✔ `fontname`: This parameter sets the font face. Possible values are `Courier`, `Dialog`, `Helvetica`, and `TimesRoman`. The default value is `TimesRoman`.

- ✔ `fontsize`: This parameter sets the point size of the font. The default is 24 points.

- ✔ `fontstyle`: This parameter sets the style of the lettering. You can use values of `plain`, `bold`, and `italic`. The default style is `plain`.

- ✔ `textcolor`: This parameter controls the color of the letters. You must set the value in hexadecimal format, although the leading # is optional. The default color is #FFFF80, a shade of yellow.

The `bgcolor` parameter sets the background color and has a default value of #4040C0, a deep blue. The value of the `shadowcolor` parameter sets the color of the drop shadow that underlies the text. The default is #000000, black. Both color-setting parameters work the same as `textcolor`.

You have to use hexadecimal color values in Quoter. You can't use named colors (like turquoise, sienna, and orchid). If you try, you won't get the colors you're looking for, that's for sure.

Speaking of drop shadows, the shadowoffset parameter determines how far away the shadow falls from the text. By default, this distance is two pixels. The single number in this parameter specifies distance both down and to the right. A setting of 0 means that no shadow is cast. The value of the shadowoffset parameter must always be 0 or a positive number, by the way, so unless you're fond of unreadable text and bizarre visual effects, don't try to use a negative number.

Although larger numbers increase the feeling of depth, you probably want to keep this value relatively small — say, 4 or lower — unless you're using very large fonts.

The following three parameters adjust spacing:

- hspacing: This parameter sets the space between characters. Its default value is 1.0. Yes, that's right, people — this one can take a fractional value for fine control. You can set it at 1.1, 1.2, 1.3, or even something wild like 0.9! Pretty exciting, isn't it?

- internalmargin: The value of this parameter sets the distance, in pixels, between the quotation and the edges of the box. By default, it's 10 pixels.

- vspacing: This parameter sets the amount of space between two sentences. Like hspacing, it also has a default value of 1.0 and takes fractional values.

The following two parameters control how fast the whole thing works:

- chardelay: This parameter takes care of how much time the applet spends between the drawing of one text character and the next one. The value is the number of milliseconds (thousandths of a second), and the default is 50.

- timedelay: This parameter controls the amount of time between quotations. It's also set to 50 milliseconds by default, but it's a little more complicated than that. After all, 50 thousandths of a second wouldn't even give Evelyn Wood a chance to read a sentence. The actual calculation goes like this: [(timedelay * character count) + 5,000 milliseconds. So what you get with the default, assuming that you've got a quotation with 80 characters in it, is [(50 * 80) + 5,000] or [4,000 + 5,000] for a total of 9,000 milliseconds, which is — ta da! — nine seconds.

Because the character count is involved in setting the delay between quotations, a longer quotation means a slightly greater delay.

You can make the next quotation appear without delay — even before the current one finishes being drawn — by clicking the applet. It's a good idea to mention this fact to your visitors on the page that contains the applet.

There is one odd little parameter that you don't need to use if you're putting the applet up on the World Wide Web, but we figure that we better mention it just in case. It's intranet, and it's for — you guessed it again — operating the applet on an intranet with no connection to the Internet. You set the value of the parameter to true in that case. The default value, of course, is false.

Finally, we come to the last of the parameters. (Sad, isn't it? We'll miss these guys.) The quotefile parameter specifies the text file from which the quotations are loaded. If you're going to use quotes.txt as the filename, you don't need this parameter at all. So why bother with it? Why not just use the default text file name? Paul Lutus, the author of this applet, has a marvelous suggestion for taking advantage of this capability.

You can place the applet on different pages throughout your Web site. For each different one, you create a different quotation file. Then you specify which file to use for each page by setting this parameter on each one, giving your visitors some variety — and a very good reason to spend time roaming all around your Web site.

Here's all the code in one great big pile of PARAMs:

```
<APPLET code=quoter.class name=quoter width=500 height=300>
<PARAM name="fontname" value="Helvetica">
<PARAM name="fontsize" value="18">
<PARAM name="fontstyle" value="italic">
<PARAM name="textcolor" value="#FF0000">
<PARAM name="bgcolor" value="#FFFFFF">
<PARAM name="shadowcolor" value="#000000">
<PARAM name="shadowoffset" value="3">
<PARAM name="vspacing" value="1.5">
<PARAM name="hspacing" value="1.3">
<PARAM name="internalmargin" value="15">
<PARAM name="chardelay" value="45">
<PARAM name="timedelay" value="40">
<PARAM name="intranet" value="true">
<PARAM name="quotefile" value="alternate01.txt">
</APPLET>
```

Okay, now we come to the text file itself. If you take a look at quotes.txt, you can see how simple it is. Here's the first line, for example:

```
It is appallingly obvious that our technology exceeds our
            humanity.\n\n>-- Albert Einstein
```

The first part of the code is, of course, the sentence that's being quoted. If you've ever done any programming, you'll recognize the next bit — \n\n — as a pair of *newlines*. Newlines are line feeds — that is, they move the next bit of text down one line each. The example includes two of them because that's how the author felt like setting up the text display, but you can use one of them or three — or however many you like.

You can apply a newline in the middle of a quotation if you want to force a line break at a particular point.

The > is a command character — if it's the first character following a newline, that is. Otherwise, it's just a greater-than sign. It means to place the following text at the right margin. You might notice that the author's names in the quotations are right aligned; this is why they show up that way. If you want a line to start at the left margin, you use < instead. If you want to center it, you use ^.

After you apply a command character (>, <, or ^), its effect applies to all lines after that. In other words, if you right-align a new line, all the lines that come after it are right-aligned, too, unless you subsequently use a different command character. The hyphens in the quotation are just plain old hyphens. If you run the applet and look at the quotations, you can see that the ones that come with Quoter always have two hyphens before the name of the quotation's author.

Your quotations may not fit within the applet if you aren't careful with the length of the quotations and the combination of parameters, such as margins, the size of the box, and the size of the fonts. If you customize these items, make sure that you run the applet and click through all the quotations before going public.

Because Quoter simply displays text from a file that you create, you don't actually have to use it for quotations. You can also use it for displaying one-liner jokes, for example. You can put anything that you want in the box, as long as it can fit.

Setting Up EasyPostcard on Your Site

We all send cards to other people — birthday cards, Christmas cards, Hug An Australian Day cards, or whatever. But instead of trotting down to the local Hallmark store or drugstore, we can now send them from different Web sites. Why not make your site one of them?

EasyPostcard (at www.easypostcard.com, of course) is a free service that lets you set up a page where visitors can design their own e-postcards. They can choose different images, backgrounds, and songs and then type a personal message. When they're done, EasyPostcard sends them an e-mail message telling them where to view the card. The recipients click the link in the message, and their Web browsers load the page that holds the card.

To set up EasyPostcard's service on your site, follow these steps:

1. Go to www.javasky.com/postcardcenter/download.html.

2. **Enter your name and e-mail address in the appropriate text boxes (and, optionally, you can also enter your city and country names).**

3. **Click the Process Now button.**

4. **On the resulting page, click the Download EasyPostcard button.**

5. **Unzip the** `easypostcard.zip` **file.**

6. **Edit the** `postcard.html` **file by replacing all references to** `YourSite.com` **with the actual address of your Web site's postcard files and upload it to your site.**

7. **Go to** `http://javasky.com/postcardcenter/registration.html` **and register your postcard site by entering its URL and clicking the Process Now button.**

   EasyPostcard sends you an e-mail message to remind you to register the site.

8. **Upload** `postcard.html` **(as an ASCII file) and** `pickup.gif` **(as a binary file) to your Web server.**

The finished Web page looks like the one shown in Figure 11-10

REMEMBER

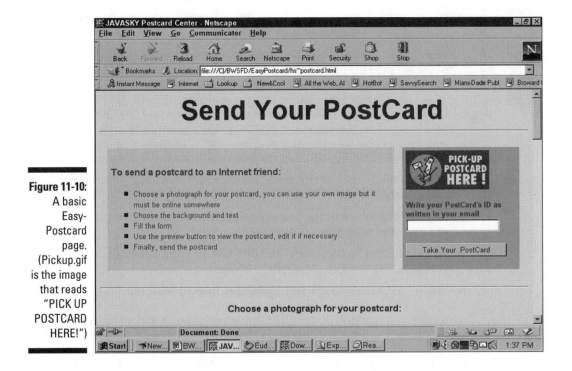

Figure 11-10:
A basic Easy-Postcard page. (Pickup.gif is the image that reads "PICK UP POSTCARD HERE!")

To modify your Web page so that it displays your own pictures or background images instead of the samples, you need to do a few more things, as the following steps describe:

1. **Add your own image files to the directory where you have the** `postcard.html` **file.**

   The images need to be small enough to fit in the cards. You have some latitude here, so feel free to experiment with size, but EasyPostcard recommends a size of 360x270 pixels. The sample images are 320x256 and 248x310. If you stay in that ballpark, you should do fine.

   Each image also requires a smaller version for use as a sample image. These aren't true thumbnail images because the small version isn't linked directly to the large version, but the basic intent is similar — to allow visitors to get an idea of what the full-sized images look like without having to wait for them to download or to have them take up the whole screen. (See Chapter 2 for information on thumbnail images.) The recommended size is 100x75 pixels.

   Any graphics program provides you with the capability to resize an image. After you resize the image, simply save it under a new filename to create a thumbnail image of the original.

2. **Replace the** `IMG SRC` **code in the form in** `postcard.html` **with the URLs of your own thumbnail images.**

   The image files used to make your postcards are on your server, but the postcards are actually created on EasyPostcard's server. That means that you must use a full URL, such as `http://www.mycardsite.com/myimage.jpg`. *Relative* URLs, such as `myimage.jpg` or `graphics/myimage.jpg`, don't work here because you can only use them to find files located on the same server. If you don't use the full URL, there's no way for EasyPostcard to find your images. If the images aren't yet on your site, put in the URL that they will have when you do upload them.

3. **Replace the values of the card_number radio buttons with the full URLs of the full-sized images.**

4. **Replace the value of the background radio buttons with the full URLs of your own background images.**

5. **To change the music, insert the full URL to your MIDI files as the values of the** `OPTION` **elements.**

6. **Upload all your images and MIDI files to your Web site.**

You now have a working postcard shop on your site. When visitors go to your postcard page, they see the thumbnail images and can select the ones they want to use for the main image and the background on the postcard they create. Likewise, they can choose among the MIDI files you uploaded to supply background music for the postcard.

Now that the postcard shop is up and running, you will probably want to modify its appearance to make it blend with the rest of your site. As long as you don't change the FORM element's action attribute or the name attribute of any of the elements within the form, you should be safe in making other changes. If you do change either of those, you'll partially or completely disable the postcard shop. The action attribute points to the remotely hosted CGI script that makes the shop work, and that script is programmed to recognize the name attributes that come in the sample postcard shop. For example, if you changed the name attribute of the radio button that controls text color so that its value was anything other than textcolor, the CGI script wouldn't know how to process that choice.

Always keep a backup copy of any important file when making changes to it.

Goofing Off with Games

Tracking down online games was grueling work. We had to keep flogging ourselves to get on with it. But we love our readers, and we kept at it. Only for you guys. Really.

Downloading free games from Loonyverse

Connie King's Loonyverse (at www.loonyverse.com) is a refreshing Web site. If you're really, really tired of seeing This site best viewed with Internet Explorer or This site best viewed with Netscape everywhere on the Web, you'll get a kick out of her saying: Best viewed at my house on my monitor.

Loonyverse has lots of interesting stuff, but because this section is about games, we'll stick to that for now. Loonyverse currently provides 18 different games that you can add to your own site for free. To get directly to the Loonyverse games page (see Figure 11-11), go to http://loonyverse.50megs.com/games.html or, if you're already at the site, just click the Games link on the main page.

To play a game, click any of the graphical links. To download a game, scroll down to the text links and click the name of the game that you want to download. Each game comes with full instructions on how to add it to your Web site.

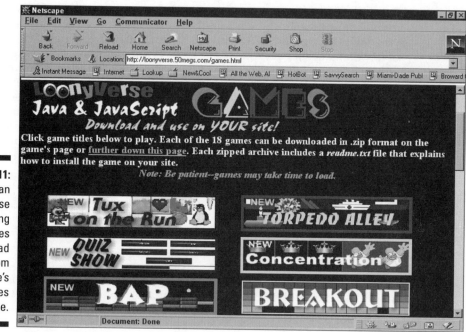

Figure 11-11:
You can choose among 18 games to download from Loonyverse's Games page.

Playing games Jagex style

Jagex (at www.jagex.com) is a software firm that makes some wonderful games. They're not only graphically attractive, but they're also really fun to play. In fact, these games are totally addictive. Figure 11-12 shows Meltdown, an arcade game by Andrew and Ian Gower. Pop in to www.jagex.com/service.html and try Meltdown and other games.

These games aren't free or even cheap. If you're running a commercial site, however, they're well worth the cost. How much do these games set you back? Well, you can license Meltdown for your Web site for only £499. (That's in *pounds*, by the way, not dollars.) That's $743.26 at today's exchange rates. The other games go for £899, or $1,339.06. These are nonexclusive licenses. If you want the company to design a custom game for your Web site, Jagex is glad to do it for you, but it costs a bit more — probably about £1,999 to £4,999. (That's $2,977.51 to $7,446.01 in colonial money.)

Wonder how we did those conversions so quickly? Check out Chapter 14 for information about how to add currency conversion to your site.

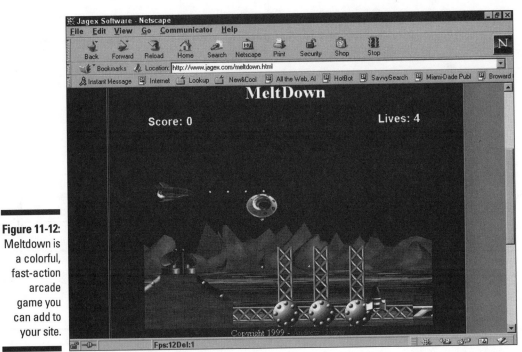

Figure 11-12:
Meltdown is
a colorful,
fast-action
arcade
game you
can add to
your site.

Meltdown by www.jagex.com

Online Sources

Table 11-1 lists some places on the World Wide Web where you can find more resources like the ones that we cover in this chapter.

If you sign up with a service that supplies jokes or quotations, you have no control over the content of the material. Make sure that you check out samples from the content provider before you commit, because some of the topics may not fit your site's theme.

Table 11-1	Online Resources
Web Site Name	**Web Address**
Dropcard	www.dropcard.com
HyperGames	www.hypergames.net
Jokes2U.com	www.jokes2u.com/webmasters.htm

(continued)

Table 11-1 *(continued)*

Web Site Name	Web Address
My Postcards	http://mypostcards.com
On Your Site Jokes	http://onyoursite.com/jokes
On Your Site Quotables	http://onyoursite.com/quotes
Radiocards	www.radiocards.net/yourradio/index.html
Today in History	www.io.com/~rga/scripts/cgitoday.html
WebWorld's Postcards	http://misc.webworld.nu/postcard

Chapter 12

Using Content Providers

In This Chapter

▶ Posting news feeds

▶ Adding weather information

▶ Carrying comic strips on your site

▶ Using public-domain text

*O*ne thing keeps people coming back to a Web site: fresh content. No matter how great your site is, no matter how wonderful your prose and how fabulous your graphics, very few people are going to visit it over and over again just to see what they've already seen.

If your Web site provides a repeatable service, like automated translations or HTML validation, you can get away with leaving your site alone. For the vast majority of sites, though, if you can't give your visitors new material from time to time, you lose 'em.

It's a treadmill that you can never get off; you've got to keep updating your site's material or your site dies. All Webmasters want high-quality content for their Web sites, but it isn't always the easiest thing to keep on generating that content yourself. Fortunately, plenty of people crank out all sorts of stuff that you can use.

Whether you know it or not, you're already familiar with this sort of material. Your daily newspaper typically consists of a little bit of locally produced material and lots of items from content providers. The comics, most — if not all — of the columns, horoscopes, and many of the articles in the newspaper come from people who don't work for that paper. The folks who do this sort of thing for a living — these companies are known as *syndicates* — are latching onto the Web as the newest and best market for such canned content.

The prices for canned content range from absolutely free to somewhere between "Oh, no!" and "You've got to be kidding!" A large amount of the free material comes in the form of *marketing information.* (Translation: thinly disguised get-rich-quick schemes.) But after you cut through the dross, you can find plenty of high-quality, free material out there. So if you're running a small Web site, you don't need to break open your piggy bank to get the good stuff.

Adding News to Your Web Site

More and more these days, people turn to the Web for the latest news. It sure beats waiting for the 11 o'clock news on TV to keep you up on the day's events. Unless you want your visitors surfing other sites to get their news, you need to add it to your own Web site. But you don't need to connect with a bunch of CNN reporters or spend all your time collating tons of reports from distant parts of the world to provide your visitors with the latest new breaks. Just plug in some of the ready-to-use news services that we describe in the following sections.

Taking advantage of 7am News

The first news-content provider that we ever ran across was 7am News (www.7am.com) — and as far as we're concerned, it's still the best service of its kind. The basic service is, and always has been, free and is supported by advertising, but now the company's branching out into alternative approaches for a small fee. And we do mean small — as in around $50 a month for no advertising to a maximum of $95 a month for providing customized news solutions, which is more than likely to fit into just about any commercial budget.

The 7am News site offers two basic services: FreeWire (www.7am.com/wires) and News Ticker (www.7am.com/ticker). We cover FreeWire first.

FreeWire offers a fixed-format, magazine-style setup with a main story taking up the bulk of a Web page, while other stories are accessible through links along the side (see Figure 12-1).

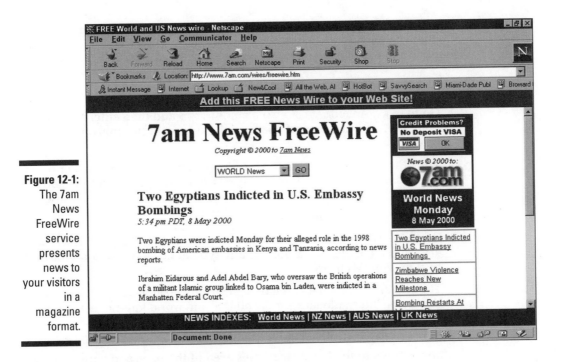

Figure 12-1:
The 7am
News
FreeWire
service
presents
news to
your visitors
in a
magazine
format.

To add the 7am News FreeWire service to your Web site, follow these steps:

1. **Go to** `www.7am.com/wires/apply.htm` **and then scroll down to the Essential Information area of the page.**

2. **Enter your name, the name and URL of your Web site, the type of content on your site, and your e-mail address in the appropriate text boxes.**

3. **Scroll down to the Customization Information area and enter a title for the news page in the appropriate text box.**

   You also have the option of specifying the background color, text color, link color, and visited link color of your news page in the appropriate text boxes. If you want to just go with the default colors, leave these blank.

4. **Click the Register button.**

The other basic news service that 7am News offers, News Ticker, is a Java applet that presents a series of scrolling headlines in a text box on your site. A visitor to your site clicks a headline that interests them and goes to a page displaying the full story. The stories come from various sources, so the page a visitor goes to may be located at any news site from CNN to the BBC.

7am News e-mails you a message with a link to a page containing the HTML code that you need to set up the news page on your site. Typically, it takes only about half an hour to get the e-mail message, but it may take up to 48 hours.

To add News Ticker to your pages, follow these steps:

1. **Go to** `www.7am.com/ticker/register.htm` **and then enter the URL of your site, your name, and your e-mail address in the appropriate text boxes.**

   The other information that the form requests, such as the number of visitors your site gets on a typical day or what you like or don't like about 7am News, is optional. All information is kept confidential by 7am News.

2. **Click the Submit button.**

3. **On the new page that appears, scroll down to the Channel Selections area and click the check box for any type of news that you want to host on your Web site.**

   The channels available at the time of writing include such choices as U.S. news, international sports, and U.S. and world Internet news. Click the Full Descriptions link at the top of the Channel Selections area for, well . . . full descriptions of the channels.

4. **Move down to the Local Headlines area of the page and enter a headline and URL for anything that you want to plug in the appropriate text boxes.**

   This is a free opportunity to add your own private advertising to the 7am News Ticker, so don't neglect it. You can add up to four separate Web pages here. Enter the headline that you want to appear first and the URL of the Web page you want to associate with that headline next. The ads will run in the ticker just like the ones that 7am News has, and your visitors won't be able to tell any difference. These ads will only show up on your Web page, though — they don't go out with the 7am News broadcast to their other member sites. That's why they're called local headlines.

5. **Scroll down to the How To Link area and select the radio button that best describes the way you want the headline link to work.**

   You can choose for the linked page to open in the current browser window, in a new window, or in a named frame.

6. **Scroll down to the Excluded Domains area and type the URLs of any domains you *don't* want to display a link from into the text boxes.**

   Say, for instance, that for some reason you don't want any headlines from CNN to show up on the 7am News Ticker on your page. Just enter `www.cnn.com` in one of the text boxes, and any input from that domain will be blocked from your site's display of 7am News.

7. **Click the Go button at the bottom of the page.**

8. **At the next page, copy the HTML code that appears there and paste it into your own Web page at the place where you want the 7am News Ticker to appear; then upload your page to your Web server.**

Getting to know Moreover.com

The news service that you can get for your site from Moreover.com consists of a series of links similar to those you get from 7am News, but Moreover.com uses a JavaScript-based interface instead of a Java applet. So, if you don't care for Java, here's another alternative for you — and the basic service is free. If you want something beyond the service's normal material, however, Moreover.com sets up a customized solution for you, but that solution costs a minimum of $1,500 a month.

But you don't really need to go for the custom job unless you have a really good reason to do so — and a hefty budget for your site. Moreover.com's normal, free news material offers far more than you (or any of your visitors) can read even if you spend all day at it. The service features more than 250 different news categories to choose from, including the following topics:

- ✔ Natural health
- ✔ MP3
- ✔ Personal finance
- ✔ Venture capital
- ✔ Foreign policy
- ✔ Genetics
- ✔ UK law
- ✔ Construction
- ✔ Firearms
- ✔ Travel
- ✔ Top Internet stories

And that's just a quick sampling of the service's news categories. Moreover.com offers an unbelievable amount of impressive stuff that you can tap. It's worth your while to take the time to browse through the whole list.

Adding Moreover.com's headlines to your Web site is about as simple as anything can get. Just follow these steps:

1. **Go to** www.moreover.com **and then click the** <u>Webmasters . . .</u> **link near the top of the page.**

    This opens the Webfeed Wizard, as shown in Figure 12-2.

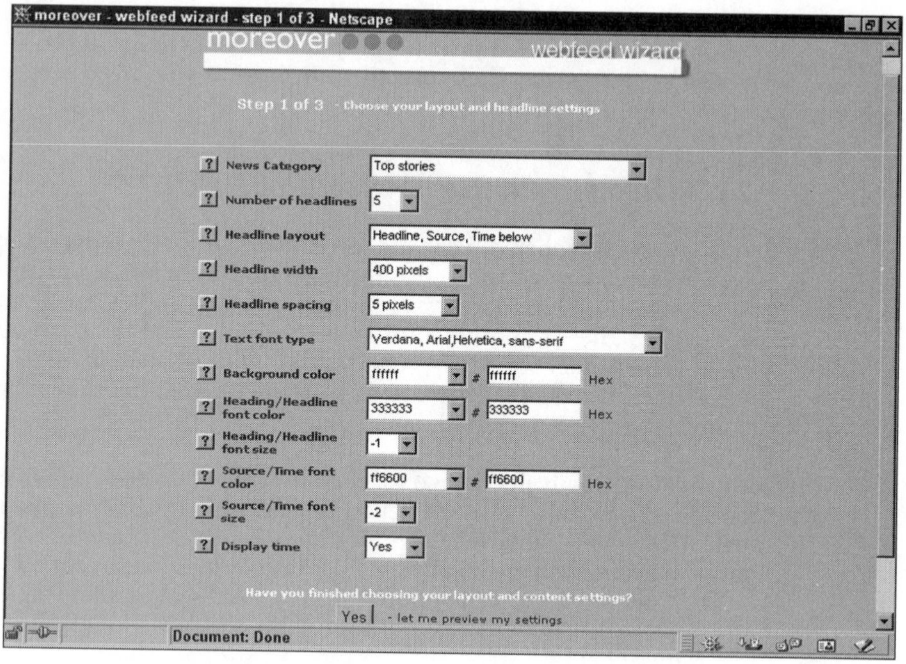

Figure 12-2:
Moreover.
com's
Webfeed
Wizard
enables you
to choose
the layout
and head-
line settings
for your
news feed.

Moreover.com uses JavaScript, and its wizard does, too. If you have dis-
abled JavaScript in your browser, the wizard can't work.

2. Choose a News Category from the first drop-down list.

The default choice is Top stories.

There's a button with a question mark on it to the left of each option.
Click these buttons for help with a particular option.

3. Select a number from the Number of Headlines drop-down list.

The default option is 5, but you can choose 1, 3, 5, 10, 15, or 20. The
number of headlines that you want to have on your page depends on
both your design intentions and the amount of room you have to spare.

The limits on the number of headlines you can place on your site can be
a bit annoying. If you want a large selection of headlines in a very small
space, check out 7am News' scrolling Java headlines in the preceding
section.

**4. Choose how you want the headlines to look by selecting an option
from the Headline Layout drop-down list.**

The default selection is to run the headline on the first line and the
source and time on another line below that. You can also choose to have
all three items on one line, but in our opinion, that layout doesn't look as
eye-catching as the default one does, and it tends to wrap around to a
second line anyway.

5. **Select a value from the Headline Width drop-down list.**

   Values range from 50 pixels to 400 pixels. Obviously, the smaller the area in which you put the headlines, the shorter you need to make them.

6. **Choose a value from the Headline Spacing drop-down list.**

   Headline spacing refers to the amount of vertical spacing between two different headlines. Values range from 5 to 30 pixels.

7. **Select a text style for the headlines from the Text Font Type drop-down list.**

8. **Pick a background color for your news feed from the Background Color drop-down list.**

   You can choose a named color from the drop-down list, or choose Custom and type the hexadecimal value in the accompanying text box.

9. **Set the color for the headline text by selecting one from the Heading/Headline Font Color drop-down list.**

   The process for selecting a color for the headline font is the same as for setting the background color.

10. **Pick a size for the headline fonts from the Heading/Headline Font Size drop-down list.**

    The options are –1, –2, +1, +2, or +3.

11. **Set the font color and font size for the source/time listing by selecting a color from the Source/Time Font Color drop-down list and a value from the Source/Time Font Size drop-down list.**

    These processes are the same as those for choosing the headline's font color and size, as we describe in Steps 9 and 10

12. **If you don't want to show the publication time of the item, select No from the Display Time drop-down list.**

    If you do want the time to show, just leave it at the default setting, which is — you guessed it — Yes.

13. **To move to the next stage of the wizard, click the Yes button at the bottom of the page.**

    After a few moments, the results of your choices appear on a preview page.

14. **If you don't like it and want to change something, click the No button to go back to the previous page and make your changes; if you like what you see, click the Yes button to go to the last stage of the wizard.**

15. **On the final page of the wizard, enter your e-mail address in the appropriate text box so that Moreover.com can send the code for the news feed to you after you finish.**

    Moreover.com keeps this address confidential.

16. **Type the URL of the page you want to put the code into.**

17. **If you want to receive updates from Moreover.com, leave the Yes radio button selected; otherwise, click the No radio button.**

18. **If you have any last-minute changes in mind, click the No button at the bottom of the page to return to the news-feed options and make your changes; if you're ready to go, click the Yes button instead.**

After you receive the e-mail from Moreover.com containing the code for your news feed, copy and paste the code into your Web page and upload it to your Web server. You're off and running!

You can set up multiple news feeds for your Web site. Run the wizard for each news category that you want to add or copy the HTML code from your first news category, paste it back in below the original on the same page, and alter the feed URL to match the desired category. You can find the feed URLs at w.moreover.com/categories/category_list.html (and no, that lone *w* at the beginning of the URL isn't a typo).

Adding Weather Forecasts to Your Site

We figure that most of the people on the Net spend almost all their free time indoors, but amazingly, they still maintain a fascination with what's happening outside. Okay, we admit that we have to drive through it sometimes, and the guys from marketing often take their laptops and cell phones to the beach to "work." But all you really need to know is whether a thunderstorm's coming your way, right? And if that bright flash and the sudden puff of smoke from your modem doesn't tell you that, what can? Still, you just can't please some folks, and if your visitors want to check out the latest weather conditions and forecasts, who are we to stand in the way?

Using Weather Underground

Weather Underground (www.wunderground.com) has lots of ways for you to add current weather information to your own Web site. They have both freebies and, uh — costies? For some reasonably priced customized weather options for your site, you can go to Weather Underground's commercial page at www.wunderground.com/autobrandinfo. To take advantage of its freebies, follow these steps:

1. **Go to** www.wunderground.com **to access the Weather Underground site and then type your location in the text box at the top of the page, underneath where it reads Find the Weather for any City, State, or Zip code, or Country.**

   Unless you enter a city name or a ZIP code, you don't get the option to add weather data to your page.

2. **Click the Fast Forecast button to get the forecast for the area you chose.**

3. **After the forecast page appears, scroll down until you see the box that reads <u>Add this sticker to your home page!</u> and click that link.**

   You now see a large selection of different weather graphics, like the ones shown in Figure 12-3.

4. **Click the graphic that you like best.**

   You now go to a page that shows that graphic and, beneath it, the HTML code you need to put it on your Web site.

5. **Copy the HTML code from the page and paste it into your own Web page; then upload it to your Web server.**

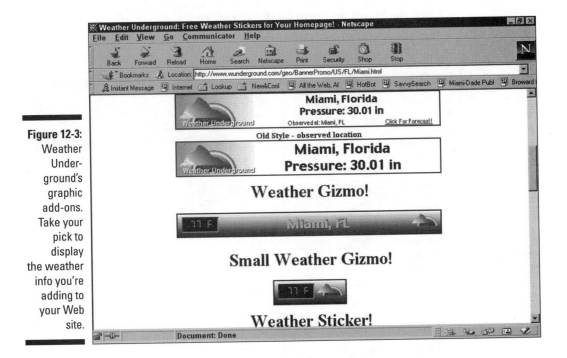

Figure 12-3: Weather Underground's graphic add-ons. Take your pick to display the weather info you're adding to your Web site.

Using Weather.com

Weather.com (at www.weather.com, of course) is the online version of The Weather Channel. If you're not familiar with that channel, you obviously don't get cable TV. It offers what they call an affiliates program, although it doesn't directly generate any income for you. (See Chapter 15 for information on affiliates programs.) The program does, however, offer some really nice weather graphics that you can put on your Web site, including radar and satellite maps, as shown in Figure 12-4.

To add all this wonderful weather wizardry to your site, follow these steps:

1. **Go to the Weather On Your Site page at** http://oap.weather.com/oap.

2. **Scroll down the page and click Weather Viewer.**

   You can click Weather Magnet or Weather Logo as well, but these don't provide the same graphical impact.

3. **On the Legal Agreement page, click the Accept radio button and then click the Continue button.**

4. **Click the Sign Up button on the Login page.**

   This takes you to the New User Registration page.

Figure 12-4: The Weather Channel's maps on its Web site, Weather. com.

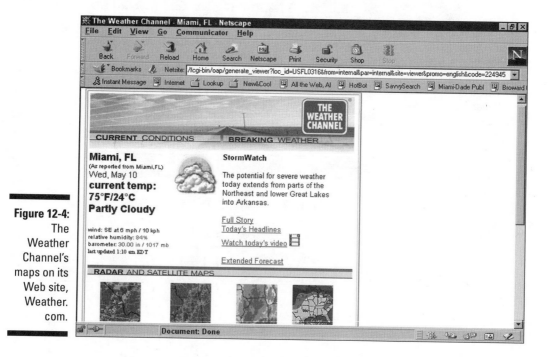

5. **Enter all the information, such as name and address, that the site requires in the appropriate text boxes.**

6. **Deselect the check box next to any statement that you don't agree with.**

   In particular, you may want to deselect the check box that says The Weather Channel Can Provide Your Information to Its "Select Partners," because agreeing to this one means that you're giving up your privacy and they can share your name, address, and other information you provide with other companies.

7. **Click the Continue button.**

   The next page displays the information that you entered on the previous pages.

8. **Click the Continue button to proceed.**

9. **Select the region that you want your site to cover (weather for Europe, the Caribbean, and so on) from the list box and click the Select Region button.**

10. **Choose the country that you want from the list box and then click the Select Country button.**

    If you choose the United States as the country, you must next select a state.

11. **Pick the state that you want from the list box and then click the Select State button.**

12. **Choose the desired city from the list box and click the Select City button.**

13. **Enter the URL of your weather page in the appropriate text box and select a site category, such as Entertainment or Personal Website, from the drop-down list.**

    You can optionally enter the name of your company, too.

14. **Click the Continue button.**

15. **Copy the HTML code from the next page that appears and paste it into the source code for your Web page.**

You can copy and paste two different versions of HTML code to your site. The first one creates a simple search text box in which visitors can enter their city or ZIP code to get weather information for their locations. It also includes a text link underneath the search text box that you can click to see all the glitzy stuff you just signed up for. All in all, this version's rather plain-looking and not entirely satisfactory.

The second version creates a framed page that shows your visitors the nice weather graphics right off the bat and enables you to add an advertisement of your own, too.

Placing Cartoons on Your Web Site

The Internet has shaken up a lot of different industries, especially the ones that consist of nothing but middlemen. (Sorry, make that middlepersons. Middlepeople? Whatever.) Anyway, the syndicates that formerly wielded total control over whether the work of cartoonists ever saw publication don't enjoy that kind of hold any more. Nowadays, artists can go right onto the Net with their cartoons, and everyone who likes their work can keep on seeing it as long as their mouse buttons and Web connections hold out.

Not In My Backyard

Dale Taylor is one of the artists who's chosen to forsake the syndicated route, and his work is just as good as the strips you see in your local newspaper. You can find his strip "Not In My Backyard" at www.notinmybackyard.com on the Web. It's a Monday-through-Friday multipanel strip that tells the story of a group of pets and wild animals that live together in the backyard. (See Figure 12-5 for a typical comic strip.) Even better than just reading the strip, however, is the fact that you can add it to your own Web site for free.

Figure 12-5:
A typical "Not In My Backyard" comic strip that you can host on your own Web site for free.

@ Dale Taylor

To set things up so that this comic strip appears automatically on your Web site, go to www.notinmybackyard.com/run-this-strip and copy the HTML code that you find there. Then paste the code into your own Web page. That's all you need to do to enjoy "Not In My Backyard" on your own site. Whenever the strip changes on its home site, it changes on yours, too, so the current strip is always showing on your Web site.

Toy Trunk Railroad

"Toy Trunk Railroad" (www.toytrunkrailroad.com) is about the adventures of some railroad people. Well, sort of. The strip blends reality and unreality in a charming way. The railroad itself is a scale model set up on a tabletop, and some of the characters live in the house that holds the model railroad. But some of the other characters live in the world of the railroad itself, including the engineer and the railway's founder. (Well, actually, the founder passed away a long time ago, but his spirit inhabits his statue and is always good for a wry crack or two.) Figure 12-6 shows a typical "Toy Trunk Railroad" comic strip.

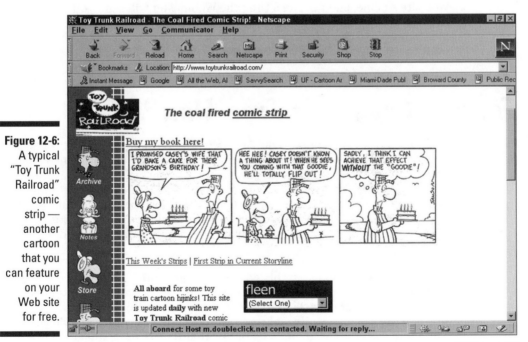

Figure 12-6: A typical "Toy Trunk Railroad" comic strip — another cartoon that you can feature on your Web site for free.

@ Erik Sansom 2000

"Toy Trunk Railroad" is a black-and-white multicolumn comic written and drawn by Erik Sansom. If you love the old-style trains, you'll really enjoy this strip. Even if you're not into coal-fired trains, you'll find yourself laughing out loud. New strips come out Monday through Friday — Saturday and Sunday are taken up with "classic strips" from the past. To add the strip to your site (it's free, so don't worry about the cost), go to `www.toytrunkrailroad.com/update.asp` and copy and paste the HTML code. The current strip will always update automatically on your page.

The Deep End

"The Deep End" is a more-or-less daily one-panel cartoon that you can view at `www.deep-end.com`. As you may guess from the name, the humor is much like that of Gary Larson's "The Far Side." In one cartoon, for example, a fish mops the bottom of his aquarium next to a sign that reads "Caution — Dry Floor."

To get this free strip for your site, check out the instructions for signing up at `www.deep-end.com/freetoon.htm`. You'll need to provide your name, your Web site's name, and the site's URL; the Webmaster will send you back the HTML code to enable you to insert the cartoon on your page. Both color and black-and-white versions exist, so you can choose how much bandwidth you want to eat up. Like the others, it'll update itself automatically.

Finding Copyright-Free Material

In addition to the people who deliberately provide material for Web sites, you can tap a mine of content from folks who surrender their copyrights by deliberately placing their work in the public domain. You can also find an abundance of material that was once copyrighted but has fallen into the public domain because of its age. The fact that it's old, however, doesn't mean that it isn't of interest to modern audiences. People enjoy authors such as Beatrix Potter and characters such as Dracula just as much today as they did years ago.

The particular advantage to this content is that, unlike syndicated content, it isn't being sent out to a million other Web sites at the same time it's being sent to you. The drawback, however, is that you have to track it down yourself, and the authors rarely make any kind of commitment to provide you with more material (assuming, of course, that they're even still alive). We provide a couple sources for you in the following sections to get you on the right track, but what you really have to do to keep this approach going is to work the search engines on a regular basis. Search for phrases like `"public domain"`, `"no copyright"`, or `"copyright free"`. Sift through the results to find what you can use on your site.

The other Krishnamurti

Need some quotations for your site? Here's one:

"Stop thinking and start living."

You can find plenty more where that one came from, and they're copyright-free. U.G. Krishnamurti (`www.ugkrishnamurti.org`) is a controversial philosopher whose works are available to you for free. As the man states in his remarkably unusual copyright notice on his Web site at `www.ugkrishnamurti.org/ug/copyright/index.html`, "My teaching, if that is the word you want to use, has no copyright. You are free to reproduce, distribute, interpret, misinterpret, distort, garble, do what you like, even claim authorship, without my consent or the permission of anybody."

Many people have written books and articles about U.G. Krishnamurti. Their stuff is usually covered by their own copyrights, so don't go grabbing material from his biographers (unless you really like running into legal trouble). And you must be especially careful not to confuse his work with that of J. Krishnamurti, another person who was in the same line of work. Just make sure that it's U.G., not J., and you'll be all right.

The following list provides a bunch of quotations from "the unguru" that you can use to grace your Web pages. We're still trying to figure most of 'em out, but a spiritual friend of ours assures us that they're quite profound.

- ✔ "The questioner is nothing but the answers."
- ✔ "You have to touch life at a point where nobody has touched it before. Nobody can teach you that."
- ✔ "As long as you are doing something to be selfless, you will be a self-centered individual."
- ✔ "Thought is something dead and can never touch anything living. It cannot capture life, contain it, and give expression to it. The moment it tries to touch life it is destroyed by the quality of life."
- ✔ "Consciousness is so pure that whatever you are doing in the direction of purifying that consciousness is adding impurity to it."

Project Gutenberg

One of the largest sources of public domain texts is Project Gutenberg (www.promo.net/pg/). You can grab — and use — nearly everything on this Web site. (You do run into a few rare exceptions, but the site clearly notes these.)

The great thing about Project Gutenberg's selections is that you can get your hands on such a wide variety of really great material. Want to put *Captain Blood*, the classic pirate tale by Rafael Sabatini, on your Web site? Go right ahead and do so. Do all six volumes of Gibbons' *History of the Decline and Fall of the Roman Empire* impress you? They're yours. Like the suspense movie *The Thirty-Nine Steps?* Try the book by John Buchan. Got a kids' site? How about adding *The Great Big Treasury of Beatrix Potter?* The following list gives you a quick sampling of some of the other material you can get from this great site:

- George Eliot's *Middlemarch*
- Helen Keller's *The Story of My Life*
- Machiavelli's *The Prince*
- Howard Pyle's *Adventures of Robin Hood*
- Bram Stoker's *Dracula*
- Henry David Thoreau's *Walden*
- Tolstoy's *Anna Karenina*
- Lew Wallace's *Ben-Hur*
- H.G. Wells' *War of the Worlds*

You can download the files in either plain text or zip format.

The materials Project Gutenberg has are public domain under U.S. law. If you live in another country, or if the server that houses your site is in another country, check with a lawyer before you post any of this. International copyright law is a very tricky area. As a matter of fact, you should probably double-check the copyright status even if you're under U.S. law, just to play it safe. If you don't want to use a lawyer and don't mind a lot of detail work, you can do it yourself. See "How to Investigate the Copyright Status of a Work" at www.loc.gov/copyright/circs/circ22.html.

Online Sources

Table 12-1 lists some places on the World Wide Web where you can find more information on the topics that we cover in this chapter.

Table 12-1	Online Resources
Web Site Name	*Web Address*
AccuWeather	www.accuweather.com
Article Resource Association	www.aracopy.com
ComicExchange	www.comicexchange.com
dotmusic Webmaster Zone	www.dotmusic.com/community/webmasters
EzineArticles.com	www.ezinearticles.com
Ezine News Wire	www.ezinenewswire.com
Gibbleguts.com	www.gibbleguts.com
News Harvester	www.webreference.com/headlines/nh
NewsHub	www.newshub.com/affiliates/g.cgi
News Index	www.newsindex.com
Pipeline News	www.aphrodigitaliac.com/pipeline
selfPage.com	www.selfpage.com/addtick1.html
The Naked Word	www.crosswinds.net/~freee-books/nakedword
The Weather Guys	weatherguys.com
Weather24	www.weather24.com
U.G. Krishnamurti	www.well.com/user/jct

Part IV
Raking in the Bucks

The 5th Wave   By Rich Tennant

"You know, it dawned on me last night why we aren't getting any hits on our Web site."

In this part . . .

In this part, we take a look at making money from your site. Chapter 13 explodes the myths about Internet income and shows you how to really make a profit. Chapter 14 tells you how to get set up with a credit-card merchant account. And Chapter 15 shows how to work both ends of the affiliates game.

Chapter 13

Stalking the Wild Dollar

In This Chapter

▶ Finding your niche

▶ Delivering the goods

▶ Designing for orders

More pure bull hockey's floating around about Internet commerce than about practically any other topic in the world. If you haven't found thousands of e-commerce Web sites promising you the moon — and a moon made of gold and platinum at that — you aren't looking.

According to these self-proclaimed gurus of e-commerce, all you need to do is put up a Web page — not even a site, just a page — and the money comes rolling in. You can vacation in Acapulco this weekend and sun yourself on the Riviera by Monday. The secret to this success? Well, of course, they can't just *tell* you what it is. That kind of information is worth some real money, you know.

This "get-rich-quick-over-the-Internet" scheme reminds us of an ad that used to run in the back of cheap magazines many, many years ago. For 25 cents, the ad promised, you could discover how to make a fortune fast. After you sent in your quarter, you got back a pamphlet that, boiled down to its basics, told you to put an ad in a magazine asking people to send you a quarter. Today's get-rich-quick schemes are no more solid than that one, even if they are draped in the latest finery of high technology.

So is there any truth at all to the glowing promise of Internet commerce? Yes, there is. The Internet represents the greatest market that's ever existed, and the opportunity is very real. You *can* make a fortune in e-commerce, just as you can make a fortune in any other kind of commerce. But success takes a combination of brains, toughness, marketing savvy, luck, and — most of all — a determination to succeed. In this chapter, we show you how to be a real Internet marketer.

Learning the Real Secret to Internet Success

Are you ready for the real "secret of success" in any business? Here it is:

Put the right product or service in front of the right audience at the right time for the right price.

There ya go. That's all you need to do to succeed. Well, okay, implementing this advice isn't always all that easy. And when it comes to e-commerce, there are some special considerations.

Developing the attitude

If you go into Internet commerce figuring that you don't need to do any real work — that it's just something that you can play with between football games or pay attention to if you happen to feel like it — you're better off going fishing. At least that way, you may end up with food on your table.

To win in any kind of business, you need a whole different kind of attitude than you need to hold down a job. Let's face it, the whole point of most jobs is merely to keep a paycheck coming in. Most people work in jobs they don't care about — even jobs that they hate. They stick with the job solely because they have bills to pay. (Honestly, would you show up for work if you won the lottery? No? Neither would most people.)

If you run your own business, though, work's different. If you're sick and tired of rush hour, wearing suits and ties or high heels, and having bosses stand over your shoulder demanding that you work harder than they do, the Internet may be your ticket to financial independence. But you must pay a certain price. To run your own business, you must work harder than you ever did before. And you need to take a good, hard look at who you really are.

Notice that we're not saying "what you really want" but "who you really are." There's a good reason for that. If you're going to win in business, you win not because you're doing something, but because you're being yourself. In our case, if we won the lottery, we'd take a few days off to meet with our attorneys and accountants and get everything nicely in order, but we'd go back to work as soon as possible. We can't help it, because we're book people. Winning enough money to afford even more books can't change that fact.

What do you love most in the world? Whatever's your true passion is also your natural business. If you do anything else with your life, you can't give it the same kind of energy. That's plain old human nature. Who can give 100 percent all the time if they don't care about the outcome? If you're stuck in a job at a desk in a cubicle and the company you work for experiences a crisis, what you do usually doesn't matter. The situation isn't your doing, and you're not in charge anyway. Even if you do manage, by superhuman effort, to overcome the situation and save the day, you know you probably won't even get a raise out of it. After all, you're just doing your duty.

If you want to make a break from the old working world, you must make a clean break from the employee attitude, too. An Internet business is different — it's yours. It's a part of you, and if you listen to your inner voice, it's a natural extension of your own self. It's not what you do — it's who you are.

Focusing on your line

Many people believe that you can sell anything on the Internet. After all, zillions and zillions of people are on it, so anything that you create is sure to appeal to someone. Well, that belief's more or less true, but it doesn't mean that you can make money from your creation.

If you're serious about making money, you must remember the key factor in Web site appeal: focus, focus, focus. If you run your site as a hobby or a public service, you can afford to drift a bit, but if you depend on it for your living, you must stay fully on target. Any drift off the mark costs you money.

What we're talking about here is *specialization*. When it comes to general merchandise, the Internet is pretty much already lost to you. Why? Because it's got JCPenney and Kmart and Sears and all those other well-established companies with very deep pockets. You're not going to put them out of business in a physical shopping mall, and you're not going to take them out on the Internet either. They already enjoy the kind of name recognition that takes decades to build. And they can spend more money on one ad than the average online business has in its annual budget.

Even if you do have the kind of bucks that going up against the big outfits like that takes, we advise you to put it into specialized stores. The future of e-commerce lies in smaller companies that can focus all their energies on a relatively small market. Here's where the size of the Internet really comes into play for you — a "relatively small market" on the Internet is much larger than you can find even in a large city.

Indianapolis, the capital of Indiana, for example, is the 12th-largest city in America. In round numbers, more than 800,000 people live in the city and about another 700,000 dwell in the greater Indianapolis area. Some people we know run a go-kart supply shop near Indianapolis. In their local area, they can possibly draw on an absolute total of 1,500,000 people as customers. Yet about 100,000 go-karters come to visit their business every year. That's not because one out of every 15 people in Indianapolis race go-karts, either. They attract such a large customer base because of their Web site (at `www.kartshop.com`), which caters to the entire go-kart community (see Figure 13-1). Anyone with an interest in kart racing can visit the shop on the Web and find what they need, regardless of where they live or where the shop is located.

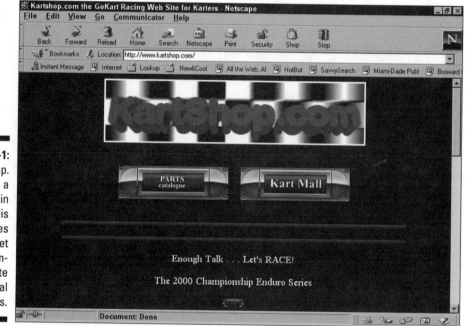

Figure 13-1: KartShop.com is a shop in Indianapolis that uses the Internet to accommodate nonlocal customers.

Reaching customers all over the globe is the Internet's greatest strength. Like the telephone and air travel before it, the Net is making the world — especially the world of commerce — much smaller than it was even ten years ago. By targeting a particular submarket, you can tightly focus your business efforts and still reach more people than you ever could reach by running a local business. And a functional Web site is much cheaper than even a small physical store. You can indeed start successful businesses on a shoestring if you use the Net.

Even if you do need some kind of physical facilities for your operation, such as storage space for your products, you don't need to concern yourself with its appearance and attractiveness. For most online businesses, renting a small warehouse space does just as well as a fancy, glitzy store in a major shopping mall. In many cases, you can just start with a spare room in your own house. If you end up needing more room to handle all the merchandise that people are ordering . . . well, we should all have such problems, right?

Getting supplies flowing

Okay, so now you know what your online business is all about. If you choose wisely, you probably already know plenty about the field. You know all the major suppliers, your competition, and all sorts of other little things that outsiders know nothing about. You know what's been done, what works and what doesn't, and how your potential customers feel about it all.

Depending on your field, you need to either create your product or line up some good, low-cost sources of supply. If you create your own product or market your own service, you're already there. If you rely on outsiders, though, you must do some research. Even if you already have a supplier in mind, you'll probably be able to find a better deal or get more or better services if you ask around.

Track down everyone who makes what you want to sell. Use search engines to find their Web sites and print them out. Make folders for each one (the manila kind, not the hard-drive kind) and arrange the hard copies neatly so that you can refer to them at a moment's notice.

If a site you're researching offers a <u>Contacts</u> link, follow it to see whether its information is useful to you. Different companies provide different degrees of contact data. Some of them have confusing and relatively worthless listings or nothing significant at all. Others provide fully detailed breakdowns of their operations by department and by significant personnel, including everything from phone numbers to e-mail and snail-mail addresses, to descriptions of people's job functions. You're looking for the director of sales and marketing. In the unlikely event that one isn't listed, go for the shipping manager.

The <u>Contacts</u> link may say something different, such as <u>About Our Company</u> or <u>Regional Offices</u>. Be creative and explore the site exhaustively when you're looking for contact info.

If you can't find the information you're looking for on the company's Web site, you can turn to one of the many business phone-number databases on the Web. We list some for you in Table 13-1.

Table 13-1	Phone Number Sources
Web Site Name	*Web Address*
555-1212.com	www.555-1212.com
At Hand Network Yellow Pages	www.athand.com
AT&T AnyWho Info	www.tollfree.att.net/tf.html
BigBook	www.bigbook.com
BigYellow	www.bigyellow.com
InfoSpace Yellow Pages	www.infospace.com/info/index_ylw.htm
Switchboard	www.switchboard.com
Telephone Directories on the Web	www.teldir.com/eng
Yahoo! Yellow Pages	http://yp.yahoo.com

Try the AT&T AnyWho Info Web site that we list in Table 13-1 before you commit to spending money on long-distance calls. It's a source of toll-free business phone numbers. Even if the company you're looking at doesn't list a toll-free number on its own site, it may still have one that would show up in the AT&T listings.

After you get a phone number and/or e-mail address, check with the company to find out whether it uses drop shipping. (*Drop shipping* is an arrangement in which you gather the orders and submit them to the company; the company then sends the merchandise off to the customer with your return address on it. You, of course, must pay the company for the merchandise, but you pay them a wholesale rate and keep the rest for your profit.)

If the company doesn't drop-ship, find out the minimum order that you can place and what kind of discount you get for different sizes of orders, if any. In either case, make sure that you find out how long the company normally takes to fulfill your orders. You need to know this so you can specify how long you will take to deliver to your customers. (Now you know why so many order forms say something like "Takes 4 to 6 weeks for delivery.")

If you get stuck with delivering the product to your customers yourself, you need to establish a business account with at least one shipping company. Most companies use UPS for shipping merchandise, although offering more alternatives to your customers doesn't hurt. You can also use the U.S. Postal Service. Table 13-2 lists the URLs for some of the major shipping companies' Web sites.

Table 13-2	Major Shipping Companies
Web Site Name	*Web Address*
Airborne Express	`www.airborne.com`
DHL Worldwide Express	`www.dhl.com`
Federal Express	`www.fedex.com`
Purolator Courier Ltd.	`www.purolator.com`
United Parcel Service	`www.ups.com`
United States Postal Service	`http://new.usps.com`

Make sure that you find out from your shipping company if you can get discounts for volume shipping.

By the way, PackTrack.com offers a nice tool that you can add to your site to save you a lot of headaches. Everybody always wants to know "Where's my package?" The handy little gizmo shown in Figure 13-2 checks the status of any package you're shipping from all the major players, as well as from a few of the middle ones.

Figure 13-2:
PackTrack.
com's
package
tracker
enables you
to track any
package
that you
ship via
the major
carriers.

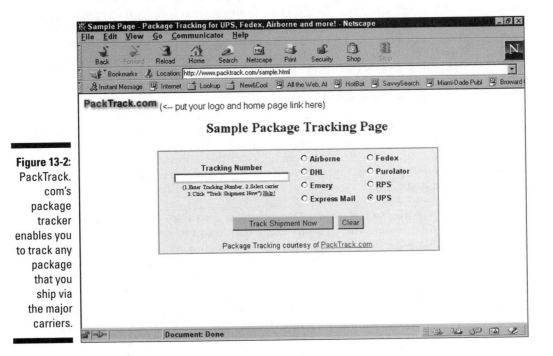

You can add PackTrack.com's tracking tool to your site by just following these steps:

1. **Go to** `www.packtrack.com/sample.html` **and then save that page to your computer.**

2. **Load the file into your HTML editor.**

3. **Change the content of the** `TITLE` **element to suit your site.**

4. **Replace the** `A` **and** `IMG` **elements in the first line after the start of the form with your own or delete them entirely; change or delete the text that reads** (`<-- put your logo and home page link here`) **as well.**

5. **Alter the Sample Package Tracking Page text to your preferences.**

6. **Save the modified page and upload it to your server.**

Designing for E-Commerce

You may understand Web site design in general, but that's not necessarily enough for e-commerce. Face the fact — if you're building a shopping mall in the "real world," do you want an architect who specializes in houses or one who's built stores all their life? Store design involves its own special needs.

Yes, your Web site must display a pretty face. Yes, it must perform all the functions you need to show your wares and process orders. But the key point to Web design is this one rule:

It must be simple to use.

If customers face any kind of hitch in the process, you're going to lose money. That's guaranteed — 100 percent. As you plan the site design for an e-commerce store, you must approach it from the perspective of making it totally easy and painless. Regardless of what you sell, here's the basic breakdown of what you need to cover:

✔ **Getting to the product description:** If you sell some type of merchandise, make sure that you include at least one picture. This is a classic situation calling for the use of thumbnail images instead of full-sized ones so that the basic product page doesn't take too long to load. (Customers may lose interest if they must wait too long for the site to load.)

✔ **Getting more detailed information:** This one depends on the nature of what you sell. With many products, the total information is so little that you can easily fit it all into the product's description. On the other hand, providing additional information also provides you with an opportunity to sing the product's praises at length, even if it's not totally necessary.

✔ **Finding the cost:** You may think that we really don't need to state this requirement, but you'd be surprised how often we've followed link after link on e-commerce sites without ever finding this one fundamental fact clearly stated. Put the price right out in the open where everyone can see it.

✔ **Buying the product:** If you're using shopping-cart software for multiple products, make sure that it's easy to use and doesn't require a bunch of back-and-forth steps to work. If you sell a single product or service, make sure that your site can quickly accommodate the customer's decision to buy. Put a Buy This Now link right at the top of the page — and put one at the bottom, too. Don't ask a bunch of extra questions on the order form, either. Keep it down to the basics such as name, address, payment method, and shipping options.

Online Sources

Table 13-3 lists some places on the World Wide Web where you can find more information about the topics that we cover in this chapter.

Table 13-3	Online Resources
Web Site Name	*Web Address*
Freightworld	www.freightworld.com/exp_geo.html
Internet Tools for Package Tracking	www.copresco.com/pkgtrack.htm
Shipment and Parcel Tracking	http://remarkablegifts.com/ Services/shipping.htm
Transportation Solutions Web Links	www.transportationsolution. com/links.html
Website Success Monthly newsletter	www.irsmarketing.com/ newsletter_home.htm

Chapter 14

Love That Plastic:
Taking Credit Cards

In This Chapter

▶ Becoming a merchant

▶ Avoiding pitfalls

▶ Using e-cash and phone checks

▶ Converting currencies

*I*t's a pretty easy matter to take in money if you're operating a regular store. Cash, checks, credit cards, debit cards — you name it, and there's some well-established process in place to handle it. From night-deposit drops to armored car pickups, the bricks-and-mortar merchant is already well covered when it comes to getting paid.

There are no cash registers online, though, so you need to look at other options. The major approach is to take credit cards. But, you can arrange to be paid in other ways, like accepting checks by phone or using digital money. However, none of the other ways can really compete with the power of plastic.

By the way, after you're set up to take credit cards, you probably want to slap the credit card logos onto your site. Table 14-1 shows you sites from which you can download this artwork.

Table 14-1	Credit Card Icon Sources
Credit Card	*Web Address*
American Express*	`http://home5.americanexpress.com/merchant/profit/profit_default.asp?profit_body=logos_body`
MasterCard	`www.mastercard.com/business/brand/online.html`

The American Express site also has MasterCard, VISA, and Discover logos.

Getting a Merchant Account

You know that old line of Groucho Marx's? The one that went something like, "I wouldn't want to join any club that would have someone like me as a member." Well, if you're just getting started and don't have any kind of business or financial track record, you may have to settle for a credit card merchant account — which gives you the capability to accept credit cards — that doesn't necessarily give you the best deal.

Even if you're really good at what you do, and even if you're going into all this with your eyes wide open, the odds are pretty good that a financial analyst will classify you right alongside the starry-eyed dreamers who don't have a chance — unless you have a solid business plan, a proven staff, and some serious money behind your operation. That doesn't necessarily mean that you can't get a merchant account — after all, some credit card companies will give merchant accounts to businesses that they consider high-risk clients, just as there are loan companies that give a loan to someone with poor credit. But it probably means that you'll end up paying more for the privilege than a well-established firm would. Maybe lots more.

So what do you need to do to get established? And what are the pitfalls you have to guard against?

Local banks versus online specialists

If you think that you have a good relationship with your local bank, going into e-commerce might make you think again. Bankers are notoriously conservative. This is a good trait, of course, in people whom you need to trust with your money. But that conservative streak isn't so nice when you find out that the conservatism means that they don't get the whole e-commerce idea.

When we entered into our first e-commerce venture, we trotted merrily into the bank we'd done business with for around 15 years, confident that they could handle our needs. Talk about running into a brick wall! When we told the bank officer what we wanted, we got a flat answer: "We don't allow merchant accounts for online businesses." "But," we protested, "you know us, and we know this field inside and out. It's not like we're high risk. Besides, you're online yourselves!" Nothing, no argument at all, including the hypocrisy of the bank having its own Web site — especially that — would budge her. It was a matter of Policy. Our banker suggested that we try the bank across the street. "That bank," she said, looking like she was talking about some unspeakable sin, "handles online accounts."

So we trotted across the street. Would that bank give us a merchant account for an online business? "Sure. Just deposit 20 gazillion dollars in the bank, and we'll issue an account to you. Only, you have to pay double the fees that a normal business pays." We got the strong feeling that the banker expected us to kiss her feet for offering us even that "deal."

Even if your bank isn't Internet friendly, there are still tons of places you can turn to. There's no way that you can get accepted directly by MasterCard or VISA. You'll have to go through some kind of intermediary, called a *merchant account acquirer,* along the way. These acquirers are usually banks that take care of your transactions, although many banks also have independent sales agents who work on their behalf to bring in more business. Most of the companies offering online credit card services, in fact, are really sales organizations that front for the real credit card processing companies and get a cut for bringing in new customers — pretty much like an affiliate program. (Ironically, many of these acquirers now run their own affiliate programs for Webmasters.) Acquirers just take applications and pass them on to the banks that set up the merchant accounts and do the actual transaction processing.

The individual banks then deal with an *interbank,* which takes care of all the transactions that member banks send to them, but that's a level you'll never have to deal with. To find out whom you can talk to about getting set up as an Internet merchant, check out some of the official sites of the major credit card companies. Table 14-2 lists MasterCard's official merchant sites for different countries and areas.

Table 14-2	Directories of MasterCard Acquirers
Region or Industry	***Web Address***
Australia and New Zealand	`www.mastercard.com/cgi-bin/auacq/au`
Canada	`www.mastercard.com/canada/business/merchant`
Middle East/ North Africa	`www.mastercard.com/cgi-bin/meacq/me_en`
Singapore	`www.mastercard.com/sg/business/merchant/ sg_acquirers.html`
USA	`www.mastercard.com/cgi-bin/usacq`

The VISA listings for the U.S. are found at `www.visa.com/pd/cards/us/ main.html`. VISA recommends using First of Omaha Merchant Processing as a way to get started. The First of Omaha site is secure, so you need to make sure that you use the `https` instead of the `http` beginning to the address: `https://www.foomp.com/applications/online_app.htm`. First of Omaha doesn't have an online international directory of its merchant account providers, but it does have one for credit card applications. Many of the same banks that issue credit cards are also merchant account providers, so you can track them down by going to www.visa.com/pd/cards/main.html and clicking the appropriate region on the world map there.

American Express is refreshingly simple — you apply to American Express. Drop in to www.americanexpress.com/homepage/merchant.shtml and go at it. If you prefer to keep everything under one roof, you can usually also sign up with American Express through the same merchant account provider you use for MasterCard and VISA. Or check out both approaches and see which method will give you the best deal.

The American Express Web site is one fine example of design. It's both functional and attractive. Anyone could learn a lot about Web design and structure from studying it.

In addition to the official Web sites, there are so many acquirers online that it'll make your head spin. Go to any good search engine and type the phrase **accept credit cards**. You should get more than 100,000 results. Even allowing for duplicate listings and bad links, that's a lot to dig through. We've pared the list down a bit for you, though. Check out the section "Online Sources," at the end of this chapter, for some of the major acquirers.

So which card should you take? Or which cards? Well, the obvious answer is this: all of them. But the obvious isn't always the best. MasterCard and VISA for sure. They're the real biggies that everyone has. Beyond that, though, each one that you sign up for usually adds to your expenses. Most credit card firms charge you for just being able to offer to take the cards, even if you never process a single transaction with them. American Express doesn't. Well, actually, American Express has two plans: With the first one, you don't pay American Express any monthly fee, but you do pay the company a percentage of the take. The second plan is just the opposite — American Express doesn't get a cut, but you pay a flat fee every month. It's up to you.

If you're dealing with the general public, American Express is mostly useful for high-end purchases. If you're dealing with the business market, though, it's another story. Zillions of businesses have corporate American Express cards, and you can lose a significant amount of money if you can't take orders with these corporate cards, even for low-priced items. When it comes to the smaller cards, like Discover and Diner's Club, you should probably take them only if you're a really big company that does millions of dollars in sales. It's just not worth it for a typical small business because not many of your customers will have Discover or Diner's Club and not also have VISA, MasterCard, or American Express.

How to sign up

After you decide which acquirers you want to sign up with, contact them and ask for an application. From that point, the exact details vary somewhat from one company to the next — make sure that you ask each company about the process before you get involved so that you'll have everything ready ahead of time — but the basic procedure goes something like this:

✔ **Fill out application forms.** Tons of sheets of them. And those forms are always too long to photocopy the whole sheet at once, so you'll have to keep turning them around and shooting them again to make a copy of the whole thing. You'll also need a magnifying glass to read some of it. These people take fine print seriously.

Most merchant account providers now have an online application form. You fill it out and submit it online; then the providers mail a printed copy to you for your signature.

When you're getting ready to fill out the forms, don't neglect to have the information handy about where the credit card company should send the money you make — your bank name, business account number, and ABA routing code (ask your bank).

Some merchant-account providers require you to open an account in a bank of their choosing. Run, don't walk, away from this kind of arrangement. It's a lot easier to handle your money if it's in your own bank.

✔ **Provide copies of your business documentation.** This may include a business license, corporate papers or partnership agreement, licenses to perform various services, or even copies of tax returns. Remember that merchant accounts are issued to companies, not individuals. Even if you're running a one-person shop, you have to do whatever your locality requires to be a legal business.

✔ **Estimate how many credit card orders you will process each month and how much money they will involve.** This is rough with a startup business, but it's important because the merchant account provider will set a limit on how much you can submit for processing. If you end up making more than you thought, you have to ask the provider's permission to submit more orders than you signed up for. Most people deliberately overestimate the number of orders and the amount of money they expect, just to avoid this problem.

✔ **Have an on-site inspection.** That's right. Even though your business may not have a physical location but exists only in Cyberspace, you could have to put up with someone coming out to your house to look at it. They'll even take a picture of your computer as your "place of business" for the record. This is nothing but a bit of red tape left over from the days before e-commerce.

What to watch out for

Top of the list of things to watch out for: fees. Merchants pay for the privilege of taking credit card orders, and the credit card companies have all sorts of little ways of sticking it to you. Here's a sampling:

- **An application fee:** This is pure gravy for the bank or — more likely — the sales agents, for whom it may be the main source of income. Double-check whether the application fee will be refunded if you don't get account approval and take the answer with a grain of salt. Get it in writing. Better yet, stay away from companies that charge one. There are plenty of companies out there that don't charge you just for looking at your application.

- **A setup fee for starting the account:** Again, lots of companies will set you up for nothing. Try to avoid the ones that charge you for the simple act of becoming a customer.

- **Monthly statement fee:** This is a charge that the credit card companies levy on you because they have to keep track of how much money they're making from you. You'd think that they'd be glad to do this for nothing, but that's not the case.

- **A percentage of each sale:** This is called the *discount rate.*

- **Transaction fee:** Yes, you're already paying a percentage. But the company still wants a few more cents.

- **Minimum monthly charge:** If you don't make enough sales for the credit card company's cut to meet a certain minimum amount, you have to pay the minimum amount anyway. Hey, it's not going to lose money just because you might. American Express has a refreshing difference — it doesn't have a monthly minimum.

- **Equipment charges:** If you're strictly online, you don't need any kind of equipment. Don't get suckered into buying a point-of-sale system or anything else you're not going to use.

Leaving off equipment, because it's unnecessary and wildly variable in cost, Table 14-3 shows the lowest costs typically associated with these fees. Lots of places claim to offer lower costs, but those firms must be running charities because these are the minimums that MasterCard and VISA charge Internet companies. (They do offer lower rates for more "stable" traditional bricks-and-mortar firms, however.)

Table 14-3	Low Internet Company Fees	
Fee	**Amount**	**When Paid**
Application	$0	One-time
Setup	$0	One-time
Statement	$9	Monthly
Discount rate	2.30%	Per transaction
Transaction	$0.30	Per transaction
Monthly minimum*	$20	Monthly

* If company's income from your transactions doesn't reach this amount.

How do you pay all this and still make a profit? The same way every other merchant does — you raise your prices and pass the increase on to the consumer.

Some companies, of course, actually care about your business and have nice, helpful people working for them. The best way to find out whom you're dealing with — before you sign up for a merchant account with any company — is to talk to some of its current customers. You can ask the company for references, but its employees steer you only to people they know will say nice things about the company. Think about the references on your own résumé. You don't include the boss who thought you were a turkey or the coworker who always tried to take the credit for your work, do you? The credit card companies wouldn't want to send you to the people who are mad at them either.

Well, it's kind of hard to track down the clients of a company without asking someone at the company, so why not do it the other way around? Every single Web site that takes credit cards has to be doing business with an acquirer. And almost all of those acquirer sites have an e-mail link to the Webmaster. Just surf the Web and keep leaving messages. "Who do you use? How do you like them? Have you had any problems with them?" (And that kind of thing.) Pretty soon, you start to build up a consensus about which companies are currently the best to do business with.

Beware of the bad companies

In addition to looking out for how much it's going to cost you to take orders, you also have to beware of dealing with a badly run company. We once had a merchant account with a company that was a royal horror story from beginning to end. It's not one of the ones in this book, so don't worry — we wouldn't steer you to an outfit like that. But it's a good illustration of the kinds of things you may have to put up with.

First of all, the guy the company sent out for the site inspection was about as rude as can be. And ignorant, too. While we listened to comments like, "In my day, we had to do *real* work for a living," we had to point out the computer to him because he didn't know what one looked like. We really wanted to get that account, so we took it with a smile, but it was a severely strained smile.

We were required to buy a credit-card imprinter to get the account, despite the fact that online businesses never even see their customers, let alone have an opportunity to actually handle a customer's credit card. Still, it did make a lovely paperweight.

After paying many hundreds of dollars for the software, you'd figure it would be a pretty decent package, right? Wrong. It was obsolete and originally designed for an older operating system. It was badly designed and clumsy to use. It wouldn't work on the Internet; instead, it would only connect with the company's system via a direct dial-up connection. You had to key in the orders by hand. It didn't maintain any sort of database beyond what was necessary to send in the current batch of orders.

One day, we went to use the alleged software, and it just plain didn't work. We reinstalled it from the original disks. Didn't work. We reinstalled it from backup disks. No go. We tried it on different computers, different phone lines, and different modems. Nothing. So we did what any dimwitted fool would do — we called up the credit card company's tech-support line for help. We explained the situation and our equipment setup in clear and simple terms and waited for their enlightening response. They asked us what a modem was.

We'd had just about all we could take by then, so we cancelled the account. Guess what the company did? They sent us a bill for $300. So we got back on the phone again. What was the bill for? For closing the account. Where in our contract did it say they could charge us for closing it? Well, nowhere; at least not in the original one, but they had unilaterally decided to change the terms. When were we notified of this? Well, they must have notified us, they were sure of that. We offered to introduce them to a wonderful lawyer, and after a further exchange of letters, they backed off. We never talked to them again and never looked back either.

The worst problem, though, is credit card fraud. So what does happen if you get a bad order? The answer's simple — you don't get paid. It's called a *chargeback* — the folks who handle your account issue a debit instead of a credit, and the amount of the bad charge is deducted from your business bank account. The same thing happens if a customer complains to the credit card company, saying that you didn't fulfill your duties (like if they never received their order, or the product didn't work). And if you get too many chargebacks, you can lose your merchant account. Worse, you can get charged big-time fees. That's right — another fee. Not only do you lose the money from the sale, but if more than 1 percent of your sales in one month comes back as chargebacks, the credit card companies jack up your discount rate, which means that your profit on future sales shrinks. And even if you successfully dispute the chargeback, you still have to pay a processing fee to cover the credit card company's expenses in falsely accusing you. Then comes the ultimate "insult to injury" stunt — if you keep getting lots of chargebacks, the company charges you to "review" your account. And that review can run into many thousands of dollars — MasterCard chargeback fees can even go up to $100,000 in a single month for repeat "offenders." Not many Internet companies can eat that kind of expense.

The problem here is that Internet companies — like mail order or telephone order ones — have no way of ever seeing the credit card or the person who uses it. Normal fraud prevention wisdom (like watching to see if the credit card comes out of a wallet or a pocket) can't work. Nor, except in rare cases where people mail in Web pages they printed out, can Internet companies get a signature on an order form. All the company can do is accept a credit card number. There's no way to prove who provided that number. That's the nature of the Net. No doubt, this will be resolved in some manner some day; but for now, that's the way it is. Credit card companies have a phrase for this: *high risk.* That's right: MasterCard and VISA consider every company on the Internet to be a high risk. Well . . . not every company. If you're successful enough to make zillions of dollars, they pretend that you're not in the same boat as everyone else on the Net, even though nothing but the amount of profit is any different. Short of that, though, they've got the entire e-commerce world in their sights.

Obviously, this hostility is kind of a self-defeating attitude because the Internet is rapidly becoming the driving force behind the twenty-first century's economy. It's an issue that needs to be addressed by some form of government intervention with the credit card industry in the near future, and we strongly urge you to write your legislators about resolving this problem.

Check out the Inter@ctive Week article on this issue at `www.zdnet.com/intweek/stories/news/0,4164,2524002,00.html`.

Okay, off the soapbox. In the meanwhile, make sure that the software you're using to process credit cards has an anti-fraud feature called *address verification.* Because the credit card issuer knows where it sends the bill, the address on the order can be checked against the credit card issuer's records. If it's not the same, you may not want to fulfill that order. Some companies, such as florists and fruit shippers, pretty well have to handle such orders because many of their products get ordered by one person to be sent to another person at another address. If you do decide to take a risk like that, at least have two address areas on your form. One should be for the address to ship to, and the other one should be for the purchaser's home address if it's different from the address the item's being shipped to. It's not perfect protection, but it's a step in the right direction. And always make sure to require a signature for delivery. That way, you can prove the item reached the right address — assuming you ship a physical product anyway.

Online Malls

Many online malls also provide merchant account services. And most of the virtual and dedicated server providers (see Chapter 16) have some sort of shopping-cart software available as well. If you're looking for an all-in-one solution to your e-commerce needs, you should check out some of the sites in Table 14-4.

Table 14-4	Online Malls
Mall	*Web Address*
Americart Cart Shopping Service	www.cartserver.com/americart/
AMS I-Stores	www.merchant-accounts.com/rates.html
Electronic Merchant Systems	www.emscorporate.com
ExciteStores	www.excitestores.com
Hiway Technologies, Inc.	www.hiway.com
HyperMart	www.hypermart.net/index.gsp
Key Merchant Services	http://info.KeyMerchants.com/ecommerce/yourstore/index.html
Yahoo! Stores	http://store.yahoo.com

Many of the malls offer complete e-commerce solutions — Web sites, merchant services, integrated shopping carts, and so on — and have some pretty sophisticated antifraud capabilities. In fact, they may be a better option for many small companies than going the traditional route.

Checking Out Alternative Payment Methods

We said at the beginning of this chapter that credit cards were king. And we stand by that. If you do nothing but take MasterCard and VISA, you're pretty thoroughly covered. Nearly everyone who can afford a computer has one or both of them. Toss in American Express for the high-end customer and the business client, and you're all set. But there are alternatives out there, and you may want to add some or all of them to your own setup.

E-Cash

Digital wallets. Sounds cool. Nice, easy-to-understand metaphor. You use digitally signed certificates online just like you'd use cash in the non-Net world. But it really hasn't worked out. There's no standard yet, although something called *ECML* — the Electronic Commerce Modeling Language — seems to be the first fitful attempt at one.

The most telling thing, though, is that no one's telling. What we mean is that when you ask the folks who are trying to market e-cash exactly how many customers they have, exactly how many merchants are using their systems, and exactly how profitable this all is, they clam up real fast. This is not a good sign. When people are winning, they generally like to trumpet it to the world. But e-cash has nothing to show so far but hype and broken promises.

Phone checks

Here's the scenario — you print checks with other people's account numbers on them, take them to your bank and deposit them, and then watch the money roll in. It's not some kind of criminal operation, either. It's a perfectly legitimate business practice — as long as you have permission from your customers to do it.

The way it works is that your customers give you authorization to create a *draft* on their accounts. A draft is a check. You ask your customers to give you the information off their checks — bank name, check number, those little bank and account numbers across the bottom, and so forth — and then you enter that information into a check-writing program. Next, you toss some special *safety paper* into your printer — that's the kind of paper checks are printed on — print those checks, and you've gotten paid.

Figure 14-1 shows a sample check made with Quick Pay Office Pro from www.checksbyfax.net. See the "Online Resources" table, at the end of the chapter, for more sources.

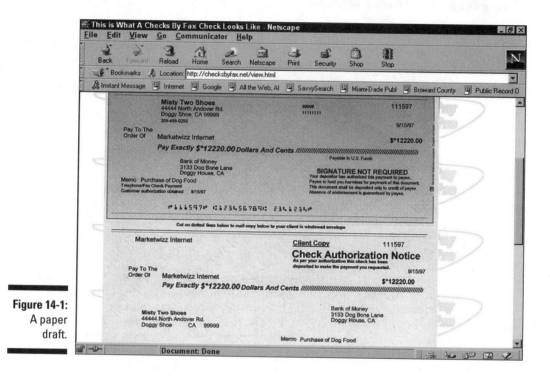

Figure 14-1:
A paper
draft.

This is one of those systems that you really should have in place. It has only two drawbacks. One is that few people are familiar with this system, but that situation is changing rapidly. The other is that the customers are paying the full amount up front (where, with a credit card, they can repay the purchase price over time in small amounts).

There's one thing you just can't beat about this payment approach. All you pay for is the software and the paper (which you can get at any good office supply company). You have no monthly fee, no minimum charges, no discount rate, no nothin' that you've gotta put up with when you deal with credit card companies.

Phones, faxes, and snail mail

You should always give your customers some way to purchase from you offline. Even if you've got a fully secure system, there are still plenty of people who are uncomfortable with entering their financial information online. If you can have someone answering the phone (at least during normal business hours), put that phone number on the order form. If you have a fax, put your fax number on there, too. And don't forget to add a physical address. That way, anyone who wants to order, but fears online security gaps, can still do so in the old, traditional ways.

If you work from your home and don't want to give out your home address, you can easily get an office address by renting a private mailbox for about a buck a day at most package-shipping companies. (Not the big ones like UPS that drive trucks around, but the small storefront operations like Pak Mail, Mail Boxes Etc., and Mailboxes USA that wrap and send packages for you.)

Converting Currencies

Whatever you're up to with e-commerce, your audience is global. Even if that's not your intent, you're going to have people looking at your stuff who aren't necessarily familiar with the current value of a U.S. dollar. Is there a solution? Oh, yeah. A really good one.

The Universal Currency Converter (UCC) from Xenon Labs is pretty much a must-have for any commercial site that expects to handle international business. Like most free services, it has a banner ad built into it, but you can negotiate with Xenon Labs to remove it for a fee. The converter lets anyone convert any amount in any currency to the equivalent amount in any other currency.

The basic module has only the major world currencies in it. Don't sweat it, though — if you need to include others, it doesn't cost you anything. This limitation is only for practical reasons. After all, nearly every transaction takes place in one of the top currencies, and the more options you add, the slower things get. Really, how often do you need to figure out how many Seborga Luiginos are equal to 800 Uzbekistan Soms?

To add the converter to your Web page, follow these steps:

1. **Go to** www.xe.net/ucc/customize.htm.

2. **Read through the terms of use.**

3. **Fill out the required form with your URL and contact information.**

   Notice that the URL must be the address of the Web page on which you will actually put the converter, not just the general URL of your domain.

4. **Click the button that says I Accept These Conditions.**

   You need to register each page you use the converter on.

5. **On the resulting page, click the Fast Track Instructions button.**

   Now, you're back on the earlier page, right below the form you filled out. Yes, it's a roundabout way to get there, but the registration process is legally required if you want to use the converter.

   From here, you have two options. Both of them work fine, so it's just a matter of how you like to do things.

6. **Download the compressed file for either Windows or Mac, in which case you need to unzip it and load the resulting HTML page into an editor before you can use the code, or click the <u>Click Here to See the Raw HTML</u> link and just copy the code off your browser screen.**

   If you download the file, you'll see that the enclosed Web page, samp-ucc.htm, has none of the usual elements you're used to — HTML, HEAD, and BODY. Yet it will still load into any browser and will work just fine. That's because, as useful as those elements are for envisioning the structure of your Web page, they're not technically required under the HTML standard. We're not recommending that you leave them out of your pages, and we're sure that Xenon Labs did it just because the purpose of that page is only to hold the code for you to copy and paste. But it's a decent bit of tech trivia you can amaze and amuse your friends with.

7. **Whichever way you get your hands on the code, paste it into your own Web page and save the file.**

8. **Upload the page to your Web server and try it out.**

   Figure 14-2 shows the converter on a Web page.

Now, this is one fine service as is. But it can be customized, too. Practically anything about it can be changed by Xenon for a fee, but the company has also built plenty of options into it that you can use on your own.

If you know the country from which most of your foreign customers come, you may want to set the converter so that it's ready to convert from their currency to yours right away. Say, for example, that you're in America, and you know that almost every one of your overseas customers is from the United Kingdom. You'd probably do well to set the conversion to default values of dollars to pounds in that case. This wouldn't prevent anyone from another country from still using the converter in the normal way — all it does is set which currencies are selected at the start, so visitors can still choose other currencies if they want.

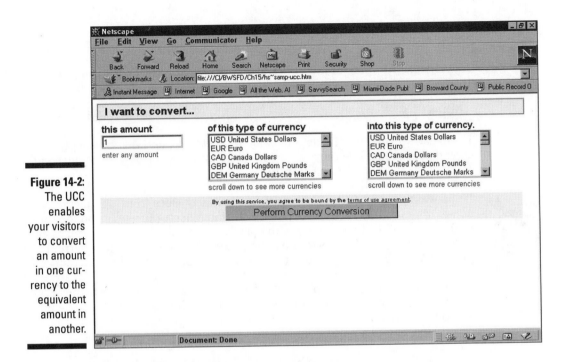

Figure 14-2:
The UCC
enables
your visitors
to convert
an amount
in one cur-
rency to the
equivalent
amount in
another.

This is what you need to do to set the default currencies in the converter:

1. **Go into the HTML source code and find the** SELECT **elements.**

    The one whose name attribute has a value of From is — you guessed it —
    the currency to convert from. The one whose name attribute has a value
    of To is the currency to convert to.

    One of the OPTION elements in each has the selected attribute. In the
    original version, the default From currency is Canadian Dollars, and the
    default To currency is U.S. Dollars.

2. **To change the default, you can just delete the word** selected **from
    the** OPTION **elements for the current currency and add it to the ones
    you want to use.**

    Simple, ain't it?

Now, what if you have only one product, or what if all your products are the
same price? At any rate, you have a price of USD$49.95 that most people are
going to want to convert to some other currency. Having already set the From
currency to U.S. dollars, you can now set the default amount to 49.95. This
default makes it really easy on your customers — all they have to do is pick
their native currency, and they're off and running. To do this, look for the following code line near the beginning of the form:

```
<INPUT TYPE="text" NAME="Amount" VALUE="1" SIZE=10><BR>
```

Just change the value of the `value` attribute. To set it to 49.95, change it to this:

```
<INPUT TYPE="text" NAME="Amount" VALUE="49.95" SIZE=10><BR>
```

Users can still change the default value to anything they want by simply typing over it, just like they can select different currencies by selecting something other than the default selections.

If you want to change the order of the currency choices from alphabetical to some other method — such as placing the most likely currencies on the top of the list — all you have to do is to cut and paste the OPTION elements that reflect the currency values in the listings. Remove them from their current positions and paste them into their new positions. That's all there is to it.

If, for some reason, you don't want to give your users any choice in these things, UCC accommodates your wishes through the use of hidden variables. To do this, you add some INPUT type="hidden" elements right after the <FORM> tag and just before the <TABLE> tag.

To set the From currency so that it can't be changed, use the following code:

```
<INPUT type="hidden" name="From" value="xyz">
```

The placeholder xyz would be replaced by the three-digit code for the currency — such as USD for U.S. dollars or GBP for United Kingdom (or Great Britain) pounds.

To set the To currency, you do the same thing, but the line would read as follows:

```
<INPUT type="hidden" name="To" value="xyz">
```

To set the value so that it can't be altered (which prevents people from using your version of the UCC for test purposes unrelated to your site), you'd add the following line of code:

```
<INPUT type="hidden" name="Amount" value="xyz">
```

Replace the placeholder xyz with the amount to be converted (for example, 49.95).

If you want to add more currencies, check out the Full Currency Converter at www.xe.net/ucc/full.shtml and copy and paste the appropriate currency to your version. Just add a new OPTION element under the To and/or From SELECT element for each new currency.

If you want to delete currencies from the listings, you need to delete the entire line for that currency, beginning with the <OPTION> tag and ending with the </OPTION> tag.

If you want to customize the default results page that appears after a currency conversion calculation, as shown in Figure 14-3, you need to go a bit deeper. Customization requires creating not just an element or an attribute, but a *header* and a *footer*. The header contains HTML that is displayed before the calculation results, and the code in the footer goes in after them.

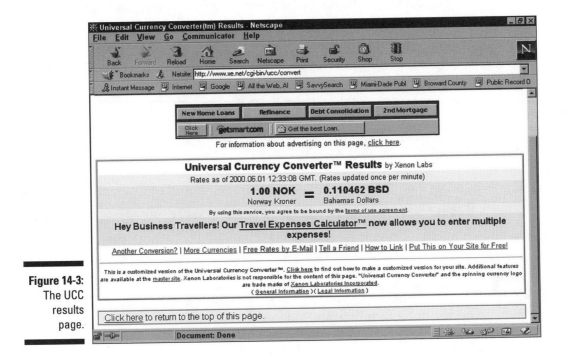

Figure 14-3:
The UCC results page.

To set up the header and footer, you need to think your HTML code out ahead of time, as well as consider the variations that the UCC demands of you. The header has to go right after the line with the <FORM> tag and has to include the [HTML], [HEAD], [/HEAD], and [BODY] tags. Notice anything weird about these? Yeah, the brackets aren't the regular angle brackets, they're regular brackets. That's so that a Web browser that reads this code won't get confused by encountering two identical tags such as <HTML> in the same page. You put these odd-looking quasi-HTML elements in as values of a hidden INPUT element, and the UCC software reinterprets the squared brackets just as though they were angle brackets when it comes time to create the results page.

So if you wanted to put in the following regular HTML code as your header . . .

```
<HTML>
<HEAD>
<TITLE>
This is a currency converter.
</TITLE>
</HEAD>
<BODY>
```

. . . you'd add it to the line in the currency converter code, like this:

```
<INPUT TYPE="hidden" NAME="Header"
        VALUE="[HTML][HEAD][TITLE]This is a currency
        converter.[/TITLE][/HEAD][BODY]">
```

Then comes the regular output of the converter. After that comes the footer. If you wanted to add the following HTML code to it . . .

```
<B>Thanks for using the converter!</B>
</BODY>
</HTML>
```

. . . you'd do it like this:

```
<INPUT TYPE="hidden" NAME="Footer" VALUE="[B]Thanks for using
        the converter![/B][/BODY]">
```

The Shopper's Currency Converter (www.xe.net/ecc/shoppers) provides the same functionality as the UCC, but it's embedded into an IFRAME (inline frame) element. However, inline frames work only on Internet Explorer, so Xenon has also included the code for a JavaScript pop-up version to ensure compatibility with Netscape Navigator.

Online Sources

Table 14-5 lists some places on the World Wide Web where you can find more information on the topics we cover in this chapter.

Table 14-5	Online Resources
Web Site Name	*Web Address*
AIS Merchant Services	www.aismerchantservices.com/index.htm
Bridgeview Bankcard	www.bvbankcard.com/englishframe.htm
CheckQuick	www.checkquick.com
ClickBank	www.clickbank.com/acceptcards.html
Direct Checks	http://ecd2.com/data/home.htm
Discover Business Services	www.novusnet.com/merchant/data/main.htm
ePayment Solutions	www.epaymentsolutions.com/indexframe.htm
EZ Merchant Accounts	www.ezmerchantaccounts.com
Fifth Third Bank	www.mpsnet.com/business/merchant/credit_card.htm
First Bank of Beverly Hills	www.fbbh.com
First Charter Bank	www.fcbankbeverlyhills.com/charter/sections/merchant1.html
Harris Bank	www.harrisbank.com/smallbiz/c_merchant.html
Heartland Payment Systems	http://bcnet.com/internet.htm
Instant Check	www.easydesksoftware.com/check.htm
Mellon Small Business	www.mellon.com/smallbusiness/merchant/
MiniVend	www.minivend.com/iri/mvend.html
Paymentech	www.paymentech.com/home/paym_ecs.html
Skipjack Merchant Services	www.skipjack.com/sjweb/default.asp
Total Merchant Services	www.totalmerchantservices.com

Chapter 15

Examining Affiliates Programs

In This Chapter

▶ Understanding payment plans

▶ Finding the right match

▶ Making a profit

▶ Acquiring affiliates

*W*hatever you call them — affiliates, associates, independent agents — businesses that operate on the World Wide Web have turned in a big way to letting other people do their sales for them. Why should you care? Because you can make money at it. They don't just want you to plug their stuff. They're willing to cut you in for a piece of the action.

Zillions of companies are jumping on the affiliate bandwagon, where you sell another company's products and services for a slice of the pie. Everybody from one end of the Web to the other is lining up to ask you to be his sales agent. And the good news is that they don't want any of your money.

Table 15-1 lists a few major companies with affiliate programs.

Table 15-1	Major Companies with Affiliate Programs
Company	*Web Address*
Amazon.com	www.amazon.com/exec/obidos/subst/associates/join/associates.html
CBS SportsLine	http://affiliate.linksynergy.com/owa_share/owa/sreg.sregister?mid=602
PETsMART	www.petsmart.com/affiliates/index.shtml
Stamps.com	www.stamps.com/affiliates/
Staples Office Supplies	www.staples.com/services/affiliates/befree/

Yeah, Sure, It's Free

No, really, it's true. Joining an affiliate program doesn't cost you a bloody thing. The folks who offer the affiliate programs would be crazy to ask you for money. If you sign up as an affiliate, you already work for nothing, so what more could they ask? Any company that asks you to put up money in order to become an affiliate is probably running some kind of scam. It doesn't cost them anything for you to sign up for their program, and there's always the possibility that your Web site may actually make them some money.

Affiliate programs are just like most sales organizations. Salespeople don't get paid unless they produce money for the company. If a salesperson sells a product, they get a percentage of the profit. Lots of people swear by that approach. After all, you may never starve on a regular paycheck, but you rarely feast either. If you're on commission, the sky's the limit. If you make enough sales, you can certainly manage a feast or two. A salaried employee who does a great job makes no more money than the one who does a lousy job. The salesperson who does a great job has something solid to show for their efforts.

Not all affiliates are paid a percentage of the profit, however. Sometimes, they get a flat fee instead. Either way, you get your slice of the pie every time it's cut. Okay, your slice goes into the fridge, so to speak. You don't get it right away. Don't panic, this is just one of those accounting things, as annoying as it is. Remember how we said that it doesn't cost a merchant anything to have you become an affiliate? Well, it's ironic, but it does cost merchants something when you actually drive business their way. It costs money to run an accounting system to keep track of how much they owe you and to cut checks and mail them to you. If you manage to generate only five bucks in commissions, it's not worth their accountants' time to pay you. Sad, but true.

But don't panic — you do get paid. It's only a matter of earning a certain minimum amount. How much is that? It depends on the merchant. Once you do reach the minimum amount, the check is cut on a specific schedule. Many programs don't pay monthly, but quarterly. Make sure that you understand the fine print before you sign up as an affiliate. Table 15-2 shows the payment schedule and minimum income necessary to trigger a payment from some representative affiliate programs.

Table 15-2	Payment Triggers	
Company	*Schedule*	*Amount Required*
Amazon.com	Quarterly	$100
Borders.com	Quarterly	$50

Company	Schedule	Amount Required
Focalex.com	Monthly	$5
Paytrust.com	Quarterly	$50
Rackunits.com	Monthly	$50
SnackExchange.com	Quarterly	$25

If you don't earn the minimum amount by the time a check would be cut, the amount you earned carries over into the next pay period. In other words, if you need to make $50 to get a check sent out and you make only $30 by the deadline, you need to make only $20 more to meet the minimum for the next deadline. You may never get paid at all if you don't ever meet the minimum requirement.

So what's the best program to sign up with? Well, obviously, it's one that pays lots of money, doesn't have a high minimum amount before it issues a check, and issues checks more often than other programs. But you need to consider a lot of other factors, too. First off, you've got to find a program.

Can I Join?

Yes, of course, you can join an affiliates program. A company would be crazy to say that you couldn't join. After all, it's possible that you might send some business its way, and it doesn't cost the company anything to sign you up. Actually, about the only way not to get approved for an affiliates program is to run a Web site that the company finds objectionable — like a XXX adult site or one that tells how to rob banks with a homemade nuclear weapon.

Finding partners

So who's running affiliates programs? Where do you go to sign up? The short answer is that just about everyone's doing some kind of affiliate program these days. If you just use your Web browser's page-search function, you can hunt for the word on the sites that you visit in the normal course of your surfing, and you're guaranteed to trip over tons of them. Many of the outfits that we list in other chapters of this book offer them, too.

There are lots of Web sites where you can go to find out the lowdown on affiliate programs. Table 15-3 lists some of the best sites for finding up-to-date news on the latest and greatest of these programs (and see Figure 15-1 for one of them).

Table 15-3	Top Affiliate Information Sites
Company	**Web Address**
Associate-it	http://associate-it.com
ClickQuick	www.clickquick.com
LinkShare	www.linkshare.com
Refer-It	www.refer-it.com

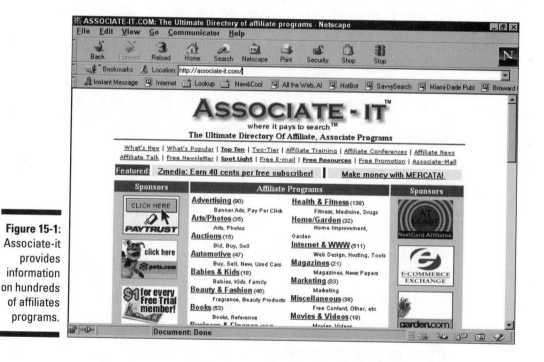

Figure 15-1:
Associate-it
provides
information
on hundreds
of affiliates
programs.

It's not a bad idea to cruise the search engines on a regular basis and hunt down any new programs that have come up since you last looked. In addition to keywords limiting things to your own site's subject area, try some of these search terms: affiliate program, associate program, bounty program. Don't forget the *program* part, or you'll spend the rest of your natural life trying to dig out from under all the responses.

Working with a network

It didn't take too long after the idea of affiliates programs for people to get the idea of affiliates-program networks. Program networks aren't just Web sites that offer you a large choice of programs to sign up for. They actually take care of nearly everything for you. All you do is go to a network's Web site, sign up, and state what kind of companies you want to sign up with. The network advises you and sets you up with some good ones. It's kind of like an e-commerce dating service.

LinkShare (www.linkshare.com) is an affiliate network that brings several programs together under one roof (see Figure 15-2).

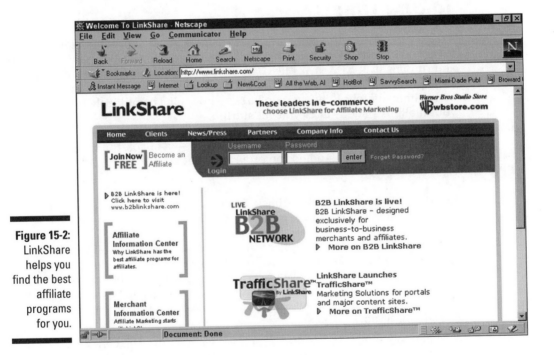

Figure 15-2: LinkShare helps you find the best affiliate programs for you.

You can find Commission Junction, a service similar to LinkShare's, at www.cj.com. Check out both Web sites to see what they can offer you.

Profiting from Your Program

Most affiliate programs depend simply on the vast number of people they can get to advertise products or services for them. But there's no guarantee that you'll actually make any money at all — let alone any significant money — if you do sign up with them. The odds, after all, are all with the affiliate programs. (See the section "Running Your Own Affiliates Program," later in this chapter.) But there are some things that you can do to make it a lot more likely that you'll actually find a check or two in your mailbox. And, if you really do it up right, that check will be more than a joke.

Taking time

It's easy to get caught up in a heady rush and sign up with every affiliate program you can find right away. After all, you could JOIN RIGHT NOW and be up and running in JUST A FEW MINUTES! If you're wise, though, you'll take it slow and easy. Trust us, you're not missing the key to instant riches by not acting immediately. Billions of dollars are not going to suddenly flow into your mailbox the day after you get started.

If you're going to make a profit — and you can — a big part of the reason will be that you carefully studied the programs that are out there and made the right choice for you.

Use this checklist to get some basic answers about an affiliate program before you commit your time and energy to it:

✔ Go to the Web site that offers the program and read the affiliate FAQ (Frequently Asked Questions) and legal agreement. If it doesn't have a FAQ or it doesn't have clear answers to obvious questions, you should be a trifle suspicious of its intentions. All the legal agreements are more or less obscure to nonlawyers, however, so that's no true indicator of the program's purpose.

✔ Find out exactly what the program pays for. Does it pay for someone to just click a link on your site? Or does it pay only if that person places an order?

✔ How much does the program pay and how often does it issue checks?

✔ What's the minimum amount that you can earn and still get paid?

✔ How good is the program's support? Does it provide you with anything besides an advertising banner?

✔ Can you monitor, in real time, how much the program owes you?

✔ Does the program list others who are currently signed up for it? If so, have you gone to those Web sites and e-mailed the Webmasters to ask them how satisfied they are with the program?

✔ How long has the program been in operation? Are there any complaints filed against it with the Better Business Bureau, Direct Marketing Association, or any regulatory agencies?

Working the audience

First off, you need a Web site that appeals to the kind of people who would buy the product or service. It does you no good to sign up with a gardening supply house's affiliate program if you run a Web site that details the naval conflicts of the Napoleonic Wars.

If you do run a gardening site, go to www.garden.com and click the <u>Affiliate Program</u> link at the bottom of the main page (see Figure 15-3). For Napoleon, well, we're still looking. Maybe one of the book chains.

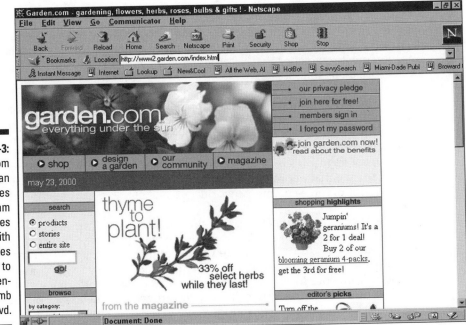

Figure 15-3: Garden.com has an affiliates program that goes well with Web sites that cater to the green-thumb crowd.

You could sign up with any program at all — very few affiliate programs really care who their agents are — but what's the point if you're not likely to be profitable? Being an affiliate is just like running a business, and just as with any other business, it's best to be involved in something that you already love and know very well.

What if you find an affiliate program that you like but you're not already running a site that fits in with its products? The short answer: Create a new site. With the incredibly low cost of starting an online site, running anywhere from totally free up to a few hundred bucks a year, you'd be crazy to walk away from a program that excited you.

In that case, it's a matter of you doing some research. If the subject matter turns you off, run — don't walk — away. Regardless of the potential rewards, you can't turn on your visitors if the topic doesn't excite you. If it does catch your heart and get you genuinely interested, though, you have a real chance to make something that people want to visit.

Adding value to your site

Even if your site's visitors are likely to be interested in the topic you're signed up for, you need to be especially vigilant about giving them full value for their visits. After all, even if you haven't planned primarily for an e-commerce site, you must remember that, after you join an affiliate's program, you're running an online business.

You've got to keep the visitors happy and keep them coming back for more. To do that, you have to give them a site that's worth their time. If all you do is set up a page with a bunch of links to programs that pay you if someone clicks their links or even buys their products, you've lost your focus. The focus of any Web site must be on the people who visit it. If you forget that or fail to take that approach for any reason, you're setting up for total failure — in or out of the e-commerce world.

You have to offer something that no one else in the world can — your own unique viewpoint and outlook on the topic or your own personal contacts. If you sell books, do a book review site, not just a book listing site. (Don't forget to add this book!) If you sell baby products, try to get something in print from your local pediatrician — someone whom you know but isn't already on other Web sites. If you sell gardening supplies, get out in the yard and get your hands dirty so that you can tell it like it is.

People visit your site more than once only if you give them a reason to.

Focusing on the topic

Tons of affiliate programs offer *two-tier* payment plans, which means that if you get someone else to sign up for the same program, you get a percentage of that person's income in addition to your own. Of course, that amount is smaller than what you make by direct purchases from your own site, but it still sounds like a pretty good deal. And it probably is, but a hazard's involved — you could get so caught up in trying to sign up other people that you forget what affiliates are for: getting your visitors to buy the products or services you're advertising for the program. If you overlook that fact, you start to see your own profits heading for the basement. When it comes to two-tier programs, take anything over your own direct involvement as gravy, because you have to rely on repeat customers, just like any business does. And you probably aren't going to get anybody to sign up as an affiliate twice.

Running Your Own Affiliates Program

It must have occurred to you by now that this affiliates bit is a pretty good thing to use if you set up your business online. We couldn't agree more. In fact, if anything, it's better for the business owner than it is for the affiliates.

Doing the math

Just look at the numbers — say, for example, that you're selling a product for $20 that costs you $10, so you make $10 per sale. You pay your affiliates a 10 percent commission on each sale. If you have 1,000 affiliates selling your product, and each one generates a single sale in a month, you're getting an extra $20,000 income per month, and it costs you only $2,000 to generate it. Take off the $10,000 for your costs and the $2,000 for the affiliates, and that's $8,000 per month profit — or $96,000 per year of free money. For a lot of small e-businesses, that's enough to justify their existence. The individual affiliate, though, gets just $2 per month.

Of course, a savvy affiliate makes more than that, but it does show that the affiliate system is heavily weighted in favor of the merchant.

Using software to host affiliates

Some software is designed to enable you to host your own affiliates program (see Figure 15-4). Table 15-4 shows some of the products that you can get. As with reciprocal linking, you have to hunt up the people you're going to be connecting with. On top of that, you have to manage everything. Rather than running all the tedious details yourself, though, you may want to consider letting someone else do all the work.

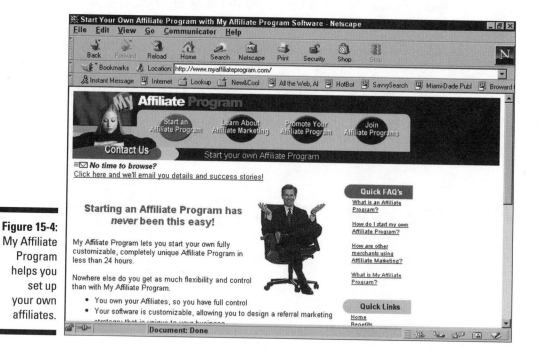

Figure 15-4:
My Affiliate
Program
helps you
set up
your own
affiliates.

Table 15-4	Affiliates Program Software
Web Site Name	**Web Address**
My Affiliate Program	www.myaffiliateprogram.com
The Affiliate Program	www.thedotcom.com.au/tap.html
Ultimate Advertiser	www.groundbreak.com
Webscape 2000	http://webscape2000.com/affiliatesoftware.html

The Affiliate Tracking Network (www.AffiliateTracking.com) occupies a kind of gray area here — it sells the software for you do it yourself but also offers to do it for you. Both LinkShare and Commission Junction (see Figure 15-5) are mentioned as sources of income for affiliates in the section "Working with a network," earlier in this chapter, but they're also a prime source of affiliates. Hey, they've got both sides of this street well covered.

Refer-It (www.refer-it.com) maintains a list of other firms that can help you set up a program. Limber up your fingers and go to www.refer-it.com/main.cfm?screen=info/build/software to check it out.

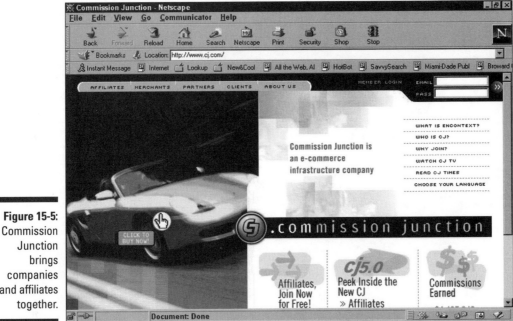

Figure 15-5:
Commission Junction brings companies and affiliates together.

Online Sources

Table 15-5 lists some places on the World Wide Web where you can find more information on the topics that we cover in this chapter.

Table 15-5	Online Resources
Web Site Name	*Web Address*
Affiliateguide.com	www.affiliateguide.com
Affiliatematch.com	www.affiliatematch.com
AffiliatesDirectory.com	http://affiliatesdirectory.com
AffiliateWorld.com	www.affiliateworld.com

(continued)

Table 15-5 *(continued)*

Web Site Name	Web Address
Associate Search	www.associatesearch.com
AssociatePrograms.com	www.associateprograms.com
ATL Network	http://atlnetwork.com
Cyberbounty	www.cyberbounty.com
DirectLeads Network	www.directleads.com
ValueClick	http://valueclick.com
Websponsors.com	www.websponsors.com

Part V

Publishing and Publicizing Your Site

The 5th Wave   By Rich Tennant

"So far our Web presence has been pretty good. We've gotten some orders, a few inquiries and nine guys who want to date our logo."

In this part . . .

This part discusses getting your site online and letting people know you're there. Chapter 16 gives you everything you need to know about different Web-hosting options. Chapter 17 covers getting your Web site listed in the search engines and establishing reciprocal links with other sites. And Chapter 18 shows you how to keep in touch with your visitors after they've left, without falling into the spam trap.

Chapter 16

Letting the World In

· ·

In This Chapter

▶ Choosing a host

▶ Finding free Web-site providers

▶ Picking and registering domain names

· ·

*1*f you don't already have a Web site or if you're not happy with your current Web space provider, you have several options. You can run your own Web server, of course. With a DSL connection and Linux, it's even possible to put together a creditable setup in your own home. But that's a lot of work — ask any network administrator just how much leisure time they have.

If you want to focus on developing and maintaining your site, you're best leaving the day-to-day grunge work of keeping the server up and running to someone else.

Practically every Web hosting provider offers all sorts of extended services in addition to plain Web space. These often include some form of e-commerce hosting, ranging from simply supplying the software to setting up a complete turnkey solution for you.

Going Live

You have three basic options when it comes to Web hosting:

▶ ISPs

▶ Virtual servers

▶ Dedicated servers

ISPs

The same people who provide you with your Internet access can also be your Web space provider. Almost certainly, you have at least some room for Web pages as part of your basic service. If you're not interested in a very extensive site or in one that has tons of glitzy features, the basic setup they give you will probably suffice. Even if you don't have any kind of CGI access (see Chapter 4), you can probably still use remotely hosted services, like the ones we describe in this book, to enhance your site.

Virtual and dedicated servers

Virtual servers are actually nothing more than directories on a hard drive. If that hard drive is on an existing Web server that supports virtual server capabilities, however, the Webmaster can make each one of those directories seem as though it were a fully functional Web server.

Other than being a really clever example of how you can use computer technology, does this have a practical application for you? It depends on your budget and your site's traffic expectations. It's certainly one of the cheapest ways to get your site up and running. You could pay for a couple of months' worth of a typical virtual server by skipping one good dinner at a decent restaurant. Some of them are so cheap that you could pay for it just by skipping dessert.

On the other hand, you're sharing one physical server with lots of other virtual servers. Any physical server's performance degrades as it gets busier, with more and more people connecting to it and placing demands on it. But if you're on a virtual server, that scenario has a slightly different meaning. People visiting a Web site on one of the other virtual servers that's hosted on the same physical server as yours are putting a drain on your resources, too, because those resources are shared. Basically, if someone else's site gets too busy, yours can look like a turtle in molasses. And vice versa.

Nearly every company that handles virtual servers also leases dedicated ones. A *dedicated server* is a step up — your very own physical computer holding your Web site, with nobody else on it.

Both virtual and dedicated servers offer more than just Web hosting. For example, they also handle e-mail. We focus only on the Web hosting aspect because this book is about Web sites.

Dedicated servers used to cost a small fortune, but a combination of generally lower computer prices and competitive pressures has dropped the expense of leasing one. At around $300 per month, they're still a bit pricey for a private individual, but for any serious commercial operation, that's a great bargain. After all, that's only $3,600 a year, while hiring a single network administrator to work at your own company would set you back 20 times that or even more.

Why compare those two costs? Aren't they apples and oranges? No, not at all. When you lease a dedicated server, the people you're leasing it from take care of keeping it up and running, which is what a network administrator does. Dedicated servers, like virtual servers, are located at the facility of a Web space provider, such as Covesoft (see Figure 16-1), and you don't have to worry about regularly backing up your data, restoring after a crash, upgrading things like Linux kernels, or any of the million things that keep technical staffs hopping.

Figure 16-1:
Covesoft specializes in keeping your Web site running without breaking the bank.

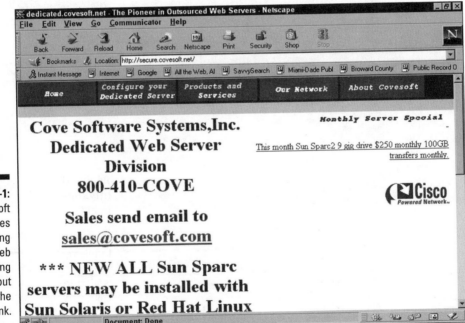

Finding your match

You can always run through the standard search engines and site guides looking for information on Web hosts. Some search engines, however, such as HostIndex (www.hostindex.com), are specifically intended to help you track down the right host for you (see Figure 16-2). The Web sites in Table 16-1 will help you do some comparison shopping.

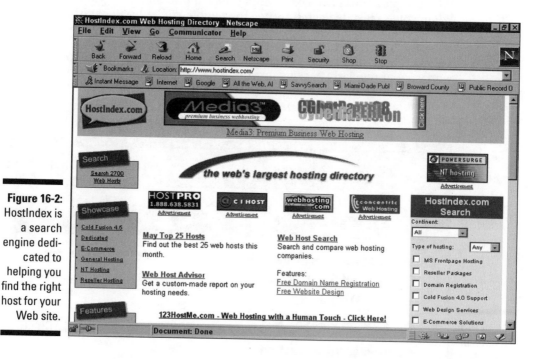

Figure 16-2: HostIndex is a search engine dedicated to helping you find the right host for your Web site.

Table 16-1	Web Hosting Indexes
Web Site Name	*Web Address*
budgetweb.com	www.budgetweb.com/budgetweb/index.html
c|net	www.webhostlist.com/html/aisles/ Web_Hosting.asp
FindAHost.com	www.FindAHost.com
HostReview.com	www.hostreview.com/power_search.html

Keeping It Cheap: Free Web Site Providers

More than 23 zillion Web space providers have an unbeatable price, which you probably guessed already from the title of this section. If you set up a personal site, free Web space providers may be the way for you to go. You can get lots more space than your local ISP provides. It's not unusual to get 50 or more megabytes of Web storage space without having to pay a dime for it.

If you plan on running any sort of professional site, though, the free Web space providers aren't really the ticket for you. You need your own domain name — .com, .org, or whatever — in order to be taken seriously. (See the section "Getting Your Own Domain Name," later in this chapter.) Also, free Web hosts make their money by slapping ads onto your site, and you can't usually put up your own in competition with them.

Having to post a free Web host's ad on your site means you may not be able to use any remote add-ins that feature their own banner ads either.

One refreshingly different free Web host that you might want to take a look at, though, even if you're running a commercial Web site is Crosswinds (http://home.crosswinds.net). It has a business model we'd like to see more of on the Web. Crosswinds offers unlimited Web space — that's right, unlimited. And it doesn't clutter up your pages with ad banners. It doesn't insist on intrusive pop-ups or locking your pages into its frames. It doesn't do any of the annoying things you have to put up with from its competitors. It gives you everything you could want for free, and it makes money strictly from the banner ads on its own pages, not on yours. On top of all that, Crosswinds doesn't care if it's a business or personal site you want to set up.

Table 16-2 lists some other free Web hosts.

Table 16-2	Free Web Hosts
Web Site Name	**Web Address**
Angelfire	http://angelfire.lycos.com
Bounceweb	www.bounceweb.com
Freeservers	www.freeservers.com
TopCities	http://topcities.com
Tripod	www.tripod.lycos.com
Virtual Avenue	www.virtualave.net

Getting Your Own Domain Name

Domain names, like idgbooks.com, are the addresses of sites on the World Wide Web. Picking and registering your own domain name are two of the most critical phases in your site planning, and we show you how to do both in this section. When you tell your Web browser to go to www.idgbooks.com, it's obvious where you're going to end up — at IDG Books' Web site. Your computer doesn't know that, though. It can't actually go to a named site, but asks a Domain Name Server (DNS) to translate that name into a more computer-friendly set of numbers known as an *IP address*. It's like getting into a cab and telling the driver to go to the Acme Building. He asks you where it is and you tell him it's at 1123 Main Street.

Domain extensions — the final letters at the end of an Internet address — are known as the *top-level domain*, or TLD. They're called "top level" because you read Internet addresses from right to left, with the part after the last dot being the highest step in a hierarchy that eventually leads down, step by dotted step, to the particular computer you're going to. The four main domain extensions you'll probably deal with are

- **.com:** Commercial operations
- **.edu:** Educational institutions
- **.net:** Internet Service Providers (ISPs)
- **.org:** Nonprofit organizations

Seven new TLDs may come into usage some day. When that day will come, no one seems to know. They've been officially approved, but that was back in 1997. Anyway, here they are:

- **.arts:** Arts and entertainment sites
- **.firm:** Business firms
- **.info:** Information services
- **.nom:** Private individuals' sites (short for *nom de plume* — pen name)
- **.rec:** Recreational and entertainment sites
- **.store:** Sites that sell products
- **.web:** Sites that focus on the Web itself

One problem with any new approach is that the general public identifies old standards with reliability and some may tend to see the lesser-known alternatives as misprints or typographical errors. "Dot what? Don't you mean 'dot com?'" The phrase *dot com* has, in fact, come into colloquial usage as meaning an Internet-based company.

The funny thing about all these TLDs, though, is that there's no requirement at all for people to use any of them in the manner in which they were intended. Plenty of nonprofit organizations have .com addresses, and quite a few .nets have nothing at all to do with ISPs. Go figure.

The domain extensions that we mention in the bulleted lists are called *generic TLDs*, but there's another kind of TLD as well — the *country-level TLD*. These specify the country in which the Web site is based. That's not necessarily where the Web server that holds the site is located, thanks to the global nature of the Internet. It can be very useful to register the same name in many countries if you're an international organization with multiple languages to support. That way, you can have a Spanish-language page at `mysite.es`, a Japanese-language page at `mysite.jp`, and so on.

If you're into alphabet soup, you can toss around such terms as *gTLD* and *CLTLD* for the generic and country-level extensions. Why it's a small "g" but an uppercase "CL" before the TLD parts is one of the Internet's great mysteries.

Picking a name

In the early days, it was so easy to create a domain name — there weren't all that many of them in use yet. Today, though, if you want to pick a three- or four-letter abbreviation or a single word for your domain name, you're likely to be out of luck. Everything short is already taken. The solution? Forget the acronyms and short names. Use phrases instead. The basic idea is to go for anything long enough that it's unlikely to have been used yet, but short enough to remember.

To find out whether a name is available, you use a WhoIs utility. One of the most familiar ones on the Web is the Network Solutions page at `www.networksolutions.com/cgi-bin/whois/whois`. You might also try the nice set of tools at `www.whois.net` (see Figure 16-3) or use a stand-alone tool like WhoIs Ultra, which you can get your hands on at `www.analogx.com/contents/download/network/whois.htm`.

Take your time and poke around the AnalogX site while you're there. You can get some other wonderful utilities there, too.

What do you do if you've come up with a great domain name, but it's already taken and you've just gotta have it? Well, it depends. If you're a company that already has a trademark, the domain name may well already "belong" to you as a matter of course, even if you haven't registered it yet. Well, at any rate, it can't legally be used by anyone else. If you've been doing business as, say, Joe's Acme Fabuloso Garbanzo Beans and Unicyle Maintenance Company, and that name's your registered trademark, anyone running a site named `www.JoesAcmeFabulosoGarbanzoBeansAndUnicycleMaintenanceCompany.com` is probably easy game for your lawyers.

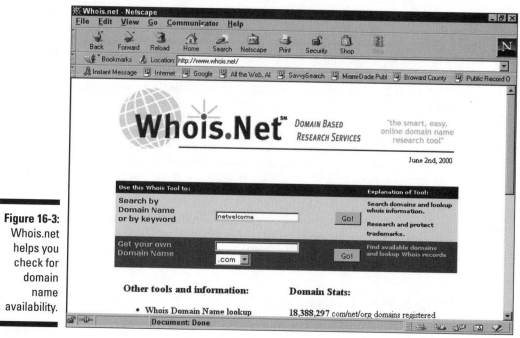

Figure 16-3:
Whois.net
helps you
check for
domain
name
availability.

You can often buy a domain name from the person or organization who's currently using it. It can't hurt to ask, anyway.

Another factor you need to consider when picking a domain name, besides the fact that some organization that's actually using the name has already registered it, is that some companies exist to do nothing but think up good names and register them. They seem to have no intention of ever actually running a real Web site that uses that name, but only to . . . — well, it's hard to think of it as anything but holding the name hostage. The only purpose they have is to own the name and sell it to you. And if you think you'll get it away from them for $70, think again. Hundreds of dollars at least — and the upper end? Limitless for a good name.

Finding a registrar

After you pick a name, you need to register it so that nobody else can use it. This task is usually handled for you by your Web space provider, who's used to the job and probably fills out zillions of these applications every year.

The best-known registrar of domain names in America is Network Solutions (www.networksolutions.com). They register your domain name for $35 a year if you've already got a Web server lined up, or $40 a year to hold your name for you until you're ready to use it. That's called *reserving* or *parking* a domain name, by the way.

For a long time, Network Solutions was the only registrar on the block, but this is no longer the case. Today, many other registrars compete with them. The prices vary a little bit, but not significantly.

It used to be that you had to pay for the first two years at once, but in early 2000, this changed so that you can pay for only one year if you prefer. Many sites that offer assistance in registering your domain name still say that you need to cough up two years' money.

The organization that accredits domain name registrars is the Internet Corporation for Assigned Names and Numbers (ICANN). They maintain lists of the outfits that are authorized to register your domain name.

To register one of the generic TLDs, go to `www.icann.org/registrars/accredited-list.html` and pick one of the registrars in your region.

To register one of the country-level TLDs, go to `www.iana.org/cctld/cctld-whois.htm` and click the name of the country; you find the URL of the country-level registrar at the bottom of the resulting page.

If you decide you don't like your current registrar, you can change. Any of the others will happily take your business away from its competitors.

Online Sources

Table 16-3 lists some places on the World Wide Web where you can find more information on the topics that we cover in this chapter.

Table 16-3	Online Resources
Web Site Name	**Web Address**
Better-Whois.com	`www.betterwhois.com`
FreeISP Directory	`www.freedomlist.com`
FreeWebspace.net	`www.freewebspace.net`
Netcraft	`www.netcraft.com`
ServerWatch	`http://serverwatch.internet.com/webservers.html`
WebServer Compare	`http://webcompare.internet.com`

Chapter 17

Publicizing Your Site

● ●

In This Chapter

▶ Choosing keywords wisely

▶ Getting listed

▶ Checking rank

▶ Trading links

▶ Using banner ads

● ●

*S*earch sites (also called search engines) are a critical part of the World Wide Web. Without them, it's nearly impossible for most people to find what they're looking for. Therefore, it's important for people who're really serious about their own Web sites to know as much about search sites as possible (like by hands-on, real-life experiences). And you can't do much better than trying each of the search sites out. By trying out different search sites, you can see which ones give helpful responses to your particular queries and which ones return nonsense.

Table 17-1 lists the major search sites.

Table 17-1	Major Search Sites
Search Site	*Web Address*
All the Web	www.ussc.alltheweb.com
AltaVista	www.altavista.com
Ask Jeeves	www.ask.com
Direct Hit	www.directhit.com
Excite	www.excite.com
Google	www.google.com

(continued)

Table 17-1 *(continued)*

Search Site	Web Address
HotBot	`http://hotbot.lycos.com`
Lycos	`www.lycos.com`
Northern Light Search	`www.northernlight.com`
Snap	`www.snap.com`
Webcrawler	`www.webcrawler.com`
Yahoo!	`www.yahoo.com`

If you're tired of slow search response times, try All the Web. It gives you answers so fast that your head spins.

To make sure that people know your Web site exists, you should have it listed in lots of search engines. How many you should list in is a matter of opinion. There's certainly no harm in going for broke and listing with every search engine, but there are about 1,500 of them out there, and most of them aren't very well known. In our opinion, after you're listed with all the ones in Table 17-1, any more effort runs into the law of diminishing returns. Yes, you will generate more visits by listing at even more search sites, but you don't get anywhere near as many visits from obscure search sites as you do from the more popular ones.

Using search sites isn't the only way of getting the word out, though. You can also work out reciprocal link arrangements with other Web sites, either on a personal level or through the agency of a banner-link exchange. (See the section "Investigating Reciprocal Linking," later in this chapter.)

Working Keywords

The search sites have different ways of going about gathering information on the content of Web sites. Some of them are put together by human effort, while others are fully automated. In the first case, people visit Web sites with URLs that have been submitted to them and manually categorize the sites. In the latter case, programs called *robots* or *spiders* surf the Web, cataloging their findings and adding Web pages to the search site's database. Robots and spiders don't just note the URL of a page, though. They also index all the words on the page. When someone runs a search, the search terms are compared with these indexed words. Links to whatever sites match the search terms are then shown to the person doing the searching.

In addition to the words in the text of your page (and sometimes in the alt text fields of images and other elements as well), meta keywords are indexed.

Adding meta tags

The META element is one of the most versatile ones in HTML because it's one of the most poorly defined ones. Some would just say it doesn't have many limits. Its name and content attributes let you put a lot of different kinds of information into your HTML documents.

META always goes within the HEAD element, and it has no end tag.

You can have all the META elements you want, but there are only two uses that can matter to a search engine: as a page description, and as a list of keywords. Neither one is essential. In fact, despite the great frenzy about META keywords, your page description and your TITLE element are actually more useful for search engines.

When someone makes a search that returns a hit to your site, the response usually shows your page title and a little bit from the beginning of your page. This response underscores the importance of a good title, but if the first sentence of your page doesn't describe all its contents, that might not be the best possible enticement for someone to visit it. If your page has a META description, however, that will be used to — you guessed it — describe your page.

Imagine that you have a page titled "The Love Letters of Grover Cleveland." Well, that title might not mean much to a lot of folks, and if the first sentence is something like a tame quotation from one of those letters, you're not doing too well. But a good description could fix that:

```
<META name="description" content="The secret life of the 24th
          President">
```

Keywords are added in much the same way:

```
<META name="keywords" content="Grover Cleveland, 24th
          President, Buffalo, New York, Mugwumps">
```

Mugwumps? Trust us — it's a Grover Cleveland thing.

Writing for keywords

The META keywords just aren't that important because the content of the page itself should already have the important terms in it. Some search engines don't even look at keywords. Where keywords are really useful is in a special situation that can't be easily solved in the visible page content without looking silly — you need to intentionally misspell words.

It's a fact: Lots of people have trouble spelling or typing or both. Therefore, you should also add common spelling errors to your list of keywords. If you list *flying saucers* and someone's looking for *flying sossers*, they won't be able to find your site. Well, you may not want them to, but we're not going to get into that. You should also cover yourself for any legitimate spelling variants. For example, if you sell tires and don't want to miss out on the British market, you should also list "tyres" among your keywords.

When it comes to choosing keywords, don't neglect synonyms. One person may look for "car parts" while another searches for "automotive accessories."

The actual content of your Web pages is much more important than META keywords. In fact, it's critical, both to your search engine ranking and to visitor retention. When you write the copy for your pages, make sure to throw in as many terms that accurately describe your topic as you can. As far as the search engines are concerned, the more often you can reasonably include relevant keywords, the better. After all, search engines do rank your Web site by how much the contents of your pages match up with the search term that someone enters.

Writing for your audience

When it comes to the human visitors to your pages, as opposed to the robotic ones, you need to write in a way that entertains your audience. As professional writers, we always try to avoid using the same phrase too often. When we need to refer to the same thing or action over and over again, we strive for new ways to say it. We practically live for synonyms and pronouns.

It can be a difficult balancing act to satisfy your human visitors while at the same time catering to the needs of search engines. You don't want to bore your readers by endlessly repeating the same terms, but you do want to nail down the ranking you deserve. To start with, make up a list of terms that you think that someone might use if they searched for your page. Then go ahead and write your content without paying any attention to your list. Writing your content first is very important because if you stare at your list of terms while you're working, you may stifle your creativity. After you've finished writing your page, take the list and mark down how many times the terms have been used. Go over your page and see where the ones that *weren't* used could be worked in. Then, see where the ones that *were* used might be used again without really screwing up the flow of the writing. After you've done those things, toss the list in the trashcan and reread your page. If it's still good, go with it. If it doesn't read too well, you may have to sacrifice some of the terms to make it more reader-friendly.

Avoiding traps

The traps, in this case, are some of the perfectly normal Web site design approaches. If you use frames or image maps, you're asking for trouble with the search engines. Why? Because many of the search engines don't navigate frames properly, and none of them can read the text in an image map. The same problem crops up when people use images containing text.

Does that mean that you can't do things like putting text-filled images in a table for layout purposes? No, and you don't have to give up on frames or image maps, either. But you do have to provide a plain old text link alternative approach to these fancier methods. Lots of Web designers do so anyway in order to accommodate old or off-brand Web browsers.

If you're using frames, make sure to include NOFRAMES content with all the same links the folks who go through the framed version get. If you're using image maps or image links, toss in a text link somewhere on the page that leads to another page that has text-link versions of all the links from the images.

Playing games with keywords

Lots of the get-rich-quick sites advise you to raise your ratings with the search engines by stacking the deck. Typically, this involves putting the same phrase over and over again into your meta tags, like this:

```
<META name="keywords" content="computer books, computer
          books, computer books, computer books, computer
          books, computer books, computer books">
```

Another common trick is to put content like that into the text of the page itself. Often, Webmasters hide this bogus text from their human readers by setting its color to the same as the page's background color or by making the text so small that it's barely visible or both.

This common trick is not the same thing as legitimately using the same terms and phrases several times in different places within the real context of your Web page. If you run a site that deals with airports, for example, the word *runway* may show up hundreds of times on one page, and anyone searching for that term will rightly find your page.

So why not use the trick method? Well, for starters, it doesn't work. Playing these kinds of games with keywords is a fast way to get dropped from the major search engines altogether. The people who run search engines aren't stupid, and they're fully aware of this type of stunt. They don't much care for sites that try to stack the deck because they're in the business of providing good results, and these kinds of tricks skew the results. You don't want to make enemies of the search engine folks; it's much better to keep on their good side.

Even if you do manage to find a workable trick that artificially boosts your ranking, you're not doing yourself any favors. What if you end up number one on every search but your actual content isn't what you said it was (it's all just a clever use of keywords)? Do you think that the people who drop into your site are going to be coming back? After they find out that you're not delivering what you promised, they'll be off to other destinations before you can blink, and they won't pay any attention to your listing after that, even if it does turn up on top in their next search.

Some of the Web sites that come up on the first page of search results turn out to be dead links. If those sites had paid more attention to site design fundamentals than to search engine ranking, they might still be around.

Analyzing keywords

Getting a look at what other people are doing with and about keywords can be instructive. There are plenty of ways to find out just what people are searching for; if some of those terms fit in with what you're doing, you may want to work them in.

Don't just toss in popular search terms in an attempt to generate bogus hits. Adding *sex* and *MP3* to a site that's about walrus migration patterns won't bring you the kind of visitors you're looking for.

One Web site you may want to get a look at is searchterms.com (www. searchterms.com). This site lists the top 100 search terms gathered from an unnamed major search site. The lack of specificity about the source and methodology used is a bit annoying, but the results on the list do tend to make sense when compared to the results on similar sites.

Another good site to check is The Lycos 50 Daily Report (http://50.lycos. com), as shown in Figure 17-1. These results of the most popular user searches come from Lycos, of course, and they're tallied at the end of every week. This listing is particularly informative because it shows the rank for each term in the previous week as well, and it also shows how many weeks each term has been in the top 50.

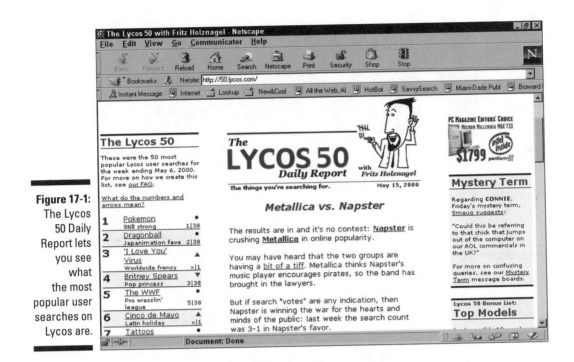

One of the best programs you can lay your hands on is Keyword Live, as shown in Figure 17-2. It runs a check on several search engines to see what keywords people are typing in and shows you the top 100 for each in real time. That's right — not yesterday's news, not what was hot last week, but right now. You can download it from www.analogx.com/contents/download/network/keyword.htm. Try it. You'll like it.

After you get that one, check out Keyword Extractor by the same author. It can be found at www.analogx.com/contents/download/network/keyex.htm. Keyword Extractor lets you analyze Web pages just like search engines do. It indexes all the words on the page and assigns weights to them depending on their frequency of use and position on the page. One of the best ways to use this program is to perform a search at one of the major search sites, follow the links to the top-ranked pages, and run Keyword Extractor on each of those pages. Study the results and you see how those pages earned their rank.

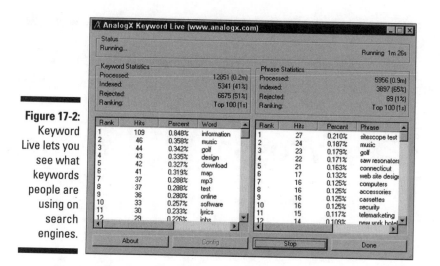

Figure 17-2:
Keyword
Live lets you
see what
keywords
people are
using on
search
engines.

Submitting to the Search Sites

You can just sit around and wait for a spider or robot to trip over your site. Sooner or later, that'll probably happen all by itself. But being proactive and making certain that your site is listed is a lot smarter. You can submit your site on your own, or you can use services that do it for you.

Do it yourself

Why bother doing it yourself when you can pay someone else to do it for you? Well, there's the obvious advantage of saving money. If you're on a shoestring budget, that can matter. If not, you're likely going to say something like, "It'll cost me more money in lost work to do it myself because I can't be doing anything else while I'm doing this." Well, there's something to be said for that reasoning, too.

But there's nothing like making sure that the job gets done right. And it's a wise Webmaster who gets thoroughly familiar with the many variations on how the search engines want Web page URLs to be submitted. We strongly recommend that you try submitting to at least a few of them yourself. Table 17-2 gives the URLs of the submission pages for several major search sites.

Table 17-2	Search Site Submission Pages
Submission Page	**Web Address**
All the Web	`www.ussc.alltheweb.com/add_url.php3`
AltaVista	`www.altavista.com/cgi-bin/query?pg=addurl`
Ask Jeeves	*
Direct Hit	`www.directhit.com/util/addurl.html`
Excite	`www.excite.com/info/add_url`
Google	`www.google.com/addurl.html`
HotBot	`http://hotbot.lycos.com/addurl.asp`
Lycos	`www.lycos.com/addasite.html`
Northern Light Search	`www.northernlight.com/docs/regurl_help.html`
Snap	`www.snap.com/LMOID/resource/0,566,-1077,00.html?st.sn.ld.0.1077`
Webcrawler	`www.webcrawler.com/info/add_url`
Yahoo!	`http://docs.yahoo.com/info/suggest`

Send an e-mail message to `url@askjeeves.com`. In the message, give a brief description of your site and its URL.

Submission services

You get what you pay for, you know? When it comes to Web site submission services, that saying really hits home. Very few of the free services submit your URL to anywhere near as many search sites as the paid ones do. One of the rare exceptions is *the promoter* (`www.thepromoter.com`). The folks there pop you into about 40 search engines and more than 7,000 free listings sites for no charge, except a plug on the page you're listing. Many of the paid services submit your info to lots more search engines, but there's not much payback from listing in all the obscure ones, so the promoter provides a pretty nice deal.

Many Web site submission services fall into kind of a gray area, offering limited free services but charging more for anything extra. iSubmitter.com (`www.isubmitter.com`), for example, has half a dozen different grades of service, including a free submission to ten search engines.

The paid services may or may not be worthwhile, depending on how well they know their stuff. If you're going to part with your hard-earned bucks, you have the right to ask them a few questions first. Make sure that the people you're dealing with understand the differences among the search engines. If they can't tell you things like which ones accept HTML coding in their listings or how long a description is acceptable at a particular search site, you may not be getting much bang for your buck. You may be better off using site submission software like SitePromoter (www.sitepromoter.com).

ProBoost (www.proboost.com), as shown in Figure 17-3, is one really classy example of folks who know what they're all about. With ProBoost, you don't just fill out a form. You can actually work with real-live people who are committed to your success. They have a toll-free support line and a chat room where you can ask questions in the middle of the night.

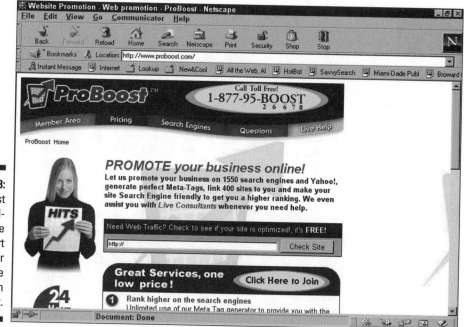

Figure 17-3: ProBoost offers excellent service and support for your Web page submission effort.

Keeping out of the search sites

Not everybody wants all their pages indexed and offered to the general public at a search site. There are two ways to keep a search engine's robot from indexing your site. One may require the assistance of your network administrator or Internet service provider. The other you can do yourself.

For a long time, the only way to lock a search engine out was to use a file called `robots.txt`. This file, located in the top-level domain directory (the same one your home page goes into), lists all banned robots and all directories that can't be searched. The reason you might need some professional help here is that unless you run your own dedicated server, you may not have access to the top-level domain directory. Putting `robots.txt` anywhere else doesn't do any good at all. If your Web site is housed on your ISP's server or on a virtual server, it's really in a subdirectory of a dedicated Web server. What you need to do in this case is to let the person who runs your HTTP server know which directories you don't want searched. They'll take care of the rest, which consists of simply listing those directories in a text file. The following example shows how to block all robots from searching two sample directories:

```
User-agent: *
Disallow: /~mine/private/
Disallow: /~mine/personal/
```

Someone who wants to pry into your site can get a good start by looking at the contents of your `robots.txt` file. After all, it contains a list of all the directories and files you don't want the world to see. If there's anything confidential in those areas, `robots.txt` is a road map pointing straight to it.

If you want to grab control yourself, or if you just want to avoid using `robots.txt`, you can turn to our good old friend, the `META` tag. Remember that we said that tag was versatile. Well, this is another useful application for it. By assigning the `name` attribute a value of `robots` and adding one or more variables to the `content` attribute, you can specify your desires about the page it's in.

By default, a search robot will both index your page, adding the words in it to the search site's database, and follow all the links on the page. If you want to disallow both of these behaviors, you add the following HTML code in the `HEAD` element of your file:

```
<META name="robots" content="noindex,nofollow">
```

You can accomplish the same thing by using a value of `none`:

```
<META name="robots" content="none">
```

Technically, you can do the opposite of this, allowing both options, by using a value of `all`, but there's no point to doing that. If you want both options working, just don't do anything.

To allow the indexing, but keep robots from following your links, you use this line of code:

```
<META name="robots" content="nofollow">
```

Remember that robot's indexing and the link following are default behaviors, so you don't need to specify either one if you're allowing it. Thus, the preceding code doesn't mention indexing at all. You could, if you want to be pedantic about it, say the same thing like this:

```
<META name="robots" content="index,nofollow">
```

To allow a robot to follow your links, but deny it from indexing, use this code:

```
<META name="robots" content="noindex">
```

Checking Your Search Site Position

You need to follow up on your submissions to make sure, not only that you are listed (different search sites take different lengths of time to react), but also to find out where you land in the rankings when your keywords are used in a search.

Manual checking

Obviously, the fastest way to find out both of these things is to log on to the search engines you've submitted to and check things out. First off, enter the name of your site and see if it comes up at all. If not, and it's been more time than the search engine is supposed to take, you might want to resubmit to them.

This is also a great way to find out which other Web sites have links to yours because any page with your site's name on it will show up in the search results. (See the section "Investigating Reciprocal Linking," later in this chapter.)

If your site does come up, you'll want to enter the keywords from your site as search terms. This shows you real fast just where you fall in the rankings. Assuming that some other sites show up on top of your own, it's worthwhile to take a look at their source code to see what keywords they use. Also, don't forget to look their pages over very carefully. This is one of those rare instances where your competitors' techniques are literally an open book.

ScoreCheck

Most Web site submission services will also check up on your ranking for you after the submissions are complete. If your service doesn't do this, if you've done your own submissions, or if you just plain want a change of pace, take a look at ScoreCheck (www.scorecheck.com). You can try that company's service out for free; it's shown in Figure 17-4. ScoreCheck will run your Web site's URL through ten major search engines and report to you where you rank with each of them.

Actually, the folks at ScoreCheck do quite a bit more than that. You can also compare your site's ranking with other specified sites, check to see who's using your trademarked or copyrighted material, and track down good sites to set up reciprocal links with. This is another site that you'd be well advised to check out.

Figure 17-4:
ScoreCheck finds out where your Web site ranks with major search engines.

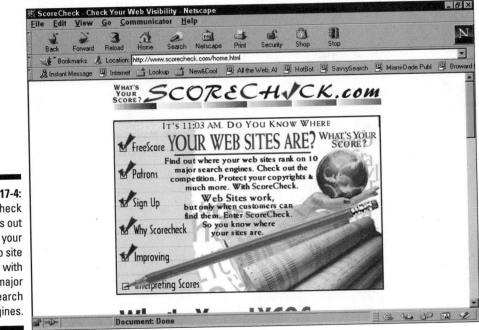

Investigating Reciprocal Linking

Reciprocal linking is the Net's equivalent of "You scratch my back, and I'll scratch yours." The way it works is this: You put in a link on your page to another Web site, and the other Web site returns the favor by putting in a link to yours. Even directly competing sites can benefit from a link to one another, just as two restaurants can happily exist side by side.

So whom do you want to link with? Well, the simple answer is "Anybody and everybody." The smart answer, though, is "The best and most popular sites in my category." What's best is a matter of your own opinion, but it's pretty easy to find the most popular ones, and you can use this technique to piggyback on their success.

What you need to do is to spend some time working the search engines. Here's the drill:

1. **Enter the keywords you think people would use to find your site.**

2. **Follow the links in the results to the other sites that are similar to your own.**

   All search engines will return some poor responses, so don't automatically assume that all the results will be good reciprocal link sources for your Web site.

3. **Look for an e-mail link to the site's owner.**

   Typically, this type of link will be found at the bottom of the page, but it may be anywhere.

4. **Click the link and send the site's Webmaster a message politely suggesting that you both link up.**

It doesn't hurt to take the time to put in a link to the other site first. That way, you can say something like, "I've linked to your site and would appreciate a return link from yours." This takes the discussion out of the realm of the hypothetical and puts the other site's Webmaster under an obligation to respond in kind. No guarantees, but most people do.

Sometimes, there isn't any kind of contact info at all on a Web site, no matter how hard you look. If that's the case and you really want to set up a reciprocal link with that site, you can run a search on the site's domain name by using a WhoIs service. WhoIs identifies the administrative, billing, and technical contacts for a domain. The best known one is at Network Solutions (www.networksolutions.com/cgi-bin/whois/whois). Or you can do it from your own system with software such as WhoIs ULTRA from AnalogX (www.analogx.com/contents/download/network/whois.htm).

Another worthwhile program you may want to check out is Link Trader (www.net-matrix.com/linktrader). You use Link Trader to create a database of all the people you've set up reciprocal links with, and it checks those sites to verify that the link back to you still exists. Keep the database up to date and run the program on a regular basis, and you can quickly spot any sites that drop your link. Then you can e-mail the Webmasters and ask them to put the link back in. For only $20, it's a worthwhile purchase.

Many search engines consider the number of other sites with links to yours when determining how high you rank. This means that of two sites, with everything else being equal, the one with more links leading to it from other sites shows up before the other one in search results. Think about it. Reciprocal linking is one powerful tool that you can use to legitimately boost your own site's ratings.

Joining Web rings

Web rings are a kind of super reciprocal link arrangement. Instead of making a reciprocal link between two sites, you make it with an entire group of similar sites at a time. Web rings can be found on just about any topic you care to name, and many such rings can be found at www.webring.org or www.ringsurf.com. You can also start your own Web ring if you want to.

The weakness of Web rings is that they link in a ring. In other words, each one links to the previous one in the list and the next one in the list. If any one site drops out of the ring, that messes up the whole thing, just as if you broke a link in a chain.

Joining a banner exchange

In a *banner exchange,* each member creates a banner ad and submits it to a central site. That site, the exchange itself, automates the process of displaying all the members' ads on all the other members' Web sites. A banner exchange sounds like a great idea, but in practice, few banner exchanges survive for very long. Make sure, when considering joining one, that you ask how long it's been in operation. Also make it a point to contact current members and see how satisfied they are with the exchange.

That said, joining a banner exchange is an easy task. You fill out a simple application form on the exchange's Web site; then you send the exchange your banner and place some HTML code on your site. That's all there is to it — everything else is handled by the exchange. There are several reputable banner exchanges listed in "Online Sources."

Online Sources

Table 17-3 lists some places on the World Wide Web where you can find more information on the topics we cover in this chapter.

Table 17-3	Online Resources
Web Site Name	**Web Address**
Ask Jeeves Peek Through the Keyhole	www.askjeeves.com/docs/peek/
Banner Ad Network	www.banneradnetwork.com
BannerExpress	www.bannerexpress.com
BannerPromo.com	www.bannerpromo.com
Cyber-Pro	www.cyber-pro.com
Dynamic Submission 2000	www.submission2000.com
EIS Banner Exchange	http://einets.com/stats/gsa
Guerilla Marketing Online	www.gmarketing.com/cgi-bin/main.pl
HitExchange	www.hitexchange.net
LinkBuddies Banner Exchange	www.linkbuddies.com/banners/index.html
Magellan Search Voyeur	http://voyeur.mckinley.com/cgi-bin/voyeur.cgi
MetaSpy	www.metaspy.com
SavvySnoop	www.savvysearch.com/snoop
Search Engine Report Newsletter	http://searchenginewatch.com/sereport/index.html
Search Spy	www.searchspy.com
SmartClicks	www.smartage.com/promote/smartclicks

Chapter 18

Keeping in Touch

● ●

In This Chapter

▶ Using autoresponders

▶ Distributing electronic newsletters

▶ Spreading the word about new content on your Web site

● ●

*W*hen someone initially visits your site, you naturally want them to keep on coming back. One of the natural ways to do that is to keep in touch, let the visitor know what's new, and remind them that you're there. The problem is *spam* — no, not the canned meat — it's Internet slang for unsolicited commercial e-mail. If you haven't gotten plenty of it already, you probably don't have an e-mail address at all. Get-rich-quick schemes, health products that make you live forever, and all sorts of other garbage zoom back and forth across the Net, clogging mailboxes and raising hackles.

So how do you keep in touch without spamming? The answer is simple — you only send e-mail messages to those visitors who request them. That way, everybody's happy. You get to build up a following among your visitors, and they get to receive the information they ask for. This chapter presents tools that make it easy for your visitors to keep up with what's going on at your site while keeping you out of the doghouse with your Web space provider.

Using Autoresponders

Autoresponders are programs that automatically send an e-mail message to a visitor who requests one. The visitor makes the request either by sending an e-mail to your autoresponder address or by making the request through a form on your Web site.

Okay, so what? Well, it all depends on what your message says. Say, for example, that your e-mail message contains your current catalog or the sale of the week. Sound like something useful?

You can even set up several different documents that people can request. This technique is useful if the things you sell or talk about can be easily organized into categories. Thus a Web site that sells software might put together one gigantic catalog or set up several links, such as <u>Click here to receive our productivity catalog</u> and <u>Click here to get information on graphics software</u>.

So far, so good. What you have is a perfectly spam-free way for people to get detailed information on demand, and the autoresponder does all the work for you. All you do is write up the documents and upload them once. From then on, the autoresponder takes care of all the drudgery.

But another feature of autoresponders borders on spammishness. You can set them up so that they send not only one message but several different messages over a period of time. The basic idea is that it often takes more than one contact to close a sale, which is true, as anyone in sales knows. The problem is that the person making the request for the first document isn't requesting a whole series of messages over several weeks or months. It's a gray area, and you should probably be well advised to carefully consider whether to use that feature.

Check with your Web space provider to see whether they have autoresponders available as part of your basic service.

WebMailStation.com

WebMailStation.com (www.webmailstation.com) has both free and paid autoresponders. The basic difference between them is that there's no advertising in the paid version. With either version, you can have up to ten different messages sent to the requestor. The autoresponders avoid the spam problem by adding a link that allows the customers to remove their names from the mailing list in each message. The autoresponder also automatically sends a copy of every request to you so that you can respond personally if necessary.

To sign up for WebMailStation.com's service, follow these steps:

1. **Go to** www.webmailstation.com **and click the <u>Sign Up Now!</u> link.**

2. **Read the material on the resulting page, scroll to the bottom of it, and click the I Accept button.**

3. **Enter a member name, password, and password double-check question on the next page; click the Forward button.**

4. **On the next page, enter your personal information and click the Forward button.**

   The final page shows your username and password and includes some important links. This information is also sent to the e-mail address that you use to register.

To set up your autoresponders with WebMailStation.com, follow these steps:

1. **Go to** www.webmailstation.com, **enter your username and password, and click the Go button.**

2. **On the resulting page, click the** Edit Your Responders **link.**

3. **Click the** Reply #1 **link.**

4. **Set the delay to 0 (zero) because this is the first message and you want it to go out right away (see Figure 18-1).**

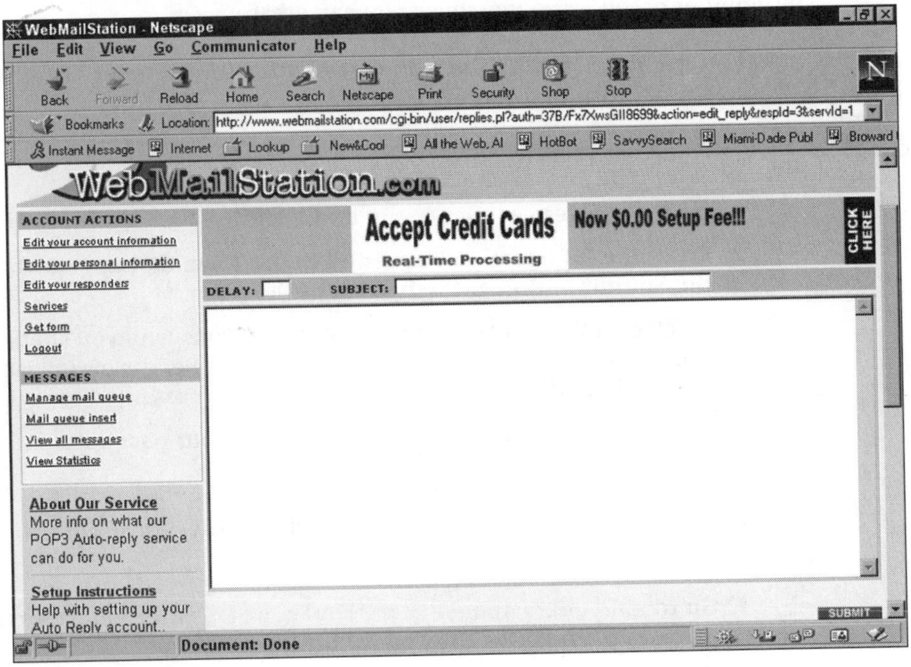

Figure 18-1:
You can set
WebMail
Station.com
responses
to suit your
situation.

5. **Enter your subject in the Subject text box and paste your response in the text area.**

6. **Scroll down and click the Submit button.**

7. **To create a follow-up message, click the Add New button.**

8. **Enter the number of days between this response and the previous message in the Delay text box.**

9. **Enter your subject and paste your response into the text area.**

10. **Scroll down and click the Submit button.**

11. **Repeat Steps 7 through 10 for any subsequent responses.**

The delay value for follow-up messages at WebMailStation.com sets the amount of time to wait between messages. If you want to send a daily message, for example, you set the first delay at 0, the second at 1, and all subsequent ones at 1 as well.

GetResponse.com

GetResponse.com (www.getresponse.com) is another autoresponder service that provides both free and paid services. There is no limit on the number of follow-up messages you can create.

If you decide to go with the paid version of autoresponder, GetResponse.com offers a 30-day money-back guarantee.

To sign up with GetResponse.com, follow these steps:

1. **Go to** www.getresponse.com **and click the Sign Up For Free button.**

2. **Enter the information requested in the form that appears and click the Submit button at the bottom of the page.**

   You face a Web page filled with all the reasons why you should switch from a free to a paid service. No response is necessary unless you want to switch. In that case, click any of the links presented to you.

   You receive an e-mail message containing your password and a couple of useful links.

To set up your autoresponder message with GetResponse.com, follow these steps:

1. **Go to** www.getresponse.com/login.html, **enter your username and password, and click the Log In! button.**

2. **On the resulting page, click the Edit messages link.**

3. **Scroll down past the upgrade information to get to the message form.**

4. **Enter your subject in the text box and paste your response message into the text area.**

5. **Enter 0 in the Delay text box so that the message goes out as soon as it's requested.**

6. **Click the Save Message button.**

   After you have some messages, you can get to them by choosing one from the drop-down list under Select Message, as shown in Figure 18-2. After it's selected, you can either edit or delete it.

7. **Repeat Steps 2 through 6 for any subsequent messages.**

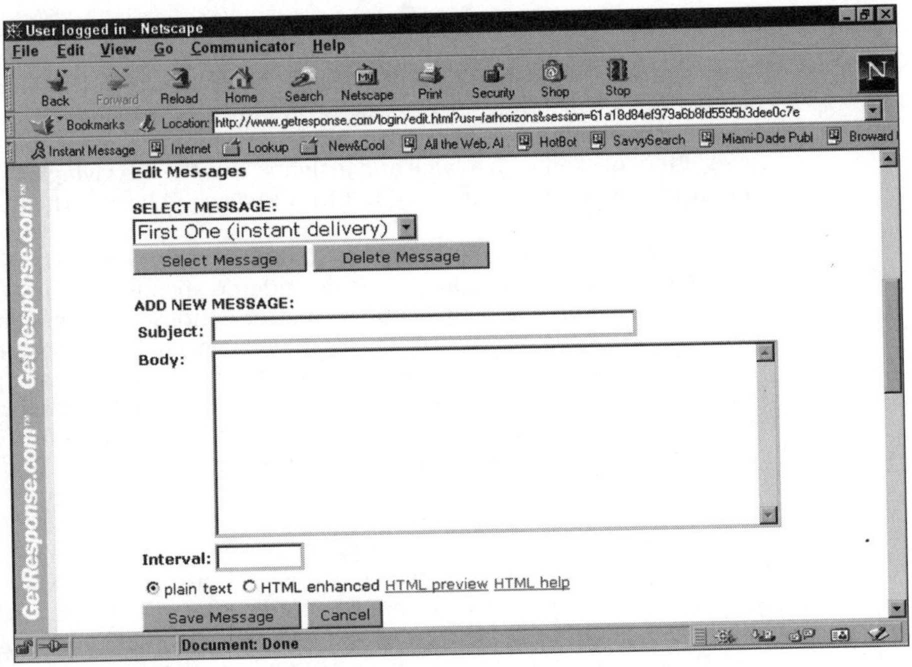

Figure 18-2:
You can
easily edit
or delete
your mes-
sages by
using the
Select
Message
drop-down
list.

The delay value for follow-up messages at GetResponse.com sets the amount of time to wait from the date of the first request, not the amount of time between each message. So if you want to send a message every day, your first message should have a delay of 0, your second one should have a delay of 1, the third should have a delay of 2, and so on.

Opt-In Newsletters

Newsletters are short, privately produced publications that focus on a single topic. They've been around for hundreds of years, but rising postage costs drove many of them out of business. Now that e-mail is such a common part of life, they're making a major comeback. In its purest form, a newsletter is dedicated to covering current situations, like a newspaper does, but it usually provides a deeper analytical approach. Many newsletters, however, have nothing to do with news but deal with business or professional interests. Because they're often written by one person or a small team of people, they tend to be informal and highly opinionated.

We once received a remarkably honest item that looked a great deal like a newsletter. Under the title, the masthead bore the motto "A Catalog Thinly Disguised as a Newsletter." That's probably the single most common use of newsletters. Even if they're not directly offering products for sale, they're still a sales and marketing tool. Many consultants, for example, send out monthly newsletters packed with advice and insights. Yes, they're giving away a little bit of their services for free this way, but they're also publicizing their expertise.

Many services let you send messages to their own targeted lists of e-mail addresses. Normally, this practice is considered spamming, but if the lists are generated from opt-ins, that's another matter entirely. *Opt-in* mailing lists are much less intrusive or prone to errors than normal mailing lists, because the safeguard makes it impossible for anybody to sign someone else up for one. With an opt-in system, a person enters their e-mail address in a form. They then receive a message in their mailbox that asks them to confirm their subscription. If they don't reply to that message, their address doesn't go into the system.

The problem with other people's lists is that because you didn't run the opt-in service yourself, there's no way to know for sure that all the names on the list are legitimate. And some of the companies that offer these "opportunities" also seem to be heavily into hype and get-rich-quick philosophies. You have to be very careful not to get caught up in spamming.

The services that we list in this section don't adhere to get-rich-quick schemes and spamming. They help you run your own opt-in system off your own site, while taking most of the workload off you. This setup gives you the best of both worlds.

Although you're using an opt-in system, it's still a good idea to begin your newsletter with something like this: *"For subscribers only.* You received this newsletter because you filled out the opt-in form for XYZ News at `www.xyznewsoptin.com`. We keep our subscriber information completely confidential. If you have any questions, e-mail us at `subscriptions@xyznewsoptin.com`."

Eurofreebies

Eurofreebies (`www.eurofreebies.com`) mailing list service is a rarity — a free service that doesn't hang advertising on your messages. So how do they make any money? Ads are involved, as you'd expect, but they don't involve you at all. If someone subscribes to your newsletter through Eurofreebies, they're shown a thank-you page after they click the form's button. This page has an ad banner at the top of it. Your newsletter, though, doesn't carry any ads unless you put in some of your own. In our opinion, this system is painless and definitely not intrusive, and we wish more people would use something like it.

To set up a free account with Eurofreebies, follow these steps:

1. **Go to** `www.eurofreebies.com/maillist/subscribe/step1.mv.`

2. **Enter the required information (such as name, e-mail address, and so on) in the form that appears and click the Submit button.**

3. **Click the Proceed To The Next Step button.**

   On the next page, you see examples of two forms for people to use to subscribe to your newsletter.

4. **Click the radio button next to the form you want to use on your site; then scroll down and click the Make Your Choice button.**

5. **Click the Proceed To The Third Step button that appears next.**

   Now you need to enter a welcome message that appears to people on the Web page that is shown after they subscribe, as well as one that goes to their e-mail addresses. Enter the first one in the text area at the top of the page. Enter the subject of the e-mail message in the text box in the lower portion of the page and the message itself in the text area below that text box.

6. **After you finish typing your message, click the Proceed To The Fourth Step button at the bottom of the page.**

   At this stage, you have some options to choose. If you want to get an e-mail message that tells you every time someone signs up for your newsletter, select the first check box. If you want to add a signature file to your outgoing newsletters, select the second check box and enter the sig in the text area right under it. Although the opt-in approach is the default method, you can also click the Use Direct Subscription radio button. Finally, you click the radio button next to the date format you want to use.

7. **When you finish selecting the options you want, click the Proceed To The Last Step button.**

   A Web page appears that gives you some HTML code to copy and paste into your own page. There are also two links underneath the code. The first is the link to the Eurofreebies page where you'll manage your newsletter. The second link leads to a form for unsubscribing from your newsletter.

8. **Copy and paste the HTML code into your own page and then bookmark the first link and add the second link to your Web page.**

To manage your account, go to `www.eurofreebies.com/login.html` and enter your username and password; then click the Submit button. The resulting page has all the bells and whistles you'll ever need. Well, actually it only has buttons. But there are lots of buttons, and they all lead to simple and intuitive forms. There are buttons that let you display your subscriber list, add and delete people, view archived messages, change your options, get a copy of the HTML code for your page, and just about anything else you can imagine.

Eurofreebies sends you an e-mail message when you first sign up, containing both the HTML code and the URLs you need.

To send a newsletter, for example, you click the Send a Message or a Newsletter button. In the resulting form, you can choose to send a test message. With the test-mode option, you can fire off your newsletter without having any of your subscribers see it. Only you get the resulting e-mail message, and it's not added to the archive. That way, you can double-check that your newsletter looks exactly the way you want it to after it appears in your subscribers' mailboxes.

You can also choose whether to use HTML in the outgoing message or keep it as plain text. Other than that, all you have to do is enter a subject and paste your newsletter into the text area. Then click the Send the Newsletter button beneath the newsletter text (see Figure 18-3).

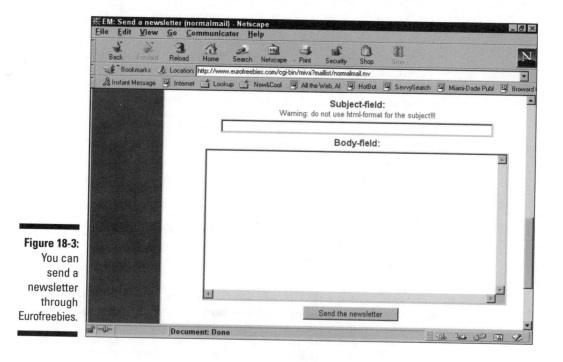

Figure 18-3:
You can send a newsletter through Eurofreebies.

OakNet Publishing

OakNet Publishing (www.oaknetpub.com) is a professional e-mail newsletter service. It doesn't write your newsletter, but it takes care of everything else. And we do mean *everything*.

After you sign up, they send you the HTML code for a form you put on your site to enable people to subscribe and unsubscribe. OakNet has a strict policy of supporting only opt-in situations and doesn't tolerate any spamming. All you have to do is copy and paste the code into one or more of your Web pages.

OakNet keeps track of who is a subscriber and removes anyone who unsubscribes. It takes care of returned mail and deletes bad e-mail addresses. Of course, you can check out the number of subscribers and snag a copy of the addresses for your own records.

They also store your back issues. Your visitors can order any of the back issues of your newsletter right from your site by using the same form they used for subscriptions.

So how hard is it for you to use OakNet to send out a newsletter? Well, you have to log on to the site and paste your newsletter into a form. Then you click a button. Tough job, isn't it?

Did we mention that all this service isn't free? But, the good news is that it's not expensive either — $35 a month for each 10,000 subscribers. You should easily be able to generate more than that in increased business due to the newsletter.

Even if you can't, though, you still may be able to turn a profit through OakNet. Although they don't require you to carry any advertising, they're more than happy to get you some ad money — what pals! All you do is paste a short ad into your next newsletter. Of course, there's no guarantee that anybody will advertise in your newsletter, but if you put together a good newsletter, and build up thousands of subscribers, the odds are pretty good. The financials are pretty good, too — in fact, they're better than almost any affiliates program can manage. OakNet keeps a cut and sends you two-thirds of the ad money — the day your newsletter goes out. That's right. Not months later. Right away.

Sound good? Why are you waiting? Here's how to sign up:

1. **Go to** www.oaknetpub.com/services/welcome.html.

2. **Scroll down and click the Order Form button.**

3. **On the resulting order page, click the <u>Check Out Now</u> link, as shown in Figure 18-4.**

Don't click the <u>Continue Shopping</u> link. If you do, you go back to the Web site. If you then click the Order Form button again, you find that the shopping cart thinks that you ordered two accounts. If you already did so before reading these instructions, click the Decrease Quantity button on the shopping cart form to get back down to one account.

4. **On the next page, click the top button if you plan to telephone in or snail mail your credit-card information; click the bottom button if you plan to use OakNet's secure online-order system.**

5. **Enter the required information into the form and click the Submit Secure Order button at the bottom of the page.**

Keeping Visitors Updated with Mind-it

So you made some changes to your site. You worked hard on them from the conception to the follow-through, and you're just thrilled with the results. Well, personal satisfaction is nice, but what about all those people who have already visited your site? Are they going to know about all the improvements that you made?

Figure 18-4: OakNet Publishing offers newsletter services at a reasonable price.

They notice if you use an update notification service such as Mind-it. Mind-it is a great service from NetMind (www.netmind.com). It not only keeps track of and reports on changes to your page, but your visitors can even set it up to watch for specific words that you're adding. For example, if you run a sports site, visitors can set it up to notify them whenever you add something about their favorite team.

Update notifications aren't for every site, however. A well-run general news site that changes several times a day would drive people crazy with a deluge of e-mails. For the average site, however, it's one of those things that you wake up every day thankful to have.

To add Mind-it to your site, follow these steps:

1. **Go to** www.netmind.com/html/wmmindit.html **and click the** <u>Get Started Now!</u> **link.**

   Two buttons are on the resulting page. The Start Wizard button leads to a series of steps that help you implement options. The Basic Features button skips the details and goes straight to a page with the HTML code to include Mind-it on your site. Because all you have to do is copy and paste the code, you follow the wizard's path here.

   The first page in the wizard asks for basic information, such as your name and URL.

2. **After you enter the facts that the wizard asks for, click the Next button at the bottom of the page.**

   On the second page, you need to choose a password and fill out some information about your Web site.

3. **After you finish filling out the info, click the Next button at the bottom of the page.**

4. **On the third page, select which button type you want to put on your site (see Figure 18-5).**

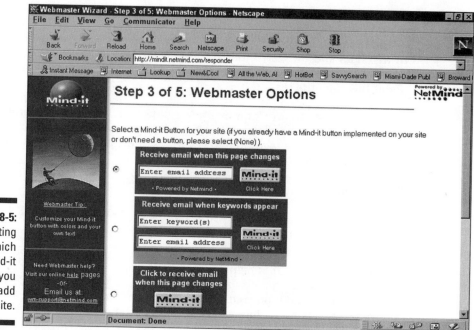

Figure 18-5: Selecting which Mind-it buttons you want to add to your site.

You can get more buttons at `www.netmind.com/html/webmaster_buttons.html`.

Scroll down under the button options, and you find a text area. If you want to include your own message, perhaps something like "We're always on the job keeping you up to date," enter it here.

There's also a text box into which you can enter a URL. Normally, after a visitor registers your site with Mind-it, they're returned to the Web page on your site that they started from. If you'd rather they return to a different page, put its URL in this box.

Way down at the bottom of this page, you find your Publisher ID, which you may need later if you want to manually add a customized message to the update notification.

5. **Save and/or print a copy of the Publisher ID page so you have a record of that ID. Click the Next button at the bottom of the page.**

   The fourth page simply lists some of the information you've already entered.

It's easier to add the customized message by just running this wizard again and pasting the new code over the old code. If you're an incurable tinkerer, though, or if you just like typing, you can get the full instructions at www.netmind.com/html/admin_central.html#embed.

6. **If you entered some wrong information, click the Back button to go back and fix it; if everything's okay, click the Next button.**

   The fifth and final page lists the HTML code that was generated as a result of the answers you gave earlier in the process.

7. **Copy the HTML code and paste it into your own Web page; then click the Finish button.**

Mind-it e-mails the HTML code to you, along with a list of important links that you can use.

There are some situations — maybe many of them, depending on your site — where you don't want everyone to get an e-mail message every time something changes. Mind-it has that base covered. You can set off a section of your page by using a couple of custom tags. There are both HTML and SGML versions, and you can use whichever ones your Web-page editor likes best.

The HTML version:

```
<mind-it-ignore>
Content to be ignored goes here.
</mind-it-ignore>
```

The SGML version:

```
<!--$mind-it-ignore$-->
Content to be ignored goes here.
<!--$/mind-it-ignore$-->
```

Online Sources

Table 18-1 lists some places on the World Wide Web where you can find more resources like the ones that we cover in this chapter.

Table 18-1	Online Resources
Web Site Name	*Web Address*
60kOpt-In	www.dollarsontheweb.com/60kOptIn.htm
AUTORESPONDERS.ORG	http://autoresponders.org
AWeber Systems	www.aweber.com
NO SPAMM Opt-In Mailing List	www.themarketingedge.com/nospamm
SendFree	www.sendfree.com
Websitings	www.websitings.com

Part VI
The Part of Tens

The 5th Wave   By Rich Tennant

"Hold your horses. It takes time to build a home page for someone your size."

In this part . . .

Well, it just wouldn't be a For Dummies book without The Part of Tens. Chapter 19 shows you where to go when you need to find out the answers to everything from business and legal issues to grammar. Chapter 20 is a guide to some of the best things an e-commerce site can add. And Chapter 21 is a potpourri of ten more great add-ins.

Chapter 19

Ten Great Places to Get Advice

In This Chapter

▶ Web Watch

▶ MyService Experts Avenue

▶ grammarNOW!

▶ geek/talk Forums For Webmasters

▶ The Small Business Advisor

▶ LawGuru.com

▶ Bizy Moms

▶ Ezine Factory

▶ Poor Richard's Web Site

▶ eBoz!

*W*e all need advice from time to time. Even if you're terribly independent, as nearly self-sufficient as can be, there are times when you need to turn to others for assistance. Well, here are ten Web sites where you can go if you feel the need to ask for help. Each site has its own special feeling and its own particular set of standards. But somewhere in this chapter, you're gonna find a few places that you'll be so happy to know about that you'll just thank us from here to there for including them. Trust us. We like you. We wouldn't lead you astray.

Web Watch

Web Watch is an e-commerce e-zine with a difference: It's actually worth reading. Granted, it doesn't have as many neat links as we've packed into this book, but against competition like us, who stands a chance? (For the humor-impaired, that's a joke — consider yourself officially notified.) You can visit Web Watch, as shown in Figure 19-1, at the following address:

```
www.cozahost.co.za/WebWatch/default.htm
```

Seriously, folks, the links at Web Watch, although fewer than you find on some sites that have a lot less to offer, are premium. It's worth your time to follow them. If they're internal links, they lead to good articles on Web work; if they're external, they lead to decent tools that you should consider adding to your own repertoire.

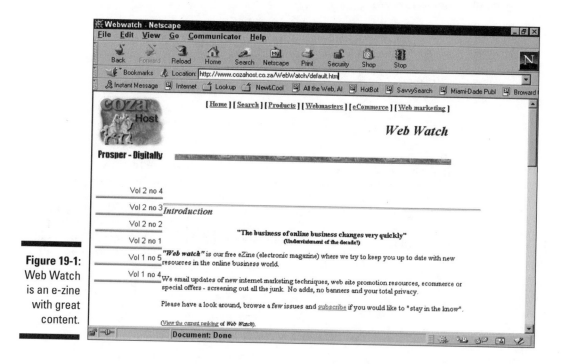

Figure 19-1:
Web Watch
is an e-zine
with great
content.

MyService Experts Avenue

This one is a great place to get answers on a wide variety of topics, ranging from businesses to computers (see Figure 19-2). It's also a great source of information on lots of things that Web people need to know. Want to start a home-based business? Want to know about tax liabilities? Or about e-commerce or Web design? Ask 'em. Just enter the following URL into your browser to access the site:

```
http://myservice.com/MyService/advice/index.html
```

They've got the people who know all the answers, and they'll get back to you quickly with good, solid information.

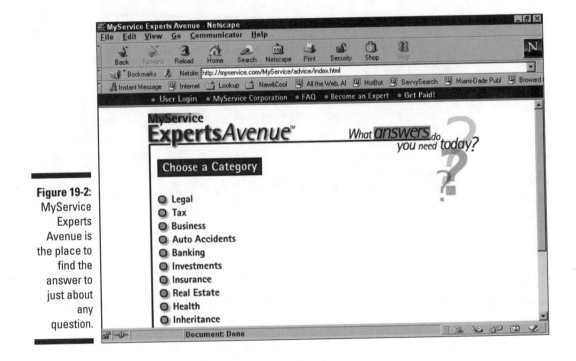

Figure 19-2:
MyService
Experts
Avenue is
the place to
find the
answer to
just about
any
question.

grammarNOW!

Do your participles dangle embarrassingly? Are your diphthongs out of style? If you ever stay awake wondering about these mighty questions, grammarNOW! (see Figure 19-3) is your kind of site. This site is one place where you can get free answers to those embarrassing questions with complete confidentiality. The folks who run this site e-mail you an answer without showing the world that you don't know what to do about the ablative absolute. To access the site, just go to the following Web address:

www.grammarnow.com

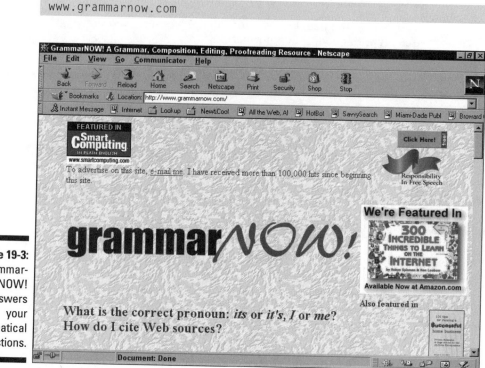

Figure 19-3: grammar-NOW! answers your grammatical questions.

If you're really out on a limb, you'll be happy to know that not only can you get a quick answer for free, but you can actually hire the brains behind this site to go over your whole Web site with a fine-tooth comb and clear up any grammatical problems on it. And their list of grammar links is well worth exploring on its own.

geek/talk Forums For Webmasters

Ah, fellow geeks! This is the place where you can let it all hang out. The geek/talk bulletin board (see Figure 19-4) is for those of us who just *love* technical stuff, who absolutely live for the last bit that we can squeeze out of HTML, who . . . well, you get the idea. Actually, you're welcome to pop in even if you have the simplest questions in the world. Even if you don't know the first thing about HTML, this site is the place to ask your dumbest questions and expect a civil answer. Just hop on over to the following address:

```
http://geekvillage.com/ubb/Ultimate.cgi
```

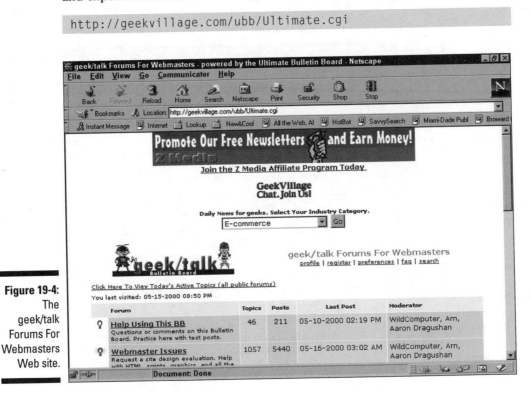

Figure 19-4:
The geek/talk Forums For Webmasters Web site.

This wonderland is a great place to visit. Here, there are folks who are interested in all the same things you are, from Web design to e-commerce. And you can find a different BBS (bulletin board service) for just about any topic you care to discuss.

The Small Business Advisor

The Small Business Advisor is one handy little resource for all of you who're even thinking about opening up your own business (see Figure 19-5). It covers everything from taxes to insurance and has business news that actually makes sense to small-business people (and tall ones, too). Their free e-mail newsletter is a prime source of savvy advice, useful information, and links that you'll want to click. Just visit the following URL:

```
www.isquare.com
```

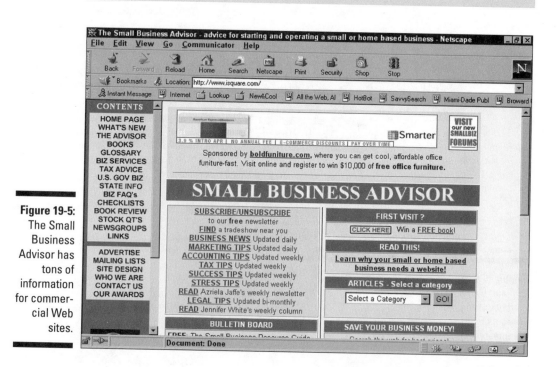

Figure 19-5:
The Small Business Advisor has tons of information for commercial Web sites.

The site's various checklists alone are worth the visit — they cover everything from choosing a business partner or a bank to working with an attorney. Lists of business-oriented newsgroups, Internet-specific business commentary, and state-specific contact information are just a few of the tidbits that this site offers.

LawGuru.com

We figure that we're kind of uniquely qualified to comment on this site, seeing as how we did our own law firm's site (which is `www.coberlaw.com`, by the way — tell 'em we sent ya). Anyway, LawGuru.com is a nice source for legal research (see Figure 19-6). You can check out everything, from that money you forgot you were owed to the latest U.S. Code revisions. Pop on in to the following address:

```
www.lawguru.com
```

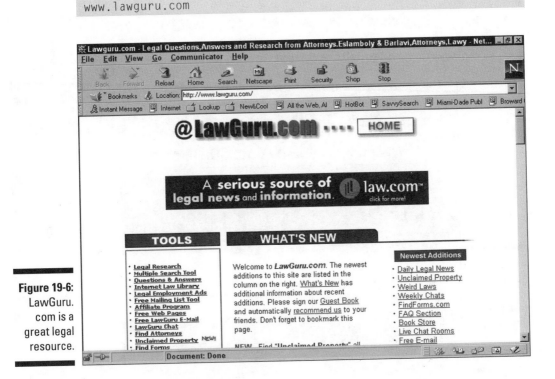

Figure 19-6: LawGuru. com is a great legal resource.

They've got a huge database of legal questions and answers, and if you can't find what you're looking for in it, you can submit your own questions to them. They've also got chat rooms for both attorneys and normal people and a no-nonsense FAQ (Frequently Asked Questions) on copyright.

Bizy Moms

Despite its name, this site appeals to both the mother and father who want to work from home while raising a family (see Figure 19-7). Live chats on issues such as "The Internet, Money, and You" or "Business on a Shoestring" are constantly taking place. Bizy Moms is the best place to go if you want to know about free postage, Internet marketing, or just about anything else of interest to the home-working parent. To check out the site, go to the following Web address:

www.bizymoms.com

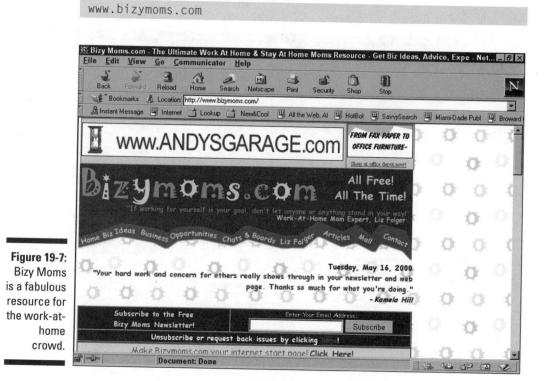

Figure 19-7:
Bizy Moms is a fabulous resource for the work-at-home crowd.

Toss in the advice on time management and paperwork control from those who've been there, and you're just beginning to explore this site.

Ezine Factory

Okay, so Ezine Factory's got the usual salesmen with mustaches — it's still a good source of advice on Internet marketing, with worthwhile links to things like the Tell-a-friend Broadcaster, which lets people recommend your site to others. Really, this site is different. It makes sense. It's got good stuff on it. The Ezine Factory is shown in Figure 19-8, and you can see it for yourself at the following URL:

```
www.ezinefactory.co.za
```

Figure 19-8:
The Ezine Factory's Web site offers great advice on Internet marketing and a number of worthwhile links to explore.

The one thing that's both annoying about the site and a treasure trove is the collection of articles written by outsiders. Although you've got to sift through them carefully to find the diamonds hidden in the rest of it, it's worth your time.

Poor Richard's Web Site

Now, you just *know* that we hate to plug another author, don't you? Especially if he writes for a different publisher. Well, that gives you a slight idea just how good Peter Kent (Poor Richard) is. He's got a fabulous newsletter, great ideas on Web site promotion, and lots of other goodies. You can visit Poor Richard's Web Site, as shown in Figure 19-9, at the following address:

```
http://poorrichard.com
```

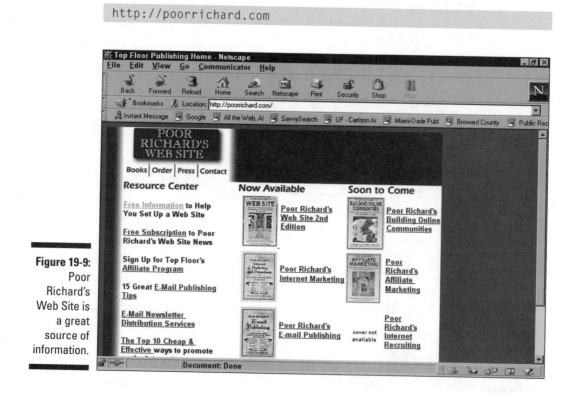

Figure 19-9:
Poor
Richard's
Web Site is
a great
source of
information.

Make sure that you check out his <u>Free Information</u> link. It contains articles and links that you'll want to explore, such as the Top 10 Mistakes and Add A Shopping Cart links.

eBoz!

Well, granted, its name's kind of weird, but if you're interested in Web design, this site's a pretty nice place to stop in and absorb things. And eBoz!, shown in Figure 19-10, even has its own Webmaster forums, including Web site critiques and discussions about topics like Web site awards and Web site programming techniques. Visit eBoz! at the following URL:

`www.eboz.com`

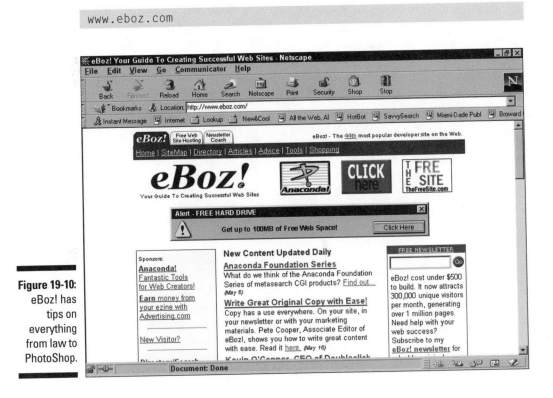

Figure 19-10:
eBoz! has tips on everything from law to PhotoShop.

You can find articles on e-commerce, marketing, and Web design and a list of other online newsletters, just to name a few of the features of this premier site.

Chapter 20

Ten Fabulous Tools
for E-Commerce

In This Chapter

▶ suite 7

▶ AllCommerce

▶ HumanClick

▶ BayBuilder

▶ ECommerce Guide

▶ MapQuest

▶ S&H Greenpoints

▶ Systran Translation Software

▶ TRUSTe

▶ DMA Privacy Policy Generator

*Y*ou simply must try this blend of programs, add-ins, and services if you're into e-commerce. Even if you're not, some of the items in this chapter, such as HumanClick, MapQuest, or the Direct Marketing Association's Privacy Policy Generator, may come in handy. Some of these items are freebies, some cost serious money, and others offer a combination in which you can get a lesser version at no charge.

suite 7

What you get in suite 7 is a nicely designed collection of interlocking e-commerce tools. It's definitely not for the shoestring operator, however, at a price of nearly $4,000 for the entire toolbox. The good news for the smaller business is that you don't need to buy all seven tools. The entire system is modular, and you can buy just what you want now and add to it if you need to later. Check it out at the following Web site:

`www.suiteseven.com`

The two key elements of suite 7 are its advertising and e-commerce tools. The advertising tool is for both outgoing and incoming ads. It manages banners and generates detailed reports about the effectiveness of each ad. The e-commerce module is a hot program. It combines a shopping cart for your customers to use and a sophisticated account-management system for you. On top of that, it even manages your affiliate program and can handle any kind of tax situation from percentage taxes to VAT.

The remainder of the tools includes standard items on many Web sites: forms processing, forum management, guestbooks, jump menus, and surveys.

You can download a fully functional trial version of suite 7 from `www.suiteseven.com/download`, or just go to the suite 7 home page and click the Download button, as shown in Figure 20-1. It's good for 30 days, which should be plenty of time to fall in love.

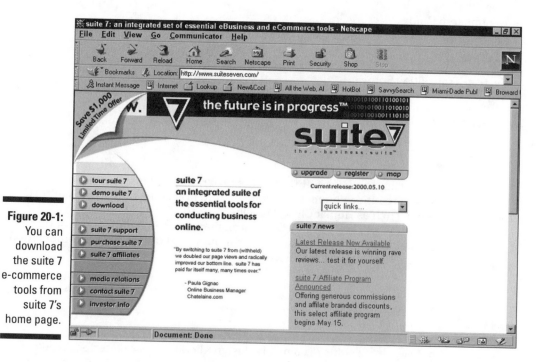

Figure 20-1: You can download the suite 7 e-commerce tools from suite 7's home page.

AllCommerce

OpenSales has a deal that's hard to refuse — you can download its AllCommerce software (formerly known as OpenMerchant) for zero dollars with no limits, no time constraints, no nothing. It's open-source software, which means that it's not only free, but you also get to play with the source code and change it to suit yourself. Ah, yes, that's the catch. If you're not a Perl programmer or don't have one on staff, you may get in a bit over your head with this software; if you are or do, however, you can download this software at the following Web address:

```
www.opensales.org/html/source.shtml
```

Still, even without custom modifications, using this package is a worthwhile way to get your store up and running. It handles everything from product page creation to shipping management and just about anything that you can imagine in between. It's easy to use, too. Figure 20-2 shows the management interface for an AllCommerce site.

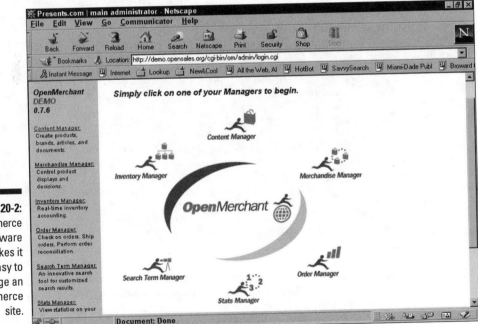

Figure 20-2: AllCommerce software makes it easy to manage an e-commerce site.

HumanClick

HumanClick is a fantastic way to add a human touch to your Web site. It's a free service that enables you to respond instantly to your customers' needs. Imagine: You're looking at a page on someone's site, and you have some questions about the products you see. An icon there reads, <u>Click for a real person</u>. You do so, and you go into a chat with someone who can answer your questions. Pretty nice, eh? Yep, this one's a must-have. Drop everything and go to this Web site, as shown in Figure 20-3. Click the <u>See it work!</u> link and think about how nice having this feature on your site could be. Just visit the following URL:

www.humanclick.com

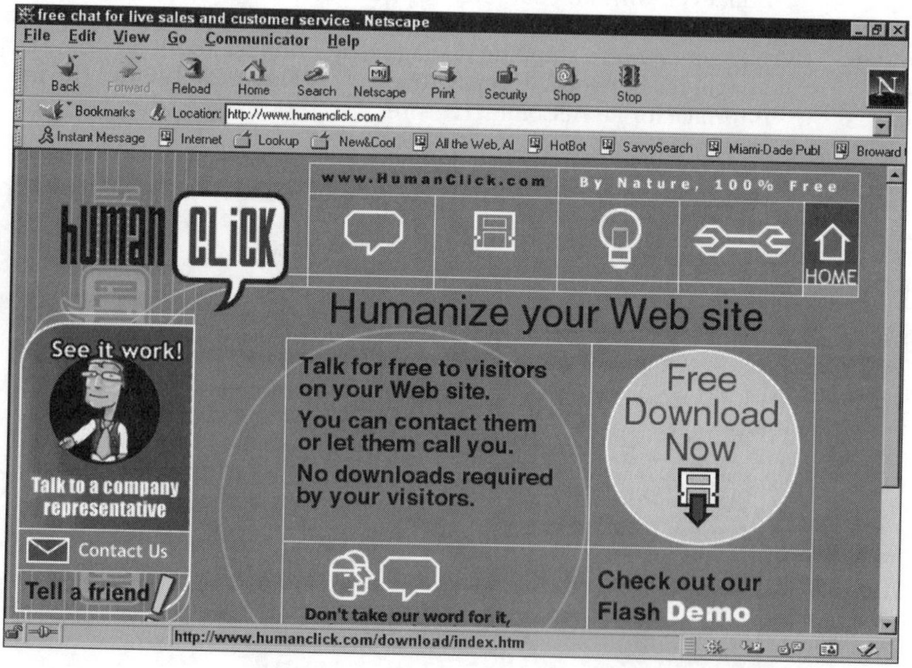

Figure 20-3:
HumanClick is a must-have for your Web site because it enables your visitors to speak to an actual person.

This service is definitely something you want on your Web site — and you don't even need to keep your people available 24 hours a day to use it. During the times that nobody's around to answer questions, you just tell the HumanClick client program on your computer that you're unavailable, and the icon on your site changes to read Leave a message.

As if all that's not enough, the service places no burden on your customers because HumanClick is JavaScript that's embedded in your pages. It works with every major Web browser. Your visitors don't need to download anything to make it work.

BayBuilder

Want to get into the online auction frenzy? Well, as you can imagine, setting one up isn't the easiest thing in the world to do. Unless you go to BayBuilder — and then it's a piece of cake. You can set up either private or public auctions. (At private auctions, you're the only one selling things.) If your company makes less than a million bucks a year from online revenues — and the odds are pretty good that's the case — you can sign up for free. If you're a major corporation, you must cough up some money. Go to the following address to sign up:

```
www.baybuilder.com
```

Before you sign up with BayBuilder, we suggest that you create a logo 60 pixels high by 200 pixels wide and upload it to your site. You need to supply the URL for the logo, as well as for your Web site as you fill out the registration form, as shown in Figure 20-4. BayBuilder uses these URLs to place the logo and a link to your Web site on your auction site, which is hosted on BayBuilder's server. You can get to the form from the site's main page by clicking the Get Started button, or you can go directly to `www.baybuilder.com/register.cfm`.

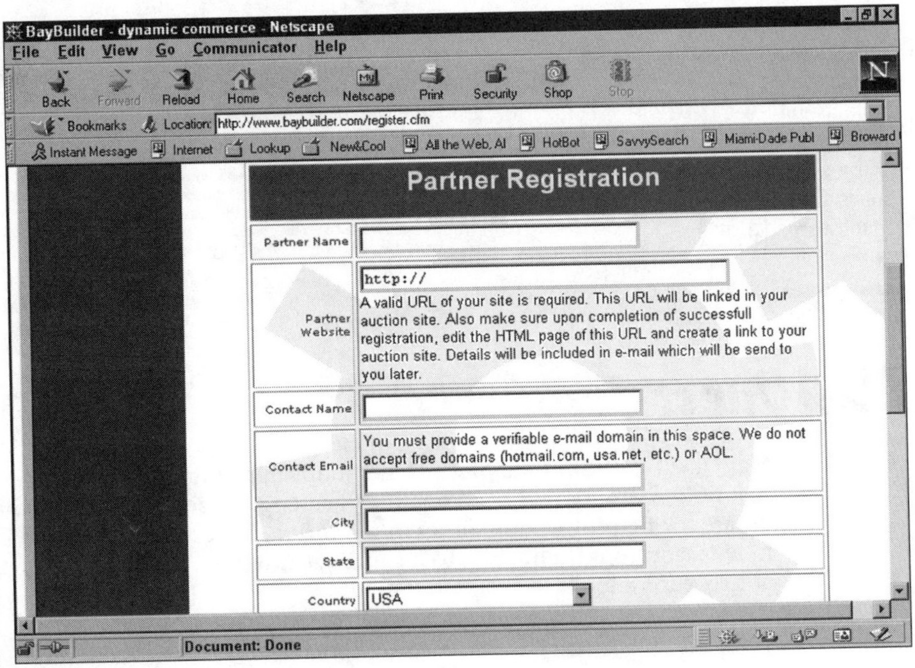

Figure 20-4:
You can join BayBuilder and hold auctions on its server simply by filling out the registration form on its site.

ECommerce Guide

The ECommerce Guide is an e-zine that's a truly valuable resource for anyone involved in e-commerce (see Figure 20-5). It's got reviews of online store software, the latest news for e-sales, and some really, really good columns. If you're not checking out this site, at the following URL, you're missing out on a lot of useful information:

```
ecommerce.internet.com
```

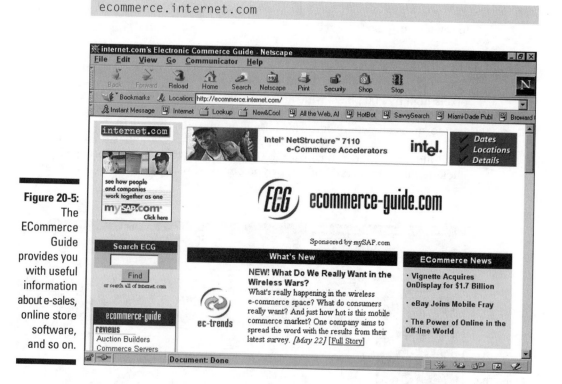

Figure 20-5: The ECommerce Guide provides you with useful information about e-sales, online store software, and so on.

MapQuest

MapQuest is a fabulous place to get maps. No kidding — maps. But not just plain old road maps. These beauties are customized maps that you can create for helping people find your location, for example, or showing them how to get from their hotel to a tourist attraction. Go to the following Web address for a look:

```
www.mapquest.com
```

Although MapQuest charges for plenty of things on its site, it also offers a couple of free services that you may want to take a look at: MapFree and LinkFree. MapFree enables you to use the site to make anywhere from 1 to 25 customized maps. You're free to place these maps on your own site. LinkFree links your site to the main MapQuest site so that your users can take advantage of its cartography services.

To access the MapQuest free services page, use `www.mapquest.com/cgi-bin/stat_parser?link=b2b/b2b_our-services_free` instead of the main address. Really — no kidding. But if you'd rather not type such a long URL, you can get there with just a few mouse clicks: First, go to MapQuest's main page at `www.mapquest.com`, as shown in Figure 20-6. Click the yellow strip at the top of the page that reads <u>Business Services: Add maps and directions to your company's Web site</u>. Then click <u>Our Products and Services</u>. Finally, scroll down and click the <u>Free Services</u> link.

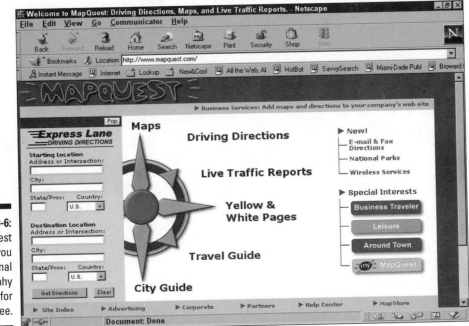

Figure 20-6: MapQuest gives you professional cartography services for free.

Don't neglect that tantalizing <u>Web Site Applications</u> link. The applications that you find there aren't free, but they're worth considering, especially if you have a physical location in addition to your Web presence.

S&H Greenpoints

Ah, remember how you used to collect S&H Green Stamps? Okay, ask your parents about it. Maybe your grandparents? At any rate, someone you know will remember. Believe it. It used to be that you'd go to the grocery, fill your cart, and pay for your purchases. Then, along with your change, you'd get a certain number of stamps from the cashier, depending on how much money you'd just spent. You'd toss the stamps in the grocery bag along with your receipt and trot on home. You'd put the stamps in a kitchen drawer until there were so many stored there that you couldn't open the drawer any more without stamps spilling out all over the floor.

When things reached that stage, you'd have to face the odious task of licking all of them and pasting them into the books that you also picked up at the grocery. When you had a whole bunch of books filled, you'd sit down with the S&H catalog and go on a shopping spree. We got everything from our pet carriers to a nice, warm quilt that way. The closing of the S&H Redemption Center was a sad event for us, but now the Internet is reviving this grand old piece of Americana. But this time around, you don't have to lick all those stamps! Now, it's S&H Greenpoints, a new form of digital reward — kind of like the Web equivalent of frequent-flyer miles.

We have a major hunch that this arrangement is going to work out well for both online shoppers and e-merchants. If you're into any kind of e-commerce, look into this site (see Figure 20-7). Drop on in and visit the site at the following URL (or skip the preliminaries and send an e-mail to `bd-online@greenpoints.com` saying that you want to get on board):

```
www.greenpoints.com
```

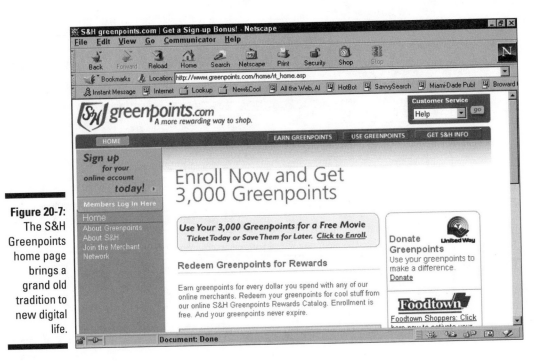

Figure 20-7:
The S&H Greenpoints home page brings a grand old tradition to new digital life.

Systran Translation Software

One of the hottest sites on the Web is AltaVista's Babel Fish translation page. It works with Systran Translation Software, and you can go right to the source and set up your very own translation system. The basic service costs nothing, although customized solutions are available for a fee. Anyone who's serious about e-commerce must deal with the fact that the World Wide Web is just that — a global setup. Your storefront is an international business, and although English is widely spoken, it's hardly the only language in the world.

With Systran Translation Software working on your site, visitors quickly translate your pages among half a dozen major languages: English, French, German, Italian, Portuguese, and Spanish. And Systran doesn't stop there. The service is already working on adding Chinese, Japanese, Korean, and Russian to the mix. So hurry up already and pop into Systran's Web site, as shown in Figure 20-8. The whole world is waiting. Run — don't walk — to the following URL:

```
www.systransoft.com
```

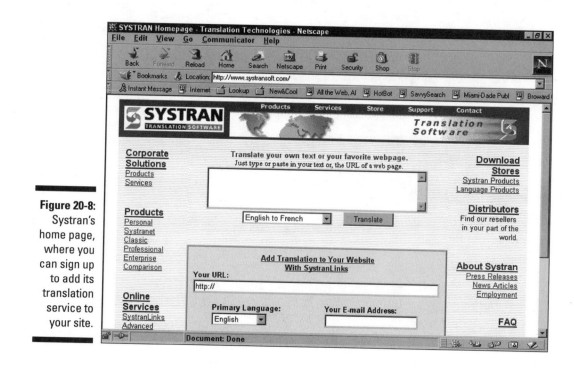

Figure 20-8:
Systran's
home page,
where you
can sign up
to add its
translation
service to
your site.

TRUSTe

This site's kind of an open question. What question is that? Well, whether paying hundreds or even thousands of dollars to an outside group to certify that your privacy policy means what it says is worth the price to your organization. To solidly quantify how much a trustmark such as the TRUSTe seal means in terms of extra sales is impossible, just as it is with things such as Chamber of Commerce or Better Business Bureau logos in a store window.

If you collect any kind of potentially embarrassing personal information, such as criminal records or health status, getting TRUSTe certification is probably worth the cost. Without it, people may prove reluctant to provide honest answers to such questions. Still, unless you're in the employment or insurance business (or something similar), you're not likely to gather any kind of information other than names, addresses, phone numbers, credit card numbers, and so on.

Visit the TRUSTe site and read over all the materials there to decide for yourself whether its service is right for your situation (see Figure 20-9). You also find valuable advice there on creating a privacy statement. TRUSTe does provide an automated wizard to help you create such a statement (at `www.truste.com/wizard`), but it's currently in the process of "format improvements." You can access the site's home page at the following URL:

`www.truste.com`

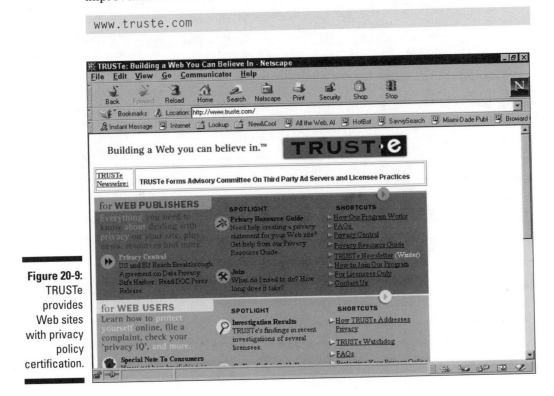

Figure 20-9:
TRUSTe
provides
Web sites
with privacy
policy
certification.

DMA Privacy Policy Generator

The Direct Marketing Association (DMA) assists you in creating a privacy statement with its DMA Privacy Policy Generator, a simple, easy-to-use online form, as shown in Figure 20-10. By filling out the form and selecting the check boxes that apply to your company's situation, you provide the basic material for your privacy statement. After you finish, you can have the completed statement e-mailed to you as plain text or as a ready-to-use Web page that you can drop into your site. Use the following URL to go directly to the Privacy Policy form:

`www.the-dma.org/policy.html`

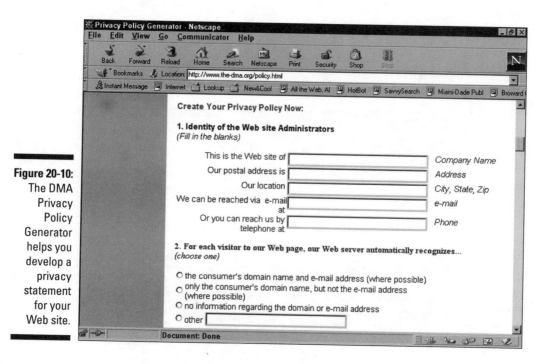

Figure 20-10:
The DMA
Privacy
Policy
Generator
helps you
develop a
privacy
statement
for your
Web site.

Chapter 21

Ten More Great Add-Ins

In This Chapter

▶ Intel Web Applets

▶ Merriam-Webster

▶ iSyndicate

▶ Leonardo MediaBank

▶ Recommend-It

▶ Server Rat

▶ @Watch

▶ VoiceBlast

▶ Tough Media

▶ eCal*Now!*

*W*ell, you just know that every book has to have a final chapter. We'd like to keep on going forever, but we can't, so we're using these last few pages to point you toward some more great Web site add-ins and services.

Intel Web Applets

Intel's Web site offers a nice selection of sophisticated applets. The Photo Album II applet, for example, features some really addictive image transitions. One image may fold itself up into a paper airplane and sail off into the next picture, and that one might find itself pulled into a black hole and sucked off the screen, while the next one — well, you get the idea. It's well worth a look. You can find it and the other Intel Web Applets at the following URL:

```
www.intel.com/home/funstuff/webapplets/index.htm
```

The 3D Photo Cube applet displays half a dozen images on a free-floating, rotating cube that changes direction depending on where you place your mouse pointer. Clicking an image stops the cube and rotates that image to the front in full size. Double-clicking an image takes you to a linked page.

The Image Carousel is another way of showing linkable images. It also rotates a series of images, but it does so by looping them into a circle, as though the images are hardcopy photographs placed vertically along the rim of a carousel. Each image scrolls by, curls at the edges, and loops around. You can even see the reverse of the image faintly as it passes along the far side of the circle. One Image Carousel loops vertically and another loops horizontally (see Figure 21-1). With either one, the visitor can interactively change the direction of movement — left and right or up and down, depending on which applet you use — and click an image to go to a linked page.

If you prefer text to images, you may want to try the 3D text applet, which rotates a text string either horizontally or in the full 360 degrees. In addition to setting the text size and color, you can also specify shadow and background colors. The text is linkable to a URL as well.

Figure 21-1:
The horizontal Image Carousel applet displays images as if they were on a merry-go-round.

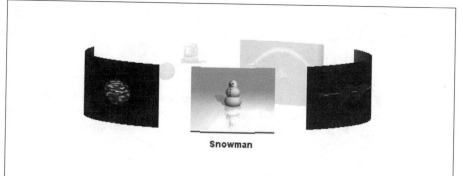

Snowman

Merriam-Webster

As you probably expect, Merriam-Webster offers dictionary and thesaurus services, and you just know from the nature of this book that you can latch onto those services for your own site, right? You can just go to the Merriam-Webster site, click the <u>Put a free dictionary search box on your Web site</u> link, and fill out a simple form. Then you choose from among a selection of search boxes and paste the code into your Web page (see Figure 21-2). What could be simpler? Check it out at the following Web address:

```
www.m-w.com
```

Okay, if you're a stickler for form, you can type the following URL and get to the same site (but why bother with all those extra letters?):

```
www.merriam-webster.com
```

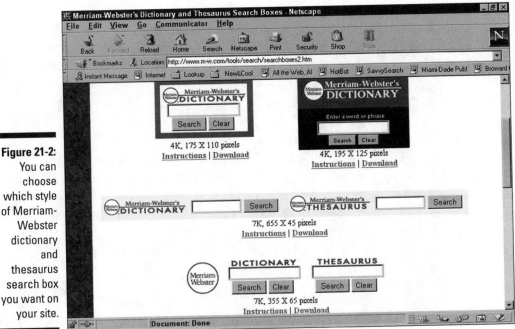

Figure 21-2:
You can choose which style of Merriam-Webster dictionary and thesaurus search box you want on your site.

iSyndicate

The content provider iSyndicate offers plenty of great material that you can add to your site, including *Rolling Stone* and *Salon Magazine*. You can find zillions of different categories of stuff, and it's all professionally produced. Figure 21-3 shows a sampling of some of the products that you can tap into here. The down side? Well, some of it's not free. The company provides a number of different programs that range in price from free content to $99 per month, and on up to $1,299 per month. And we have a strong feeling that, if any of its ready packages don't cover your needs, iSyndicate's willing to work with you to develop a customized program that does suit you. Check iSyndicate out at the following address:

`www.isyndicate.com`

To get the freebies that the company offers, go to `affiliate.isyndicate.com/join` and fill out the form. The rest, as they say, is history.

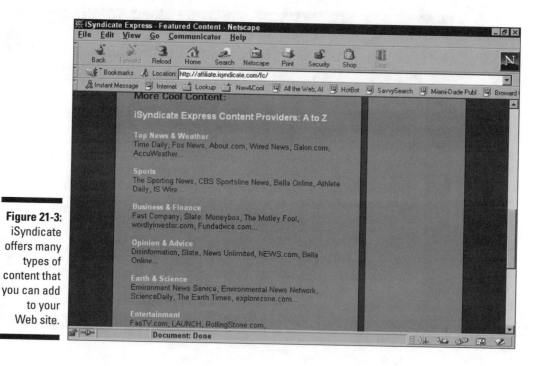

Figure 21-3:
iSyndicate offers many types of content that you can add to your Web site.

Leonardo MediaBank

Leonardo MediaBank is a must for anyone involved in the travel industry. But even if your site isn't travel-oriented — if you just need some great content about tourist destinations around the world — you must see this place. It's like going on a shopping spree in a chocolate boutique.

One person's vacation spot is another person's banking center or technology mecca . . . or whatever.

These folks provide photos, recordings, video, and just about anything else you can imagine. Drop in, sign up, and take a look around the stuff shown in Figure 21-4 by entering the following URL into your browser:

```
www.leonardo.com
```

Figure 21-4:
You can get images, sounds, and so on of everything from cruise lines to car rentals at Leonardo MediaBank's Web site.

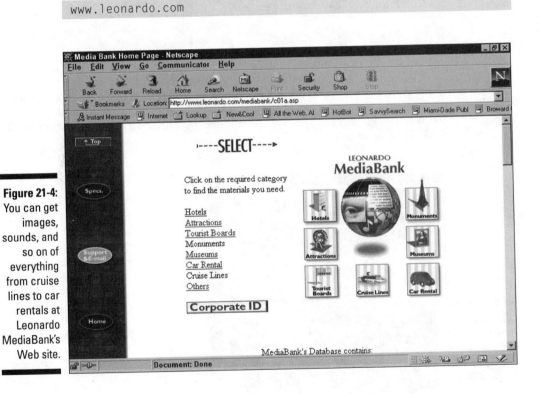

Recommend-It

You see billions and billions, if not absolute zillions, of Web sites that display a <u>Recommend This Site To A Friend</u> link. You have good reason to include a link like this one on your own site because there's no more powerful sales tool than a personal recommendation. If people hear from someone they trust about a Web site that they ought to look at, they're a lot more inclined to check it out. With any other method, you have to ask people to rely on the word of strangers or maybe even just a search engine.

Even if you're not involved in e-commerce, you still want to attract quality visitors. And you still get more of the right people visiting your site if you help your current visitors tell their friends how much they like it. One of the easiest ways to do so is to use the free Recommend-It service (see Figure 21-5). Just go to the following Web address:

```
www.recommend-it.com
```

One of the benefits of the Recommend-It service is that they offer prizes, which is an extra incentive for people to make a recommendation. One of the drawbacks to Recommend-It is that they're trying to get people to sign up for their newsletter, but even that's got a silver lining. If people do sign up, Recommend-It pays you as an affiliate. (See Chapter 15 for information about affiliate programs.)

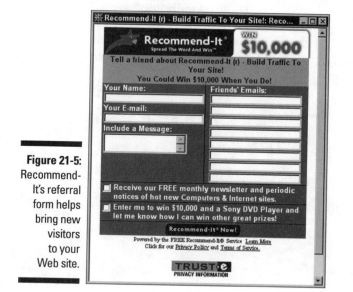

Figure 21-5: Recommend-It's referral form helps bring new visitors to your Web site.

Server Rat

Aside from having one of the cutest logos on the Web, Server Rat is one nice little service (see Figure 21-6). It's a Web server monitoring service that "rats" on your server if it goes down. As the company says, "Our Server Rat just loves to find out if your ISP is up to something cheesy!" The service costs you nothing, but you must accept a once-a-week e-mail from the company. Not much of a price to pay for such a neat feature. The Server Rat site's Web address is as follows:

```
www.serverrat.com
```

Server Rat checks your site every 15 minutes and informs you through e-mail, AOL, or ICQ whenever the site doesn't respond. It also maintains a pie chart of your server's uptime and downtime on its site, and after you log in, you can check the stats for your site. Server Rat is a relatively new service, managing something around 800 sites at press time. The company plans to add more in the way of services over time, ultimately meaning to keep a worldwide database of Web server efficiency.

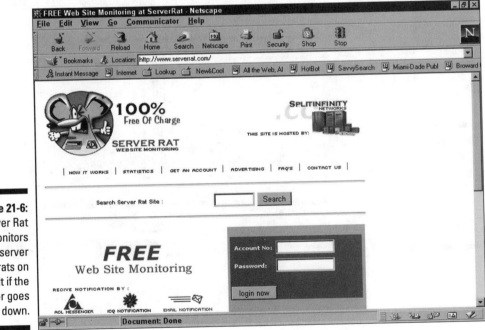

Figure 21-6: Server Rat monitors your server and rats on it if the server goes down.

@Watch

If you have deeper pockets and need a more detailed analysis than Server Rat offers (at least right now), you may want to take a look at @Watch at the following URL:

www.atwatch.com

@Watch offers three different program levels: @Watch Lite ($19.95 to $99.95 per month), @Watch Pro ($102.95 to $182.95 per month), and @Watch Enterprise ($186.95 to $266.95 per month). Prices decrease if you sign up for a year at a time, and you get volume discounts for multiple URLs.

Figure 21-7 shows an availability report from @Watch.

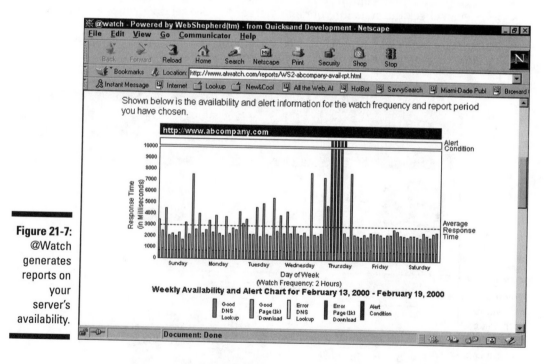

Figure 21-7: @Watch generates reports on your server's availability.

VoiceBlast

Not many things are more persuasive than a human voice. VoiceBlast enables you to add your recorded voice to your Web site (see Figure 21-8). You can hook up a microphone to your local computer or call in the voice content via a toll-free phone line (within the U.S.). If you use the local microphone option, you need to download a Java archive file. For details, visit VoiceBlast at the following URL:

```
www.voiceblast.com
```

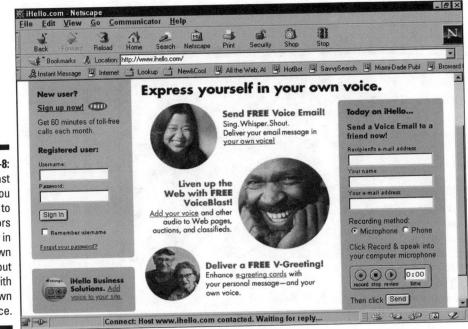

Figure 21-8: VoiceBlast enables you to speak to your visitors not only in your own words, but also with your own voice.

Tough Media

Everyone loves to use Macromedia Flash for making Web animations, but it's not exactly the easiest or least expensive tool in the old box. Tough Media gives you an intermediate option, helping you create Flash-enabled Web sites without the bother and expense of owning and learning to operate Flash. You can give Tough Media a try by visiting its site at the following address:

```
www.toughmedia.com
```

Figure 21-9 shows one of the free Flash pages that you can make at Tough Media. Unfortunately, the company saves the best for its paid services, but even those aren't exactly bank breakers at $9.95 and $12.95 a pop.

Figure 21-9: Tough Media's Star Sector IV — one of the free animated Flash pages you can create at its Web site.

eCalNow!

This applet is one of the best add-ons that you can have on your site — period. It's a free version of the famous eCal online calendar system, and it's available to any site that gets less than a million visitors per month. Just go to the following URL:

```
www.ecalnow.com
```

We could write an entire book about all of eCal*Now!*'s features because it includes so many great tools. Figure 21-10 gives you a quick idea of some of the minor capabilities of this awesome service.

Aside from the fact that it's something you're likely to want to use yourself, eCal*Now!* is an incredible facility to offer your Web site visitors. It's advertiser supported, so you end up hosting some banners on the calendar site, but you can set things up so that it blends in perfectly with your own site's layout, including adding your own logo to the calendar site.

Figure 21-10:
You can explore the many available features of eCal*Now!* on its Web site.

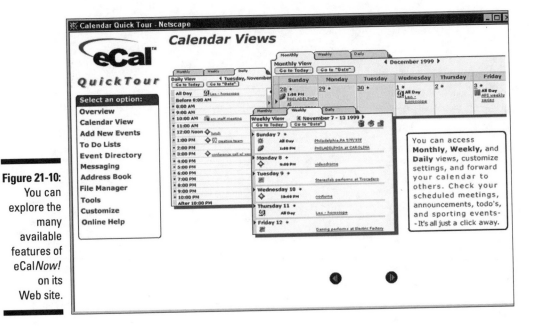

Part VII
Appendixes

In this part . . .

*A*ll the new terms that have been invented to describe the Internet could drive even Daniel Webster nuts, so we put together a glossary of them for you. And we wouldn't want to leave you guessing about what's on the CD-ROM that's tucked into the back of this book, so we tossed in an appendix about that, too.

Appendix A
Glossary

aardvark: A type of anteater — its name means earth pig.

acquirer: See *merchant account.*

active link: See *link.*

Address Verification System (AVS): An antifraud feature for credit card transactions in which the address to which the credit card issuer sends the monthly bill is compared to the address on an order form. If the two addresses aren't the same, the probability of fraud is higher.

applet: Major programs are known as *applications.* Short programs, especially those written in the Java programming language for use on the World Wide Web, are called by the diminutive *applet.*

ASCII (American Standard Code for Information Interchange): Common method for representing textual characters.

attachment: A file that is sent along with an e-mail message. Most e-mail clients place an attachment into a separate directory from the one where they store the e-mail messages. E-mail attachments are one of the primary means of spreading viruses.

authentication: Verifying the identity of a person or service, usually through digital IDs.

autoresponder: A program that automatically responds to an e-mail message by sending back a preprogrammed e-mail message of its own. Autoresponders are useful for providing price lists, back issues of newsletters, and so on.

AVS: See *Address Verification System.*

banner: An image link that appears on a Web page (generally at the top of the page) and contains advertising for a sponsor.

Bertie Wooster: The employer of the famed fictional butler, Jeeves.

binary file: A program file. In transferring files through FTP, you must be careful to send program files as binary files rather than as text files because text files have a different format.

cat: A creature that deigns to permit humans to inhabit the same planet.

CGI: See *Common Gateway Interface.*

chargeback: A debit issued against your merchant account by a credit card company because of a dispute over the validity of a transaction.

chat room: A place where people meet online and exchange messages in real time.

client/server: A computer that provides resources to other computers over a network. The main computer provides a network service and is known as a server. Computers that use the services of a server are clients. You also use the term *server* to refer to the software that provides the service. The software that accesses the server is also known as the client or client agent.

Common Gateway Interface (CGI): A program that can take information gathered from information users provide in a Web page form and can pass that information to other programs for processing.

compile: The source code that you create with languages, such as Java or C, is run through a *compiler* that prepares a stand-alone, ready-to-run program.

copyright: The right to make copies. The creators of works such as books, paintings, songs, or computer programs own the copyrights to those works unless they transfer their rights to another person or company.

dedicated server: A computer that is reserved for the use of a single person, company, or organization. See also *virtual server.*

default: Failure to pay bills. Seriously, defaults are the normal settings for software and hardware as they come from the manufacturers. In most cases, you may change the default settings to suit yourself.

demographics: Information that you gather from visitors to your site. Commonly, demographics include such things as the computer systems that visitors use, their income levels, and any other information that you require to understand your audience. Be careful about gathering data on age, race, sex, ethnicity, religious persuasion, and such, though, because this may lead to discrimination charges. Make sure that, if you do ask for any of this type of information, you make clear that such disclosures are purely optional. And never, never, *never* make any of this information available to anyone else, except as a lump-sum total. You need to keep the individual input absolutely confidential.

Denmark: A country in northern Europe, of which about 75 percent is composed of farms.

digital ID: An encrypted identifier that you keep on file at a central repository known as a *Certificate Authority,* which certifies that you *are* who you say you are (just in case you're wondering).

Digital Subscriber Line (DSL): A popular method of high-speed Internet access that utilizes existing telephone lines. Normal telephone operation is also possible on the same line, so you can still use phones and fax machines while the DSL connection is active. The DSL connection doesn't interfere with normal phone signals because it goes out at a different frequency.

discount rate: A percentage of each sale that you pay to the bank that processes credit card transactions.

DNS: See *Domain Name System.*

domain extension: See *top-level domain.*

Domain Name System (DNS): A system to translate the human-readable domain names, such as www.dummies.com, into the numerical IP addresses that computers understand (in this case, 38.170.216.18).

dot com (or dotcom): Colloquial expression meaning an Internet-based company.

download: Transferring a file to your computer from another computer. Also refers to the file that you download. See also *upload.*

draft: A check that you print to draw funds from another person's account after the person provides you with account information and authorization.

drop shipping: An arrangement by which you gather orders and submit them to another company; that company then sends its merchandise to your customer with your return address on it. You pay the company at a wholesale rate and keep the difference as profit.

DSL: See *Digital Subscriber Line.*

Emerald City: The home base of the Wizard of Oz.

end tag: See *tag.*

Fargo: A city in North Dakota.

feed: The transmission of information from a server to either its clients or another server.

File Transfer Protocol (FTP): A method for transferring files from one computer to another across a network or the Internet.

flame: A message that contains insults or inflammatory material.

flame war: An extended exchange of messages containing flames. Flame wars disrupt the normal process of communication in mailing lists, newsgroups, message boards, and chat rooms.

font: A complete set of letters, numbers, punctuation, and special characters that all have a particular look and shape. For example, **this** is in the Arial font, whereas **this** is in the Courier New font.

frame/frameset: A method enabling you to display multiple Web pages on a single browser screen. Framesets set off different areas of the screen. Each area is known as a *frame*, and each frame contains its own Web page.

FTP: See *File Transfer Protocol.*

GIF: Image files that follow the standards of the *G*raphics *I*nterchange *F*ormat. You commonly use GIFs for limited animation.

guillemot: A type of sea bird famous for waddling.

high risk: The category into which credit card companies place businesses that they believe are particularly prone to suffering from fraudulent transactions.

hit: A single access of a Web page.

Horace Greeley: Newspaper editor, most famous for the phrase, "Go west, young man, go west." He wasn't actually the person who said that, but nobody remembers John Soule, who did.

horizontal rule: A line across a Web page that you use to visually separate one section of a page from another. The HR element in HTML creates a horizontal rule.

HTML: See *HyperText Markup Language.*

HTML editor: Text editor with special features designed to assist you in creating Web pages.

HTTP: See *HyperText Transfer Protocol.*

hyperlink: See *link.*

hypertext: Text on a computer that includes links to other text, images, sound, and so on.

HyperText Markup Language (HTML): The native language of the World Wide Web, which you use to construct Web pages.

HyperText Transfer Protocol (HTTP): System for transferring files across the World Wide Web.

ICANN: See *Internet Corporation for Assigned Names and Numbers.*

image: General term for any picture or artwork on a Web page. Web images are usually stored in GIF, JPEG, or PNG formats.

image map: An image that contains multiple links. Users viewing an image map select different links by moving the mouse pointer to different parts of the image and clicking. You must carefully design the images that you use in image maps to provide visual clues to the links that they contain.

image repository: A Web site that contains a large amount of digital art, mostly simple icons. Image repositories typically gather these files without any attention to avoiding copyright and trademark violations.

interbank: An organization that processes merchant credit card transactions for its member banks.

Internet: Short for *Internetwork*. The Internet consists of several different computer networks that all link together into a "network of networks."

Internet access: The capability to connect to the Internet; usually an ISP provides this capability.

Internet Corporation for Assigned Names and Numbers (ICANN): The organization that accredits domain-name registrars.

Internet Service Provider (ISP): Company that provides Internet access, usually by dial-up connections, although many also offer high-speed dedicated connections.

interpret: Source code from languages such as JavaScript and Perl is read by another program (such as a Web browser or Web server). That program then interprets the instructions in the code and carries them out. See also *compile.*

IP address: The numerical equivalent of a domain name.

Isopoda: A type of crustacean with a small head.

ISP: See *Internet Service Provider.*

Java: A programming language that is often used to create applets for the Web. See also *applet.*

JavaScript: A simple but powerful programming language that programmers use to create scripts for Web pages. See also *script*.

JPEG: Also known as *JPG*. Image files that follow the standards of the *Joint Photographic Experts Group*. JPEG files are generally smaller than other file formats but maintain a high-quality image nonetheless.

JPG: See *JPEG*.

John of Lancaster: Admiral of the British fleet in 1422.

keyword: A word or phrase that search engines use to locate Web pages containing matching terms.

Klondike: Area in Alaska where gold was discovered in the late nineteenth century.

link (hyperlink): A connection between a Web page and another Internet resource. Usually, a link contains the URL (Internet address) of another Web page, but it can also link to other resources, such as images. By convention, links appear as blue underlined text that, after you activate it (usually by a mouse click), causes a Web browser to load the linked resource. You also often use images as links; by convention, a thin blue border surrounds image links to differentiate them from normal images. An *active link* is one that you're currently clicking, while a *visited link* is one that you activated previously.

list owner: The person who manages a mailing list. Usually, the list owner is the person who conceives and launches the list. This person is also known as a *list manager* and may be the *moderator* of the list as well. See also *moderator*.

list server: Program that processes the e-mail messages that compose a mailing list. The list server usually also handles such routine administrative matters as subscribing and unsubscribing list members if they send it a message containing the appropriate commands.

locomotive: A specialized type of railroad car, also known as an engine, that propels other railroad cars along the track.

log file: A file that records activity. A Web server log file, for example, records the origin of anyone who looks at a Web page, the type of browser the person's using, and so on. Log-file analyzer programs, such as Statbot, are useful to Webmasters in figuring out peak times of usage, number of hits per day, what other sites are referring visitors to this site, and so on.

mailing list: A discussion group in which the members post messages that a list server relays to them via e-mail. Open mailing lists can be joined by anyone; closed mailing lists require approval to join.

merchant account: An arrangement with a bank or a bank's sales organization for you to accept credit cards in payment for goods or services.

message board: Similar to a newsgroup but operates on an individual Web site. Message boards, sometimes known as graffiti walls, enable site visitors to leave messages for other visitors to read.

modem (*mo*dulator/*dem*odulator): Device that enables a computer to send signals over a telephone line.

moderator: Person who controls the content of a mailing list or newsgroup. In extreme cases, this control can amount to censorship, but moderate moderation simply results in the removal of extraneous material, such as sales pitches for products and services that don't relate to the topic. A moderator may also play peacemaker, attempting to keep tempers in check among the members of the mailing list or newsgroup, thus avoiding flame wars.

Modesty Blaise: Popular adventure character first appearing in a 1962 comic strip and later the subject of about a dozen novels and at least one movie.

Netiquette (Inter*net* et*iquette*): A series of customs that enable people to get along while living in Cyberspace. Basically, you want to be nice and consider how your actions may affect other people.

newline: A programming instruction in the form of \n to move the next bit of text down one line.

Northwest Passage: Channel leading from the Atlantic to the Pacific ocean north of North America. Much sought after since the fifteenth century, but not successfully negotiated until 1906.

Ogdensburg: City in New York State at the meeting of the Oswegatchie and Saint Lawrence rivers.

online service: Sort of a mini-Internet, services such as CompuServe, America Online, and so on provide many of the functions that the Internet does but on a smaller scale. In recent years, the online services have lost much business to the Internet and now provide Internet access as part of their services.

opt-in mailing list: A mailing list that you subscribe to by entering your e-mail address in a form. You then receive a message in your mailbox asking you to confirm the subscription. If you don't reply to that message, your address doesn't go into the system. This sign-up method makes it difficult for anyone else to sign you up for the list.

page generation program: Software that uses a WYSIWYG (What You See Is What You Get), point-and-click interface for creating Web pages.

parameter: Information that you add to the HTML code that calls a Java applet. This information sets variable values for the applet's use, and you add it through the PARAM element.

parking: See *Domain Name System.*

password: Secret word that you use to gain computer access. Sometimes you choose a password; sometimes someone else assigns you one. Two schools of thought on passwords offer contradictory advice. One says to make them so difficult to imagine that no one else can possibly guess yours in a million years. The other school of thought says to make them easy enough that you can remember your password.

Pausanias: General of the Greek army in the Battle of Plataea in 479 B.C.

public domain: The group of all created works that copyright law no longer protects (or never did).

Quimper: French city on the Odet River.

reciprocal link: A link to a Web page that also displays a link back to your own Web page. Hyperlinking is a common practice for building traffic among Web sites. If you want to establish a reciprocal link with someone else's site, add a link to that site on your own and then send an e-mail message asking the site's owner to reciprocate.

registrar: A company approved by the Internet Corporation for Assigned Names and Numbers (ICANN) to keep track of domain names on the Internet. A domain name that you register must point to an active Web site. You may also *reserve* or *park* domain names if you have no current site active for that name but you still want to prevent anybody else from registering the name. See also *Domain Name System; Internet Corporation for Assigned Names and Numbers.*

reserving: See *Domain Name System.*

RGB triplet: A method of denoting colors by specifying the amount of red, green, and blue in the color. Java applets often utilize this method. The possible values range from 0 to 255. Thus, if you want red lettering, you use a value of 255,0,0. This setting tells the applet to use as much red as possible but no green and no blue.

ring: A series of Web sites that connect together through links that lead from one to the other until visitors who follow all the links go full circle and return to their starting place.

robot: A program, also known as a *spider*, that automatically surfs the Web, indexing Web pages and adding information from them to a search site's database.

Runic alphabet: Characters that the Teutonic peoples of early Europe used; also known as *futhark*.

safety paper: The kind of paper on which you print a draft or check.

Samuel Langhorne Clemens: Real name of writer known to history as *Mark Twain*.

script: A short program.

server: See *client/server*.

server-side includes (SSI): The capability of a server that processes a CGI script to include data of its own that it sends back to the Web browser.

shopping cart: A program that visitors to your site use to keep track of which items they want to purchase. The shopping cart metaphor extends to the visitor's capability to put items into the cart and remove them before making a final purchasing decision.

sleep: A common practice utterly unknown to authors trying to meet a deadline.

spam: Unsolicited e-mail messages that someone sends in bulk quantities to several addresses; also the same message posted to multiple newsgroups simultaneously.

spider: See *robot*.

SSI: See *server-side includes (SSI)*.

standard: Also known as *specifications*. Generic term for anything that lots of people agree on. It may apply to a way to transfer files from one system to another one, the exact structure and function of a computer language, or a method of compressing video images. If a recognized, organized group develops it, it's known as an *official standard*. If it's just something that the market leader develops, and most of the people in a particular field use it, it's known as a *de facto standard*.

start tag: See *tag*.

subscriber: A member of a mailing list. Also known, amazingly enough, as a list member.

syndicate: A content provider that represents several different sources of content, such as comics, opinion columns, horoscopes, and articles.

tag: You indicate the beginning of each element in HTML by placing the name of that element within angle brackets. This part of the element is known as a *start tag*. You indicate the end of the element by using an *end tag*, which looks just like the start tag except that you add a slash before the element's name. The start and end tags for the TABLE element, for example, are <TABLE> and </TABLE>.

telepathy: Ability to transfer thoughts from one mind to another.

text editor: A simple form of word processor that saves text files without formatting.

text file: A file of text. (No kidding.) In transferring text files via FTP, you want to be careful to send them as such rather than as binary files because text files often require conversion in transferring between Windows and Unix systems, which use slightly different text formats. See also **ASCII**.

thread: Hierarchy that shows the relationship of a series of messages on a message board. See also **message board**.

tiling: The repetition of a background image across a Web page until it reaches the edge of the screen. It then begins tiling again in the next available space below the first line of images — and so on until it fills the entire page with multiple copies of the image.

top-level domain (TLD): The final letters at the end of an Internet address. You consider them "top level" because you read Internet addresses in steps from right to left, with the part after the last dot on the right being the highest step in a hierarchy that eventually leads down, step by dotted step, to a particular computer. The four most common TLDs are *.com*, *.net*, *.edu*, and *.org*. These TLDs are known as the *generic TLDs* or *gTLDs*, while those that specify a country in which a site originates are known as *country-level TLDs* or *CLTLDs*.

traffic: The number of visits to an Internet site, as in "Our traffic increased by 100,000 visitors last week."

Uncertainty Principle: Fundamental theorem of quantum physics that states that knowing both the direction of travel and the location in space-time of an atomic particle is impossible.

Uniform Resource Locator (URL): The address of a file (or other resource) on the Internet. The URL for a file on a Web server is formed by putting together a series of directions to the file, as in the following example:

```
http://www.someschool.edu/graphics/logo.png
```

The `http://` in the preceding line specifies the Hypertext Transfer Protocol (the Web's native method of information exchange). The `www` tells you that the computer that holds the file is a Web server. Actually, you already know that from the first part — that's why a lot of Web sites don't use the `www` prefix anymore. The `someschool` segment gives the *subdomain*, which is what people usually think of as the name of the Web site. The IDG Books Web site, for example, is located at `www.idgbooks.com`, and its subdomain is `idgbooks`. The three-letter extension represents the *top-level domain*. In this case, the subdomain is followed by `.edu`, meaning that this Web site is in the education domain. The `graphics` part leads to a particular directory on the specified Web server, and the final portion, `logo.png`, is a file within that directory.

Files located within the same server as a Web page can be referenced in a simpler way by using *relative URLs*. Instead of fully specifying how to find the file from anywhere on the Internet, relative URLs only specify how to find it from the Web page that refers to it. The file in the preceding example could be linked to from the school's home page by using the following relative URL:

```
<IMG src="graphics/logo.png">
```

Because the Web browser that you use to view the home page already knows where it is, it can perform a bit of cutting and pasting to come up with the right URL. The browser "reasons" that it is currently viewing a Web page located at `http://www.someschool.edu/index.html`. It strips off everything after the final slash to arrive at `http://www.someschool.edu/` and then adds `graphics/logo.png` to that to arrive at `http://www.someschool.edu/graphics/logo.png`. See also *top-level domain*.

upload: To transfer a file from your computer to another computer. Also the file that you upload. See also *download.*

URL: See *Uniform Resource Locator.*

Van de Graaff generator: A primitive device that generates millions of volts of static electricity.

virtual server: A directory on a computer that simulates the existence of a separate computer. See also *dedicated server.*

visited link: See *link.*

Web ring: See *ring.*

Web site: Any presence on the World Wide Web. Usually applies to a collection of Web pages.

Webmaster: The person in control of a Web site. A Webmaster may be an individual with only a single Web page or the manager of a large team of developers who create and maintain Web sites.

William Kidd: Eighteenth-century English privateer who went down in history as the pirate *Captain Kidd.* He provided documents to political authorities that showed that he'd attacked only ships carrying papers that showed they were at war with England, but the papers were lost until the 1970s.

xylem: The central core of plant roots.

ytterbium: A rare earth element that you often find in combination with gadolinite.

zymurgy: The study of the fermentation process.

Appendix B

About the CD

*H*ere is some of the cool stuff that you'll find on the *Building a Web Site For Dummies* CD-ROM:

- ✔ An incredible array of evaluation, trial, and freeware versions of Web-site creation tools: Dreamweaver, HomeSite, BBEdit, Fireworks, and Paint Shop Pro.
- ✔ A collection of stunningly beautiful artwork that you can use on your own sites.
- ✔ Java applets to make your images stand out.

System Requirements

Make sure that your computer meets the minimum system requirements in the following list. If your computer doesn't match up to most of these requirements, you may experience problems in using the contents of the CD:

- ✔ A PC with a Pentium or faster processor or a Mac OS computer with a 68040 or faster processor.
- ✔ Microsoft Windows 95, Windows NT 4.0 or later or Mac OS system software 7.5.5 or later.
- ✔ At least 16MB of total RAM installed on your computer. For best performance, we recommend at least 32MB of RAM installed.
- ✔ At least 300MB of hard drive space available to install all the software from this CD. (You need less space if you don't install every program.)
- ✔ A CD-ROM drive — double-speed (2x) or faster.
- ✔ A sound card for PCs. (Mac OS computers have built-in sound support.)
- ✔ A monitor capable of displaying at least 256 colors or grayscale.
- ✔ A modem with a speed of at least 14,400 bps.

If you need more information on the basics, check out *PCs For Dummies*, 7th Edition, by Dan Gookin; *Macs For Dummies*, 6th Edition, by David Pogue; *Windows 95 For Dummies,* 2nd Edition, or *Windows 98 For Dummies*, both by Andy Rathbone (all published by IDG Books Worldwide, Inc.).

Using the CD in Windows

Follow these steps to access the software on the book's CD:

1. **Insert the CD into your computer's CD-ROM drive.**

2. **Open your browser.**

   If you do not have a browser, we have included Microsoft Internet Explorer as well as Netscape Communicator. They can be found in the Programs folders at the root of the CD.

3. **Click Start⇨Run.**

4. **In the dialog box that appears, type** D:\START.HTM

   Replace *D* with the proper drive letter if your CD-ROM drive uses a different letter. (If you don't know the letter, see how your CD-ROM drive is listed under My Computer.)

5. **Read through the license agreement, nod your head, and then click the Accept button if you want to use the CD — after you click Accept, you'll jump to the Main Menu.**

   This action displays the file that will walk you through the contents of the CD.

6. **To navigate within the interface, simply click on any topic of interest to take you to an explanation of the files on the CD and how to use or install them.**

7. **To install the software from the CD, simply click on the software name.**

   You'll see two options — the option to run or open the file from the current location or the option to save the file to your hard drive. Choose to run or open the file from its current location and the installation procedure will continue. After you are done with the interface, simply close your browser as usual.

To run some of the programs, you may need to keep the CD inside your CD-ROM drive. This is a Good Thing. Otherwise, the installed program would require you to install a very large chunk of the program to your hard drive space, which would keep you from installing other software.

Using the CD with Mac OS

To install the items from the CD to your hard drive, follow these steps:

1. **Insert the CD into your computer's CD-ROM drive.**

   In a moment, an icon representing the CD you just inserted appears on your Mac desktop. The icon probably looks like a CD-ROM.

2. **Double-click the CD icon to show the CD's contents.**

3. **Double-click the Read Me First icon.**

   This text file contains information about the CD's programs and any last-minute instructions you need to know about installing the programs on the CD that we don't cover in this appendix.

4. **Open your browser.**

   In case you don't have a browser, we included the two most popular ones for your convenience — Microsoft Internet Explorer and Netscape Communicator.

5. **Choose File⇨Open and select the CD titled Building a Web Site For Dummies.**

6. **Click the** Links.htm **file to see an explanation of all files and folders included on the CD.**

7. **With the programs that come with installer programs, you simply open the program's folder on the CD and double-click the icon with the words** Install **or** Installer.

   After you install the programs that you want, you can eject the CD. Carefully place it back in the plastic jacket of the book for safekeeping.

What You Find

Here's a summary of the software on this CD.

Authors' links

For Mac and Windows. This file is a set of all the links from every chapter in the whole book. Saves you a bunch of typing.

BBEdit and BBEdit Lite

For Mac OS. BBEdit is a demo version and BBEdit Lite is a freeware version. Two versions of the famed Mac HTML editor from Bare Bones Software are on this CD. One is BBEdit Lite 4.6, which is freeware. The other is a demo version of the full program, BBEdit 5.1.1.

For more information and updates, visit the Bare Bones Software Web site: www.bbedit.com/free/free.html.

Bookshelf applet

For Mac and Windows that support Java. Freeware version. The Bookshelf applet is a Java applet that makes graphical Web site navigation a breeze by representing each link as a book on a shelf.

For more information and updates, check out Nikolai Sakva's Web site: www.aha.ru/~sakva.

Dee Dreslough's Art Gallery on CD-ROM Web page graphics

For Mac and Windows. Freeware version. Some stunning graphics for your Web pages.

To get a look at where these came from, check out Dee Dreslough's Web site: www.dreslough.com/dee/colorgalleries.htm.

Dreamweaver

For Windows and Mac. Trial version. This is the famous WYSIWYG Web site creation tool from Macromedia.

For more information and updates, visit the Dreamweaver Web site: www.macromedia.com/software/dreamweaver/trial.

Fire applet

For Mac and Windows that support Java. Freeware version. The Fire applet is a Java applet that turns the light areas of an image into a roaring inferno.

To get a look at more great applets by David Griffiths, check out his Web site:
www.spigots.com.

Fireworks 3.0

For Windows and Mac. Trial version. This is the sophisticated Web graphics program from the same folks who make Dreamweaver.

For more information and updates, visit the Fireworks Web site:
www.macromedia.com/software/fireworks/trial.

Goddess Art of Jonathon Earl Bowser

For Mac and Windows. Freeware version. Some truly fabulous artwork for your Web pages.

To get a look at where these came from, check out Jonathon Earl Bowser's Web site: www.jonathonart.com.

HomeSite

For Windows. 30-day evaluation version. This program is one of the best Windows HTML editors available.

For more information and updates, visit the HomeSite Web site:
www.allaire.com/products/homesite/index.cfm.

Lake applet

For Mac and Windows that support Java. Freeware. The Lake applet is a Java applet that turns the bottom half of an image into a reflective lake.

To get a look at more great applets by David Griffiths, check out his Web site:
www.spigots.com.

Lindy's Graphics

For Mac and Windows. Shareware. These images are some of the most enchanting artwork on the Web.

To get a look at where these came from, check out Melinda Hoehn's Web site: www.theiowa.net/lindy.

Linkbot Pro and Linkbot Enterprise Server

For Windows. Linkbot Pro and Linkbot Enterprise Server are both 15-day trial versions. Linkbot tracks down broken links automatically and generates detailed reports on them. It also checks for dozens of problem areas on your site and warns you where you need to tighten things up a bit. The Enterprise version utilizes an SQL database and is for Web sites with more than 100,000 links.

For more information on this and other programs from Watchfire, visit its Web site: www.watchfire.com.

Macrobot

For Windows. 15-day trial version. Macrobot records interactive Web-site application scenarios that the program can play back unattended on any pre-defined schedule.

For more information on this and other programs from Watchfire, visit its Web site: www.watchfire.com.

Metabot

For Windows. 15-day trial version. Metabot is a META-tag generator and management system from the folks who brought you Linkbot.

For more information on this and other programs from Watchfire, visit its Web site: www.watchfire.com.

Microsoft Internet Explorer 5.0 Web browser

For Mac and Windows. Commercial product. Provides the best support to date for Dynamic HTML and CSS. You can use this program to test your work when you take advantage of the most powerful features in Dreamweaver.

This program is updated frequently, so check out the Microsoft Web site at www.microsoft.com.

Netscape Communicator 4.7 Web browser

For Mac and Windows. Commercial product. Communicator 4.7 provides some support for Dynamic HTML and CSS. It's a good idea to test your work in both Communicator and Internet Explorer to ensure that your pages look good to viewers using either program.

This program is updated frequently, so check out the Netscape Web site at home.netscape.com.

Novagene's tiled background images

For Mac and Windows. Freeware. These background images are some of the best you've ever seen.

To get a look at where these came from, check out Gene Lyons' Web site: www.novagene.com/gallery_lobby.html.

Paint Shop Pro

For Windows. Evaluation version. This is the well-known Windows paint program.

For more information and updates, visit the Jasc Web site: www.jasc.com/download_4.asp.

Snow applet

For Mac and Windows that support Java. Freeware. The Snow applet is a Java applet that turns any image into a winter scene.

To get a look at more great applets by David Griffiths, check out his Web site: www.spigots.com.

Statbot

For Windows. Evaluation version. Statbot is a log-analyzer custom made for this book that crunches all the information in your Web-server log and gathers it into useful categories. It even makes maps showing which countries your visitors come from.

For information on other versions of Statbot, visit the Moorglade Design Group's Web site: www.moorglade.com.

WS_FTP Pro

For Windows. Trial version. This is the easy-to-use FTP program.

For more information and updates, visit the Ipswitch Web site: www.ipswitch.com/cgi/download_eval.pl.

If You've Got Problems (Of the CD Kind)

We tried our best to compile programs that work on most computers with the minimum system requirements. Alas, your computer may differ, and some programs may not work correctly for some reason.

The two likeliest problems are that you don't have enough memory (RAM) for the programs you want to use, or you have other programs running that are affecting installation or running of a program. If you get error messages like Not enough memory or Setup cannot continue, try one or more of these methods and then try using the software again:

- ✔ **Turn off any antivirus software that you have on your computer:** Installers sometimes mimic virus activity and may make your computer incorrectly believe that a virus is infecting it.

- ✔ **Close all running programs:** The more programs you run, the less memory is available to other programs. Installers also typically update files and programs. So if you keep other programs running, installation may not work correctly.

- ✔ **Have your local computer store add more RAM to your computer:** This step is, admittedly, drastic and somewhat expensive. However, if you have a Windows 95 PC or a Mac OS computer with a PowerPC chip, adding more memory can really help the speed of your computer and enable more programs to run at the same time.

If you still have trouble installing the items from the CD, please call the IDG Books Worldwide Customer Service phone number: 800-762-2974 (outside the U.S.: 317-572-3342).

Index

• *Numbers and Symbols* •

10 Questions About MP3, 120
3D Photo Cube applet, 336
3D text applet, 336
555-1212.com Web site, 230
60kOpt-In, 308
7am News, 206–209
@Watch, 342
  (nonbreaking space), 38

 tag, 36
<P> tag, 36–37
</P> tag, 36–37

• *A* •

A (anchor) element, 43
  onClick attribute, 58
aardvark, 349
aBooth Web site, 162
AccuWeather, 221
acquirer, 349
action attribute, 79, 201
active links, 349, 354
  color, 43
add-ins
  @Watch, 342
  eCalNow!, 345
  Intel Web Applets, 335–336
  iSyndicate, 338
  Leonardo MediaBank, 339
  Merriam Webster, 337
  Recommend-It, 340
  Server Rat, 341
  Tough Media, 344
  VoiceBlast, 343
address verification, 243
Adobe PageMill, 33
adults-only sites, 66
Adventures of Robin Hood, 220
advice
  Bizy Moms, 318
  eBoz!, 321
  Ezine Factory, 319

  geek/talk Forums For Webmasters, 315
  grammarNOW!, 314
  LawGuru.com, 317–318
  MyService Experts Avenue, 313
  Poor Richard's Web Site, 320
  Small Business Advisor, 316
  Web Watch, 312
The Affiliate Program, 264
affiliate programs
  adding value to site, 262
  audience and, 261, 262
  companies with, 255
  costs, 263
  FAQ (Frequently Asked Questions) and legal
    agreement, 260
  finding partners, 257–258
  hosting, 263–265
  joining, 256–257
  minimum payments, 257
  payment for, 256
  payment triggers, 256
  profiting from, 260–263
  studying before signing up, 260–261
  two-tier payment plans, 263
  working within network, 259
Affiliate Tracking Network Web site, 264
Affiliateguide.com Web site, 265
Affiliatematch.com Web site, 265
affiliates, 255
AffiliatesDirectory.com Web site, 265
AffiliateWorld.com Web site, 265
aGNeS News Forum, 182
Airborne Express, 231
AIS Merchant Services, 253
alink attribute, 43
All the Web, 279–280, 287
AllCommerce, 325
AltaVista, 279, 287
AltaVista's Babel Fish translation page, 331
alternative payment methods, 245–247
Alxpoll
  Create a Polling page, 147
  linking to your home page, 147
  location of survey form, 148
  mailing lists, 146, 148
  modifying form, 151–152

Alxpoll *(continued)*
  poll creation, 146–148, 150
  Quick Sign-Up form, 146
  sending backup copy of HTML code, 147
  Sign Up-Page 2, 148
  viewing poll, 150
  wizard, 146
Alxpoll Web site, 146, 151
Amazon.com, 255–256
American Cart Shopping Service, 244
American Express, 235, 238
American Express Web site, 238
AMS I-Stores, 244
AnalogX Web site, 275, 285, 292
Angelfile, 273
animated GIFs, 130
The Animation Factory Web site, 129–130
Anna Karenina, 220
Anvil Studio, 120
Applause, 116
APPLET element, 60–61, 63
applets, 51, 349
applications, 59, 349
Arachnophilia, 30
Article Resource Association, 221
Artigen Web site, 192
ASCII (American Standard Code for Information
    Interchange), 349
Ask Jeeves, 279, 287
Ask Jeeves Peek Through the Keyhole, 294
ASP (Active Server Pages), 9
Associate Search, 266
Associate-it, 258
AssociatePrograms.com Web site, 266
At Hand Network Yellow Pages, 230
AT&T AnyWho Info, 230
ATL Network, 266
Atomz.com search engine
  adding to site, 75
  Contact Information page, 70, 73
  excluding pages, 70
  HTML Overview page, 75
  indexing your site, 75
  joining, 70, 73
  reports, 70
  Service Agreement page, 70
  Site Information page, 73
  sites with more than 500 pages, 69
  Welcome page, 70, 73
attachments, 349
attributes, 28
audience, 17
  affiliate programs and, 261–262
  appealing to, 18

  clothing preferences, 19
  visual design requirements, 18
  world view of, 19
  writing Web pages for, 282
authentication, 349
autoresponders, 295, 349
  GetResponse.com, 298–299
  multiple messages for, 296
  WebMailStation.com, 296–298
Aweber Systems, 308

• B •

backcolor attribute, 186
background attribute, 46
background color, 43
background images, 46
Banner Ad Network, 294
banner exchange, 293
BannerExpress, 294
BannerPromo.com Web site, 294
banners, 349
Bare Bones Software Web site, 364
Barry's Clip Art Server, 44
BayBuilder, 327
BBEdit, 364
Ben-Hur, 220
Beseen Quizlet, 162
Better-Whois.com Web site, 277
bgcolor attribute, 43
Big Yellow, 230
BigBook, 230
binary files, 350
Bizy Moms, 318
Boardhost, 170–173
  Account Creation page, 171, 173
  activation code, 171
  ad-free service upgrade, 173
  administrative postings, 177
  administrative replies, 177
  advanced options, 176
  banning IP addresses, 178
  Boardhost Administration page, 172–173
  canceling message board, 173
  colors for message board, 175
  customizing labels, 176
  default number of message, 174
  duplicating HTML code, 173
  e-mail address for message board, 174
  Edit Account Settings page, 174–175
  Edit Appearance page, 175–176
  Edit Headers/Footers page, 176
  Edit Meta Tags page, 177

Enter Administration link, 172
features, 170
font selection, 176
formatting messages with HTML, 175
header for index page, 176
header for message board, 174
HTML Codes page, 172
including images in messages, 175
IP address stamping, 175
keyword search feature, 175
message board owner name and
    password, 174
message posting notification, 174
modifying message board, 172, 174–178
password protection, 178
Personal Info page, 174
public message board listing, 173
quoted messages, 175
removing messages, 178
replies only to messages, 175
reply e-mail messages, 175
setting up message board, 170–172
smiley faces converted to images, 175
terms of service, 173
Terms of Service page, 170
title of message board, 174
user name, 170
viewing message logs, 178
Boardhost Web site, 170
Boards2Go, 182
Bobby Web site, 141
BODY element, 33, 35
    alink attribute, 43
    background attribute, 46
    bg color attribute, 43
    forms, 89
    JavaScript scripts, 58
    link attribute, 43
    onload attribute, 58
    text attribute, 43
    triggers for JavaScript scripts, 58
    vlink attribute, 43
Bogglers, 187
    adding to Web site, 187
    default code, 188
Bogglers.com Web site, 187
bold text, 39
Bookshelf applet, 364
Borders.com payment triggers, 256
Bounceweb, 273
Bowser, Jonathon Earl, 365

 tag, 36
Bradbury, Nick, 29
brainstorming, 13

brainteasers, 187–188
BrainWavesTM Center, The, 14
Brandi Jasmine's Digital Art Gallery, 104
Bridgeview Bankcard, 253
broken links, 125
Browser Check Web site, 136
Buchan, John, 220
budgetweb.com Web site, 272
Building a Web Site For Dummies
    CD-ROM, 361
    Art Gallery on CD-ROM v.1.12 Web page
        graphics, 364
    authors' links, 363
    BBEdit, 364
    Bookshelf applet, 364
    Dreamweaver 3.0, 364
    Fire applet, 364
    Fireworks 3.0, 365
    Fireworks trial version, 45
    Goddess Art of Jonathon Earl Bowser, 365
    HomeSite 4.5, 30, 365
    Lake applet, 365
    Lindy's Graphics, 366
    Linkbot Pro 5.5 and Linkbot Enterprise 2.0, 366
    Linkbot Pro demo, 128
    Macintosh OS, 363
    Macrobot 2.0, 366
    Metabot 3.0, 366
    Novagene's tiled background images, 367
    Paint Shop Pro 6.0, 367
    Paint Shop Pro trial version, 45
    problems with, 368
    Snow applet, 367
    StatBot Micro, 17
    Statbot Micro 1.0, 367
    system requirements, 361–362
    Webshelf applet, 80
    Windows OS, 362
    WS_FTP Pro, 368
Burn All GIFs Web site, 94
business
    attitude, 226
    secret of success, 226

• C •

Cakewalk, 120
Captain Blood, 220
careware, 194
cartoons, 216
    The Deep End, 218
    Not In My Backyard, 216–217
    Toy Trunk Railroad, 217–218

CBS SportsLine, 255
censorship, 165
Certificate Authority, 351
CFML (Cold Fusion Markup Language), 9
CGI (Common Gateway Interface), 51, 350
  access to, 51, 52
  commercial remote Web-space provider, 53
  finding provider, 53
  free Web-space providers, 53
  virtual server, 53
CGI Free, 54
CGI Resource Index, 63
CGI scripts
  adding, 54, 56
  changes necessary to run, 54
  comments, 54
  downloading, 54
  file extensions, 56
  files necessary for, 56
  HTML code, 55
  instructions, 54
  ISPs Internet Service Providers, 52
  plain text files, 55
  problems with, 55–56
  readme.txt file, 54
  remotely hosted, 53
  security, 52
cgi-bin folder, 52, 56
CGI: Why Things Don't Work, 63
chargeback, 242, 350
chat rooms, 178–181, 350
checking links, 126–127
CheckQuick, 253
The Choral Public Domain Library, 117
.class files, 60, 62
Classical Piano Free Downloads, 117
Classiclips, 116
ClickBank, 253
ClickQuick, 258
client/server, 350
Clip Animations, 44
Clip Art Connection, 44
clip art sources, 44
CN FormBuilder, 162
Coda Music Technology, 120
codebase attribute, 61
Coffee Cup HTML Editor, 30
color, 42
  active links, 43
  background, 43
  CSS (Cascading Style Sheets), 42
  fonts, 42
  HSL (hue, saturation, and luminance)
    model, 98
  links, 42
  RGB (red, green, and blue model), 96, 98
  text, 43
  unvisited links, 43
  visited links, 43
color attribute, 188
ComicExchange, 221
comments, 54
Commission Junction Web site, 259
companies with affiliate programs, 255
Compendium of HTML Elements, 48
compile, 350
Composer, 31
compressing graphics files, 128–133
concerts, 106
consistent layout, 11
content, 28, 282
  appealing to audience, 18
  consistency, 11
  fresh, 205
content attribute, 289
converting currencies, 247–252
cookies, 120
Cool Archive Free Clip Art, 44
Cool Edit, 121
CoolNotions.com, 104
CoolText.com, 95–96, 98
copyright-free material, 218
  Project Gutenberg, 220
  U.G. Krishnamurti, 219
copyrights, 350
  graphics, 91–92
  logos, 95
  music, 115
country-level TLDs, 275, 277, 358
CountZ.com Web site, 182
Covesoft, 271
Creating a Successful Web Site, 14
creativity, 13
credit cards, 235
  acquirer sign-up, 239
  application fee, 240
  badly run acquirers, 242
  chargeback, 242
  discount rate, 240
  downloading logos for, 235
  equipment charges, 240
  fees, 240–241
  fraud, 242–244
  high risk, 243
  information about acquirer, 241
  merchant account, 236–241, 243–244
  merchant account acquirers, 237–238
  minimum monthly charge, 240

monthly statement fee, 240
setup fee, 240
software address verification, 243
transaction fee, 240
types to accept, 238
Crosswinds Web site, 273
CSS (Cascading Style Sheets) and color, 42
custom logos and banners, 94
custom music, 115
Cyber-Pro, 294
Cyberbounty, 266
c|net, 272

• D •

dedicated servers, 270, 350
  Web hosting, 271
Dee Dreslough Web site, 364
Dee's Art Gallery, 104
The Deep End, 218
default fonts, 38
defaults, 350
demographics, 350
designing Web sites for e-commerce , 232–233
DevSearch, 14
DHL Worldwide Express, 231
DHTML (Dynamic HTML), 9
digital IDs, 351
digital wallets, 245
Direct Checks, 253
Direct Hit, 279, 287
DirectLeads Network, 266
discount rate, 351
Discover Business Services, 253
DMA (Direct Marketing Association), 333
DMA Privacy Policy, 333
DNS (Domain Name Server), 274
DNS (Domain Name System), 351
do-it-yourself
  logos, 95–96, 98
  search site submissions, 286–287
Doctor HTML Web site, 141
Documentation Validation Service, 141
domain extensions, 274
domain names, 274
  country-level TLDs, 275
  finding registrar, 276–277
  generic TLDs, 275
  phrases as, 275
  purchasing already registered, 276
  reserving or parking, 277
  selecting, 275–276
  TLDs (top-level domains), 274–275
  trademarks, 275

doodling, 13
DoReMix, 116
dot com, 351
dotmusic Webmaster Zone, 221
downloading, 351
  CGI scripts, 54
  games, 201
  GIF files, 129
  logos for credit cards, 235
Dr. Watson Web site, 141
Dracula, 220
drafts, 245, 351
Dreambook, 182
Dreamweaver, 31, 33
Dreamweaver 3 For Dummies, 42
Dreamweaver 3.0, 364
Dreamweaver Web site, 364
drop shipping, 230, 351
Dropcard, 203
DSL (Digital Subscriber Line), 351
Dynamic Submission 2000, 294

• E •

e-cash, 245
e-commerce
  alternative payment methods, 245–247
  attitude toward, 226–227
  converting currencies, 247–252
  credit card merchant account, 236–241,
    243–244
  credit cards, 235
  designing Web sites for, 232–233
  detailed product information, 232
  drop shipping, 230
  e-cash, 245
  focus, 227, 229
  KartShop.com, 228
  minimum orders, 230
  online malls, 244
  phone checks, 245–246
  prices, 233
  product description, 232
  product line, 229
  secret of success, 226
  shipping companies, 230
  shopping-cart software, 233
  simple-to-use Web sites, 232
  specialization, 227, 229
  suppliers, 229–232
  telephone, faxes and mail, 246
  tracking shipments, 231–232
  working harder , 226
e-commerce sites, 10

e-commerce tools
AllCommerce, 325
BayBuilder, 327
DMA Privacy Policy, 333
ECommerce Guide, 328
HumanClick, 326
MapQuest, 328–329
S&H Greenpoints, 330
suite 7, 323–324
Systran Translation Software, 331
TRUSTe, 332–333
EasyPostcard, 198, 200
EasyPostcard Web site, 198
easypostcard.zip file, 199
eatsleepmusic.com, 111
eBoz!, 321
eCalNow, 345
Echelon Guestbooks, 182
Echo Web's Web Development Articles, 25
ECML (Electronic Commerce Modeling
    Language), 245
ECommerce Guide, 328
EIS Banner Exchange, 294
electronic cards, 198, 200–201
Electronic Merchant Systems, 244
elements, 28, 33, 35
Eliot, George, 220
end tag, 28
ePayment Solutions, 253
Eurofreebies mailing list service, 300–301
EX Merchant Accounts, 253
Excite, 279, 287
ExciteStores, 244
Explorer-style menu, 85
EXPolls, 162
Ezine Factory, 319
Ezine News Wire, 221
EzineArticles.com Web site, 221

• F •

faxes, 246
Federal Copyright Office Web site, 95
Federal Express, 231
feed, 351
Fifth Third Bank, 253
files, 29
filtering messages, 169
FindAHost.com Web site, 272
finding
  information on Web hosts, 272
  partners for affiliate programs, 257–258
  registrar for domain names, 276–277
Fire applet, 99–100, 364
Fireworks, 44
  image mapping, 47
Fireworks 3.0, 365
Fireworks Web site, 365
First Bank of Beverly Hills, 253
First Charter Bank, 253
First of Omaha Merchant Processing, 237
flame wars, 352
flames, 352
flaming images, 99–100
Focalex.com payment triggers, 257
focus, 227, 229
FONT element, 39–40
fontcolor attribute, 186
fonts, 38–40, 352
  bold text, 39
  color, 42
  italic text, 39
foreign currencies, converting, 247–252
FORM element
  action attribute, 79, 201
form makers, 159
  FormSite.com, 159
  privacy policy, 161
  Response-O-Matic, 159–161
  security, 162
FormMailer, 162
forms
  drop-down lists, 88–89
  polls, 145–148, 150–153, 155–159
  Response-O-Matic creation, 160–161
  Thank You page, 161
  width attribute, 151
FormSite.com Web site, 159
frames, 352
  horizontal, 35
  search engines and, 283
  size of, 35
  vertical, 35
framesets, 35, 352
Franklin, Benjamin, 192
fraud and credit cards, 242–244
Free Grafix Web site, 104
free graphics, 91
free Web site providers, 273
Freedback.com Web site, 162
FreeFind, 66–69
Freepolls.com Web site, 162
Freeservers, 273
Freewarejava.com, 63
FreeWebspace.net, 53, 277
Free I SP Directory, 277
Freightworld, 233

fresh content, 205
Fresh Music Library, 116
friendly critiques, 11
FrontPage, 33
FrontPage Express, 31
FTP (File Transfer Protocol), 352

• G •

games, 201
   downloading, 201
   Jagex, 202
   Loonyverse, 201
Garden.com Web site, 261
geek/talk Forums For Webmasters, 315
Gene Lyons Web site, 367
Genealogy Online For Dummies, 18
generic TLDs, 275, 277, 358
GetResponse.com, 298
Gibbleguts.com Web site, 221
GIF (Graphics Interchange Format) file format,
      43, 93–94, 352
   legal problems, 94
GIF files, 129, 132
GIF Wizard, 141
GIFBot image file optimizer, 136
GIFBot Web site, 136
GIFWorks, 128–131
Gliebster.com, 104
Glory's Form Maker, 162
Goddess Art of Jonathon Earl Bowser, 104, 365
GoldWave Digital Audio Editor, 121
GoLive, 31, 33
Google, 279, 287
Gower, Andrew, 202
Gower, Ian, 202
grammarNOW!, 314
Graphic Maps, 44
graphics. *See also* images
   conditions for use of, 92
   copyrights, 91–92
   custom logos and banners, 94
   do-it-yourself logos, 95–96, 98
   file formats, 93
   for free, 91
   free logos, 94
   GIF (Graphics Interchange Format) file
         format, 93
   as horizontal lines, 41
   icons in color coordinated suites, 94
   JPEG (Joint Photographic Experts Group) file
         format, 93

MNG (Multiple Network Graphics) file
      format, 93
   PNG (Portable Network Graphics) file
      format, 93
Graphics Attic, 104
graphics files, reducing size, 128–133
graphics programs, 44–45
Graziana Web site, 94
The Great Big Treasury of Beatrix Potter, 220
Griffiths, David, 99, 101, 365, 367
grouping links, 21, 23
Guerilla Marketing Online, 294
guestbooks, 166–168
Guestcities
   displaying user answers, 167
   displaying visitor ratings, 168
   guestbook setup, 166–167
   HTML code backup, 168
   rating sites, 168
   user message, 168
Guestcities Web site, 166
GuestForum.com Web site, 182
GuestVote.com, 163
guillemot, 352

• H •

Harris Bank, 253
HEAD element, 33, 35
   JavaScript drop-down lists, 88
   JavaScript scripts, 57–58
   pasting Informatron TV script, 107
headings, 38
Heartland Payment Systems, 253
height attribute, 61
high risk, 352
high-roller site theme, 10
*History of the Decline and Fall of the Roman
      Empire,* 220
hits, 352
Hiway Technologies, Inc., 244
HomeSite, 365
HomeSite 4.5 For Dummies, 29
HomeSite Web site, 365
horizontal
   frames, 35
   lines, 40–41
   rule, 40, 352
hosting affiliate programs, 263, 265
HostReview.com, 272
Hot Dog PageWiz, 33
Hot Dog Professional, 31
HotBot, 280, 287

HoTMetaL PRO, 33
HR element, 40
href (hypertext reference) attribute, 43
HSL (hue, saturation, and luminance) color
    model, 98
HTML (HyperText Markup Language), 9, 27,
    29, 353
  checking syntax, 127
  elements, 28
  latest specifications for, 28
  tags, 28
  WC3 standard, 124
HTML Assistant Pro, 31
HTML Check Web site, 136
HTML editor, 352
HTML element, 33, 35
.html files, 61–62
HTML Goodies, 48
HTML Specification, 48
HTML Web Tips, 25
HTML Works, 142
HTML Writer's Guild, 48
HTMLed Pro, 31
htmlGear, 182
HTTP (Hypertext Transfer Protocol), 353
HumanClick, 326
HyperGames, 203
hyperlinks. *See* links
HyperMart, 244
hypertext, 352

• I •

ICANN (Internet Corporation for Assigned
    Names and Numbers), 277, 353
icons in color coordinated suites, 94
Image Carousel applet, 336
Image Mapper, 48
image mapping, 47
image mapping programs, 48
image maps, 283, 353
image repositories, 104
image repository, 353
images, 43–47, 353. *See also* graphics
  background, 46
  checking links, 126
  clip art sources, 44
  conditions for use of, 92
  copyrights, 43, 91–92
  Fire applet, 100
  flaming, 99–100
  links, 43
  obtaining, 43

reflective surface at bottom, 101–104
  snowing, 100–101
  special effects, 131
  tiling, 358
IMG element, 45
  checking links, 126
  src attribute, 45
Index DOT Html, 48
Informatron News, 106, 109–111
Informatron TV, 106–107
InsideTheWeb, 182
Insta-Poll, 163
Instant Check, 253
Intel Web Applets, 335–336
Intel Web site, 335
Interactive Scoreboard, 106, 108–109
interbanks, 237, 353
Internet, 353
Internet access, 353
Internet Explorer, 27, 365
Internet Tools for Package Tracking, 233
interpret, 353
interviews, 106
intranets and Quoter applet, 197
Intro to CGI, 63
Introduction to HTML, 48
IP addresses, 274, 353
Ipswitch Web site, 368
iShell, 118–120
Isopoda, 353
ISPs (Internet Service Providers), 353
  CGI scripts, 52
  Web hosting, 270
iSubmitter.com Web site, 287
iSyndicate, 338
italic text, 39

• J •

Jagex, 202
.jar file, 80
Jasc Web site, 367
Java, 353
Java applets, 51, 59–60, 62
Java Boutique, 63
Java page for Sun Microsystems, 59
JavaScript, 51, 56, 354
  adding to Web pages, 57–58
  drop-down lists, 88–89
  external files, 57
  free code, 56
  hiding code, 185
Moreover.com, 209–210

problems with, 58
triggering scripts, 58
JavaScript For Dummies, 2nd Edition, 58
JavaScript Made Easy, 63
JavaScript Source, 56
joining affiliate programs, 256–257
Jokes2U.com Web site, 203
Jonathon Earl Bowser Web site, 365
JPEG (Joint Photographic Experts Group) file
    format, 43, 93, 354
JPEG files, optimizing, 132
.js file, 57

• K •

karaoke rooms, 111
KartShop.com, 228
Keller, Helen, 220
Kent, Peter, 320
Key Merchant Services, 244
Keyword Extractor, 285
Keyword Live, 285
keywords, 281, 354
    analyzing, 284–285
    tricks with, 283–284
    usefulness of, 281–282
King, Connie, 201
Klondike, 354
Krishnamurti, J., 219
Krishnamurti, U.G., 219

• L •

La Rochefoucauld, Duc de, 192
Lake applet, 101–104, 365
LawGuru.com, 317–318
Learn HTML Home, 48
left brain, 13
Left vs. Right: Your Brain Takes Sides!, 14
Leonardo MediaBank, 339
level of comfort, 11
LicenseMusic, 116
Lindy's Graphics, 104, 366
line break tag, 36
link attribute, 43
Link Check Web site, 136
Link Trader, 293
LinkAlarm, 142
LinkBar, 90
Linkbot Pro, 126–127
Linkbot Pro 5.5 and Linkbot Enterprise 2.0, 366
LinkBuddies Banner Exchange, 294
linkcolor attribute, 186

LinkFree, 329
LinkPolice, 126
links, 43, 354
    as bookshelf, 79
    broken, 125
    checking, 126–127
    color, 42
    grouping, 21, 23
    Mind-it service, 126
    reciprocal arrangements, 280, 292–293
    thumbnail image, 21
    unnecessary, 21
LinkShare, 258
LinkShare Web site, 259
list owner, 354
list server, 354
LiveImage, 48
Load Check Web site, 136
local banks versus online specialists, 236–238
locomotive, 354
log files, 136–138, 140, 354
    processing, 139
logos
    copyrights, 95
    Cutout style, 96
    downloading for credit cards, 235
    free do-it-yourself, 95–96, 98
    style options, 96
Loonyverse, 201
low-cost bargain site theme, 10
Lutus, Paul, 194, 197
Lycos, 280, 287
The Lycos 50 Daily Report, 284

• M •

Machiavelli, 220
Macintosh OS
    authors' links, 363
    BBEdit, 364
    Building a Web Site For Dummies
        CD-ROM, 363
    Dreamweaver 3.0, 364
    Fireworks 3.0, 365
Macrobot 2.0, 366
Macs For Dummies, 6th Edition, 362
Magellan Search Voyeur, 294
MAGIX software, 117–118
MAGIX Web site, 118
mail, 246
mailing lists, 146, 354
    opt-in, 300, 355
Mapedit, 48

MapFree, 329
MapMaker, 48
MapQuest, 328–329
marketing information, 206
Marx, Groucho, 236
MasterCard, 235
MasterCard official merchant sites, 237
Media Builder Web site, 129
meditation, 13
Melinda Hoehn Web site, 366
Mellon Small Business, 253
merchant account acquirers, 237–238, 242
merchant accounts, 355
merchant accounts for credit cards, 236, 238
  local banks versus online specialists, 237–238
Merriam Webster, 337
message boards, 169, 355
  Boardhost, 170–178
  fields of interest, 169
  filtering messages, 169
  hierarchy of messages, 169
  modifying, 172–178
  threads, 169
  topic line for messages, 169
messages, 169
META element, 177
  content attribute, 281, 289
  disallowing robot behaviors, 290
  name attribute, 281, 289
Meta tags, 281, 283
  keyword tricks, 284
Metabot 3.0, 366
MetaSpy, 294
Middlemarch, 220
MIDI Radio, 113–114
Mind-it, 305–307
Mind-it service, 126
MiniVend, 253
MNG (Multiple Network Graphics) file
    format, 93
modems, 355
moderators, 355
modifying elements, 28
Moorglade Design Group Web site, 136–367
Moreover.com, 209–212
Moyra's Web Jewels, 104
multimedia
  iShell, 118–120
music, 113–114
  copyrights, 115
  custom, 115
  electronic cards, 200
  MAGIX software, 117–118
  obtaining, 115–116, 118

professional music suppliers, 115–116
  public-domain, 115–117
  royalty-free, 115–116
  user-created, 117–118
Music 2 Hues, 116
My Affiliate Program, 264
My Postcards, 204
MyForum, 182
MyService Experts Avenue, 313

• N •

name attribute, 61, 201, 289
napping and creativity, 14
NavBar, 90
navigating between pages, 11
navigation
  clear and easy ways to reach pages, 21
  designing, 20
  grouping links, 21, 23
  link back to main page, 20
  thumbnail image links, 21
  welcome mat, 20–21
navigational tools, 79
  JavaScript drop-down lists, 88–89
  VMaxNav, 85–88
  Webshelf, 79–85
Netcraft, 277
netiquette, 355
NetMechanic, 134–136
NetMechanic Web site, 133
NetMind Web site, 305
Netscape Communicator, 366
Netscape Navigator page, 27
NetVotes, 163
Network Solutions Web site, 275–276
newline, 197, 355
news, 109–111, 206
  7am News, 206–209
  Moreover.com, 209–212
News Harvester, 221
News Index, 221
newsletters, 299
  Eurofreebies mailing list service, 300–302
  OakNet Publishing, 303–304
Nikolai Sakva Web site, 364
Nixon, Richard, 192
NO SPAMM Opt-In Mailing List, 308
Noetic Art, 44
nonbreaking space, 37
Northern Light Search, 280, 287
noshade attribute, 41
Not In My Backyard, 216–217

Novagene's tiled background images, 367
Novagene's Web Oasis, 104
Nytebyte's Online Form Maker, 163

• O •

OakNet Publishing, 303–304
OBJECT element, 63
On Your Site Jokes, 204
On Your Site Quotables, 204
onClick attribute, 58
online malls, 244
online service, 355
onload attribute, 58
onMouseOut attribute, 58
onMouseOver attribute, 58
OpenSales Web site, 325
opt-in mailing lists, 300, 355
OPTION element
  selected attribute, 249
orphan pages, 20
orphan Web pages, 127

• P •

<P> tag, 36–37
</P> tag, 36–37
page generation programs, 355
page-building programs, 28–29, 31, 33
Paint Shop Pro, 44
Paint Shop Pro 6.0, 367
Painter, 45
paleomammalian, 13
ParaChat, 182
paragraph elements, 36, 38
paragraphs, 36
PARAM element, 61
parameters, 356
parking domain names, 277
Partners In Rhyme, 116
passwords, 356
Paymentech, 253
Paytrust.com payment triggers, 257
PBTM Library, 116
PCs For Dummies, 7th Edition, 362
PD Info, 117
PDMusic.org, 117
peripheral material, 12
Perl, 51
Perl CGI scripts, 76, 78–79
Perl Primer, 63
Perl scripts as external files, 57

PETsMART, 255
PG Music, 121
phone checks, 245
phone number Web site sources, 229
Photo Album II applet, 335
PhotoShop, 45
Pipeline News, 221
planning Web sites, 15, 17
PNG (Portable Network Graphics) file format,
  43, 93
polling visitors, 145–148, 150–153, 155–159
Pollit.com Web site, 163
Poor Richard's Web Site, 320
postcard.html file, 199
postcards, 129
PostMasterDirect.com, 148
Prime Cuts!, 116
The Prince, 220
privacy
  form makers, 161
  Weather.com, 215
ProBoost Web site, 288
product line, 229
professional music suppliers, 115–116
profiting from affiliate programs, 260–263
programs
  Adobe PageMill, 33
  Arachnophilia, 30
  autoresponders, 295–299
  Coffee Cup HTML Editor, 30
  Composer, 31
  Dreamweaver, 31, 33
  Fireworks, 44
  FrontPage, 33
  FrontPage Express, 31
  GIFWorks, 128–131
  GoLive, 31, 33
  graphics, 44–45
  HomeSite, 29, 31
  hosting affiliate programs, 263, 265
  Hot Dog PageWiz, 33
  Hot Dog Professional, 31
  HoTMetaL PRO, 33
  HTML Assistant Pro, 31
  HTMLed Pro, 31
  Image Mapper, 48
  image mapping, 48
  iShell, 118, 119, 120
  Keyword Extractor, 285
  Keyword Live, 285
  Link Trader, 293
  Linkbot Pro, 126–127
  LiveImage, 48

programs *(continued)*
Mapedit, 48
MapMaker, 48
Netscape Communicator, 31
page generation, 355
page-building, 28–29, 31, 33
Paint Shop Pro, 44
Painter, 45
PhotoShop, 45
Quick Pay Office Pro, 246
RealPlayer, 106
SitePromoter, 288
Spinwave, 132–133
Statbot, 136–138, 140
text editors, 28–29, 31
Ulead Web Razor Pro, 45
Web Hotspots, 48
WhoIs ULTRA, 292
Windows Notepad, 29
WYSIWYG (What You See Is What You Get)
editors, 28, 31, 33
Xara WebStyle, 45
Project Cool, 14
Project Gutenberg, 220
the promoter Web site, 287
public domain, 92, 356
Public Domain Music, 117
public-domain music, 115–117
publicizing sites, 279–280
Purolator Courier Ltd., 231
purpose, 15–16
Pyle, Howard, 220

• *Q* •

Quick Pay Office Pro, 246
QuickChat, 179–180, 181
QuickChat Web site, 179
quotations, 192–194, 196–198
The Quote Machine applet, 192
Quoter applet, 194, 196–197
quoter.class file, 194
quoter.txt file, 194
quoter.zip file, 194

• *R* •

Rackunits.com payment trigger, 257
radio stations, 105
Radiocards, 204
Random Riddle, 184, 186
readme.txt file, 54

RealPlayer, 106
RealPlayer Web site, 106
reciprocal link arrangements, 280, 292–293
reciprocal links, 356
Recommend-It, 340
reducing graphics files size, 128–133
Refer-It, 258
Refer-It Web site, 265
reflective surface at bottom of image, 101–104
registrar, 356
regular Web pages, 33
relative URLs, 200
religious sites topics, 10
remotely hosted CGI scripts, 53
repeat customers, 12
level of comfort, 11
reserving domain names, 277
Response-O-Matic, 160–161
Response-O-Matic Web site, 159
return visits, frequency of, 11–12
RGB (red, green, and blue) color model, 96, 98
RGB triplet, 356
RiddleNut Web site, 184
riddles, 184–187
right brain, 13
ring, 356
Ring of Lake Applets Web sites, 102
Ringsurf Web site, 293
robots, 280, 357
robots.txt file, 289
Rolling Stone, 338
Royalty Free Music, 116
royalty-free music, 116
rule. *See* horizontal lines
rules for building Web sites, 24–25

• *S* •

S&H Greenpoints, 330
Sabatini, Rafael, 220
safety paper, 245, 357
Sakva, Nikolai, 79, 364
Salon Magazine, 338
Sansom, Erik, 218
SavvySnoop, 294
ScoreCheck, 291
Script Archive Web site, 76
scripts, 51, 357
Search Engine Report Newsletter, 294
search engines, 65, 279–280, 292. *See also*
search sites
accepting credit cards search, 238
Atomz.com, 69–70, 73, 75

avoiding traps, 283
frames, 283
FreeFind, 66–69
image maps, 283
list of keywords, 281
listing Web sites, 280
page descriptions, 281
tricks with keywords, 283–284
search sites, 279–280. *See also* search engines
checking with ScoreCheck, 291
gathering information, 280
keeping Web sites out of, 288, 290
keywords, 281–282
manual submissions to, 280
manually checking submissions, 290
Meta tags, 281
robots and spiders, 280
submission pages, 287
submitting to, 286–288
Search Spy, 294
Searchbutton, 90
searches, allowing, 11
searchterms.com Web site, 284
security
CGI scripts, 52
form makers, 162
selected attribute, 249
selfPage.com, 221
SendFree, 308
Server Rat, 341
ServerWatch, 277
services required by Web site, 17
shelf.jar file, 80
Shipment and Parcel Tracking, 233
shipping companies, 230
Shopper's Currency Converter, 252
shopping carts, 357
shopping-cart software, 233
Simple Search, 76–79
Simple Server Shout, 121
Site Check, 142
SiteGadgets.com Web site, 163
SitePromoter, 288
size attribute, 41
Skipjack Merchant Services, 253
Small Business Advisor, 316
SmartClicks, 294
SnackExchange.com payment trigger, 257
Snap, 280, 287
sniffer programs, 162
Snow applet, 100–101, 367
snowing images, 100–101

SoftStep, 121
sound
capability to turn off, 106
concerts, 106
interviews, 106
iShell, 118–120
karaoke rooms, 111
music, 113–118
sound files, 105
SoundSurf, 116
spam, 295, 357
specialization, 227, 229
specifications, 357
Spell Check Web site, 136
spiders, 280, 357
Spigots Web site, 99
Spinwave, 132–133
sports scores, 108–109
src attribute, 45
SSI (Server Side Includes), 52, 357
Stamps.com, 255
standards, 357
Staples Office Supplies, 255
start tag, 28
Statbot, 136–138, 140
StatBot Micro, 17
Statbot Micro 1.0, 367
Steal My JavaScript, 64
Stoker, Bram, 220
The Story of My Life, 220
streaming-video content, 106–107
structure of Web pages, 33, 35
submission services, 287–288
submitting to search sites, 286
do-it-yourself, 286–287
submission services, 287–288
subscribers, 357
suite 7, 323–324
suppliers, 229–232
Survey Engine, 163
Switchboard, 230
syndicates, 205, 358
Systran Translation Software, 331

• *T* •

tabwid attribute, 186
tags, 358
end, 28
line break, 36
start, 28
taking break and creativity, 14

TallySite.com
   background image URL, 158
   banner advertising, 152
   color selection for items, 155
   customizing voting results page, 157–158
   default colors changes, 156–157
   deleting previous statistics, 159
   modifying surveys, 155
   My Polls page, 154–155
   survey form creation, 152–153, 155
   User Profile page, 152–153
Taylor, Dale, 216
tbcolor attribute, 188
Telephone Directories on the Web, 230
telephone numbers, 246
television, 105
testing Web sites, 133–136
text
   color, 43
   fonts, 38–40
   headings, 38
   horizontal lines, 40
   links, 43
   paragraph elements, 36, 38
text editors, 28–29, 31, 358
text files, 29, 358
text link alternatives, 283
theme, 10
The Thirty-Nine Steps, 220
Thoreau, Henry David, 220
threads, 169, 358
thumbnail image links, 21
tiling, 358
TITLE element, 281
TLDs (top-level domains), 274–275, 358
Today in History, 204
TopCities, 273
topics, 10, 12, 16
Total Merchant Services, 253
Tough Media, 344
Toy Trunk Railroad, 217–218
traffic, 358
transparent GIFs, 131
Transportation Solutions Web Links, 233
Tribeworks Web site, 118–120
Tripod, 273
trivia, 189–191
Trivia Blitz, 189–191
TRUSTe, 332–333
Ty Hafan Children's Hospice Web site, 99

• U •

U.G. Krishnamurti Web site, 221
UCC (Universal Currency Converter), 247–248,
   250–252
Ulead Web Razor Pro, 45
Ultimate Advertiser, 264
underlying theme, 10
Unisys Corporation, 94
Unisys Web site, 94
United States Postal Service, 231
unnecessary links, 21
Unseengraphics Web site, 104
unvisited links
   color, 43
updates, 12
uploading, 359
Uproar.com Web site, 189
URLs (Uniform Resource Locators, 43, 359
User Friendly Web site, 21, 23
user-created music, 117–118

• V •

Validator Web site, 124
value attribute, 250
ValueClick, 266
vertical frames, 35
Virtual Avenue, 273
virtual servers, 360
   CGI (Common Gateway Interface), 53
   Web hosting, 270–271
Virtual Sheet Music, 117
Virtual Stampede, 142
VISA merchant listings, 237
visited links, 43, 354
visitors, 65
   keeping in touch with, 295
   links to data about, 17
   newsletters, 299–304
   polls, 145–148, 150–153, 155–159
   requesting e-mail messages,
      295–299
   site update notification, 304–307
vlink attribute, 43
VMaxNav applet, 85, 87
VoiceBlast, 343
volatile topics updates, 12

• W •

W3C (World Wide Web Consortium)
  HTML validation service, 123, 125
  Web site, 28
W3C CSS Validation Service, 142
Walden, 220
Wallace, Lew, 220
War of the Worlds, 220
Watchfire Web site, 366
WDG HTML Validator, 142
WDVL: The Perl You Need to Know, 64
The Weather Channel, 214
weather forecasts, 212–215
The Weather Guys, 221
Weather Underground, 212–213
Weather Underground Web site, 212
Weather.com, 214–215
Web browsers
  default fonts, 38
  JavaScript scripts and, 59
  not supporting Java applets, 61
  page appearance, 27
Web hosting, 269
  dedicated servers, 270–271
  finding information on, 272
  free providers, 273
  ISPs (Internet Service Providers, 270
  virtual servers, 270–271
Web Hotspots, 48
Web pages
  BODY element, 33, 35
  content, 282
  elements, 33, 35
  fonts, 38–40
  frames, 33
  HEAD element, 33, 35
  headings, 38
  HTML element, 33, 35
  links, 43
  meeting WC3 standard, 124–125
  navigation, 20
  navigating between, 11
  organized, 19
  orphan, 127
  paragraph elements, 36, 38
  regular, 33
  structure, 33, 35
  too much good stuff, 19
  Web site purpose and, 20
  writing for audience, 282

Web Pages That Suck, 25
Web rings, 293
Web Site Garage, 133, 142
Web sites, 360
  avoiding design traps, 283
  censorship, 165
  e-commerce design, 232–233
  frames, 35
  free providers, 273
  friendly critiques, 11
  karaoke rooms, 111
  keeping out of search sites, 288, 290
  level of comfort, 11
  limiting user postings, 165
  links to visitor data, 17
  list of keywords, 281
  listing with search engines, 280
  log files, 136–138, 140
  orphan pages, 20
  page descriptions, 281
  phone number sources, 229
  planning, 15–16
  purpose, 15–16
  reciprocal link arrangements, 280, 292–293
  repeat customers, 11–12
  rules for building, 24–25
  search engines, 65–70, 73, 75
  searching for qualified candidates to build, 17
  storing, 18
  submitting to search sites, 286–288
  testing, 133–136
  text link alternatives, 283
  topics, 10
  underlying theme, 10
  value provided by affiliate program, 262
  welcome mat, 20–21
Web Watch, 312
Web-based television, 106–107
Web-site surveys
  Alxpoll, 146–148, 150–152
  new site feature requests, 145
  political candidate preferences, 145
  product quality feedback, 145
  social issue opinions, 145
  TallySite.com, 152–153, 155–159
Webcrawler, 280, 287
WebMailStation.com, 296, 298
Webmaster, 360
Webring Web site, 293
Webscape 2000, 264

Webshelf applet, 79
  arranging books, 81
  book link and title, 83–84
  boxes on shelves, 84
  changing width and height values, 80
  .class files, 80
  clicking links, 81
  color of covers and titles, 82
  completed code, 84
  dimensions of books, 82
  images on books, 84
  individual book settings, 84
  number of books, 83
  opening linked page in new browser, 81
  placeholders, 85
  SHELF_E1.HTM and SHELF_E2.HTM files, 81
  title direction, 82
Website Abstraction, 64
Website Success Monthly newsletter, 233
Websitings, 308
Websponsors.com Web site, 266
WebWorld's Postcards, 204
Wells, H.G., 220
whatUseek, 90
WhoIs Ultra, 275, 292
WhoIs utility, 275
WhoIs.net Web site, 275
width attribute, 41, 61, 151
Windows 95 For Dummies, 2nd Edition, 362
Windows 98 For Dummies, 362
Windows Notepad, 29
Windows OS
  authors' links, 363
  Building a Web Site For Dummies
    CD-ROM, 362
  Dreamweaver 3.0, 364
  Fireworks 3.0, 365
  HomeSite 4.5, 365
  Linkbot Pro 5.5 and Linkbot Enterprise 2.0, 366
  Macrobot 2.0, 366
  Metabot 3.0, 366
  Paint Shop Pro 6.0, 367
  Statbot Micro 1.0, 367
  WS_FTP Pro, 368
word processors, 55
Wright, Matt, 76
WS_FTP Pro, 368
WWWeblint Web site, 142
WYSIWYG (What You See Is What You Get)
  editors, 28, 31, 33

• X •

Xara WebStyle, 45
XML Syntax Checker, 142

• Y •

Yahoo!, 280, 287
Yahoo! Stores, 244
Yahoo! Yellow Pages, 230
Yale Style Manual, 25

• Z •

ZDNet Web site, 243
.zip files, 60
ZoneCoaster Search, 90

IDG Books Worldwide, Inc., End-User License Agreement

READ THIS. You should carefully read these terms and conditions before opening the software packet(s) included with this book ("Book"). This is a license agreement ("Agreement") between you and IDG Books Worldwide, Inc. ("IDGB"). By opening the accompanying software packet(s), you acknowledge that you have read and accept the following terms and conditions. If you do not agree and do not want to be bound by such terms and conditions, promptly return the Book and the unopened software packet(s) to the place you obtained them for a full refund.

1. **License Grant.** IDGB grants to you (either an individual or entity) a nonexclusive license to use one copy of the enclosed software program(s) (collectively, the "Software") solely for your own personal or business purposes on a single computer (whether a standard computer or a workstation component of a multiuser network). The Software is in use on a computer when it is loaded into temporary memory (RAM) or installed into permanent memory (hard disk, CD-ROM, or other storage device). IDGB reserves all rights not expressly granted herein.

2. **Ownership.** IDGB is the owner of all right, title, and interest, including copyright, in and to the compilation of the Software recorded on the disk(s) or CD-ROM ("Software Media"). Copyright to the individual programs recorded on the Software Media is owned by the author or other authorized copyright owner of each program. Ownership of the Software and all proprietary rights relating thereto remain with IDGB and its licensers.

3. **Restrictions on Use and Transfer.**

    (a) You may only (i) make one copy of the Software for backup or archival purposes, or (ii) transfer the Software to a single hard disk, provided that you keep the original for backup or archival purposes. You may not (i) rent or lease the Software, (ii) copy or reproduce the Software through a LAN or other network system or through any computer subscriber system or bulletin-board system, or (iii) modify, adapt, or create derivative works based on the Software.

    (b) You may not reverse engineer, decompile, or disassemble the Software. You may transfer the Software and user documentation on a permanent basis, provided that the transferee agrees to accept the terms and conditions of this Agreement and you retain no copies. If the Software is an update or has been updated, any transfer must include the most recent update and all prior versions.

4. **Restrictions on Use of Individual Programs.** You must follow the individual requirements and restrictions detailed for each individual program in Appendix B of this Book. These limitations are also contained in the individual license agreements recorded on the Software Media. These limitations may include a requirement that after using the program for a specified period of time, the user must pay a registration fee or discontinue use. By opening the Software packet(s), you will be agreeing to abide by the licenses and restrictions for these individual programs that are detailed in Appendix B and on the Software Media. None of the material on this Software Media or listed in this Book may ever be redistributed, in original or modified form, for commercial purposes.

5. **Limited Warranty.**

   (a) IDGB warrants that the Software and Software Media are free from defects in materials and workmanship under normal use for a period of sixty (60) days from the date of purchase of this Book. If IDGB receives notification within the warranty period of defects in materials or workmanship, IDGB will replace the defective Software Media.

   (b) IDGB AND THE AUTHOR OF THE BOOK DISCLAIM ALL OTHER WARRANTIES, EXPRESS OR IMPLIED, INCLUDING WITHOUT LIMITATION IMPLIED WARRANTIES OF MERCHANTABILITY AND FITNESS FOR A PARTICULAR PURPOSE, WITH RESPECT TO THE SOFTWARE, THE PROGRAMS, THE SOURCE CODE CONTAINED THEREIN, AND/OR THE TECHNIQUES DESCRIBED IN THIS BOOK. IDGB DOES NOT WARRANT THAT THE FUNCTIONS CONTAINED IN THE SOFTWARE WILL MEET YOUR REQUIREMENTS OR THAT THE OPERATION OF THE SOFTWARE WILL BE ERROR FREE.

   (c) This limited warranty gives you specific legal rights, and you may have other rights that vary from jurisdiction to jurisdiction.

6. **Remedies.**

   (a) IDGB's entire liability and your exclusive remedy for defects in materials and workmanship shall be limited to replacement of the Software Media, which may be returned to IDGB with a copy of your receipt at the following address: Software Media Fulfillment Department, Attn.: *Building a Web Site For Dummies*, IDG Books Worldwide, Inc., 10475 Crosspoint Blvd., Indianapolis, IN 46256, or call 800-762-2974. Please allow three to four weeks for delivery. This Limited Warranty is void if failure of the Software Media has resulted from accident, abuse, or misapplication. Any replacement Software Media will be warranted for the remainder of the original warranty period or thirty (30) days, whichever is longer.

   (b) In no event shall IDGB or the author be liable for any damages whatsoever (including without limitation damages for loss of business profits, business interruption, loss of business information, or any other pecuniary loss) arising from the use of or inability to use the Book or the Software, even if IDGB has been advised of the possibility of such damages.

   (c) Because some jurisdictions do not allow the exclusion or limitation of liability for consequential or incidental damages, the above limitation or exclusion may not apply to you.

7. **U.S. Government Restricted Rights.** Use, duplication, or disclosure of the Software by the U.S. Government is subject to restrictions stated in paragraph (c)(1)(ii) of the Rights in Technical Data and Computer Software clause of DFARS 252.227-7013, and in subparagraphs (a) through (d) of the Commercial Computer–Restricted Rights clause at FAR 52.227-19, and in similar clauses in the NASA FAR supplement, when applicable.

8. **General.** This Agreement constitutes the entire understanding of the parties and revokes and supersedes all prior agreements, oral or written, between them and may not be modified or amended except in a writing signed by both parties hereto that specifically refers to this Agreement. This Agreement shall take precedence over any other documents that may be in conflict herewith. If any one or more provisions contained in this Agreement are held by any court or tribunal to be invalid, illegal, or otherwise unenforceable, each and every other provision shall remain in full force and effect.

Installation Instructions

The *Building a Web Site For Dummies* CD offers valuable information that you won't want to miss. To install the items from the CD to your hard drive, follow these steps.

For Microsoft Windows users

1. **Insert the CD into your computer's CD-ROM drive.**

2. **Open your browser.**

3. **Click Start⇨Run.**

4. **In the dialog box that appears, type** D:\START.HTM.

5. **Read through the license agreement, nod your head, and click the Accept button if you want to use the CD. After you click Accept, you'll jump to the Main Menu.**

6. **To navigate within the interface, click any topic of interest to take you to an explanation of the files on the CD and how to use or install them.**

7. **To install the software from the CD, click the software name.**

For Mac OS Users

1. **Insert the CD into your computer's CD-ROM drive.**

2. **Double-click the CD icon to show the CD's contents.**

3. **Double-click the Read Me First icon.**

4. **Open your browser.**

5. **Click File⇨Open and choose the CD titled Building a Web Site For Dummies. Click the Links.htm file to see an explanation of all files and folders included on the CD.**

6. **Some programs come with installer programs. With those, you open the program's folder on the CD and double-click the icon with the word** Install **or** Installer.

For more complete information, please see Appendix B, "About the CD."

IDG BOOKS WORLDWIDE BOOK REGISTRATION

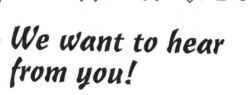

We want to hear from you!

Visit **http://my2cents.dummies.com** to register this book and tell us how you liked it!

- ✔ Get entered in our monthly prize giveaway.

- ✔ Give us feedback about this book — tell us what you like best, what you like least, or maybe what you'd like to ask the author and us to change!

- ✔ Let us know any other *For Dummies*® topics that interest you.

Your feedback helps us determine what books to publish, tells us what coverage to add as we revise our books, and lets us know whether we're meeting your needs as a *For Dummies* reader. You're our most valuable resource, and what you have to say is important to us!

Not on the Web yet? It's easy to get started with *Dummies 101*®*: The Internet For Windows*® *98* or *The Internet For Dummies*® at local retailers everywhere.

Or let us know what you think by sending us a letter at the following address:

For Dummies Book Registration
Dummies Press
10475 Crosspoint Blvd.
Indianapolis, IN 46256

BESTSELLING
BOOK SERIES